Marveling with Mark

Marveling with Mark

A Homiletical Commentary on the Second Gospel

Steven A. Crane

WIPF & STOCK · Eugene, Oregon

MARVELING WITH MARK
A Homiletical Commentary on the Second Gospel

Copyright © 2010 Steven A. Crane. All rights reserved. Except for brief quotations in critical publications or reviews, no part of this book may be reproduced in any manner without prior written permission from the publisher. Write: Permissions, Wipf and Stock Publishers, 199 W. 8th Ave., Suite 3, Eugene, OR 97401.

Wipf & Stock
An Imprint of Wipf and Stock Publishers
199 W. 8th Ave., Suite 3
Eugene, OR 97401
www.wipfandstock.com

ISBN 13: 978-1-60899-339-0

Manufactured in the U.S.A.

All scripture quotations, unless otherwise indicated, are taken from the Holy Bible, New International Version®, NIV®. Copyright ©1973, 1978, 1984 by Biblica, Inc.™ Used by permission of Zondervan. All rights reserved worldwide.

Contents

Acknowledgments vii
Preface ix

PART ONE—WHO IS THIS MAN? (1:1—8:30)

1. Bouncing Back (1:1) 3
2. Suspending Disbelief (1:1–15) 11
3. Inherent Authority (1:16–34) 19
4. Necessary Solitude (1:35–39) 29
5. Reckless Faith (2:1–12) 37
6. Challenging Assumptions (2:13—3:6) 45
7. Unforgiven (3:7–34) 57
8. Hearing Impaired (4:1–25) 67
9. Who Is This? (4:26–41) 77
10. For the Pigs (5:1–20) 85
11. *Talitha Koum* (5:21–43) 95
12. Local Yokel (6:1–6a) 105
13. Fascinated, but Afraid (6:6b–31) 113
14. Loaves & Fishes (6:30–44) 123
15. The Near Transcendent (6:45–56) 133
16. When Rite Is Wrong (7:1–23) 143
17. Table Scraps (7:24–30) 151
18. Overwhelmed with Amazement (7:31–37) 159

19 Much Ado About Bread (8:1–21) 169

20 Seeing and Not Perceiving (8:22–30) 177

Part Two—What Did He Come to Do? (8:31—16:20)

21 Finders Weepers, Losers Keepers (8:31—9:1) 187

22 Resplendent Glory (9:2–13) 197

23 Misplaced Confidence (9:14–29) 207

24 Redefining Greatness (9:30–50) 217

25 It's Just a Piece of Paper Anyway! (10:1–12) 225

26 Camels & Needles (10:13–31) 235

27 Blind Entitlement (10:32–52) 245

28 Not a Gentle Jesus (11:1–26) 253

29 Q & A, Part One (11:27—12:17) 265

30 Q & A, Part Two (12:18–44) 275

31 Keep Watch (13:1–37) 285

32 A Beautiful Thing (14:1–11) 295

33 No Ordinary Meal (14:12–26) 305

34 Pressed at Gethsemane (14:26–52) 313

35 Deafening Silence (14:53–65) 323

36 The Great In-Between (14:66–72) 331

37 What to Do with Jesus? (15:1–20) 339

38 Glimpses from the Cross (15:21–47) 345

39 See for Yourself (16:1–8) 351

40 A "Puzzling" Solution (16:9–20) 359

41 *Missio Dei* (16:9–20) 369

Bibliography 379

Acknowledgments

WITH SPECIAL APPRECIATION TO the following:

To Russell Clum, my preaching associate—I have tried to pour my ministry experience into him and have found that I have been the one blessed.

To David Christensen, our small group minister—He has contributed a great many of the study questions found in this volume.

To Janet Colburn (my executive assistant) and Margaret Crane (my mom)—Although they sometimes get their roles reversed, they have spent countless hours trying to correct my grammar, spelling, and idiosyncracies. Any that remain only show how difficult a task they undertook.

To many others who have participated in "Sermon Club": Scott Riggan, Rick Chromey, Bill Zink, John Cole, and Will Nockles—They are responsible for many of the puns and humor (or lack thereof) throughout this volume.

To our congregation at Eagle Christian Church—They have encouraged the publication of this volume and are more than just church members—they are family.

Preface

IF YOU HAD ASKED me a few years ago to rank the Gospels according to their significance and impact, it would have been an appreciable challenge. Depending upon the situation, I can imagine circumstances where I might have varied the order of my top three, but I would have remained consistent in my lowest ranking, giving this position to the Gospel of Mark. My rationale for placing the others higher would likely have gone something like this: The Gospel of John is dramatically different from the others and has such great theological teaching (i.e., "The Word became Flesh" and the "I Am" statements) that it must be given consideration. Luke has such a detailed historical accounting from the pen of a doctor that places the message of Jesus in its rightful context. Matthew not only stresses the Kingdom of God, but has the Jewish background and Hebraisms which are necessary to confirm that Jesus is the Messiah.

My reasoning for excluding Mark from the top three would take a much different turn. Mark is just a quick overview, leaving out many important details (including two trips to Jerusalem), many significant events, and seems to randomly jump from one story to the next without rhyme or reason—or so I thought.

Actually, the Gospel of Mark is remarkably written and detailed in its presentation. While it is true that the book moves quickly (the word "immediately" is used forty-two times) and it is not always concerned with chronology (which might give the appearance of haphazardness), Mark uses several writing techniques which give remarkable structure and precision to his narrative. One such technique is called "sandwiching" where he takes two seemingly unrelated stories and places them together to form one literary unit. He starts with one story, interrupts it with a second, and then returns to the first. The two stories together make a single point of emphasis. Far from being aimlessly written, it is masterful in its technique.

This same point could be demonstrated by the book's outline. The Gospel of Mark can easily be divided into two sections. Many have assigned different titles and descriptions to these two sections, but at the core Mark seems to be asking (and answering) two questions: (1) Who is this Man, Jesus (1:1—8:30)? and, (2) What did he come to do (8:31—16:20)? The content of the Gospel is logically arranged according to this outline.

One more illustration brings clarity to the mastery of Mark. Mark uses the reputation of words to hammer home his main ideas. One example should suffice. In presenting his case that Jesus is the Christ, Mark uses seven different words repeatedly that can be translated "marvel." They include: "greatly surprised" (*ekthambeō*, 9:15; 14:33; 16:5; 16:6); "completely amazed" (*ekthaumazō*, 12:17); "amazement" (*ekstasis*, 5:42; 16:8); "surprised" (*existēmi*, 2:12; 3:21; 5:42; 6:51); "shocked" (*thambeō*, 1:27; 10:24; 10:32), "marvel" (*thaumazō*, 5:20; 6:6; 15:5; 15:44); and "astonished" (*thaumastos*, 12:11). As we look at these words it becomes clear that Mark wants us to marvel at the person and work of Jesus.

As I have studied this gospel over the last year, it has become my favorite. My hope is that as you read the words about Jesus Christ, you will also "Marvel with Mark."

PART ONE

Who Is This Man?
Mark 1:1—8:30

"Who is this? Even the wind and the waves obey him!"

Mark 4:41

1

Bouncing Back

An Introduction to Mark

The beginning of the gospel about Jesus Christ,
the Son of God. (Mark 1:1)[1]

THE BIBLE IS NOT only continually the world's best seller, but it is the most translated book in all of history, having been translated into more than two thousand languages. Within the Bible, the Gospels[2] are the most translated books. This is not surprising, since the Gospels contain the story of Jesus: his life, teachings, miracles, death, burial, and resurrection. So, it just makes sense to start your Bible translation here. Of the Gospels, Mark is the most translated—making the Gospel of Mark the most translated of all books in history!

This might lead us to the question: Why is Mark the most translated of the four Gospel accounts? Several reasons can be given. First, it is the shortest. It is a formidable task to translate any book into another language. After selecting the Gospels as a place to start, Mark can be translated most quickly. Second, it is the simplest and most multicultural.[3] Mark does not contain complicated Greek grammar like the Gospel of Luke, the deep theological statements of the Gospel of John, or the highly-Jewish flavor of the Gospel of Matthew, making it more

---

1. All Scripture is taken from the New International Version of the Bible.

2. The term "gospel" (*euangelion*) is a Greek word that simply means good news. It acquired special significance, however, for early Christians who linked it specifically to the message of salvation that is available in Jesus Christ. Later, in the second century, it was also applied to the four canonical writings attributed to Matthew, Mark, Luke, and John. Both meanings will be used in this work. The latter usage is in view here.

3. This will be discussed further in chapter 2 of this work.

applicable to various cultures. Third, Mark emphasizes the freshness and revolutionary character of the message of Jesus. Fourth, it gives an excellent introduction to the gospel message of Jesus Christ. Notice the first verse of the first chapter: "The beginning of the gospel about Jesus Christ, the Son of God" (1:1).[4] Finally, it may be the earliest Gospel written—eighty percent (80%) of it is recorded in the other Gospels.

This might lead to a second question: When was the Gospel of Mark written? Much evidence suggests that it may be the earliest of the four Gospels penned.[5] Early Church tradition says it was written during Peter's lifetime—telling us that Mark wrote while Peter spoke. Peter's death dates at AD 64 and therefore we must arrive at a date earlier than this. We also know that after spending considerable time with Peter, Mark left to spend time with the Apostle Paul in the early 60s. If Mark wrote while Peter spoke, the book necessarily dates to a time before he left to be with Paul. History again records for us that Mark and Peter were in Rome during the later part of the 50s. This would necessarily place the writing of the Gospel of Mark at the latest around AD 57–59 or possibly even earlier.

We should also ask: To whom was it written? The best answer is that the Gospel of Mark was written from Rome for the Romans, which makes it particularly applicable for us today. The Romans loved power, strength, might, force and movement, and for this reason the book is an action-packed thriller! It contains the most miracles—eighteen; it is fast paced and regularly uses the word "immediately" (*euthys*);[6] it does not contain genealogies or much Messianic language which is far less important for this audience; it is down to earth, to the point, and may be best summarized by this statement: "For even the Son of Man did not come to be served, but to serve, and to give his life as a ransom for many" (10:45).

Our fourth question may seem too obvious, but I want to ask and answer it. Who wrote Mark? While at first blush it seems elementary (after all, it is "The Gospel of Mark!"), it may not be as simple as it seems. Actually, the book does not bear his (or any other) name. That's not to say that we don't have clues or even answers. First, all the church fathers

---

4. Mark uses the word "gospel" more than any other Gospel writer (1:1; 1:14; 1:15; 8:35; 10:29; 13:10; 14:9).

5. Some suggest that this honor goes to Matthew.

6. Mark uses the word forty-two times.

agree that it was written by Mark from Rome. Second, we have extra biblical citations as early as AD 79 attributing it to Mark. Third, Polycarp—who was a disciple of John and whose writings date between AD 110 and 150—tells us that Mark wrote as Peter preached. Fourth, Papias—a student of Polycarp who also dates early in the second century—writes in *Interpretation of the Oracles of the Lord* that Mark was Peter's interpreter. Finally, Eusebius—a church father of the third century—gives us more insight when he says the early church was so challenged by Peter's preaching that they asked his companion, Mark, to write down his sermons. This explains why the Apostle Peter plays such a significant part in Mark's narrative.[7]

This leads us to one final question: Who was Mark? As just mentioned, his name was actually John Mark (John is his Hebrew name, Mark is his Roman name), and we find references to him throughout Scripture. We will examine several of these references, including mentions from the Book of Acts (the history of the church), the Gospel of Mark itself, and personal letters addressed to various individuals and churches within our New Testament.

Most of us don't get excited about dates and background information. We understand that history is important, but is it engaging? Maybe or maybe not. But let me tell you a story about Mark. His story serves as an apt introduction to the gospel that bears his name.

The story begins in approximately AD 30. Church meetings were held in John Mark's mother's home in Jerusalem when he was just a youth. Mark records for us that someone follows Jesus and the disciples to the Garden of Gethsemane, where Jesus is betrayed and arrested. All of the disciples desert him and flee. "A young man, wearing nothing but a linen garment, was following Jesus. When they seized him, he fled naked, leaving his garment behind" (14:50–52). This young man may have been Mark himself. If indeed this passage refers to John Mark, our author may have been the first known streaker!

We read next about John Mark in Acts, chapter 12, more than a decade later (AD 44). Once again we find ourselves at John Mark's home. John Mark's mother, Mary, is a wealthy woman who owns a large house in Jerusalem. The Apostle Peter is in prison and all the Christians of the area are gathered in her home praying for Peter's release.[8]

---

7. Many of the third-person narratives in Mark may be reasonably understood as representing a first-person plural of Peter's discourses': 1:21, 29; 5:1, 38; 6:53, 54; 8:22; 9:14, 30, 33; 10:32, 46; 11:1, 12, 15, 20, 27; 14:18, 22, 26, 32.

8. Some traditions hold that this house was the one in which the Last Supper was

> So Peter was kept in prison, but the early church was earnestly praying to God for him. The night before Herod was to bring him to trial, Peter was sleeping between two soldiers, bound with two chains, and sentries stood guard at the entrance. Suddenly an angel of the Lord appeared and a light shone in the cell. He struck Peter on the side and woke him up. "Quick, get up!" he said, and the chains fell off Peter's wrists. Then the angel said to him, "Put on your clothes and sandals." And Peter did so. "Wrap your cloak around you and follow me," the angel told him. Peter followed him out of the prison, but he had no idea that what the angel was doing was really happening; he thought he was seeing a vision. They passed the first and second guards and came to the iron gate leading to the city. It opened for them by itself, and they went through it. When they had walked the length of one street, suddenly the angel left him. Then Peter came to himself and said, "Now I know without a doubt that the Lord sent his angel and rescued me from Herod's clutches and from everything the Jewish people were anticipating." When this had dawned on him, he went to the house of Mary the mother of John, also called Mark, where many people had gathered and were praying. Peter knocked at the outer entrance, and a servant girl named Rhoda came to answer the door. When she recognized Peter's voice, she was so overjoyed she ran back without opening it and exclaimed, "Peter is at the door!" "You're out of your mind," they told her. When she kept insisting that it was so, they said, "It must be his angel." But Peter kept on knocking, and when they opened the door and saw him, they were astonished. Peter motioned with his hand for them to be quiet and described how the Lord had brought him out of prison. (Acts 12:5–17)

I have been told that Peter's urgent knocking at the door that day was not the basis for the popular song, "Help me Rhoda, help, help me Rhoda" (in case you were wondering).[9]

Later still (AD 46), John Mark travels along with his cousin Joseph (you may know him by his nickname, Barnabas, or "son of encouragement") on Paul's first missionary journey. In all likelihood, Barnabas sells a piece of land to make the journey possible (Acts 4:36–37). Mark's mom, Mary, also likely contributes to the missionary journeys. Initially,

---

held (cf. Acts 12:12).

9. Of course the song is actually, "Help Me Rhonda," and was written by Brian Wilson and Mike Love for the Beach Boys and recorded in March 1965 on their "Beach Boys Today" album.

Mark is said to be very helpful (Acts 13:5), but makes it only as far as Perga, where he abandons them. "From Paphos, Paul and his companions sailed to Perga in Pamphylia, where John left them to return to Jerusalem" (Acts 13:13).

We don't know why Mark leaves (we are left no commentary here), but we do know his leaving becomes a major point of contention. In AD 55, Paul tells Barnabas that he wants to go back and visit the various church plants. Barnabas wants to take John Mark along—but Paul doesn't think it wise because of John Mark's earlier desertion. Paul and Barnabas have such a sharp disagreement that they part company (Acts 15:36–39).[10] Barnabas takes Mark and sails for Cyprus, which was probably home for them before Jerusalem (the wealthy often relocated to Jerusalem as a type of pilgrimage). Paul chooses another traveling companion named Silas to take on the second missionary journey and he heads north, up the Mediterranean coast.

John Mark has developed a reputation as a quitter and a deserter. With the Apostle Paul against him, you might think the story line is over for John Mark. But, surprisingly, it isn't. The next we hear of Mark, he has actually become an associate of Peter in Rome in the mid to late 50s.

In thinking about John Mark joining Peter, Peter certainly knows what it is like to have failed Jesus and yet be restored. Remember the story of Peter denying Jesus? It shouldn't surprise us to find one of the most detailed accounts of Peter's denial recorded for us in the book of Mark.

> While Peter was below in the courtyard, one of the servant girls of the high priest came by. When she saw Peter warming himself, she looked closely at him. "You also were with that Nazarene, Jesus," she said. But he denied it. "I don't know or understand what you're talking about," he said, and went out into the entryway. When the servant girl saw him there, she said again to those standing around, "This fellow is one of them." Again he denied it. After a little while, those standing near said to Peter, "Surely you are one of them, for you are a Galilean." He began to call down curses on himself, and he swore to them, "I don't know this man you're talking about." Immediately the rooster crowed the second time. Then Peter remembered the word Jesus had spoken to him:

---

10. This in itself is interesting, considering it was Barnabas who took Paul under his wing and vouched for him immediately following his conversion to Christianity (see Acts 9:27).

"Before the rooster crows twice you will disown me three times."
And he broke down and wept. (Mark 14:66–72)

Peter, as well as anyone, understands that a person who has failed can learn and grow from that failure. (Also, in Galatians 2:13, it appears that Barnabas has been led astray either by the Jewish or Christian fringe, but brought back. This might explain why Barnabas is also willing to extend grace to his cousin.)

It is no wonder that John Mark (the deserter) becomes Peter's son in the faith, much like Timothy does for Paul (1 Peter 5:13). It is also no surprise that Mark would compile the sermons of Peter, who has helped restore him. Think for a moment about Peter's risk. John Mark has already failed Paul. But that's what the gospel is about—second chances.

But our story doesn't stop there. As we read further through the Bible we find that we are not yet finished with John Mark. Fast forward a couple of years to AD 60, Paul is now able to write, "If he comes to you, welcome him" (Colossians 4:10). Mark is once again in Paul's good graces. But more than that, we read in Philemon 23–24, "Epaphras, my fellow prisoner in Christ Jesus, sends you greetings. And so do Mark, Aristarchus, Demas and Luke, my fellow workers." Nine years after his desertion, John Mark has once again become Paul's companion and trusted fellow worker. Seven years later still (AD 67), as Paul is in prison and advancing in years, he writes Timothy saying, "Get Mark and bring him with you, because he is helpful to me in my ministry" (2 Timothy 4:11).

Peter (Mark's father in the faith), is out of the picture, having been crucified upside down at the hands of Nero. Now Paul writes to his own son in the faith (Timothy) and says . . . John Mark is more than welcome. Paul, spiritually speaking, adopts John Mark as well.

Application

John Mark has bounced back. Think about this for a moment. What would have happened to John Mark without Peter?

The church needs to be a place of second chances. People make wrong choices and bad decisions. We have all had lapses of indiscretion or shown signs of poor judgment. But this is what the gospel is about—rescuing the wandering.

We need to understand a couple of things. First, from God's perspective, no one is too far gone or too far removed. No one is too sinful to be beyond God's reach. Paul the murderer, Peter the denier, Mark the deserter—there is room at God's table for all three.

Second, people usually have one of two responses to failure: they are either too hard on themselves or too hard on others. Maybe you believe that God gives people second chances, but you don't believe it applies to you—you don't think you have any value or anything to contribute. You need to listen to the words that Mark himself pens from the book that presents the gospel more clearly than any other.

Or maybe there is someone to whom you need to extend a second chance. Maybe you have been the recipient of a second chance and you are the perfect candidate to help someone else on their journey. Maybe God is calling you right now to be the "Barnabas" or the "Peter" to someone struggling who needs a second chance. One thing I know, God is all about helping us overcome our failures and bounce back.

Study Questions

All of us have experienced failure—whether in our careers, or relationships, or even our Christianity. The short glimpses of the life of John Mark give us encouragement that, despite our failures, God can still use us in important ways.

1. Who wrote this book?
2. When was it written?
3. To whom was it written?
4. Why was it written?
5. John Mark accompanied Paul and Barnabas on the first missionary journey in AD 46. Read Acts 13:5. What is said about John Mark?
6. John Mark left Paul and Barnabas at Perga in Pamphylia (Acts 13:13). While nothing is said about *why* he left, we learn in Acts 15 that it was a major point of contention between Paul and Barnabas. Read Acts 15:36–41.
    a. According to verse 38, why does Paul not want to take John Mark on the second missionary journey?
    b. What comes to mind when you hear the word "deserted"?
    c. Notice the language of verse 39. Did Paul consider Mark's leaving significant or insignificant?

7. Barnabas is willing to give Mark a second chance.
    a. Have you ever wished for a second chance that never appeared? How did that make you feel?
    b. Have you ever been given a second chance at something that turned out well? What?
    c. Read Galatians 2:13. What event took place earlier in the life of Barnabas that may have softened Barnabas' heart to the thought of second chances?
8. By AD 55, we learn that Mark is an associate of the Apostle Peter. In the Gospel of Mark, we learn about an event in Peter's own life that might have played a role in his willingness to accept Mark. Read Mark 14:66–72.
    a. What event are we referring to?
    b. How might this event in the life of Peter have softened his heart to the thought of second chances?
9. Mark becomes "near and dear" to Peter. Note what Peter calls Mark in 1 Peter 5:13.
10. Paul also softens to John Mark. Note what is said by Paul about Mark in the following scriptures.
    a. Colossians 4:10
    b. Philemon 23–24
    c. 2 Timothy 4:11
11. What might we speculate about John Mark's life if Barnabas and Peter had not been willing to give him another opportunity?
12. Who in your life have you failed? Has the situation been reconciled? If not, is there anything that could be done to reconcile the situation?
13. Do you believe that God can redeem your failures?
14. Do you need to give someone in your life a second chance?

For Further Study

15. Read Philippians 3:12–14. How can you commit to moving forward with God?

2

Suspending Disbelief

Mark 1:1–15

The beginning of the gospel about Jesus Christ, the Son of God. It is written in Isaiah the prophet: "I will send my messenger ahead of you, who will prepare your way"—"a voice of one calling in the desert, 'Prepare the way for the Lord, make straight paths for him.'" And so John came, baptizing in the desert region and preaching a baptism of repentance for the forgiveness of sins. The whole Judean countryside and all the people of Jerusalem went out to him. Confessing their sins, they were baptized by him in the Jordan River. John wore clothing made of camel's hair, with a leather belt around his waist, and he ate locusts and wild honey. And this was his message: "After me will come one more powerful than I, the thongs of whose sandals I am not worthy to stoop down and untie. I baptize you with water, but he will baptize you with the Holy Spirit." At that time Jesus came from Nazareth in Galilee and was baptized by John in the Jordan. As Jesus was coming up out of the water, he saw heaven being torn open and the Spirit descending on him like a dove. And a voice came from heaven: "You are my Son, whom I love; with you I am well pleased." At once the Spirit sent him out into the desert, and he was in the desert forty days, being tempted by Satan. He was with the wild animals, and angels attended him. After John was put in prison, Jesus went into Galilee, proclaiming the good news of God. "The time has come," he said, "The kingdom of God is near. Repent and believe the good news!" (Mark 1:1–15)

I<small>N ONE, SHORT, PREGNANT</small> sentence, Mark announces his direction and gives an outline for his book, "The beginning of the gospel about Jesus Christ, the Son of God" (1:1). This verse serves as an appropriate outline—the gospel (the good news) about Jesus (his humanity) Christ (his divinity). Chapters one through ten (1–10) focus on Jesus and his ministry. Chapters eleven through sixteen (11–16) depict the passion week (the last week of Jesus' earthly life), where he becomes our Messiah, the Christ. You would do well to remember this outline.

But before we get started, I want you to be aware of a footnote. It is probably in your Bible at the bottom of the page, and may read as follows: "Some manuscripts do not contain the phrase "the Son of God." According to some, this is an example of one of the many "errors" that the Bible contains. Some of the earliest manuscripts do not contain this phrase and the likelihood is that it may have actually been added later by a scribe as a note in the margin. It's true—it is a variant. In fact, in terms of variances within scripture, this one, along with others like Mark 16:9–20, makes the "significant" list of Bible problems.[1] After acknowledging that fact, I've got to tell you what I really think of those who claim the Bible is in error. Here it is: Come on! Is that the best you've got? All you need to do is read down eleven verses in our text to find clarification on the subject once and for all. God himself joins the discussion when he says, "You are my Son, whom I love; with whom I am well pleased" (1:11). No footnote is needed on that verse! God has spoken.[2]

Let me state this another way. This variance is supposedly one of the most significant problems in the Bible. Critics say that it proves the Bible's inaccuracy. No, it doesn't! First of all, your Bible acknowledges it. More importantly, this poses no problem. When we speak about inerrancy of scripture, we mean in the originals. We don't believe that all copies through the centuries were miraculously penned or that God would strike someone dead with lightening if they made a transcribing error. We do believe the Bible is inerrant in the originals and that it has been remarkably preserved.

Actually, in some ways, the verse without the variant is a more precise outline. The gospel of Jesus (part one) Christ (part two). The phrase "Son of God" is just commentary. Mark's introduction is short and sweet. Contrast that with:

---

1. We will deal with the textual variant of Mark 16:9–20 in chapter 40 of this book.

2. It is interesting to find that Jesus is called Son of God only by God (1:11; 9:7), by demons (3:11; 5:7), and by one man, the centurion at the cross (15:39).

1. The Gospel of Matthew, which needs sixteen verses to announce Jesus to the Jews by way of genealogy, which was extremely important for Matthew's audience.
2. The Gospel of Luke, which begins with forty-two Greek words (actually eighty-four in the NIV) before he gets to the story.
3. The Gospel of John needs eighteen verses and uses seventeen mystical and difficult words before he gets started.

Not so with Mark. He is short and precise. He only uses five Greek words to get us started. Simple—the story of the good news, the redemptive grace of Jesus Christ—that is exactly what he wants to communicate.

Actually, this is a significant observation regarding the Gospel of Mark from which we need to make a couple of points. First, Mark is fast-paced throughout. He gives few details. "Just the facts, ma'am." The book moves rapidly, but when it stops—pay attention. Second, Mark is written in narrative. Narrative tells a story. Dialogue in a narrative passage slows the pace for a reason. So another principle to keep in mind is that whenever there is dialogue—pay attention. When people are speaking, take note of what they are saying!

So here we go. Mark has made his announcement: "The beginning of the gospel of Jesus Christ." Now, he turns from announcer to advocate. He has presented Jesus as the Christ, but can he prove his case? One legal maxim says to the defense attorney, "If your facts are strong, hammer the facts. If your facts are weak, hammer the desk." Mark hammers the facts.

In our passage, Mark gives four witnesses for Jesus Christ: 1) John the Baptist; 2) God; 3) Satan [although we are given no dialogue]; and 4) the words of Jesus himself.

Announced by John the Baptist (Mark 1:2-8)

Mark sets the stage by quoting two Old Testament prophets: Malachi and Isaiah. He mentions by name only the prophet Isaiah because he serves as a figurehead for all of the prophets. The point? The prophets predicted that one like Elijah would come and announce Christ—and here he is, John the Baptist. John the Baptist comes in prophetic style, making a statement with both his clothing and his diet. "John wore clothing made of camel's hair, with a leather belt around his waist, and he ate locusts and wild honey" (1:6).

As I read this passage, a couple of thoughts immediately come to mind. First, I must tell you, I've smelled camels many times and never once thought, "Boy, that would make a good coat." My second thought is along these lines: "Who was his public relations guy?" This is a public relations nightmare. Who would have given him this advice: "If you want to make an impact, leave Jerusalem, go to the desert, dress up like a caveman, and make a statement with your diet"? Actually, that is probably the point. John the Baptist was counterculture. The Romans expected a dignitary to announce the King—probably one riding an Italian stallion! No one expected one like John the Baptist—wearing the camel. The Jews would have probably expected an inaugural ball in Jerusalem—not grasshoppers in the wilderness. But John the Baptist came in prophetic style—like Elijah. Actually Jesus himself says of this prophet, "I tell you the truth: Among those born of women there has not risen anyone greater than John the Baptist" (Matthew 11:11).

Maybe the wilderness is a good place. It's a symbol of where we are as a people. Maybe it serves as a picture of our own day, with our empty, barren, and weary lives. It would make a good sermon—"The Desert of Human Existence." But that's not Mark's point. You can get many more picturesque details in the other gospel accounts. Mark's point comes with what is said in the dialogue. Remember, dialogue slows the pace of narrative for a reason. What is John the Baptist's message? He makes three points. First, "After me will come one more powerful than I." Second, "The thongs of whose sandals I am not worthy to stoop down and untie." And third, "I will baptize you with water, but he will baptize you with the Holy Spirit" (1:7–8).

John the Baptist would later say, "He must become greater; I must become less" (John 3:30). The one whom Jesus called the greatest prophet, called Jesus greater still. That was John's testimony.

Affirmed by God (Mark 1:9–11)

Mark next moves to the baptism of Jesus. Again, I'd draw your attention to the fact that much more detail is given to this event in the other Gospels. In Mark, we get no insight into why Jesus was baptized. Matthew tells us that it was to fulfill all righteousness (Matthew 1:15). We are not informed that John the Baptist actually refuses (at first) to baptize Jesus, but responds that he should be the one to be baptized (Matthew 1:14). We do not even get the announcement, "Look, the Lamb of God who takes away the sins of the world" (John 1:29). All this seems, and is, important. But Mark has a different purpose—to give a character witness for Jesus. Notice the dialogue.

> As Jesus was coming up out of the water, he saw heaven being torn open and the Spirit descending on him like a dove. And a voice came from heaven: "You are my Son, whom I love; with you I am well-pleased." (Mark 1:10-11)

Here we have God's word on it. We have the Father's approval of Jesus as his divine Son. This is the foundation for all we read about Jesus in Mark. This is who Jesus is.

It is interesting that we only find God speaking from heaven in three places in Scripture. First, at Jesus' baptism: "You are my Son, whom I love" (1:11). Next, at the transfiguration: "This is my Son, listen to him" (9:7). Finally, as Jesus prepares for the crucifixion: "Glorify your name, and a voice came from heaven saying, 'I have glorified it, and will glorify it again'" (John 12:27-28). Afterwards, Jesus tells the disciples, "That was for your benefit." God has spoken! Try to minimize Jesus if you will, but you are arguing with God himself.

Acknowledged by Satan (Mark 1:12-13)

Look critically at Mark's account of the temptation of Jesus and try as you might, you would be hard pressed to cover this event with fewer words—two very abbreviated sentences. In contrast, Matthew and Luke record for us the temptations of Jesus with great detail. We read about the temptation to turn stone into bread, the temptation of the kingdoms of the world, and the temptation of authority and splendor. We also learn how Jesus responds to them: "It is written, man does not live by bread alone . . . Do not put the Lord to the test . . . Worship and serve God only" (Matthew 4:1-10).

One might ask the question: Why does Mark bother with such an abbreviated account of the temptations? He simply wants to make this one point—Satan considers Jesus a formidable opponent and views him as a threat. Why else would Satan spend forty days in the desert tempting him?

I should also draw your attention to what Satan has to say about the matter. Actually, Mark doesn't include dialogue for us here. Why record the statement from the Father of Lies? Do you really want the testimony of Satan? Mark simply told of Satan's actions. Actions speak louder than words. Satan thinks Jesus is a formidable opponent and is willing to focus attention on him for forty days. Satan's actions serve as testimony to who Jesus is.

Accepted by Christ (Mark 1:14–15)

This is the crescendo of the passage. John the Baptist, God, even Satan have testified. Now Jesus gives his own words on the matter. We hear Jesus making three claims (again, notice the dialogue). First, "The time has come"—a prophetic phrase about the fullness of time (1:15). Jesus is essentially saying, "I am the fulfillment of Old Testament prophecy. What you have been waiting for is here. Moses, Elijah, Isaiah, Malachi—they were speaking about me." Second, "The kingdom of God is near" (1:15). Again, using prophetical language, Jesus is stating, "I am the one in whom the kingdom rests." He places himself as King of the kingdom. He couldn't claim kingship if it were not for his identity. And finally, "Repent and believe the good news!" (1:15). These represent the first words spoken by Jesus in the book of Mark: They give the core of Mark's teaching, and state Jesus' mission. Based on who Jesus is, what should our response be? Repent (change who you are living for) and believe. Those are the words of Jesus.

Application

What should we do with a passage like this? More importantly, what is Mark's purpose in writing this passage? His purpose is to present Jesus as the Christ, and to give testimony to the identity of Jesus.

In light of this, you need to first give yourself an opportunity to hear who Jesus is. Suspend for a moment your disbelief, at least long enough to let Mark make his argument. If you are a skeptic, if you are yet to believe—give Mark a chance. I know many people who have said, "I want to believe, but I have doubts." I would suggest to you that doubt is not the opposite of faith. Doubt is actually on the faith continuum. The opposite of belief is not doubt. The opposite of belief is disbelief. Allow Mark to answer some of your objections and give you reason to believe.

Second, understand this: all history points to Jesus. Whether it be Moses, Elijah, Isaiah, or Malachi—Jesus is the culmination of all of history and he is the fulfillment of their words.

Finally, realize that we are insignificant compared to him. He is all-powerful. He is the one in whom salvation rests. He is the Christ. The appropriate response is voiced for us by John the Baptist: "He is more powerful . . . I am not worthy . . . He must become greater, I must become less" (Matthew 3:1–12; Mark 1:1–8; Luke 3:15–18).

Study Questions

1. Who is the wildest preacher you have ever heard? How did you respond to their message?

2. In what ways does Mark 1:1 serve as an outline for the Gospel of Mark?

3. Why did John the Baptist dress so strangely (1:6)? See 2 Kings 1:8.

4. What three statements does John the Baptist make about Jesus (1:7–8)?

    a. What are the implications of recognizing Jesus as more powerful than yourself?

    b. What are the implications of recognizing your own unworthiness in comparison with Christ? How does it change your thinking about him?

5. Mark only gives an abbreviated account of the baptism of Jesus. Read Mark 1:9–11 and then compare it with Matthew 3:13–17 and Luke 4:1–13.

    a. What details does Mark omit?

    b. What is Mark's point in telling about this event? (Hint: remember the dialogue.)

6. There are only three places in the New Testament where God audibly speaks from heaven. Read the following three accounts. What do they have in common?

    a. Mark 1:11

    b. Mark 9:7

    c. John 12:27–30

7. Mark again only gives an abbreviated account of the desert temptations. Compare Mark 1:12–13 with Matthew 4:1–11 and Luke 4:1–13.

    a. What details does Mark omit?

    b. What is Mark's point in telling about this event? (Hint: why would Satan spend so much time and effort trying to tempt Jesus?)

8. Summarize in your own words what you learn about Jesus from John the Baptist, God, and Satan. What do we learn about Jesus' identity and purpose?

9. When Jesus says that "the time has come" and "the kingdom of God is near" (15), he is alluding to prophetic language about the coming Messiah and applying it to himself. How is Jesus the fulfillment of Old Testament prophecy?

10. What does it meant to "repent and believe the good news" (15)?

11. What is the good news of God (15)?

12. What is it about Jesus that makes you follow him?

For Further Study

13. Reflect on how Jesus is introduced by John the Baptist. How does it compare to a typical announcement of a Roman dignitary? How does it compare to how we would expect a foreign diplomat or the U. S. President to be introduced?

3

Inherent Authority

Mark 1:16–34

Have you ever known people who made great claims about themselves, but failed to back them up? Most of us have. As an athlete you often hear others making claims about their ability, but get them on the court and their boasts are empty—lots of talk, little game. It's usually not the one who makes great claims about their own athletic ability that worry you, it is the one who when asked, "Do you play?" responds, "A little!" But when you get one athlete saying about another, "He's got game!" you always take note.

Mark has put forward Jesus as the Christ—the Son of God. He has given us four testimonies to substantiate his claim: John the Baptist, God, Satan, and Jesus himself. But the question remains: Can Jesus deliver when it comes to these claims? In our passage, we will look at three areas of his everyday life that demonstrate and verify his authority as the Son of God.

The Authority of His Call (Mark 1:16–20)

Jesus' authority is depicted when he calls his disciples to follow him. Jesus calls them in the midst of their everyday life—where they live.

> As Jesus walked beside the Sea of Galilee, he saw Simon and his brother Andrew casting a net into the lake, for they were fishermen. "Come, follow me," Jesus said, "and I will make you fishers of men." At once they left their nets and followed him. When he had gone a little farther, he saw James son of Zebedee and his brother John in a boat, preparing their nets. Without delay he called them, and they left their father Zebedee in the boat with the hired men and followed him. (Mark 1:16–20)

Jesus initially calls two sets of brothers. This is not their first contact with Jesus, but you would not know it from Mark. John 1:35–42 records Andrew as a disciple of John the Baptist, introducing Peter to Jesus. Mark omits these details—not because he doesn't know them—they are just not essential for his point. He simply tells us that Simon (Peter) and his brother Andrew are fishing along the shore of Galilee. In all likelihood they are poor, as evidenced by their casting their nets from the shore. Jesus extends an invitation to follow and they leave their nets immediately (1:18). Mark gives few details—in typical fashion his treatment is short and sweet.

Jesus next encounters James and his brother John, sons of Zebedee. Unlike Peter and Andrew, they are likely wealthy businessmen—they have boats and a hired man. But they too, leave "without delay" to follow Jesus when he calls (1:20).

Mark's emphasis is once again not on the details, but on their immediate response. I'd like to point out two words in particular for your consideration that are repeated seven times in this section alone. Notice "at once" (1:18) and "without delay" (1:20). Actually both are the word "immediately" in Greek (*eutheōs*), but are translated various ways by the NIV (1:18–at once; 1:20–without delay; 1:23–just then; 1:28–quickly; 1:29–as soon as). Two other times the word is simply left untranslated (omitted in 1:21 and 1:30).

Jesus says to the disciples, "Follow me." Pay special attention to the dialogue. Unlike the prophets who challenged people to follow God, Jesus challenges his disciples to follow him. Unlike the prophets, whose disciples followed for the purpose of learning the Torah, Jesus' disciples have a different goal of learning from him and about him.

Also notice the language. It is an exhortational particle—a particle that expects an imperative (*akolouthein*). Simply put, Jesus does not invite the disciples to follow, he commands the disciples to do so. Jesus does not post a sign-up sheet for the curious: "Messiah: interested in a few good men." Jesus gives the command, the disciples recognize his authority, and they leave immediately. It reflects the appropriate response of a soldier reacting to an order from a superior officer.

Where they are going is not discussed, nor is it clear at this point what they will be doing. It is interesting that Jesus does not call them to be shepherds, or farmers, or laborers. But he calls his disciples to be fishermen—he speaks their language. But I wonder if this is more than a benign reference to the mission to which he calls them. When a fisherman hooks a fish, it has fatal consequences for the fish—life cannot go on as before. Jesus calls them to leave everything and life can no longer be the same.

But why tell this story? Mark tells it for a reason. Mark wants to make a single impression: the person who speaks is a figure of enormous authority. Jesus can make tremendous demands upon people and they recognize his right to do so. Someone once said, "Repentance is not ceasing to commit a sin, but turning away from what we were doing and embracing God at what he is doing wholeheartedly." The disciples embrace Jesus wholeheartedly.

It might be worth asking the question: What kind of person would it take to motivate you so completely to leave everything? Would it be a radical, or revolutionary? It likely would be someone who possesses great authority.

The Authority of His Teaching (Mark 1:21–28)

The authority of Jesus is further emphasized by his teaching.

> They went to Capernaum, and when the Sabbath came, Jesus went into the synagogue and began to teach. The people were amazed at his teaching, because he taught them as one who had authority, not as the teachers of the law. Just then a man in their synagogue who was possessed by an evil spirit cried out, "What do you want with us, Jesus of Nazareth? Have you come to destroy us? I know who you are—the Holy One of God!" "Be quiet!" said Jesus sternly. "Come out of him!" The evil spirit shook the man violently and came out of him with a shriek. The people were all so amazed that they asked each other, "What is this? A new teaching—and with authority! He even gives orders to evil spirits and they obey him." News about him spread quickly over the whole region of Galilee. (Mark 1:21–28)

Jesus and his disciples go to Capernaum,[1] home of Peter and Andrew. Capernaum becomes Jesus' base of operations in the Gospel of Mark. While in Capernaum, Jesus takes advantage of freedom of the

---

1. Capernaum was a fishing town on the northwest shore of Lake Galilee. Its Hebrew meaning is "village of Nahum." It was the home of Peter and Andrew, and possibly others of the twelve disciples (1:29). This is the headquarters of Jesus during his ministry in Galilee and a focal point in the Gospel of Mark. Matthew 11:23–24 and Luke 10:15 record Jesus' condemnation of Capernaum for their poor response to the Gospel.

synagogue,[2] a Jewish custom which permitted recognized visiting teachers to preach. There is not much here in Mark's gospel to help us understand what Jesus says (we should learn not to expect this). Mark doesn't record lengthy, sage-like discourses, but pithy statements and dramatic action. Once again the narrative is abbreviated so that the reader receives only a single impression—Jesus teaches with authority.

Again, let me point out just a couple of words for your consideration. First, as Jesus taught, "The people were amazed at his teaching" (1:22). You should ask, "Why?" You might chalk their amazement up to his style and suggest that the manner in which he spoke was dynamic and compelling. But the text refers not to the way he spoke (charisma), but to how and what he taught, "As one with authority" (1:27). Unlike the scribes who talked about God, Jesus spoke for God. The word "amazed" (*exeplessonto*)[3] is very strong. Its root means to strike or to smite. The people are astonished at what he says. Jesus does not have to quote authorities (so and so said this), Jesus *is* the authority.

Second, note that his very presence provokes a confrontation with the demonic man. "Just then a man in their synagogue who was possessed by an evil spirit cried out" (1:23). At this point, you may be saying, "Come on, you don't really believe in demon possession do you? We live in the twenty-first century! We are products of the enlightenment!" Actually, I do. I know demon possession is relegated by some to superstition—but they are the uninformed, or those who deny anything spiritual. I believe in a cosmic battle between good and evil. Paul tells us that our battle is not against flesh and blood, but powers and principalities (Ephesians 6:12).

Beyond that, studies in the occult and demonism today show that possession is not to be relegated to the bizarre—it happens. It not only happens in third world countries (in Africa or Haiti), but in major urban centers. Do you still need to be convinced? Take a trip to New Orleans. Am I suggesting that demon possession is prevalent? No! Am I suggesting it's possible? Absolutely! And the removal of God from our culture, our schools, and our way of life is assuredly making this a greater reality.

Let me give you two points to consider. First, Mark (as well as Doctor Luke) differentiates between possession and illness. He is not uninformed. Second, if demon possession is possible, if Jesus is the

---

2. The word synagogue literally means "to gather together." It is the typical name for the place where Jewish followers met for worship.

3. Mark 1:22.

ultimate spiritual authority, and if Jesus is routing Satan's realm—you should expect Satan's forces to resist. It is no wonder that we find the majority of Satanic attacks recorded for us in Scripture at the height of Jesus' ministry.

In any case, notice the outburst from this man—most would take steps to remove the man from the "church service," but Jesus delivers the man. First, the man spoke: "What do you want with us, Jesus of Nazareth?[4] Have you come to destroy us? I know who you are—the Holy One of God" (1:24).

As I read this, I wonder, is this panicked reaction? Or reverent acknowledgment? Probably both! Actually, the question, "Have you come to destroy us?" can also be translated not as a question, but as an acknowledgment: "You have come to destroy us."

Notice what happens next in this passage—Jesus orders the evil spirit to be silent (1:25). You might think that Jesus would want the free advertising. After all, the unclean spirit is right, "Jesus is the Holy One of God." But Jesus doesn't want testimony that is demonic. Throughout the book, Mark treats all the demonic utterances as unwelcome declarations.

One last phrase is worthy of consideration before moving on. After Jesus casts out the demon we read, "The people were all so amazed that they asked each other, 'What is this? A new teaching—and with authority'" (1:27). Jesus has the authority to command obedience, he teaches with authority, but he also couples his teaching with mighty deeds.

The Authority to Heal (Mark 1:29–34)

Jesus' authority is depicted through his miraculous ability to manipulate the physical restraints of our world.

> As soon as they left the synagogue, they went with James and John to the home of Simon and Andrew. Simon's mother-in-law was in bed with a fever, and they told Jesus about her. So he went to her, took her hand and helped her up. The fever left her and she began to wait on them. That evening after sunset the people brought to Jesus all the sick and demon-possessed. The whole town gathered at the door, and Jesus healed many who had various diseases. He also drove out many demons, but he would not let the demons speak because they knew who he was. (Mark 1:29–34)

---

4. Nazareth was an obscure village about seventy miles north of Jerusalem. It is not mentioned in the Old Testament.

After teaching in the synagogue, Jesus immediately leaves and enters the home of Peter and Andrew. Here we find Peter's mother-in-law[5] in bed with a fever. Jesus simply offers her his hand and, "The fever left her" (1:31). Actually, the phrase "the fever left her" (*aphiēmi*) is too mild. Literally, the fever forsakes her. It can't wait to get out of the presence of Jesus. Talk about authority! The healing is instantaneous, final, and complete. She is totally restored—there are no after effects. In fact, she gets up and waits on them. (Gentlemen, this is not to be used as a proof text that mothers-in-law should be waiting on us! I've tried it, it doesn't work!)

When Mark speaks of serving, nothing menial or insignificant is in view here. Actually, serving will become one of the main characteristics of discipleship that Jesus tries to convey to his disciples (with some difficulty, I might add).

Another verse is also striking: "That evening after sunset the people brought to Jesus all the sick and demon possessed" (1:32). With the single exception of Peter, the villagers do not bring their sick to Jesus until sundown. Mark makes a point to say the sun has set. Why? Notice also that Jesus' first two miracles recorded in Mark are on the Sabbath. Is this a coincidence? Or is Mark suggesting that the power of Jesus stands in stark contrast to the existing structures and institutions of Judaism?

We can certainly say that the same God who created the Sabbath is the one at work in Jesus. Jesus is Lord of the Sabbath. He is the one with authority. Here again we find Mark's point. Jesus has the ability to heal the sick, cast out demons, and in the next section (1:40–45), cleanse the leper—the very traits the prophets predicted of the Messiah. This is all part of the proof that Jesus is the Christ the Son of the living God.

You can see Jesus' authority in the calling of his disciples, in his teaching, and in his authority to heal. Jesus has *inherent authority* because of who he is. As such, we should listen to him.

Listen when Jesus speaks! When Jesus says, "Come follow me"—people are compelled to follow (1:17). When Jesus says, "Be quiet, come out of him"—unclean spirits are routed (1:25). When Jesus commands, "Quiet, be still"—the wind and the waves obey him (4:39). When Jesus utters the phrase, "Little girl, get up"—even the dead are raised (5:41).

---

5. In 1 Corinthians 9:5, Paul refers to Peter as married. In 10:28, Peter speaks of having "left everything" to follow Jesus. This may mean that Peter (and perhaps others of the disciples) left his family for prolonged periods to follow Jesus.

When Jesus speaks, "Be opened"—deaf ears are opened (7:34). When Jesus cries out—the temple veil is split from top to bottom (15:38–39). It's all about the authority of Jesus.

Application

In applying this passage to our lives we must understand that Jesus is the ultimate authority. This being the case, the predominant views that the world often holds cannot also be true. Pluralism (the view that there are many ways or paths we might follow) can't stand. Relativism (the view that what is right for you may not be right for me—follow your own path, do your own thing) can't stand. Self-determination (the belief that you determine truth, that you are your own boss) can't stand. There is only one hub, and you are not it.

I want to take you back to the call of Jesus: "Follow Me" (1:17). That command strikes at the heart of Christianity. Jesus is calling—how will you respond? The disciples recognize who Jesus is, and when he commands—they respond. When Jesus says to them, "Follow me," they go immediately. As I mentioned before, that's actually true repentance. Repentance is not simply ceasing to commit a sin (although this is certainly necessary). Repentance is turning away from what we are doing and wholeheartedly embracing what God wants us to do. It is following Jesus Christ completely, in every area of our lives.

Too often, we try to add "Christ" to our endeavors. We do what we normally do, just with Christ in view. That is addition without subtraction. We merely add him to what we are doing, rather than saying, "I only want what Christ wants from me." Christ is not just asking that we attend church every weekend. Christ is not suggesting that we simply act with integrity at our work place. Christ is not just asking that we remember to pray and give him praise. He doesn't want us simply to add him to what we are doing. He wants all of us.

Am I suggesting that God wants you to leave your job, change careers, sell everything you have, and become a missionary? Not necessarily, but maybe. Am I suggesting that God wants you to stop attending a secular college, change your major, and go to a Christian college? Maybe that is what God is calling you to do. Have you asked him? Am I suggesting that God might want you to leave behind some of your non-Christian friends, your non-Christian activities and follow him completely? Absolutely! I am suggesting that you follow Jesus completely! Nothing else really matters.

I want you to think for a moment about a bicycle rim—everything focuses on the hub and works out from there. Loosen one spoke (or take it out completely) and you can ride for a while, but when things get rough, or over time, you will experience trouble. Loosen several spokes and the impact will be dynamic. The same is true in your life. Without the proper center, your life is in danger. Christ needs to be the hub of your marriage, of your finances (your checkbook), of your career, of your education, of your activities, and of your hobbies. Get one or two of these out of balance and you will experience trouble. You might be able to survive for awhile, but not indefinitely. Remove several spokes from the hub and your life will be in turmoil.

You must bring Jesus back as the hub of your life. He is the one who has the authority and the power to bring things back into balance. He is the one with inherent authority.

Study Questions

1. In your experience, what product or professional service made the greatest claim/boast about their merchandise but failed to back it up?
2. Of all the people you have ever encountered, who impressed you as having the greatest authority?
3. Who has served as your best teacher? Why?
4. What does Jesus mean when he says to his disciples, "Come, follow me" (17)? How was that different from the Old Testament Prophets?
5. Should we obey instantly, or should we first count the cost (1:18)? Before you answer: It appears from Mark's account that Simon (Peter) and Andrew acted on impulse to an invitation from someone they hardly knew. A closer look, however suggests that they had known and followed Jesus in a limited way prior to this encounter. (See John 1:35–42)
6. What is your initial response when you first read the account of "a demon-possessed man" (23)? Do you relegate this to superstition or is it really possible?

7. In Scripture, the appearance of evil spirits reached a climax during the earthly ministry of Jesus. Why might this be the case? What impact did Jesus' earthly ministry have?

8. Why would a demon publicly confess who Jesus was (23–24)?

9. What does the demon say about Jesus (24)? Is it accurate?

10. Why would Jesus tell the evil spirit to be quiet even though it made an accurate statement about him (25)?

11. Looking at verses 22–27, in what two ways did Jesus' authority amaze the people? What would it take to amaze you?

12. In verses 30–31, Mark records the healing of Peter's mother-in-law. Why does Mark also include the fact that she immediately got up and began to wait on them?

13. Why did the people wait until after sunset to bring all the sick and demon-possessed (32)?

14. What does it show about their view of the Sabbath? What does it say about Jesus' authority over the Sabbath? (See 2:27–28)

15. What is true repentance? What are the implications of true repentance on specific areas of your life?

16. On a scale of one to ten, how much authority does Jesus have in your life? What needs to be submitted to Jesus to rate it a ten? How are you going to do this?

For Further Study

17. Locate Capernaum on a map of Israel. This is not only Peter and Andrew's home town, it becomes the center of Jesus' Galilean ministry and the focal point of most of the book of Mark.

18. The calling of the first disciples can also be found in Matthew 4:18–22; Luke 5:2–11; and John 1:35–42. What do we learn from these passages?

19. Matthew and Luke also tell about Jesus healing Peter's mother-in-law. Read Matthew 8:14–15 and Luke 4:38–39. What do we learn from these accounts?

4

Necessary Solitude

Mark 1:35–39

> Very early in the morning, while it was still dark, Jesus got up, left the house and went off to a solitary place, where he prayed. Simon and his companions went to look for him, and when they found him, they exclaimed: "Everyone is looking for you!" Jesus replied, "Let us go somewhere else—to the nearby villages—so I can preach there also. That is why I have come." So he traveled throughout Galilee, preaching in their synagogues and driving out demons. (Mark 1:35–39)

AS WE PICK UP our story, we need to remember that it has been a long, busy day. In all probability, Jesus has gotten up early to travel to Capernaum. He has arrived at the synagogue where he preaches (this was not your typical twenty-minute sermon). He has confronted a man with an evil spirit (1:23). He goes to Peter's house where he heals Peter's mother-in-law (1:30) and they have dinner together. After sunset, the whole town gathers at the door where Jesus heals many people late into the night (1:32).

I can only begin to imagine a day in the life of Jesus. Personally, I know what I feel like after a weekend of preaching and dealing with the demands of ministry. I need a day off—but I don't take it. There is too much to do: phone calls to make, letters to write, and meetings to schedule. I realize that most preachers do take Mondays off, but not me (sounds deeply spiritual, doesn't it?). Actually, I am so tired on Mondays that I don't want to spend my day off being tired.

You, too, know what it is like to get busy and tired. Each of our lives has certain aspects which drag us down and wear us out. Certain days of the week, or periods during the year are exceptionally busy. And I imagine, after a hard and grueling day, the first thing on your mind is, "I want to get up at the crack of dawn and spend a few hours in prayer!" Right? Probably not!

But that's what we get with the first five words: "Very early in the morning" (1:35). Well, that's a little subjective. After all, how early is very early? A teenage boy might say noon. We can, however, rule out the typical teenage response. The next five words in our passage narrow it down for us. They read, "While it was still dark" (1:35).

This morning, as I write, sunrise was about 6 a.m. That's fairly early by my standards. According to the Roman standard of keeping time (remember Mark is writing to the Romans), this would have been the last watch of the night which was the period right before dawn (usually from 3 a.m. and ending about 6 a.m.). Any way you slice it, that's early.

Jesus has had an exhausting day, but rises early to get a start on his day by praying. That goes against most people's attitude towards prayer. It's not typical. Here are some typical attitudes:

- I'm tired, I'm going to skip prayer today.

- Prayer is what we do when we have the time. (Prayer is often neglected by active people who are too busy.)

- Prayer is a last resort. Prayer is what we do when all else fails—we can always pray.

- In fact, there are probably some who would secretly think or say, "There are two different types of people—those who get things done and those who pray."

Actually, my own attitudes towards prayer must change as I reflect on this passage. I've always approached it with the mind-set, okay, Jesus prayed, it must be important (maybe even more important) for me also. But, there is much more to this than I ever imagined. I now assert that as Christians, we have no choice but to pray if we are going to accomplish God's will. Prayer is the time when we let God set our agenda and are strengthened to accomplish his purpose in our lives. Prayer is the conduit by which the power of God flows to our lives.

To get at the deeper meaning of this passage, I want to ask and answer three rather simple questions.

What Did the People Want?

"Everyone is looking for you" (1:37).

These are the words of the disciples as they find Jesus. The question is, why are they looking for him? The answer is easy. We see people coming to Jesus late into the night on Saturday night. They are back again on Sunday morning, looking for Jesus. Undoubtedly, there were varying responses for each as to why they were seeking out Jesus. Some are amazed at his teaching, others come out of curiosity, but it is likely that most are coming to be healed by Jesus or perhaps they were bringing someone whom they wanted Jesus to work on. After the account of the demon-possessed man, some men may have come to Jesus and said, "Jesus, my wife is possessed, can you possibly help me out here?" (Just kidding!)

You won't hear me condemning the people for coming to Jesus. Who could blame them for seeking him out? If you were sick, lame, blind, or had leprosy (or any other medical issue for that matter), and you heard about Jesus' healing, what would you have done? Even if you personally were healthy, wouldn't you be at least a bit curious? Any rubber-neckers out there? I've got to admit, there have been times when I have driven by the scene of an accident just to see what was going on, or even drove out to see the latest storm damage or home destroyed by fire. My neck bends with the best of them.

The people want Jesus for what he can do for them. I understand it completely and would readily admit, I'd probably do the same if I were in their sandals! Truthfully, the miracle worker scenario fits very nicely into the Jewish expectations for the Messiah. The people want a show.

What if they had gotten that Messiah? If this had been Jesus' purpose, he would have set up shop, hung a shingle out on his porch, registered with the Capernaum Better Business Bureau, and gotten started.

What Did the Disciples Want?

"Simon and his companions went to look for him" (1:36).

Again, I need to ask, why? It is interesting that Mark writes "Simon and his companions"—literally, "Simon and the others." Remember, Mark wrote as Simon Peter spoke.

It is worth asking: Are the disciples simply looking out for the interests of other people here? Jesus has been healing people late into the night. Then the disciples go to sleep. During this time (between 3 a.m.

and 6 a.m.) Jesus sneaks out to be alone and pray. When the disciples awake (probably because people are pounding on the door) Jesus is gone. Crowds have gathered and are clamoring for Jesus.

My suspicion is that the disciples aren't worried about Jesus, nor are they simply trying to help the people out. The disciples are saying, "Last night was awesome!" They don't want the miracle show to stop. They view themselves at the pinnacle of this pyramid scheme with Jesus at the top. They don't want the party to be over. They are seeking popularity, power, and prestige. They are Jesus' disciples, and Jesus has just hit it big time!

Again, I'm not being hard on the disciples. I probably would have done the same thing. In fact, this fits in well with their assumptions about the Messiah. If Jesus is the Chosen One of Israel, he is supposed to be a miracle worker. The Messiah is supposed to heal the sick and give sight to the blind. He could heal lepers (1:40–45). The disciples expect a conquering general, a ruling king, a man to usher in a new era for Israel. In the eyes of many people, Jesus has just demonstrated himself as such.

The disciples are excited. So when they go looking for Jesus, they are saying, "Jesus, where did you go? Get back here, everyone is looking for you." Mark uses an interesting phrase here. It is the word for manhunt (*katadiōkō*). They are trying to hunt him down. The idea is that of a panicked search. They've got to find Jesus, and find him now! They eventually find him and interrupt his prayers.

Let me ask you another question: What if they had gotten their way? They would have made Jesus king. They wanted a ruler with power and authority. They wanted a rock star. Which leads to my third question.

What Did Jesus Want?

"Jesus got up, went to a solitary place . . . and prayed" (1:35).

Step back one more time. Jesus is weary, exhausted, and tired. So tired that he feels the necessity to pray. Keep that in mind and then ask, why did Jesus go to a solitary place?

Before we tackle this question, I want to give you some background. The first item of interest is the word "solitary place" (*erēmos*). It is the same word used of John the Baptist's preaching and for the temptations of Jesus. Literally, it means in the desert. Mark uses this word again now (and later) and wants us to make a specific connection. John the Baptist went to prepare the way for Christ, and now Christ goes to prepare for ministry. Jesus goes into solitude to prepare himself.

This is also the first of three of Jesus' prayers in the book of Mark. We find one here at the beginning of his ministry (1:35–39); one in the middle of his ministry (6:46); and the last in the Garden of Gethsemane, just prior to Jesus' arrest (14:35–36).

In all three cases the scene is the same. Jesus is always alone, it is always at night, it is during a time of tension, and Jesus seems always to be praying to God for direction.

The only place where we actually get Jesus' words comes later. "'Abba, Father,' he said, 'everything is possible for you. Take this cup from me. Yet not what I will, but what you will'" (14:36).

Other prayers are recorded for us in the other Gospels: at Jesus' baptism (Luke 3:21); when Jesus has to deal with the crowds (Luke 5:16); during the transfiguration (Luke 9:29); and before choosing the twelve apostles where he spends the entire night in prayer (Luke 6:12). Jesus' prayers include times when he prays for individuals (Luke 9:18; 11:1; 22:32); and prays for his own decisions, especially when people want to make him King (Matthew 14:23; John 6:15). The most notable is the Lord's prayer (Matthew 6:9–15).

I mention these because we get a clue about why Jesus is praying. It isn't just as an example for the disciples to follow—actually, Jesus is sneaking away to be alone. His prayers are not for the benefit of their observation. When he prays, Jesus is seeking guidance and direction. We sometimes forget, that while Jesus is indeed "God with us," Jesus became fully human. Hebrews 2:17 says, "For this reason, he had to be made like his brothers in every way, in order that he might become a merciful and faithful high priest in service to God, and that he might make atonement for the sins of the people."

Paul wrote,

> Your attitude should be the same as that of Christ Jesus: Who being in very nature God, did not consider equality with God something to be grasped (clenched, held on to), but made himself nothing, taking the very nature of a servant, being made in human likeness. And being found in appearance as a man, he humbled himself and became obedient to death—even death on a cross! (Philippians 2:5–8)

In the Gospel of Mark, Jesus becomes tired, exhausted, thirsty, shows emotion, suffers temptation, and seeks direction. Jesus gets away from the people—because he needs to get away from the people. Jesus goes to pray—because Jesus needs to pray. Jesus goes to pray to withstand temptation and to seek power to live out God's purposes.

Let me ask you a couple more questions. If Jesus had simply remained at Peter's home and listened to the town folk, what would they have had him do? If Jesus had stayed and listened to the disciples, what advice would they have given him?

Instead of being distracted or misled by them, Jesus slips off alone to pray. Just as in every other instance, when we find Jesus at a crossroads, Jesus goes to pray. Jesus is seeking power, direction, and guidance from his Father. Jesus is not just talking to himself, he self-limits himself by becoming a man and is seeking counsel from God. It is *necessary solitude*. It is essential for Jesus to pray and he understands this. So especially when he is tired; especially when he is tempted; especially when he needs help and direction—Mark records Jesus praying.

After Jesus has prayed, he is able to say to the disciples, "Let us go somewhere else—to the nearby villages—so I can preach there also. That's why I have come" (1:38). If you are observant, you will notice that's the same purpose recorded for us earlier when, "Jesus went into Galilee, proclaiming the good news of God" (1:14).

It's not a matter of prayer being important. It was an essential part of Jesus' life and should also be a part of yours. You must pray if you are going to accomplish God's will for your life.

What Should We Do with This Passage?

We have no choice, but to pray.

1. We must make it a regular practice (as was his custom).

2. We must pray, especially at busy times.

3. We must withdraw from the noise and demands of life in order to focus.

4. We must determine to pray before times of crisis, rather than simply during times of crisis.

5. Most important, we must reflect on the priorities of Jesus, and seek God's strength and purpose for our lives.

6. When is the last time you did this? Maybe it is time to pray, "God give me the strength and ability to fulfill your purpose in my life."

Study Questions

1. Are you an early bird or a night owl? What gets you up or keeps you up?
2. When life is its busiest, what do you do to find rest? How do you relax?
3. How does busyness or exhaustion affect your spiritual life?
4. Why was "everyone" looking for Jesus?
5. What was the crowd hoping for that morning as they awoke reflecting on the night before? What might they have been expecting from the Messiah?
6. The disciples were not just looking for Jesus, but they were a part of an all-out manhunt for him. Why were they so intently looking for Jesus?
7. What were the disciples hoping for that morning as they awoke reflecting on the night before? What might they have been expecting from the Messiah?
8. When Jesus got up early that morning, what was he looking for? Why did he decide to pray that morning instead of continuing the miracles of the night before?
9. Mark tells us Jesus went to a "solitary place" to pray. That word "solitary" can also be translated as "desert" or "lonely place." In fact, Mark has already used that word twice in the book of Mark. Looking at 1:3 and 1:12, what might the significance be of Jesus' chosen location to pray? Why didn't he pray in a public place with lots of people around?
10. When Jesus is found by his disciples and they explain the situation to him, what did Jesus decide to do (1:38–39)? Why? Does anything shock you about Jesus' decisions so far? Why or why not?
11. We find that sometimes Jesus prays in order to teach his disciples (see Matt. 6:9–13 and Luke 11:1–4). This, however, does not seem to be the case in our story.
    a. Why does Jesus pray?
    b. Why didn't Jesus invite his disciples to pray with him?
    c. Does Jesus need to pray? (See Philippians 2:5–8; Hebrews 2:14–18).

12. What does Jesus' behavior communicate about his priorities? At this point in his ministry, what was Jesus' mission (see 1:14–15 and 1:38–39)? How did his view of "mission" impact his decision to pray?

13. When and why do you pray? What kinds of things keep you from praying? What kinds of things motivate you to pray?

For Further Study

14. If you had to succinctly state what you view your mission as a Christian to be, what would you say? How does that impact the way and how often you pray?

15. What would you do if God asked you to move, to simplify your life, to change careers, to be his witness in a country that is hostile toward Christians?

5

Reckless Faith

Mark 2:1-12

> A few days later, when Jesus again entered Capernaum, the people heard that he had come home. So many gathered that there was no room left, not even outside the door, and he preached the word to them. (Mark 2:1-2)

WHEN JESUS LEFT, HE left in triumph—now he returns under suspicion. Critical eyes are trying to find fault.[1] But Jesus returns, doing what he is supposed to be doing—preaching. When Jesus comes home (likely to Peter's house or another in Capernaum) the crowds gather. The room is full, even the doorway is full.

Our passage is a story told in three acts: one, focusing on a group of men outside trying to get in; the second on the thoughts of the scribes on the inside; and finally, the camera shows a panoramic view of the full crowd and their response to Jesus. I'd like to look at each in turn.

Act One: Through the Roof (Mark 2:3-5)

The story begins by depicting the faith of several men making their way towards Jesus.

> Some men came, bringing to him a paralytic, carried by four of them. Since they could not get him to Jesus because of the crowd, they made an opening in the roof above Jesus and, after digging through it, lowered the mat the paralyzed man was lying on. When Jesus saw their faith, he said to the paralytic, "Son, your sins are forgiven." (Mark 2:3-5)

---

1. This is the first of five negative responses toward Jesus recorded for us in the book of Mark, each with increasing intensity.

Notice, there are actually more than five men involved. Our passage reads, "Some men came . . . carried by four of them" (2:3). This large group really possesses a mob mentality and their story is remarkable in several ways.

First, these men carry the paralytic across town—we aren't told how far. It could be several blocks, it could be several miles, but they come carrying him. They make their way through the crowded streets to the crowded house only to find the door blocked. Amazingly, the men are undeterred and they look for another way in. They seem to have the attitude, "We have made it this far, we are not going to give up now." As I read this account, I am confronted with this question I'd like to pose to you. Do you really think their minds immediately jumped to this conclusion: "Let's dig a hole in the roof"? No! I can't imagine this was their first thought. They certainly contemplated other means. They were improvising. Surely, they first had the thought, "Let's ask others to move,"—but the others wanted to see Jesus too. Maybe they tried sending a representative in to try to bring Jesus out—unsuccessfully. I'm fairly confident they brainstormed many ideas. My experience in circumstances like this is—a bunch of guys, a little bit of duct tape, some baling wire—they think they can do anything. But nothing worked. Finally, one of them suggests a hair-brained idea: "We should dig a hole in the roof!" And here, the mob mentality kicks into play. They all buy in! If it were only two, or maybe three guys, the whole idea collapses—it's probably not going to happen. But a bunch of guys, all who obviously left their wives at home, conclude: "Sounds like a great idea!"

One more comment. Mark doesn't tell us any of the details—I wish he would. We don't know the kind of roof—if it's a flat, adobe-type roof, it probably has stairs on the outside of the house. Or, more common in Capernaum, it might have been a sloped, thatched roof with wooden cross beams, overlaid with matting of reeds, branches, and dried mud. Mark doesn't tell us, but Luke says they lifted tiles (Luke 5:19). This suggests the less common adobe-type roof which would make getting up on top easier, but the digging more difficult.[2] In either case, they get the guy up, they dig a hole (the passage literally says, "they de-roofed the roof"),[3] and they let him down.

---

2. Matthew 9:1–8 omits any reference to the paralytic being lowered through the roof.

3. *Apostegazō.*

Again, this leaves me with all kinds of questions. What did they use to dig the hole? Where did they get it? I doubt they brought it with them. How did they lower the guy down? What did they use? Where did they get it? Certainly they didn't bring these things along. Did they conveniently borrow these items from someone's open garage?

Even more perplexing is the "digging the hole and getting him down" part—can you imagine being on the inside of the house as Jesus is preaching and witnessing these events? Imagine yourself for a moment as part of the crowd listening as the debris starts falling from the ceiling on your head. Worse yet, imagine the reaction of the home owner! How would you feel if someone was digging through your drywall? Did someone in that group scream, "Property damage"? Did anyone speak up? They likely did!

It must have been startling to everyone involved: to Jesus, to the audience, to the homeowner, and to the paralytic on the mat. We do learn that the scribes are startled, but their shock comes from Jesus' words, not the hole in the roof. Jesus says, "Son, your sins are forgiven" (2:5). Which ones? He has probably committed several in just the last few minutes: trespassing, stolen property, property damage, breaking and entering!

Obviously, we know Jesus is referring to the common notion that a person reaps what he sows. If someone was paralyzed, the common understanding was that either this person or his parents had sinned. We will discuss this further in a moment.

While we know the Scribes are startled, I wonder what the friends thought about Jesus' statement: "Your sins are forgiven." They hadn't brought their friend to Jesus for forgiveness, they brought him to be healed. How would you feel if you went to your doctor because you were sick, and he simply made this pronouncement: "You're forgiven, that will be three hundred bucks"?

But notice the beginning of verse 5: "When Jesus saw their faith." Each synoptic Gospel (Matthew, Mark, and Luke) records this fact for us. What did he see? He saw unstoppable, unashamed determination to get their friend to him. Here we learn a valuable lesson—faith means more than simple belief, it shows itself in action. Faith is not thwarted by obstructions. In fact, faith by definition is obedient response. Faith is not inactive, it's active. James says he'll show us faith by what he does (James 2:18). Later in Mark, in the story of Blind Bartimaeus, the crowds are trying to deter him, but Bartimaeus is undeterred. He keeps pressing, he keeps calling, he is relentless, and Jesus finally says to him, "Your faith has healed you" (See 10:46–52).

There is another passage that always intrigues me. It comes from Matthew 11:12. Jesus is speaking and he says, "From the days of John the Baptist until now the kingdom of heaven has been forcefully advancing, and forceful men lay hold of it." I'm not confident of everything said in that passage, but it seems to suggest that Jesus is looking for people who will passionately pursue him. The paralytic's friends have shown a reckless faith.

That's Act One—men on the outside, trying to get in. Act Two focuses on some of the people already on the inside, and we learn something about them—they are questioning Jesus.

Act Two: Pessimistic Priests (Mark 2:6–9)

> Now some teachers of the law were sitting there, thinking to themselves, "Why does this fellow talk like that? He's blaspheming! Who can forgive sins but God alone?" Immediately Jesus knew in his spirit that this was what they were thinking in their hearts, and he said to them, "Why are you thinking these things? Which is easier: to say to the paralytic, 'Your sins are forgiven,' or to say, 'Get up, take your mat and walk?'" (Mark 2:6–9)

Everyone has come to hear Jesus, but not all are impressed. Luke tells us that the Scribes[4] have come from all over, including Jerusalem, and here we find a clue why Jesus said, "Your sins are forgiven" (2:5).

The Scribes falsely believe that if a person is sick or handicapped, it is because of some sin in their life. Legalists would contend that a man cannot be healed until he has been forgiven because his ailment is a result of his sin. They use this doctrine as an excuse to justify neglect for all the sick. In other places, Jesus categorically denies that sin is synonymous with sickness. He is even asked the question, "Who sinned, this man or his parents?" to which Jesus responds, "Neither" (John 9:2–3).

But Jesus sees the Scribes and knows what they are up to. Maybe for this very reason he says what he does. By doing so, he not only goads them on, but cuts right to the heart of this particular issue.

---

4. The phrase translated "teachers of the law" in verse 6 is literally "scribes." These were people who were trained in the religious law of Judaism. They were the experts of proper conduct. They appear several times in Mark in opposition to Jesus and are often seen with the Pharisees. Unlike the Pharisees, the scribes were a professional class and not a religious sect or party.

They accuse him of blasphemy (*blasphēmeō*).[5] Blasphemy simply means to show contempt or disrespect for God. It can take one of two forms. First, you can blaspheme by trying to bring God down, minimize him, or limit his importance. This is why swearing is wrong—you are actually committing blasphemy. When you take the Lord's name in vain you are bringing him down or minimizing his importance. The Hebrews were so conscious of this that they would not even speak the name of God out of reverence and took special precautions before they would even write the word. This is part of the reason I discourage using slang terms for Jesus or God.

The second form of blasphemy is actually just the opposite. It is elevating man to the status of God, or claiming abilities that belong only to God. The Roman emperors did this by calling themselves god or demanding to be worshiped. This is what we do when we want to judge others in areas that only God should judge—we put ourselves in the place of God.

Understand, the Scribes are right in their statement: "Who can forgive sins but God alone?" (2:7). Scripture is clear on this issue. The assessment of the Jewish leaders is correct (Exodus 34:6–9; Psalms 103:3; 130:4; Isaiah 43:25; 44:22; 48:11; Daniel 9:9; etc). Only God can forgive sins. Their assessment of the situation is right, but their conclusion about Jesus is wrong—they assume he is only a man.

For this reason Jesus asks, "Which is easier: to say 'your sins are forgiven' or to say 'get up and walk'?" (2:9). From a human perspective, the answer is obvious. Any quack, religious nut, or feigned religious leader could utter the words, "Your sins are forgiven"—and no one could prove otherwise. Which is easier, to make a theological pronouncement about forgiveness or provide empirical proof? From God's perspective, both are his prerogative. Actually, forgiveness of sins may be more difficult—it certainly cost him more.

Jesus simply asks the question, and then the scene changes one more time. It changes first from the paralytic and his friends, next to the Scribes, and finally, to the whole audience. Jesus addresses all who are present.

---

5. Blasphemy is mentioned in five accounts in the book of Mark. Twice the accusation is hurled at Jesus (2:7; 14:64). Once it is used for the evil that comes out of man's heart (7:22). Once Jesus warns his critics about blaspheming against the Holy Spirit (3:28–29), and once it refers to the insults hurled at Jesus on the cross (15:29).

Act Three: In Full View (Mark 2:10–12)

> "But that you may know that the Son of Man has authority on earth to forgive sins . . ." He said to the paralytic, "I tell you, get up, take your mat and go home." He got up, took his mat and walked out in full view of them all. This amazed everyone and they praised God, saying, 'We have never seen anything like this!" (Mark 2:10–12)

Jesus says, "But that you may know" (2:10). The word "you" here is plural—y'all. In order that everyone may know, Jesus backs up his pronouncement. Words are cheap. Put your money where your mouth is. The proof is in the pudding. Jesus says, "Get up and walk" and the man got up (2:11). Jesus demonstrates conclusively that he is the Son of God. He has taught with authority. He has healed the sick and cured the leper. He can make the lame walk; and he can forgive sins.

There are some who want to suggest that Jesus never claimed divinity for himself. They haven't read scripture carefully or knowledgeably. One need only look, for example, to Jesus' "I am" statements in the Gospel of John. Or, to the account of Jesus as he stands before Pilate. Actually, we don't need to look beyond Mark chapter 2. Jesus claims the authority to forgive sins.

But if you are still unconvinced, I want to point out one more detail for you. It comes in verse 10: "That you may know that the Son of Man has authority on earth to forgive sins." Jesus calls himself, "Son of Man." It is the title that Jesus used most often for himself. In the book of Mark alone, Mark records Jesus saying this fourteen times (2:28; 8:31, 38; 9:9, 12, 31; 10:33, 45; 13:26; 14:21, 41, 62). Rather than being a title of humanity (son of man), it is a title of divinity. The title itself comes from Daniel and is a prophetic designation for the Messiah.

> And there before me was one like a son of man, coming with the clouds of heaven. He approached the Ancient of Days and was led into his presence. He was given authority, glory and sovereign power; all peoples, nations and men of every language worshiped him. His dominion is an everlasting dominion that will not pass away, and his kingdom is one that will never be destroyed. (Daniel 7:13–14)

Jesus says of himself, I am the one given authority and power. I am the one who has everlasting dominion. My kingdom will never be destroyed. I am the one deserving of worship.

It is interesting to look at the response of the people as they encounter Jesus. "This amazed everyone and they praised God, saying, 'We have never seen anything like this!'" (2:12). That is the proper response to Jesus.

In Mark, we have this syllogism: only God can forgive sins; Jesus (the Son of Man) forgives sins; Jesus stands in the place of God.

With this we come to act four.

Act Four: To Be Continued

Act Four is yet to be written. In Act Four you are the star. What will be said of you?

Some of you might be like the Scribes. You have been unconvinced, skeptical. I challenge you to consider the claims of Jesus. Investigate the facts of history. Ask this question: Where else can forgiveness be found? It is only in Jesus.

All of us should be like the paralytic's friends. We should demonstrate reckless faith. Jesus is not calling us to ordinary faith. He is calling us to extraordinary faith. He is calling us to stretch beyond the ordinary—to stretch boundaries. If Jesus looked at you and your life, would he be able to say like he did to the paralytic, "I see your faith?" If not, why not?

He is also calling us to worship. Not apathetic, weak, stale worship—but vibrant, dynamic awe, and amazement. We need to realize that there is nothing else like this in the world in which we live. Jesus, the Son of Man, the sovereign power who forgives sin, whose dominion is everlasting, walked among us. We'll be praising Christ in heaven for eternity—we had better get started now.

Study Questions

1. If in a crisis, even at 3 a.m., which four friends would you call?

2. What characteristics do you value most in a friend?

3. If you were one of the paralytic's friends and you saw the crowds, what would you have done?

4. How would you feel if you were the paralytic when your friends decided to help you "drop in" on Jesus?

5. What does it mean when it says that "Jesus saw their faith" (2:5)? What are the implications of this?

6. What qualities do the four men possess that impress you the most?

7. Why did Jesus say to the paralytic, "Son, your sins are forgiven" (2:5)?

8. Why did the teachers of the law get so upset?

9. What is the answer to the teachers' question in verse 7: "Who can forgive sins but God alone?" (See: Ex 34:6–9; Ps 103:3; 130:4; Is 43:25; 44:22; 48:11; Dan 9:9).

10. From a human perspective, what is the answer to Jesus' question in verse 9, "Which is easier: to say to the paralytic, 'Your sins are forgiven?' or to say, 'Get up and walk?'"

11. According to this lesson,

    a. What is blasphemy?

    b. What forms does it take?

    c. Which are they accusing Jesus of?

    d. Is Jesus blaspheming? Why or why not?

12. What did Christ eventually do to make forgiveness available?

13. If you had friends who could take you to Jesus for healing today, what kind of healing would you ask for?

For Further Study

14. Read the parallel accounts of the healing of the paralytic in Matthew 9:1–8 and Luke 5:17–26. What additional details do you learn?

15. What would it look like if we really worshiped God with awe and amazement? What steps can we take to accomplish this?

6

Challenging Assumptions

Mark 2:13—3:6

WHAT WOULD IT TAKE to move you to murder? Personally, mess with my wife, my children, or my car, and it could certainly bring me to rage (not that I feel the same way about all three). On TV, it seems the most common motive for murder stems from someone losing everything they hold dear.

In our last passage, we were introduced to the first of five scenes where the Teachers of the Law began questioning Jesus. Mark now recites four more incidents which ultimately culminate in the Pharisees plotting the death of Jesus (3:6). I want to ask, why? What was it about Jesus and his disciples that so infuriated the Scribes and Pharisees? The simple answer to the question is that he challenged their social, cultural and religious assumptions. They thought they might lose everything!

To study this passage, I want to focus on four stories.

Story One: Look at the Disciples He Picks
(Mark 2:13–17)

Jesus doesn't hang out with the right kind of people. He hangs out with "those kinds of people."

> Once again Jesus went out beside the lake. A large crowd came to him, and he began to teach them. As he walked along, he saw Levi son of Alphaeus sitting at the tax collector's booth. "Follow me," Jesus told him, and Levi got up and followed him. While Jesus was having dinner at Levi's house, many tax collectors and "sinners" were eating with him and his disciples, for there were many who followed him. When the teachers of the law who were

Pharisees saw him eating with the "sinners" and tax collectors, they asked his disciples: "Why does he eat with tax collectors and 'sinners'?" On hearing this, Jesus said to them, "It is not the healthy who need a doctor, but the sick. I have not come to call the righteous, but sinners." (Mark 2:13–17)

Our story begins with the calling of Levi (not Levi Strauss, we are talking approximately AD 30, not 1830). You probably know him as Matthew, the author of our first gospel. Levi is his given name. It is possible that Jesus renames him Matthew (which means gift of God), as he does with Simon Peter (the rock), and James and John (the sons of thunder).

Here is the problem in the eyes of the Pharisees.[1] Matthew is a tax collector (think IRS, but worse). Matthew has been given permission by the Roman government to collect taxes, which means not only collecting dues, but adding a certain percentage (an exorbitant amount) to the top. Tax collectors were on the take. They were considered traitors by the Jews because they had sold out to the Roman government. Levi was a government-licensed extortionist and racketeer.

As such, Levi was not well liked by the Jews (or anybody else for that matter). But Jesus extends an official call to this guy to be his disciple! He calls Levi to be more than a follower; he calls him to be a leader of followers. Understand the feelings this would generate. Nationally, it might be akin to appointing a tax evader to United States Treasury, a felon to a United States Cabinet, or even an Islamic terrorist as a Supreme Court judge. In religious circles, it would be like making a blackjack dealer your preacher, or a pimp the chairman of the board of elders.

But it gets worse! Matthew throws a party for all his tax collector friends and Jesus hangs out with the whole bunch of them (not just one blackjack dealer or one corrupt judge, we get the whole casino, or the Ninth Circuit Court of Appeals).

You need to understand something else about the first century to comprehend the magnitude of the situation. You might call it table fellowship. In the first century, when you opened up your table to someone, it conveyed the idea of full fellowship or full acceptance. Your dinner

---

1. The Pharisees are the most well-known of the sects of ancient Judaism and were very influential in the synagogues. In the first century there were about six thousand members and they were highly respected for their devotion to the religious law. They advocated minute obedience to the Jewish laws and traditions. They most frequently appear as opponents of Jesus. (See Matthew 23:1–26)

guests were more than merely acquaintances, you were throwing your hat in with them. This meant more than just friendship—it was akin to family. Thinking in terms of twenty-first century parallels, it might be like taking someone on as a business partner, or sharing family vacations together.

The Pharisees and the religious leaders not only felt jealous ("Why not us?"), but also had this question: "Why them?" This is not who the Messiah should be hanging around! He is hanging out with the wrong people. How could Jesus be the one who would overthrow Rome, when he's collaborating with Roman traitors? Jesus had not only rejected the religious leaders of the day, he had adopted the scum of society as his own.

I want to stop for a moment and look at the Pharisees' question. Actually, it is a good question to ask: "Why does Jesus eat with tax collectors and sinners?" Is Jesus accepting their practices? Is he condoning their actions? No, he is calling them to a new lifestyle. He is calling them to change their lives. While Jesus meets people where they are, he doesn't leave them there. Jesus expects them to be transformed. In response to the question of "Why," Jesus responds with a statement that cuts right to the heart of their social norms: "It is not the healthy who need a doctor, but the sick. I have not come to call the righteous, but sinners" (2:17).

The Apostle Paul says it this way: "Here is a trustworthy saying that deserves full acceptance: Christ Jesus came into the world to save sinners" (1 Timothy 1:15). This didn't sit well with the Scribes and Pharisees. Jesus is challenging their social norms. He is challenging their assumptions.

Jesus is saying, "People are more important than prejudice (class, race, wealth, gender)." People who live in the park or on the avenue are no different from those who live on Park Avenue. Whenever someone is hurting, or hungry, or in need of healing, our job is to be a friend and lead that person to the Great Physician. Jesus came to save sinners, and I am so glad he did. Aren't you?

Story Two: Look at His Disciples' Attitude
(Mark 2:18–22)

> Now John's disciples and the Pharisees were fasting. Some people came and asked Jesus, "How is it that John's disciples and the disciples of the Pharisees are fasting, but yours are not?" Jesus answered, "How can the guests of the bridegroom fast while he

is with them? They cannot, so long as they have him with them. But the time will come when the bridegroom will be taken from them, and on that day they will fast. No one sews a patch of unshrunk cloth on an old garment. If he does, the new piece will pull away from the old, making the tear worse. And no one pours new wine into old wineskins. If he does, the wine will burst the skins, and both the wine and the wineskins will be ruined. No, he pours new wine into new wineskins." (Mark 2:18–22)

In story two, we find the disciples *not* doing something. They were not fasting. Again, we need more background to understand this story. The law of Moses required only one day a year to be set aside for fasting, the Day of Atonement (Yom Kippur). But over the years, the Scribes and Pharisees, in an effort to show how righteous and zealous they were, had designated many more. Some practiced fasting as often as twice a week (let's say for example, every Monday and Thursday). They would put on sackcloth, rub ashes all over their faces, and make every effort to look depressed. It was a religious show to get them noticed for their self-righteousness. They saw fasting as the best way to call God's attention (and the attention of other people) to their piety.

Fasting had become a regular, self-imposed, religious expectation. It was a core religious ritual. Some people came to Jesus and asked, "Why do John's disciples and the disciples of the Pharisees fast, but your disciples do not?" (2:18). In other words, "Why do you and your disciples flout our traditions and ignore our customs? Jesus, you should order your disciples to fast!"

Understand, the disciples weren't doing anything wrong. They simply were not following the man-made customs and traditions of the Jewish leaders. They hadn't conformed to the religiosity established by the religious elite. Maybe I should ask: Is that what Christianity is all about? Conforming to man-made rituals and trying to earn God's attention and favor?

Jesus essentially replied, "You have completely misunderstood the nature of the occasion. You live like religion is a funeral (fasting and mourning); don't you understand, it is more like a wedding. The bridegroom is here."

This was not just a rebuke of the religious leaders. It was a prophecy. "But the time will come when the bridegroom will be taken from them" (2:20). The bridegroom was Jesus himself and he was predicting a day when he would no longer be with them, but taken away. On that day there would be fasting and mourning.[2]

More than a prediction, Jesus was also describing the nature of a new relationship he came to bring. For centuries, the Jews had worshiped in the temple, practicing solemn rituals. But he was bringing a new type of worship with vitality, warmth, and intimacy that could be expressed with gladness, joy, and celebration. Sometimes we lose sight of that. Often church services are borrowed from an Old Testament concept of solemn, ritualized worship—but that is not the image of worship presented by Jesus. Worship is a feast, not a fast. It is a time of celebration, not solemnity.

Jesus underscores the difference with two word pictures: old garments and old wineskins. "No one sews an unshrunk cloth on an old garment or pours new wine in old wineskins" (2:21–22). His point is simple: a new, fresh, revitalizing relationship with Christ requires new expressions. Don't try to confine the new life in Christ into the same old forms—it won't work. The new system (our relationship with Christ) is too powerful and will destroy the old forms that try to contain it.

Jesus shows what happens when groups and individuals suddenly discover a new and vital relationship with him. In Christ, we have a living, dynamic relationship. We must not contain it in old structures, old forms, old rituals, old ideas, and old attitudes. The new has come.

The Pharisees were upset because Jesus was attacking not only their social norms, but their cultural and religious norms as well.

Story Three: Look at the Disciples' Actions (Mark 2:23–27)

> One Sabbath Jesus was going through the grainfields, and as his disciples walked along, they began to pick some heads of grain. The Pharisees said to him, "Look, why are they doing what is unlawful on the Sabbath?" He answered, "Have you never read what David did when he and his companions were hungry and in need? In the days of Abiathar the high priest, he entered the house of God and ate the consecrated bread, which is lawful only for priests to eat. And he also gave some to his companions." Then he said to them, "The Sabbath was made for man, not man for the Sabbath. So the Son of Man is Lord even of the Sabbath." (Mark 2:23–27)

---

2. There are some who wrongly think of the crucifixion as plan "B." An unfortunate mistake. Jesus predicts his crucifixion early in his ministry.

In each story the animosity of the Pharisees is heightened, and in some sense, so is their charge. Jesus is hanging out with the wrong people; his disciples have the wrong attitude; now it is the wrong actions of the disciples that draw the Pharisees' ire.

They perceive this as the worst yet. The disciples aren't just forsaking some religious norm by not fasting; in the minds of the Pharisees, they are breaking the law by breaking the Sabbath.[3] Picking grain was taboo—one of thirty-nine forbidden acts on the Sabbath.

In all actuality, the disciples aren't breaking the law, only man-made guidelines the religious rulers had built up (the law around the law). The law allowed for travelers to pick crops from the edge of the field as they traveled (the disciples are gleaning, not stealing). The law, however, prevented farmers from harvesting on the Sabbath (Exodus 34:21). This law prevented farmers from becoming greedy and ignoring God on the Sabbath. It also prevented laborers from being overworked.

So intent were the religious leaders on keeping the law, they had narrowly defined what work was (to include the picking of a grain of wheat), and were now accusing the disciples of working on the Sabbath. All in all, the religious leaders had placed a thousand and one religious restrictions on the Sabbath alone. Understand, the disciples were not breaking the intent of the law, but they were breaking the legalistic guidelines set in place by the religious leaders concerning the law.

There is one more point we need to understand. For a Jew, Sabbath breaking was the quintessential sin in the first century. Sabbath keeping is what separated Jews from everyone else (along with circumcision, but this was obviously hidden). One set of Jewish writings, called the Jubilee, said that breaking the Sabbath was punishable by death. It also records, "The Sabbath was made for the Jews."

It is interesting how Jesus responds. He doesn't actually address whether or not what the disciples are doing is legal or illegal. Rather, he gives legal precedent. Even if you want to define the law the way you do, the disciples are not guilty. David (a man after God's own heart, their

---

3. The Sabbath is the seventh day of the week (Saturday); but begins at sundown. It therefore officially begins Friday evening and runs until sundown on Saturday. The command to observe the Sabbath comes from the Ten Commandments (Exodus 20:8–11) and by Jesus' day became one of the most important symbols of obedience to God's law. Severe punishment was prescribed for Sabbath breaking—death (Exodus 31:12–17; 35:1–3).

model of righteousness, from the line of David himself, and the one whom the Messiah is supposed to be like) did far worse.[4]

In fact, Jesus in essence is saying, "I've come in Davidic fashion." By doing so, Jesus also places himself over the law. "The Son of Man is Lord of the Sabbath" (the real issue is not the Sabbath, but Christology). The point Jesus is making is clear. Jesus is attaching himself to the Davidic Messiah and sets himself above the Torah. The law around the law is being broken, but not the law itself. Jesus challenges their assumptions of their religiosity and even of the purpose of the Sabbath.

The stories, however, reach their climax in story four.

Story Four: Look at Jesus' Actions
(Mark 3:1–6)

> Another time he went into the synagogue, and a man with a shriveled hand was there. Some of them were looking for a reason to accuse Jesus, so they watched him closely to see if he would heal him on the Sabbath. Jesus said to the man with the shriveled hand, "Stand up in front of everyone." Then Jesus asked them, "Which is lawful on the Sabbath: to do good or to do evil, to save life or to kill?" But they remained silent. He looked around at them in anger and, deeply distressed at their stubborn hearts, said to the man, "Stretch out your hand." He stretched it out, and his hand was completely restored. Then the Pharisees went out and began to plot with the Herodians how they might kill Jesus. (Mark 3:1–6)

The final story takes place on the Sabbath in the synagogue. The Pharisees are looking for a reason to accuse Jesus. Is it a trap? Maybe, maybe not. It is obvious that they think they know what Jesus would do. He would heal the man with the shriveled hand; and in their minds, this would be breaking the law of the Sabbath.

Jesus knows what they are thinking and so he asks them a question: "Is it lawful on the Sabbath to do good or to do evil, to save a life or kill?" (3:4). Let me ask you the same question: Is it lawful to do good or evil on the Sabbath? What is the right answer to that question?

---

4. Some people claim that Jesus (or the Bible) is in error at this point. Our verse says, "In the days of Abiathar the high priest" (2:26), and they respond, it was Ahimelech, his father, who was high priest. But notice the phrase, "In the days of . . ." Abiathar was alive when David did this. More than that, Abiathar was David's high priest. Jesus says it was during the time, not the tenure in office.

The Jewish leaders had perverted the law so much, if their interpretation of the law was allowed to stand, the man's hand would remain shriveled. Which would be more in keeping with God's law: healing a man or allowing him to remain crippled because it was the Sabbath?

Jesus asks (not as much a question, as a statement) about their interpretation of the law. At the heart of the question is: What was the purpose of God's law in the first place? What is law for?

Notice the Pharisees are silent. They don't speak the answer, but they know it. They also know the background of the question. Being products of a modern age, we might miss the history behind Jesus' question, but they don't. They know Torah.

Jesus here uses the pinnacle phrase from the Old Testament law, from the book of Deuteronomy chapter 30. Everything in the book of Deuteronomy builds to this passage.

> See, I set before you today life and prosperity, death and destruction. For I command you today to love the Lord your God, to walk in his ways, and to keep his commands, decrees and laws; then you will live . . . This day I call heaven and earth as witnesses against you that I have set before you life and death, blessings and curses. Now choose life, so that you and your children may live and that you may love the Lord your God, listen to his voice and hold fast to him. For the Lord is your life. (Deuteronomy 30:15–16, 19–20)

They are commanded to love God and keep his commands. But in order to keep his commands, they have built a hedge around the law. They have made their own binding rules and regulations. Don't misunderstand, their original intent was good—keep the law. But they have perverted the law. The law that was meant to bring life is now being used to keep people from really living.

Let me explain it this way. Their interpretation of Torah would have kept this man crippled (don't heal on the Sabbath). Their interpretation of Torah kept men hungry (don't glean). Their interpretation of Torah kept people in mourning (fast and wail). Their interpretation of Torah kept people in sin and excluded (don't hang out with those kinds of people). Their attempt to keep the law and build a hedge around it, actually prevents them from the intent of the original law.

It is so easy to do. In fact, it is a danger of any movement. We make our own points of emphasis, we create our own ways of doing things, and we develop ritual. We take what is important to us and we put a hedge around it—and those things then determine for us what it means to be a Christian. The unspoken laws, the prescribed worship, the proper form create for us our own form of orthodoxy. The question is, are our rules what is important to God?

Think for a moment about all the traditions of Christianity that have become stale, stagnant, and ritualistic. Ponder all the proper forms and ways of doing things that have become more important than substance. When this happens, the ritual itself becomes more important than compassion; and history and precedent become more important than purpose. No movement is exempt. Neither the one steeped in old, stale tradition, nor the one opposed to tradition for whom opposing tradition becomes their practice.

Jesus looked at the Pharisees, and "was angry at them and deeply distressed[5] at their stubborn hearts" (3:5).

Understand, Jesus is never pleased with people who play religion. He is never kind to those people who play the game, go through the motions, and perform only what is expected. Jesus never delights in people who do their duty as if this is what saves them. Jesus reserves the harshest words in Scripture for those people who play religion, calling them a brood of vipers, white-washed tombs, and hypocrites. What angers Jesus most is people whose hearts are hard even though what they are doing is being done in the name of God.

Jesus has come to challenge our assumptions. He wants us to know that even the outcasts of society are welcome at his table. He wants us to celebrate life and salvation rather than mourn. There should be no crotchety Christians. Gripe-fruit is not one of the fruits of the Spirit, but "love, joy, peace, patience, kindness, goodness, faithfulness, gentleness and self-control" (Galatians 5:22). Jesus wants us to meet the needs of people, asking, "What can we do?" instead of making known what we can't do. Most of all we are to be in the business of doing good, and saving lives—spiritual lives. "It is not the healthy who need a doctor, but the sick" (2:17).

---

5. This particular word for deeply distressed (*syllypeō*) is used only here in the New Testament.

Study Questions

1. What "Sunday" restrictions, if any, did you grow up with? Do you still honor them?
2. Which of your parents' rules did you break the most?
3. Who is Levi? Do you know him by another name (See Matthew 9:9–13)?
    a. Why are the teachers of the law so upset with the calling of Levi (2:14) and the dinner at Levi's house (2:15)?
    b. What is it about being a tax collector that was so troublesome?
    c. Why does Jesus choose to dine with tax collectors and sinners?
4. The fisherman disciples (Peter, Andrew, James, John, cf 1:16–19) probably paid inflated taxes for years, maybe even personally to Levi.
    a. How would they feel when Jesus called him?
    b. Why did Jesus call Levi?
5. In the way you relate to "undesirables," are you more like Levi (inviting them to your party), the Pharisees (looking down on them), or the disciples (unsure what to do)?
6. What does Jesus mean when he says, "It is not the healthy who need a doctor" (2:17)? What does this imply for believers?
7. How are Jesus and his teaching like the unshrunk cloth and new wine (2:21–22)?
8. What are the implications of Jesus' statement in 2:28?
9. Have you ever felt the tension between obeying religious principles and helping people?
10. What prompts Jesus' anger in 3:5? Why did this make Jesus so upset?
11. Why are the Pharisees plotting to kill Jesus (3:2–6)?
12. As you try to follow Jesus, are you becoming more free to love others, or becoming more constrained by religious rules? Why?

13. How can you reach out to those whom others consider "unacceptable"?

14. How have you seen "religious rules" or "institutions" hurt people?

For Further Study

15. See Matthew 9:9–16; 12:1–14; and Luke 5:27—6:11.

7

Unforgiven

Mark 3:7–34

As we begin this passage, please remember that the Gospel of Mark is written in narrative (story) style. We have already learned a couple of principles of interpretation when it comes to narrative. First, when the pace slows—pay attention. Second, when dialogue breaks out, it slows the pace intentionally, so when characters speak—pay attention. The words of biblical characters often contain the point the author is trying to make.

In this passage, we find a third technique used by Mark, called "sandwiching." Sandwiching is a bracketing technique employed frequently by Mark, where two similar stories are tied together to make a point, with one story sandwiching the other. It is used to heighten meaning, to add emphasis, and to clarify the message (3:20–34; 5:21–43; 6:7–31; 11:12–26; 14:1–11; 14:27–52).

More than just sandwiching, the first example is actually a chiastic structure.

>   A. Crowds coming to Jesus (20)
>   B. Jesus' family thinking he is crazy (21)
>   C. Scribes' accusations (22)
>   D. Jesus' response (23–29)
>   C. Scribes' accusations restated (30)
>   B. Jesus' family comes to take charge (31–33)
>   A. Crowds sit around Jesus as new family (34–45)

Background

Our passage starts quickly with familiar themes: crowds, healing, and the demon possessed.

> Jesus withdrew with his disciples to the lake, and a large crowd from Galilee followed. When they heard all he was doing, many people came to him from Judea, Jerusalem, Idumea, and the regions across the Jordan and around Tyre and Sidon. Because of the crowd he told his disciples to have a small boat ready for him, to keep the people from crowding him. For he had healed many, so that those with diseases were pushing forward to touch him. Whenever the evil spirits saw him, they fell down before him and cried out, "You are the Son of God." But he gave them strict orders not to tell who he was. (Mark 3:7–12)

Jesus withdraws (a familiar theme in Mark), but people follow. They follow from all over Judea,[1] Jerusalem, Idumea,[2] the region across the Jordan,[3] and from around Tyre and Sidon.[4] It is important that we realize this is not hundreds of people, or even thousands of people, but most agree at times it could have reached ten thousand people.

Mark depicts a heightened sense of determination on the part of the people to get to Jesus. This determination has been building since the paralytic and his roof-remodeling friends found a way to get to Jesus. People are pushing forward to see Jesus, be near Jesus, and touch Jesus. They have become so aggressive that Jesus orders the disciples to have a boat standing ready and waiting (it will be put to good use shortly in the book of Mark). The demon possessed cry out, "You are the Son of God" (3:11), but Jesus gives them strict orders not to speak (again, we've seen this before). But take note: the people want something from Jesus—they want a miracle worker.

Jesus tries to escape again, this time to the mountains.[5]

---

1. The southern part of Palestine with Jerusalem as its chief city. It was under direct Roman control through a Roman-appointed governor (procurator) in Jesus' time.

2. The region south of Judea. It included many inhabitants of non-Jewish descent who had migrated from the area known in the Old Testament as Edom.

3. The area known in the first century as Peraea. It is roughly the same area as Gilead of the Old Testament. In the first century this area was part of Herod Antipas' domain and was occupied by the Jews. (This is modern-day Jordan.)

4. Both of these cities were Phoenician seaports and were essentially Gentile.

5. Mountains play an important role in sacred history. A few examples include the giving of the law (Exodus 19:1–25; 20:18–20); the choosing of the Twelve (Mark

> Jesus went up on a mountainside and called to him those he wanted, and they came to him. He appointed twelve—designating them apostles—that they might be with him and that he might send them out to preach and to have authority to drive out demons. These are the twelve he appointed: Simon (to whom he gave the name Peter); James son of Zebedee and his brother John (to them he gave the name Boanerges, which means Sons of Thunder); Andrew, Philip, Bartholomew, Matthew, Thomas, James son of Alphaeus, Thaddaeus, Simon the Zealot and Judas Iscariot, who betrayed him. (Mark 3:13-19)

Jesus takes select followers with him (those he wanted) and from among those he appoints twelve to be apostles. We are told why—to be with him, that he might send them out to preach, and to help meet the demands of his ministry (to drive out demons). Then we are given the list of the twelve: Peter, James, John, Andrew, Philip, Bartholomew, Matthew, Thomas, James (number two), Thaddaeus, Simon, and Judas. Other than a few nicknames and identifying markers, we are not given many details.

Jesus returns home and again a crowd gathers, so much that Jesus and his disciples are not even able to eat. Notice, we already have a distinction being made for us between the crowds who misunderstand Jesus (some want a miracle worker, some are curious, some question Jesus, and some oppose Jesus); and those who truly are following Jesus (the twelve Apostles and other disciples). This dichotomy is further illustrated by one of the largest sections of dialogue (remember dialogue?) yet in the book of Mark.

> Then Jesus entered a house, and again a crowd gathered, so that he and his disciples were not even able to eat. When his family heard about this, they went to take charge of him, for they said, "He is out of his mind." And the teachers of the law who came down from Jerusalem said, "He is possessed by Beelzebub! By the prince of demons he is driving out demons." So Jesus called them and spoke to them in parables: "How can Satan drive out Satan? If a kingdom is divided against itself, that kingdom cannot stand. If a house is divided against itself, that house cannot stand. And if Satan opposes himself and is divided, he cannot stand; his end has come. In fact, no one can enter a strong man's house and carry off his possessions unless he first ties up the strong man. Then he can

3:13-19); the transfiguration (Mark 9:2-9); the Sermon on the Mount (Matthew 5); and the Great Commission (Matthew 28:16-20).

rob his house. I tell you the truth, all the sins and blasphemies of men will be forgiven them. But whoever blasphemes against the Holy Spirit will never be forgiven; he is guilty of an eternal sin." He said this because they were saying, "He has an evil spirit." Then Jesus' mother and brothers arrived. Standing outside, they sent someone in to call him. A crowd was sitting around him, and they told him, "Your mother and brothers are outside looking for you." "Who are my mother and my brothers?" he asked. Then he looked at those seated in a circle around him and said, "Here are my mother and my brothers! Whoever does God's will is my brother and sister and mother." (Mark 3:20–34)

The story of the teachers of the law is sandwiched by references to Jesus' family. Two seemingly unrelated stories are placed together to make a similar point.

Jesus' Family

Contrary to what some theological circles proclaim, we learn that Jesus has a family. "Who are my mother and brothers" (3:33)? Later in Mark we learn that Jesus is one of at least seven children: "Isn't this the carpenter? Isn't this Mary's son and the brother of James, Joseph, Judas, and Simon? Aren't his sisters here with us?" (6:3).

Jesus' family comes to take him away. They think he is out of his mind for at least two reasons. First, they do not think he is taking adequate care of himself. The crowd makes it impossible to eat, they are constantly pressuring him, and there are even threats against his life. Second, they don't (with the exception of Mary) understand who Jesus is. To them, Jesus has become a religious fanatic. John writes, "For even his own brothers did not believe in him" (John 7:5). Of course, all this changes after the death, burial, and resurrection when his skeptical family become believers and even leaders in the church—James becomes a leader in the church in Jerusalem, and both he and his brother Jude write books contained for us in our New Testament.

The charge by the family, "He is out of his mind" (3:21), should not surprise us. This is not an unusual charge against Christians: "You are a religious fanatic. You are crazy." It is even said of the Apostle Paul after he defends the gospel. Festus says, "You are out of your mind . . . Your great learning is driving you insane" (Acts 26:24). When Martin Luther defended the supremacy of the Word of God over the traditions of men, he was regarded as a fool and one possessed by the devil. I've had people attack my beliefs, and perhaps you have experienced this as well. It is not unusual for a family member or a close friend to question the judgment of one close to them who becomes a Christian. I have even seen Christian families question the desire of a son, daughter, brother, or sister to enter the ministry.

Jesus' family, for whatever reason—whether they are concerned, worried, or unconvinced—oppose Jesus. They have different plans for him.

The Teachers of the Law

It is interesting that the teachers of the law do not deny Jesus' power to heal and cast out demons. His power is actually acknowledged. They do, however, bring two charges against him. First, they claim he is demon-possessed. The word "Beelzebub" (*Beelzeboul*) occurs in no other Jewish writing. Some suggest it means "Lord of the Dung," but this translation is based on variant spelling. Others believe it refers to Baal-Zebub (2 Kings 1:16) and means "Baal the Prince" or interestingly, "God over the House." This was the title of the God who opposed Elijah on Mt. Carmel. In Jewish demonology, he becomes the chief of the demons.

The second charge leveled against Jesus is that he casts out demons through collaboration with the prince of demons. The family criticized his judgment ("He's out of his mind"), the teachers criticized his heart and motives ("Look how he does things"). Not unlike Jesus' family, the teachers of the law have different plans for Jesus.

Jesus' Response to the Critics

Jesus responds to the accusations of his critics, first by asking a rhetorical question, then by using a three-pronged argument to show their logical error: "How can Satan drive out Satan? If a kingdom is divided against itself, that kingdom cannot stand. If a house is divided against itself, that house cannot stand. And if Satan opposes himself and is divided, he cannot stand; his end has come" (3:23–25).

Next, he uses a parable: "No one can enter a strong man's house and carry off his possessions unless he first ties up the strong man. Then he can rob his house" (3:27).

To this, my first, well-educated, and theological response is, "Huh?" The line of thinking is hard to follow until you identify the images as they are given to us. The strong man is Satan. The strong man's house is the world. The strong man's possessions are his people. The stronger man is Jesus. Now we can see the point. Jesus is saying, not only am I not working as an agent of Satan, I am binding him and carrying off his property. Jesus flatly denies the charges of the teachers of the law, then he turns their accusation against them in one of the most frightening verses (for some) in scripture. The teachers of the law have previously charged him with blasphemy, and now he says, "Whoever blasphemes against the Holy Spirit will never be forgiven; he is guilty of an eternal sin" (3:29).

Blasphemy here is specifically against the Holy Spirit and shows defiant hostility toward God. Why is it "unforgivable"? Notice their building animosity toward Jesus. First, they questioned and doubted him (2:6). Then they accused him of blaspheming (2:7). Next, they plotted to kill him (3:6), and finally, they called him Satan (3:22).

They were guilty of conscious, continuous, and deliberate rejection of what God was doing in Christ through the Holy Spirit. They showed no sorrow and they were unrepentant of their thoughts and actions. While a person remains in this state, there is no forgiveness of sins—and there cannot be. The descent to the unforgivable is a gradual and continual process of rejection, not a one-time event.

This begs the question: Can a person commit the unpardonable sin today? Absolutely! You may be asking, "Have I committed it?" If you are reading this, or asking the question, it is doubtful. Blasphemy against the Holy Spirit occurs when a person makes a conscious, continuous, and deliberate rejection of the saving power and grace of God through Jesus Christ, and refuses to repent of this sin. While a person remains in this state, he cannot be forgiven. The unforgivable sin is the complete rejection of the Holy Spirit and its power. Understand, this is not a statement of God's refusal to forgive, but of man's refusal to accept God's forgiveness.

Rather than being a terrifying verse of scripture, this passage is actually a strong statement of forgiveness: "All the sins and blasphemies of men will be forgiven them" (3:28). There is forgiveness for David's sins of adultery, dishonesty, and murder. There is forgiveness for the prodigal son and his wayward living. There is forgiveness of the triple denial of Jesus by Peter. There is forgiveness for Paul's merciless persecution of

Christians. And there is forgiveness enough for our sins, if we will accept what Jesus has done for us.

In this passage, we find a tragic and profound irony. Every time an unclean spirit comes into contact with Jesus, it identifies him as the Holy One of God. But the religious leaders of the day actually accuse him of being aligned with Satan.

Jesus' True Family

Mark then masterfully brings us back to Jesus' family. With his family standing outside Jesus says, "Who are my mother and brothers?" (3:33). Jesus is not rejecting his mom. Jesus has a tender concern for his mother, and yet, he never allows even his mother to direct him away from his mission. Jesus says, "If anyone comes to me and does not hate his father and mother, his wife and children, his brothers and sisters—yes, even his own life—he cannot be my disciple. And anyone who does not carry his cross and follow me cannot be my disciple" (Luke 14:26).

Spiritually speaking, our relationship with God is based upon doing God's will. Actually, this whole chapter is about one thing. The crowds all have their own idea about Jesus and they want him for their own purpose—they want a miracle worker. The teachers of the law have their own ideas about Jesus—they want him dead. Jesus' own family has their own ideas about him, and I want you to notice the language used about them: "They went to take charge of him" (3:21). Any attempt to derail Jesus' mission is as serious a sin as defaming him. Jesus is not at our beck and call, we are to be at his.

We must understand several things. First, there is forgiveness of sin. It is available in Jesus Christ. All sins can be forgiven except the rejection of the forgiveness of sins. Second, any attempt to redirect Jesus' mission is serious. Don't try to use Jesus for your own purposes. Finally, we must not try to fit Jesus into our agenda, we must fit ourselves into his agenda.

The question is, "Whose will are you going to do? Whose family are you going to be part of? Who will be in charge of your life?" Don't remain *unforgiven*.

Study Questions

1. Are you attracted to or repelled by large crowds? What do you do to get "away from the madding crowd"?
2. Using a map in the back of one of your Bibles, locate as many of the places from which people traveled, that are mentioned in 3:8.
    a. What is Mark's point in mentioning these?
    b. Why are these people willing to come so far to see Jesus?
3. Reading verses 9–10, do the crowds seem to be intensifying? In light of this, what does Jesus suggest the disciples do? Why? (Notice what happens in 4:1.)
4. According to verses 14–15, what was Jesus' purpose for selecting the disciples?
5. What would prompt Jesus family to think he was "out of his mind" (21)?
6. What is Jesus' family doing in Capernaum?
7. Do the religious leaders of the day deny Jesus' ability to cast out demons?
    a. What do the religious leaders suggest about his ability to cast out demons?
    b. Who is Beelzebub (22)?
    c. How does Jesus respond (23–27)?
8. Identify the "players" from Jesus' parable in verse 27.
    a. The strong man
    b. The strong man's house
    c. The strong man's possessions
    d. The stronger man
9. What does Jesus' parable suggest about Jesus' purpose?
10. If you were Jesus, what would be the hardest for you to handle: people's constant demands (20)? Your family thinking you were crazy (21)? Or, the religious leaders thinking you were demon possessed (22)?

11. What is "blasphemy of the Holy Spirit?" What would you say to someone who is afraid they have "blasphemed" the Holy Spirit?

12. Rather than being a traumatic passage filled with fear, notice what sins verse 28 suggests can be forgiven. How does this change your view of this passage?

13. According to verse 35, who are Jesus' brothers or sisters?

For Further Study

14. Whose will is really being exerted in your life, yours or God's?

15. Compare Matthew 10:1–4; 12:15–50; Luke 6:12–16; 8:19–21.

8

Hearing Impaired

Mark 4:1–25

WITH CHAPTER 4 WE come to a familiar text and well-known parable. I would caution you not to look casually at this passage, but listen well, and put what you learn into practice. In fact, the word "hear" is used nine times in this passage. It is important to listen. Listening well matters.

Every year, one of my friends takes a winter ski trip. Cal and his buddies pick a destination and spend a week hitting the slopes. A few years ago, they settled on the ski areas around Salt Lake City, Utah. When boarding the plane in Seattle, there was a certain level of excitement and anticipation. One of the guys, however, struggled during the plane trip. He was unable to get his ears to pop, which made his trip very unpleasant. If you have ever experienced this, you probably share his pain. Upon arriving in the Salt Lake basin, the problem fortunately resolved itself and the guys had a great week skiing the slopes of Snowbird, Brighton, and Park City. No more thought was given to the ear problem until it was time for the return journey.

As Cal boarded the plane, he witnessed a strange set of events. As the story goes, his buddy said something to the flight attendant as she passed by. A moment or two later, several security personnel came onto the plane, handcuffed his friend and promptly escorted him back into the terminal. The plane doors were then shut, the plane taxied down the runway, and Cal and his friends (minus one) were on their way back to Seattle.

The next day, Cal got a phone call from his buddy asking to be picked up at the Sea-Tac airport. It was only then Cal learned what had transpired. As the stewardess had walked through the plane, his friend had remembered the difficulties of the previous flight and asked a simple question: "Do you have any gum?" But instead of hearing the question properly, the stewardess heard, "I've got a gun." That changed everything. Hearing properly matters!

In our passage, the crowds are following Jesus. For many, Jesus is nothing more than a curiosity. As Jesus teaches by the Sea of Galilee, he tells a parable to determine who is listening, and to what extent. Our parable is a familiar one, but I want you to hear what the crowd hears. Ask yourself, without hearing the later explanation, what would you actually know by listening to the storytelling of Jesus?

> Again Jesus began to teach by the lake. The crowd that gathered around him was so large that he got into a boat and sat in it out on the lake, while all the people were along the shore at the water's edge. He taught them many things by parables, and in his teaching said: "Listen! A farmer went out to sow his seed. As he was scattering the seed, some fell along the path, and the birds came and ate it up. Some fell on rocky places, where it did not have much soil. It sprang up quickly, because the soil was shallow. But when the sun came up, the plants were scorched, and they withered because they had no root. Other seed fell among thorns, which grew up and choked the plants, so that they did not bear grain. Still other seed fell on good soil. It came up, grew and produced a crop, multiplying thirty, sixty, or even a hundred times." Then Jesus said, "He who has ears to hear, let him hear."
> (Mark 4:1–9)

Look closely at the passage. Don't cheat. From what Jesus says to the crowd, how much of the story would you actually get? What can you conclude? You've been told about a farmer, some seeds, the conditions of the soil, and a miraculous harvest. But what does it all mean? Be honest, the key to unlocking the meaning of this parable has not yet been given. In fact, it is never given to the crowd.

I remember hearing several Sunday school definitions of the word "parable" (*parabolē*) when I was a kid. The most common was certainly, "A parable is an earthly story with a heavenly meaning." I also heard descriptions of how parables made complicated theology simple. Actually, neither description is quite accurate. Parables are not stories which try to make the complex understandable. At times, they may actually have the opposite effect. Strictly speaking, a parable is a story thrown alongside another. The word "parable" in Greek, literally means "to throw (*ballō*) alongside (*para*)." A parable's main purpose is actually to determine who is listening and who is not. To those who are listening, explanation will be given.

Let me give you a modern-day example. If I were to say to you, "Even monkeys fall out of trees," you may not know the intended meaning. You may have a hunch or take a guess, but the meaning is not entirely clear unless you have heard the statement and its explanation before. But if I said to you, "Even experts make mistakes," the parable makes sense and the meaning becomes clear. A parable is not initially told to bring clarity, but to promote curiosity. Jesus tells a parable to the large crowd to determine who is really listening. Some were, some were not.

The disciples, who were listening, later asked, "What does this mean?" (4:10). Jesus gave an interesting and somewhat troubling response to the disciples, and then quoted the prophet Isaiah.[1]

> When he was alone, the Twelve and the others around him asked him about the parables. He told them, "The secret of the kingdom of God has been given to you. But to those on the outside everything is said in parables so that, 'they may be ever seeing but never perceiving, and ever hearing but never understanding; otherwise they might turn and be forgiven!'" (Mark 4:10–12)

Is Jesus really saying that he doesn't want people to understand, so he intentionally spoke in parables to veil his message? No! As the context of the Isaiah passage reveals, God told Isaiah to go and speak with clarity. But even if the message is clearly spoken, some won't listen—they will see, but still not perceive, they will hear, but still not understand. No matter how clearly spoken, or eloquently delivered, some still don't heed the message.

When Jesus says, "Do you bring in a lamp to put it under a bowl or a bed?" he is stating that the intent is not to hide the message, but to bring the message into the open (4:21–23). The reason Jesus speaks in parables is not to hide or conceal the message, but simply to determine who is listening. To those who are listening, explanation is given. Since the disciples were curious, Jesus gave the disciples (and us) the key to understanding the parable.

---

1. Isaiah 6:9–10.

> Then Jesus said to them, "Don't you understand this parable? How then will you understand any parable? The farmer sows the word. Some people are like seed along the path, where the word is sown. As soon as they hear it, Satan comes and takes away the word that was sown in them. Others, like seed sown on rocky places, hear the word and at once receive it with joy. But since they have no root, they last only a short time. When trouble or persecution comes because of the word, they quickly fall away. Still others, like seed sown among thorns, hear the word; but the worries of this life, the deceitfulness of wealth and the desires for other things come in and choke the word, making it unfruitful. Others, like seed sown on good soil, hear the word, accept it, and produce a crop—thirty, sixty or even a hundred times what was sown." (Mark 4:10–20)

With Jesus' explanation, we are now in the position to start unlocking the parable. The seed is the word of God and the soils represent different types of people.

Path People

The first soil represents path people. They have calloused hearts and the word of God cannot take root. The seed is scattered on hard ground and the birds (in this case Satan) pluck up the seed before it can germinate. "Some people are like seed along the path, where the word is sown. As soon as they hear it, Satan comes and takes away the word that was sown in them" (4:4, 15).

At the church where I minister, we frequently have weddings, and birdseed is often thrown at the new bride and groom as they depart. What is unique about our situation is that there is a small farm across the street with free-roaming chickens. They have figured out that weddings are synonymous with birdseed and they come running every time they see wedding dresses and tuxedos. Herein lies the answer to that age-old question: "Why did the chicken cross the road?" The sight (if not my dumb joke) is quite humorous. Between the fact that the seed is scattered on the hard pavement, and the fact that the chickens pluck up the seed with enthusiasm, one thing is certain—none will germinate.

It is not too difficult to find path people—people whose hearts are hard and are completely calloused to the word of God. There were path people in the first century, and there are still path people in the twenty-first century.

Rock People

The rocky soil represents those people with shallow, emotional hearts. The rocky soil has no depth and while the seed sprouts, it fails just as fast (4:5). Jesus explains that this soil represents people who, "When trouble or persecution comes because of the word, they quickly fall away" (4:16).

When we first moved to Idaho, we bought a new home in a new neighborhood. From the outset, you need to understand that in Idaho people do judge you by the lawn you keep. After moving in, we promptly put in a sprinkler system and planted seed—anxiously awaiting a lawn. Something amazing happened! Soon little, green sprouts sprang up from the soil. Seed germinated in two places rather quickly and curiously. One area formed a nice large circle and another area a four-by-eight rectangle. These areas grew quickly and filled in rapidly, while the rest of the lawn seemed to stagger behind. Eventually, the remaining lawn filled in and I forgot about the geometrical shapes. Later, at the end of August, the same round circle and large rectangle reappeared in the form of dry grass. The spots grew brown and the neighbors complained. I fertilized and watered to no avail. Finally, one neighbor came over and said, "You need beer!" I told him that I didn't drink and he quickly responded, "For your lawn." He brought over a six-pack and we dumped beer on the brown spots and trotted around in our golf cleats. I need to report that just like with individuals, the beer didn't cure the lawn's problems.

After trying many other remedies, I did the inevitable—I dug up the lawn only to find the source of the problem. The contractor who built the house had dug a hole in the yard, deposited all the trash from the build, covered it with a piece of Sheetrock, and layered it with a few inches of dirt. The curious circle was formed by a large piece of concrete left over from the cleaning of the cement truck.

As I think about my lawn, I see a comparison to shallow-hearted people. They seem to start out so quickly in the Christian life, but when times get tough they wither and fade. It happened in the first century, and it still happens in the twenty-first century.

Thorn People

The thorny soil (4:7) represents people with worldly hearts. These are the people who "Hear the word; but the worries of this life, the deceitfulness of wealth and the desires for other things come in and choke the word, making it unfruitful" (4:18–19).

In the first century there were people who started so well, but walked away. I think of people like Demas, or the rich young ruler. Again, it is easy to identify people whose faith seems to start well, but gets choked out. It happened in the first century and it happens in the twenty-first century.

Productive People

Of course the good soil produces a crop, multiplying thirty, sixty, or even a hundred times (4:8, 20). Good soil produces good fruit. And I've known people like this too! Haven't you? Their lives are productive and their faith is a multiplying faith.

We can easily identify soil types in the lives of people. But I would assert to you, if that is all we do with this passage, we have misinterpreted it. In rightfully understanding this passage, we will learn three life-lessons.

Lesson One: The condition of the soil determines the ability to grow.

We know this. We've seen this. We've preached this. We've always applied this to other people. But it is not about them! Jesus is speaking to his disciples: "Consider carefully what you hear" (4:24). It's not about the crowd. It's not about other people. It's about you! Your willingness to hear determines your capability to receive.

I've got to admit to you, I'm hearing impaired. Don't misunderstand me. My ears work properly, but what I hear doesn't always make it to my brain. I suffer from selective listening. I can be watching football on TV and my wife can be talking, and truth be known, on certain rare occasions, I've heard her, but her words don't register properly. My particular hearing disability is not rare. It is also hereditary—my kids have the same problem. I can raise my voice and yell across the house to no avail, but if I whisper "ice cream," they come running from the far corners of the house.

I exhibit the same problem as I listen to God. Sometimes I have a hard heart—I know what God wants, but I don't do it. I know the difference between right and wrong, and yet sometimes I choose poorly.

Sometimes I have an emotional heart. I start out excited, wanting to do what God wants me to do, but somehow over time, I fizzle and dry up. Sometimes I have a worldly heart. I lose focus on what I need to do because the temptations of the world seem to squeeze out the righteousness of Christ. Sometimes even good things rob from the truly important things in my life. I must admit, when it comes to matters of the heart, I continue to struggle with all three heart maladies. I need to hear these words from Jesus: "Consider carefully what you hear" (4:24).

But Jesus isn't finished yet—there is a second lesson we must learn. Hearing is not enough, we must produce a crop.

Lesson Two: Your willingness to hear will be evidenced by God's Word in your life.

Not all soil is bad soil. Jesus talks about good soil as well. "Others, like seed sown on good soil, hear the word, accept it, and produce a crop—thirty, sixty or even a hundred times what is sown" (4:20). Those who hear, produce a crop.

When Jesus says, "He who has an ear to hear, let him hear" (4:9), he is not simply suggesting we need an auditory response. When Jesus uses the word "hear" (*akouō*), he is using it in the same sense as your mom. When your mom used to ask you, "Did you hear me?" she was not questioning if your ears were working properly, she was suggesting that your feet start moving.

A true disciple is not simply one who *hears*, but one who *does*. Jesus said, "By their fruit you will recognize them" (Matthew 7:20) or, "This is to my Father's glory, that you bear much fruit, showing yourselves to be my disciples" (John 15:8).

There is yet another lesson to be learned from this passage.

Lesson Three: Your willingness to hear God's word and apply it now, will determine your future capacity to receive God's Word.

> "Consider carefully what you hear," he continued. "With the measure you use, it will be measured to you—and even more. Whoever has will be given more; whoever does not have, even what he has will be taken from him." (Mark 4:24–27)

This is the crux of our passage: "With the measure you use, it will be measured to you." In other words, "Fail to listen now, and it will be taken away from you." There is a phrase that is often used, especially in the realm of athletics: "Use it or lose it." It is true in many aspects of life, whether you are referring to mathematical skills you once had, or a language you once learned. I'm told that world-class athletes work for years and even decades to hone their skills, but what took years to develop, in some cases takes only weeks to atrophy. If you don't put it to use, what you once had will deteriorate. This is especially sobering when it comes to our relationship with God. "Consider carefully what you hear . . . Whoever has will be given more; whoever does not have, even what he has will be taken from him" (4:24–25).

What does this mean for those people who say, "I'm going to wait before I yield to Christ. I want to sow my wild oats now. Later, I'll return to God"? What does our passage say to people who know what they should be doing, but fail to put it into practice? Or who fail to listen?

In my office, I keep what I call my caution list. It contains a list of people I have known through the years who I've studied with and who have trained for ministry. Many of them had unbelievable potential for Christ, but for whatever reason, they are no longer in ministry. Most have walked away from their faith. I keep the list as a simple reminder to myself: How well am I listening?

Those words, "Consider carefully what you hear," were not written for the faceless crowds of fickle followers. They were not meant to be a critique of other people. They were written for you and for me. Listening well matters. How well are you listening to God?

Study Questions

1. Have you ever been accused (or accused someone else) of having selective hearing? Describe when "selective hearing" most frequently occurs.

2. Have you ever had a time in your life when you mis-heard someone and the consequences were embarrassing?

3. We've often misunderstood the purpose of a parable. We've been taught that a parable is an earthly story with a heavenly meaning—a story to explain truths in a way we can understand. Actually, the purpose of a parable is to make people think and to determine who is listening and who is not. Try an experiment for me. Pretend you

have never heard this parable and read just the parable itself (4:1–9) without explanation.

   a. What might you conclude about Jesus' story?
   b. Without an explanation, would you have reached the right conclusion?

4. The disciples want to know the meaning of the parable and ask Jesus to explain it for them. In verses 13–20, he gives the explanation. What do the following terms represent?

   a. The seed?
   b. Who is the sower in this passage?

5. While the message and the messenger are the same, the condition of the soil determines if and how the seeds will grow. What are the different types of soil and what do they represent?

6. Without mentioning names, can you think of people who are represented by these types of soil?

7. Can you identify a time in your own life best described by each soil? Which type of soil most typically describes you?

8. A seed will germinate and grow in good soil, but we are given further expectations of each plant. From verses 8 and 20, identify the expectations. What are the implications of this for our lives?

9. The key word in 4:1–25 is "hear" (listen). It is used nine times in this passage. As we now know, biblical "hearing" is more than just listening. It implies understanding, receptivity, and action. It is like your mom saying, "Did you hear me?" What she is really saying is, "Are you going to do what I told you to do?" We often think of these soils in terms of "other people." In reality, we all demonstrate each of these types of soils in our own lives in regard to different issues.

   a. What warning is given to those who don't listen carefully to God's word (25)?
   b. How should we respond to that warning?

10. How do you tell if someone is listening to you?
11. What are some characteristics of a good listener? Explain.
12. What affects your ability to truly hear and understand?

13. What keeps us from truly hearing God?
14. Hearing is worthless if it does not result in doing. Has God called you to do something that you haven't yet done?
15. What soil best describes the current condition of your heart?
16. How can you improve your hearing? What are some specific things you can do to increase your hearing?

For Further Study

17. How do Romans 10:17 and James 1:19–22 shed light on Mark 4:1–25?
18. Compare Matthew 13:1–23 and Luke 8:4–18.

9

Who Is This?

Mark 4:26–41

> That day when evening came, he said to his disciples, "Let us go over to the other side." Leaving the crowd behind, they took him along, just as he was, in the boat. There were also other boats with him. A furious squall came up, and the waves broke over the boat, so that it was nearly swamped. Jesus was in the stern, sleeping on a cushion. The disciples woke him and said to him, "Teacher, don't you care if we drown?" He got up, rebuked the wind and said to the waves, "Quiet! Be still!" then the wind died down and it was completely calm. He said to his disciples, "Why are you so afraid? Do you still have no faith?" They were terrified and asked each other, "Who is this? Even the wind and the waves obey him!" (Mark 4:35–41)

ONCE AGAIN, WE COME upon a very familiar story. Often, when this passage is preached, it is preached as an analogy. It typically goes something like this: the boat represents your life; the waves and storms depict all the troubles and hardships you face; and calming the storm equals a promise that if you only have enough faith, life will be smooth and peaceful. So when Jesus asks the disciples, "Why are you so afraid? Do you still have no faith?" (4:40) they feel he is saying, "Don't you know if you simply believe, you will never have trials, or hardship, or pain or death?" Are we really supposed to believe that Jesus will calm all the storms in our lives if we just have faith?

A quick search of the internet will produce some titles that evidence this type of approach: *Calming the Storms of Life*, *When Life Comes Crashing Down*, *The Faith to Believe*, *Steps to Smooth Sailing*, *Overcoming Obstacles*, or *Sail On*.

Let me ask again: Is Jesus really saying that if we have absolute trust in him, our ship won't sink? That if you have faith, you will not have storms in your life? That Jesus will squelch the squalls?

Many in Christianity teach this; the prosperity movement preaches it; TV evangelists bank on it—it's called the health and wealth gospel. They assert that "God wants to bless you materially and if you have not yet received God's material blessing, it is because you haven't trusted him fully. If you are not being blessed physically, it is because you must have some unconfessed sin in your life."

Is this what the story is all about? What about the young mother whose nine-month-old child is in the hospital? Or worse, has just passed away? What about the man in his middle years in middle management who just lost his job? Or the husband and father of two who was just diagnosed with terminal cancer? Or the teen who is struggling with abusive parents? Or the rape victim? And on and on.

Are we simply to respond, "Why are you so afraid? Do you still have no faith? Don't you know that if you simply have enough faith, everything will be fine?" Does Christ promise to calm all of life's storms? And if he does, what does it mean when he doesn't calm ours?

Is this historical narrative supposed to be treated like an analogy? Or does Mark have something else in mind as he records this account?

The Setting

I want you, for a moment, to look beyond the Sea of Galilee surrounded by its precipitous cliffs. Look beyond the cool air from the mountains coming down and mixing with the warm waters of the lake basin. Look beyond the storm and beyond the fact that the disciples, in part, were made up of experienced fishermen who knew the lake and storms well and yet were terrified. You've heard those sermons! I am suggesting that there is something else in play here! Something more. The key to this passage is found in the first five words: "That day, when evening came" (4:35).

The true setting to our story actually starts back in chapter 4: "Again, Jesus began to teach by the lake" (4:1). Jesus had been teaching them all day long. The question is, what had he been teaching them?

He had taught them three parables (actually more). They were kingdom parables—parables about the kingdom of God and what it would be like; and parables about Christ's kingdom, the kingdom that he would establish. We've already looked at the first. Let me briefly remind you.

Kingdom Parable #1: The Four Soils (Mark 4:1–25)

> "Listen! A farmer went out to sow his seed. As he was scattering the seed, some fell along the path . . . some fell on rocky places . . . other seed fell among thorns . . . still other seed fell on good soil. It came up, grew and produced a crop, multiplying thirty, sixty, or even a hundred times . . . The secret of the kingdom of God has been given to you." (Mark 4:3–11)

It was the parable of the four soils. The Word of God is sown by Jesus himself. The word is preached with different levels of hearing. Some hear properly, others do not. Those who properly hear the word accept it, and produce a crop—thirty, sixty, or even a hundred times what was sown. The seed is planted. In the right environment it grows remarkably and the kingdom goes forward. Not all the seed will germinate, but in good soil (those who listen carefully) it will produce a remarkable crop. Jesus then says, "Consider carefully what you hear" (4:24).

The Point: The Kingdom of God, like seed in good soil, will reproduce remarkably.

Kingdom Parable #2: The Growing Seed (Mark 4:26–29)

> "This is what the kingdom of God is like. A man scatters seed on the ground. Night and day, whether he sleeps or gets up, the seed sprouts and grows, though he does not know how. All by itself the soil produces grain—first the stalk, then the head, then the full kernel in the head. As soon as the grain is ripe, he puts the sickle to it, because the harvest has come." (Mark 4:26–29)

I've heard sermons on this passage that analyze every detail, but miss the point. Some, for example, focus on the stages of spiritual growth: grain, stalk, head, full kernel. Others notice the patience of the farmer: good things come to those who wait.

But I am going to ask you to step back for a moment. Jesus says clearly that the kingdom of God is like seed scattered. We need to ask: What happens to the seed? It grows! It grows even if you don't know about germination, photosynthesis, or the molecular make-up of an individual plant. The point is simple—the seed grows and it produces grain. When the seed is grown, the harvest comes.

The seed grows. What is the seed? We have been given the answer—it is the kingdom of God. The question we need to be asking is: What is going to happen to the kingdom of God? It will be spread, it will grow, and it will produce a harvest. That's the point.

Kingdom Parable #3: The Mustard Seed
(Mark 4:30–34)

> "Again he said, 'What shall we say the kingdom of God is like, or what parable shall we use to describe it? It is like a mustard seed, which is the smallest seed you plan in the ground. Yet when planted, it grows and becomes the largest of all garden plants, with such big branches that the birds of the air can perch in its shade.' With many similar parables Jesus spoke the word to them, as much as they could understand." (Mark 4:30–33)

Once again, I've heard many sermons that have missed the point of this passage. Some explain the ratios between the size of a mustard seed and the size of the mustard plant. Others have waxed on about how birds love to nest in mustard trees. I am not an expert on either topic, but I do know this: Jesus is saying, the kingdom of God will start very small and grow very big.

Again, we need to ask the question: What's the point? The kingdom of God will start with deceptive insignificance but grow to significance.

Three stories, all about growing seeds and the kingdom of God—growing, multiplying, and producing a harvest. All day long, Jesus has been teaching the disciples about the kingdom: how it will start, how it will grow, and how it will become significant. Not only has he been teaching them all day, our passage says, "With many similar parables Jesus spoke the word to them, as much as they could understand" (4:33). With many similar parables? He actually told them more than three! I wonder if the disciples were listening?

Stop one more time. We know that the kingdom is the kingdom of Christ, so let me ask a few questions. Who is king of the kingdom? That answer, of course, is Christ. What had Jesus promised would happen to his kingdom? His kingdom would grow remarkably. Now let me ask:

Who was in the boat with the disciples and what would happen to the kingdom if the king drowned?

Here is the point of the story. Jesus is king of the kingdom. Essentially, all of the kingdom is in that little boat at this time. Based on what Jesus has just been telling his disciples, will they drown on this day? No! Why? Because the kingdom will go forward. It will start small, but grow to significance.

Now back to our story.

On the Lake (Mark 4:38–41)

> That day when evening came, he said to his disciples, "Let us go over to the other side." Leaving the crowd behind, they took him along, just as he was, in the boat. There were also other boats with him. A furious squall came up, and the waves broke over the boat, so that it was nearly swamped. Jesus was in the stern, sleeping on a cushion. The disciples woke him and said to him, "Teacher, don't you care if we drown?" He got up, rebuked the wind and said to the waves, "Quiet! Be still!" then the wind died down and it was completely calm. He said to his disciples, "Why are you so afraid? Do you still have no faith?" They were terrified and asked each other, "Who is this? Even the wind and the waves obey him." (Mark 4:35–41)

I always wondered why Jesus was upset at the disciples when they were terrified about their very lives. He is angry because they have failed to understand what he has been telling them all day long—he is going to build his kingdom.

In our story, four questions are asked which will give us a better understanding of this passage. Two are asked by the disciples, and two by Jesus.

Question One: "Teacher, don't you care if we drown?" (4:38)

It is interesting that Jesus doesn't respond to their question. Of course he cares. Actually, the question goes deeper. The disciples are asking, "What about us? Aren't you going to take care of us? Don't we matter?"

Again, let me remind you of this one fact—the kingdom depends on the king. They are presently with the king. They are the king's seeds. While they may be small and insignificant like the seeds (fishermen, a tax collector, etc), something large will be produced.

Questions Two and Three: "Why are you so afraid? Do you still have no faith?" (4:40)

One might think that the disciples should have believed by this time. Already in the book of Mark, Jesus had healed a man who was possessed by an evil spirit (1:25). He healed Peter's mother-in-law and many others (1:31–33). He cured a man with leprosy (1:40), and told the paralytic to get up and walk (2:11). When confronted by the Pharisees, Jesus healed a man with a shriveled hand (3:5), and performed countless other miracles for the crowds. And the disciples still had no faith.

We can be hard on them, but the truth of the matter is that we've had far more opportunity to know about Jesus Christ than they. Mark writes, "The beginning of the gospel about Jesus Christ, the Son of God" (1:1). He has been presenting Jesus to us. We even have God's word on it—speaking about Jesus he said, "You are my Son, whom I love; with you I am well pleased" (1:11).

By now, shouldn't we believe? I have been asking you to consider Jesus. And to this end, the last question is the most important.

Question Four: "Who is this? Even the wind and the waves obey him." (4:41)

This is the right question. What manner of man indeed? This is not the last time Jesus would question the faith of the disciples, nor is it the last time we will be confronted with this type of question. It is interesting, however, that Mark doesn't bother to answer. That is a question that is obvious in his mind, and a question that you must answer for yourself. Who is this Jesus who has the power over nature? Who is this Jesus who heals the lepers, the demon possessed, the crippled, the sick? Who is this Jesus, who people crowd around to hear the Word of God? Who is this Jesus who died on the cross and rose from the grave? Who is Jesus to you? Is he the Savior and Lord of your life? Is he king? He should be!

In our story, the disciples' fears change their object. They have been afraid of the waves, now they are confronted with Jesus.

Application

We need to answer this question in our own minds: On whom does the kingdom depend? Understand, it depends not on us, but on the king. Jesus is king over the kingdom. He is the focal point, not you, not me.

While we may think that the kingdom revolves around us—it does not. If we fail, his kingdom remains.

Also understand, Jesus is king even through the storms of life. Even if the boat capsizes, even when life collapses, even when from a human perspective everything seems lost—Jesus is still king. When the Jim Elliotts[1] of the world are killed by the very people they are trying to reach—Jesus is still in control. When Paul is in prison, awaiting trial for preaching the gospel—Jesus is still in control. When John the Baptist is beheaded—Jesus is still in control. Above all, when Jesus is arrested and crucified, he still holds the keys to the kingdom. Even if life appears to be crashing in around you—Jesus is still king, and his promises are still true, and his kingdom will still move forward. The kingdom does not exist because of you or me, it exists because of Jesus Christ.

Do you get it? Even when things are hard, even when storms come, even when from our perspective all is lost—God's kingdom moves forward.

Study Questions

1. Have you ever been in a natural disaster? What happened? Did you question God?

2. What comes to mind when you hear the phrase "Kingdom of God" (4:26)?

3. How is the kingdom of God like a scattered seed (4:26–29) and a mustard seed (4:30–32)? What point is Jesus trying to make by comparing the Kingdom of God to a seed planted?

4. If you could ask Jesus to explain something to you from these parables, what would it be?

5. How does knowing that the growth of the kingdom is ultimately in God's hands cause you to rest or work more? Why?

6. At what stage is the kingdom in your life now? A seed? Sprouting? Producing a harvest?

7. Does having faith mean we will never have problems or be afraid?

---

1. Philip James Elliot (October 8, 1927–January 8, 1956) was a missionary to Ecuador who, along with four others, was killed while attempting to evangelize the Waodani people.

8. What do you think was the tone in Jesus' voice when he asked, "Do you still have no faith"? Why?

9. In light of the storm, why would Jesus expect the disciples to not be afraid?

10. How did the disciples' fear during the storm differ from their fear afterward?

11. How would you answer the question in verse 41: "Who is this?"

12. How does an understanding of who Jesus is affect your approach to the circumstances and realities of this life?

13. Who is ultimately in control of your life? How do you know? How would others know?

14. Jesus is king! Are you willing to submit to his ways, his timing, his will? If so, what is next for you?

For Further Study

15. See Matthew 8:23–27; Luke 8:22–25.

10

For the Pigs

Mark 5:1–20

They went across the lake to the region of the Gerasenes. When Jesus got out of the boat, a man with an evil spirit came from the tombs to meet him. This man lived in the tombs, and no one could bind him any more, not even with a chain. For he had often been chained hand and foot, but he tore the chains apart and broke the irons on his feet. No one was strong enough to subdue him. Night and day among the tombs and in the hills he would cry out and cut himself with stones. When he saw Jesus from a distance, he ran and fell on his knees in front of him. He shouted at the top of his voice, "What do you want with me. Jesus, Son of the Most High God? Swear to God that you won't torture me!" For Jesus had said to him, "Come out of this man, you evil spirit!" Then Jesus asked him, "What is your name?" "My name is Legion," he replied, "for we are many," And he begged Jesus again and again not to send them out of the area. A large herd of pigs was feeding on the nearby hillside. The demons begged Jesus, "Send us among the pigs; allow us to go into them." He gave them permission, and the evil spirits came out and went into the pigs. The herd, about two thousand in number, rushed down the steep bank into the lake and were drowned. Those tending the pigs ran off and reported this in the town and countryside, and the people went out to see what had happened. When they came to Jesus, they saw the man who had been possessed by the legion of demons, sitting there, dressed and in his right mind; and they were afraid. Those who had seen it told the people what had happened to the demon-possessed man—and told about the pigs as well. Then the people began to plead with Jesus to leave their region. As Jesus was getting into the boat, the man who had been demon-possessed begged to go with him. Jesus did not let him, but said, "Go home to your family and tell them how much the Lord has done for you, and how he has had mercy on you." So the man went away and began to tell in the Decapolis how much Jesus had done for him. And all the people were amazed. (Mark 5:1–20)

OUR STORY BEGINS AS Jesus and the disciples travel to the region of the Gerasenes, called the Decapolis—an area of ten cities on the eastern side of the sea, one of which was Damascus, capital of modern-day Syria.

To Gentile Country (Mark 5:1)

"They went across the lake to the region of the Gerasenes" (5:1).

Jesus goes to Gentile territory (one was either a Jew or a Gentile, which simply means, non-Jew). The Gentiles were pagans. Jesus goes to alien turf. The question is, why? His vacation destination is a curiosity. Actually, Jesus' purpose is not just to get away from the crowds (he can do that in Jewish territory). He chooses this spot intentionally. Why? The answer is interesting—this is the first hint in the Gospel of Mark that the gospel is for all people, Jew and Gentile, slave and free, male and female. In the back of your mind, understand: the disciples are probably already a little uncomfortable.

An Unclean Man (Mark 5:2–5)

"When Jesus got out of the boat, an 'unclean' man came to him . . ." (5:2–5).

The issue was not his lack of hygiene (although this was quite possibly a factor). This man was called unclean for several reasons. Let me give you three. First, as we have already discussed, he was a Gentile. Jews and Gentiles didn't get along (think about modern day Jews and Arabs, although the term Gentile is a much broader category). Old Testament law clearly told the Jews: don't associate with them, don't do business with them, certainly don't marry them! Most of the Old Testament is about driving the Gentiles out of the promised land. A quick survey of Joshua and Judges right down through 1—2 Samuel, 1—2 Kings, and 1—2 Chronicles paints a clear picture. Read the stories about the captivities and you will quickly be reminded that the Jews and Gentiles didn't mix well. They were like oil and water. Strike one!

Second, he lived among the tombs. Probably more specifically, in the tombs. You've got to admit it is a little creepy. Understand, a good Jew could not even touch a dead body without becoming ceremonially unclean. Ceremonial uncleanliness came with a big price tag. Among other things, you couldn't participate in social activities and religious festivities. To become clean, you first have to go through ritualistic cleansings, offer prescribed offerings, and take a mandatory leave of absence. Tombs were often made from caves and usually included a preparation room as well as a burial chamber where he lived. This man didn't just touch dead guys, they were roommates. Strike two!

Third, our man was demon-possessed. Once again, I may have lost some of you. I've opened up this can of worms before. We live in a day and age where some people question the supernatural. You might be asking, "Do you really believe in spirits and demons?" If you are referring to what you see on TV, and your question is about the superstition and fantasy depicted there—I understand your reservation. But my answer remains yes! The Bible says, "Our struggle is not against flesh and blood, but against the rulers, against the powers of this dark world and against the spiritual forces of evil in the heavenly realms" (Ephesians 6:12).

You might ask more specifically, "Do you believe in demon possession?" Again, my answer is yes. If we believe good and evil are in conflict, it shouldn't surprise us that in Bible times, demon possession reached a climax during Jesus' life on earth.

While I believe in the supernatural, I would caution you to avoid the extremes and don't deny the supernatural. First, most exaggerate the case, bringing fear and paranoia. We should always remember that Jesus is victorious. Second, some who promote demons tend to blame them for everything—the demon of alcohol, the demon of drug abuse, the demon of abusive speech. Much of what they blame on demons is simply human vice. Third, most present-day expressions of belief in demons border on the superstitious and are at best sub-Christian and should be avoided. Fourth, Scripture certainly warns us to avoid dabbling in the occult. Finally, demon possession is a rare phenomenon. People are more likely controlled by a legion of cravings and destructive impulses than by a legion of demons.

C. S. Lewis says, "There are two equal and opposite errors into which our race can fall about the devils. One is to disbelieve in their existence. The other is to believe, and to feel an excessive and unhealthy interest in them. They themselves are equally pleased by both errors."[1]

Wreaking Havoc (Mark 5:3)

"This man lived in the tombs, and no one could bind him any more, not even with a chain" (5:3).

This demon-possessed man has probably been a thorn in the side of these people for years with growing intensity. At one time, he was able to be bound, but the chains that once protected both him and the community no longer work. He creates fear, damages the trade routes, and is more than a public nuisance, crying out both day and night.

The Confrontation (Mark 5:6–13)

"When he saw Jesus . . . he ran and fell on his knees in front of him . . ." (5:6–13).

Once again we see this strange irony. When the religious leaders of Israel see Jesus, they do not recognize him, but when the demon-possessed man sees Jesus, he recognizes him immediately. The demon-possessed man comes and bows down before Jesus. Whether he is mocking with feigned worship, or is forced by the presence of Jesus to do so is unclear. He yells at the top of his voice, "What do you want with me, Jesus?" (5:7). Literally, "Why are you confronting me?" Why are you here? Why now? Why me?

After his question, the man utters the highest form of acknowledgment a non-believer can make. Mockingly? Maybe. Reluctantly? Certainly. But his statement is accurate. While a believer can call Jesus, "Lord and Savior," or rightfully pronounce God as "Father," a nonbeliever cannot. In the Old Testament, believers called God "Lord" or "Jehovah," but again these titles were limited to those who believed. But notice what the demon-possessed man says, especially in contrast to what a man with an unclean spirit previously said in the book of Mark. Earlier, the man with the unclean spirit said, "I know who you are, the Holy One of God" (1:24). Here the statement is much stronger: "Jesus, Son of the Most High God" (5:7). The phrase comes right out of the Old Testament (*el-elyon*).

---

1. C. S. Lewis, *The Screwtape Letters*, p. 3.

Other countries had gods whom they worshiped, but when confronted with the living God (the God of Jacob), they acknowledged that the God of Israel was "The Most High God." Whatever his intentions, this is what this man proclaims. He knows who Jesus is, or at least who Jesus claims to be (once again, notice how the dialogue shows us Mark's point).

When Jesus asks him his name, he responds, "Legion" (5:9). Depending on who you read, you will see different designations of the word "legion"(*legiōn*). Actually, depending on what era you are referencing, the terminology varies. In Jesus' day, it seems to represent six thousand foot soldiers and one hundred and twenty horsemen (other time periods use other numbers). I'm not sure we need to be dogmatic about how many, but we do know it was enough to make two thousand pigs crazy (5:13).

Legion is scared: "Don't send us out of the area, send us among the pigs." Jesus grants them permission (5:13). I want to stop right here and say, I've got lots of questions, and not many answers.

First, why doesn't Jesus simply destroy them or render them powerless? The answer is: maybe he does. The language is unclear. We know that the pigs are destroyed—maybe the evil spirits are destroyed as well—we don't know. But ask the question again—why doesn't Jesus render them powerless? In the life of the demon-possessed man, he does. We should also remember that this is Jesus' intent. Jesus came, "To bind up the strong man" (3:27). More than that, we know this is exactly what Jesus accomplishes on the cross. Jesus renders Satan and the forces of darkness powerless. Maybe Jesus grants their request, because it's just not time yet to render them completely powerless.

Second, why does Jesus allow them to go into the pigs? I'm sure this made the first-century animal rights activists crazy. I've got a couple of suggestions. First, the pig (wild boar) was an icon of pagan ritual worship and also held elevated status in Rome (it was symbolized on their flags). Maybe it's a statement about pagan "false" gods or even the rule of Rome. Second, maybe Jesus did this as a visual demonstration of how many demons there were and the power that had overcome this man—and how Jesus was even stronger. Or, third, maybe this was to serve as a teaching moment to point out Satan's intentions. What the demons immediately did to the pigs is exactly what they had wanted to accomplish in this man (and all men)—their purpose is to destroy.

Satan always defaces humanity and tries to destroy the image of God in man. This is his mode of operation: torment and anguish, isolation and solitude, and the practice of self-destructive behavior. Satan wants to destroy the image of God in man while Jesus comes to restore the image of God in man.

Two Responses (Mark 5:14–20)

First, notice the response of the crowd. When the people of the town and countryside hear what has happened, they come to see it. Their response is interesting: "Then the people began to plead with Jesus to leave their region" (5:17).

You might think they would be gracious and thankful for what Jesus has done. You might think they would offer him the keys to the city, but instead they offer him the cold shoulder. They ask Jesus to leave. Why? Some, undoubtedly, were upset about the pigs. This was their livelihood. I'm not an expert on what pigs are worth, but I can imagine a price around one thousand dollars. With two thousand pigs, that would be the equivalent of two million dollars today. That would be devastating to an agrarian society. The most tender spot for most people is often their wallet. Jesus has hit them where it hurts.

Still, even then, I think the people should be pleased. This man tormented their city, undoubtedly affecting the trade routes and commerce, and certainly bringing fear into the lives of many. Besides, isn't the value of a man's life worth more than a few pigs or a few dollars? It certainly is. In fact, for Jesus, the life of one man is beyond measure. The life of one man is worth giving his own.

But there is more at play than just a few pigs. Verse 15 gives us a clue: "When they came to Jesus they saw the man who had been possessed by the legion of demons, sitting there, dressed and in his right mind; and they were afraid" (5:15).

Luke's account puts it this way: "Then all the people of the region of the Gerasenes asked Jesus to leave them alone, because they were overcome with fear. So he got into the boat and left" (Luke 8:37).

What is it about a man sitting at the feet of Jesus that scares people so completely? Not just in the first century, but the twenty-first century? Say to someone in our society that you are Hindu, or Buddhist, or even Atheist, and they seem to be fine with it. Mention the names of Mohammed, Confucius, the Dali Lama, or Joseph, and few are offended.

But mention the name of Jesus Christ and you will ruffle feathers. Why? It is precisely because of who Jesus is, who he claims to be, and the power he wields. The crowds in chapter 5 are confronted with the same question the disciples were confronted with in chapter 4: "Who is this man, that even the wind and the waves obey him?" (4:35).

That's Mark's point! The first response is that of fear. But there is a second response. Notice the response of the clean man: "The man . . . begged Jesus to go with him" (5:18). It is interesting that the crowd begged Jesus to leave and he grants their request, while the man begs to go with Jesus and his request is denied. There is wisdom in Jesus' refusal, however. Jesus says, "Go home to your family and tell them how much the Lord has done for you, and how he has had mercy on you" (5:19).

Let me ask you a question. At this point in the story, how much did this man know about Jesus? Not very much. He only knows that he was once unclean, but now he is clean. It reminds me of the response of blind Bartimaeus after Jesus restored his sight: "One thing I do know, I was blind, but now I see" (John 9:25).

There is application here for us. You don't need to be a skilled theologian or a master of evangelism to share Jesus—you simply need to share what Jesus has done for you and the mercy he has had on you. The man's witness is powerful (and possible) because people could see the change evidenced in his life. This is necessary for your life as well. If you are going to be an effective witness for Jesus, others must see Jesus evidenced in your life. The man's effectiveness was due to the fact that he did go back to his family and friends.

Schweizer says this: "Jesus' answer shows how impossible it is to have a stereotyped definition of discipleship. One person is taken away from home and family, another is sent back to them contrary to his own wishes."[2]

It is interesting that the man does what Jesus asks. In the Decapolis, he begins to tell how much Jesus has done for him. And all the people are amazed.

In chapter 5 we see two responses. The response of the clean man who wants to be with Jesus, and the response of the people who want him to leave. Fast forward two chapters. In chapter 7 Jesus returns to the area of the Decapolis and guess what happens? Crowds of people come

---

2. Edward Schweizer, *The Good News According to Mark*, p. 141.

to Jesus, bringing people to him who need healing. Why does this happen? It happens because one man was willing to go and tell.

Study Questions

1. What is the most dramatic transformation you have seen Jesus Christ make in someone's life?
2. What do we learn about the demon-possessed man from this passage?
3. How does the demon-possessed man respond to Jesus' arrival (6)?
4. According to the demon-possessed man in verse 7, who is Jesus?
    a. Do you find it interesting that the evil spirits recognized Jesus, while the religious leaders did not?
    b. Does a similar thing ever happen today? How?
5. Read verse 13. What does this imply about Jesus' authority?
6. Why might Jesus allow the demons to enter into the pigs?
7. Why were the people afraid when they saw the man who had been possessed "sitting there, dressed and in his right mind" (15)? What is it today about "sitting at the feet of Jesus" that scares some people so much?
8. Why did the people ask Jesus to leave their region? Why does Jesus grant their request?
9. Which is more valuable, a man's life or that of a pig? A man's life or 2,000 pigs? How might some answer today? How would Jesus respond to the question: "How valuable is a man's life?"
10. In contrast with Jesus' earlier requests that people remain silent, why did Jesus tell this man to share with others what had happened to him?
11. When Jesus asks the formerly demon-possessed man to "go tell," how much did he know about Jesus?
    a. What do you think he said to his family and friends?
    b. How much do you need to know in order to be an effective witness?

    c. Would the formerly demon-possessed man's testimony be more effective or less effective if he went someplace else? Why?

12. Have you ever told your family how Jesus has shown mercy on you?

13. Is demon possession still possible today? Do you know of any instances of apparent demon possession?

14. Locate the region of Gerasenes on a map at the back of your Bible. Where is the Decapolis (5:20)?

For Further Study

15. See Matthew 8:28–34 and Luke 8:26–37. Mark and Luke both record a single demon-possessed man, while Matthew records that there were two. Are these passages contradictory? How can they be reconciled?

11

Talitha Koum

Mark 5:21–43

In our passage, we get another instance of Mark using a technique called "sandwiching." As mentioned earlier, sandwiching occurs when two seemingly unrelated stories are placed together in Oreo fashion with one story interrupting the first, only to return later to the original story. Although at first glance they may appear to be unrelated, closer examination reveals that the second story helps interpret the first and may even provide its primary meaning.[1] In our passage, the story of Jairus' daughter will be interrupted by a bleeding woman, and then we will return to the first story.

Before we begin, we need to be reminded of a little background which testifies to the power of Jesus. In previous chapters Jesus had demonstrated his power over nature in the narrative about calming the sea (4:35–41), and more recently demonstrated his power over demons as we learned about Legion and the herd of pigs in the region of the Gerasenes (5:1–20).

Now, Jesus demonstrates his power over disease and even death (5:21–34). In all three cases, fear is a reappearing theme.

Story One: A Story about a Synagogue Ruler (Mark 5:21–24)

> When Jesus had again crossed over by boat to the other side of the lake, a large crowd gathered around him while he was by the lake. Then one of the synagogue rulers, named Jairus, came there. Seeing Jesus, he fell at his feet and pleaded earnestly with him, "My little daughter is dying. Please come and put your hands on

---

1. For more on sandwiching, see chapter 7.

her so that she will be healed and live." So Jesus went with him. (Mark 5:21–24a)

As the story begins, Jesus and the disciples are returning to the west side of the lake—presumably back to Capernaum.[2] Here we are introduced to Jairus. Interestingly enough, Jairus is one of the few characters in the book of Mark that is given a name. Besides John the Baptist, Herod, and the disciples, few besides Blind Bartimaeus (10:46) are named. Jairus is called a synagogue ruler[3] or official (*archisynagōgos*) and was likely responsible for oversight of the facility and the planning of the worship services. Whatever his responsibilities, he was undoubtedly a respected man of the community. In our story, we find several interesting aspects about Jairus.

He Came

Most of the Jewish leaders had rejected Jesus. We have seen the Scribes and the Pharisees along with the teachers of the law looking for ways to find fault with Jesus. They have tried to discredit Jesus (2:18); accused him of being aligned with Satan (3:22); and tried to plot how they might kill Jesus (3:6).

In the best-case scenario, Jairus would be criticized for seeking out Jesus; more likely he would be ostracized and lose his position in the synagogue. But the severity of his daughter's illness trumped ridicule.

He Came Personally

Not only did Jairus seek out Jesus, but he came himself. It would have been easy for a leader of a synagogue to justify staying behind with his dying daughter and sending a servant in his place. But he realizes that his own position of authority would hold more weight. Jairus is at his wits' end. His dear little daughter's life is on the line. He dare not just send a servant, he must get a hearing with Jesus himself. In describing the girl's condition, Mark notes that she is at the point of death (6:23). Matthew says that she has just died (Matthew 9:18). Doctor Luke records that she is dying (Luke 8:42). The situation is critical and Jairus' desperation is great. He personally has to go.

---

2. See Matthew 9:1.

3. In Jesus' day, synagogues were led by a small group of laymen responsible for the conduct of services. The official was chosen locally by the members of the synagogue.

He Pleaded

The terminology used is interesting. It reflects his desperation. Jairus fell at Jesus' feet (*piptō*)—a position of great humility, especially for a man in his position. Matthew's account says, "He prostrated himself" (Matthew 9:18). The leader of the community fell humbly at Jesus' feet and pled urgently. Literally, that phrase reads, he "appealed (*parakaleō*) much (*polys*)." Any parent who has spent time in the emergency room with a sick child can relate to the agony this man felt.

His Request

His request was simple to vocalize, but should not be considered ordinary: "Come put your hands on her, that she may be healed and live" (5:23). He had certainly heard, and maybe even personally seen Jesus' power.

Jesus' Response

Like the request before it, Jesus' response is simple yet profound. Jesus is not recorded as saying anything at this point. We simply read, "So Jesus went with him" (5:24). So why would I say his response was profound? Think for a moment about all of the people who were clamoring for Jesus' attention. Why did Jesus go with this man? We can only assume that Jesus knew the full extent of this man's faith, what he had risked personally in coming, and ultimately what was at stake.

No sooner have we got caught up in the drama, the first story is interrupted by a second—building tension and suspense. Story two is parenthetical and a parallel narrative.

Story Two: A Story About a Woman (Mark 5:25–34)

> A large crowd followed and pressed around him. And a woman was there who had been subject to bleeding for twelve years. She had suffered a great deal under the care of many doctors and had spent all she had, yet instead of getting better she grew worse. When she heard about Jesus, she came up behind him in the crowd and touched his cloak, because she thought, "If I just touch his clothes, I will be healed." Immediately her bleeding stopped and she felt in her body that she was freed from her suffering. At once Jesus realized that power had gone out from him.

> He turned around in the crowd and asked, "Who touched my clothes?" "You see the people crowding against you," his disciples answered, "and yet you can ask, 'Who touched me?'" But Jesus kept looking around to see who had done it. Then the woman, knowing what had happened to her, came and fell at his feet and, trembling with fear, told him the whole truth. He said to her, "Daughter, your faith has healed you. Go in peace and be freed from your suffering." (Mark 5:24b–34)

As Jesus is heading toward the home of Jairus, a woman who has been hemorrhaging sneaks up behind him. She probably suffers from some type of menstrual bleeding or uterine disorder that would have made her ritually unclean[4] and excluded her from social contact. She had lived a wretched life as an outcast for twelve years. To put this in perspective, we learn that she has suffered the entire life span of Jairus' daughter. She has been in a continuous state of uncleanness and has been shunned by society. She has suffered every day physically, socially, and psychologically. Above all, she is a contaminant to society.

We learn that she was once a woman of means. She had sufficient finances to consult many physicians. I am humored by the phrase (probably because my brother is an M.D.), "She had suffered a great deal under the care of many doctors" (5:26). One might even conclude that they had contributed to her problems (there is a reason we say doctors "practice" medicine). Whatever the cause, she is now in desperate straits. The treatments have not only been ineffective, instead of getting better, she has steadily grown worse, and now she is in financial ruin.

This woman has obviously heard of Jesus and possesses a whatever-it-takes mentality. If she could just touch his clothes (there are probably superstitious overtones here) she might be cured. Her faith motivates her, not only to illegally pass through the crowds, but in her state of uncleanliness, to touch Jesus. Her faith propels her. It is worth noting that faith involves action. Faith that isn't put into action is no faith at all.

As soon as she touches Jesus, she is healed. Mark writes, "Immediately her bleeding stopped and she felt in her body that she was freed from her suffering" (5:39).

Jesus, not knowing who touched him, questions, "Who touched my clothes?" (5:30). The question seems pointless and even ridiculous to the disciples: "You see the people crowding against you . . . and yet you can

---

4. See Leviticus 15:25–27.

ask, 'Who touched my clothes?'" (5:31). They don't know what we have been given as an editorial comment: "Jesus realized that power had gone out from him" (5:30).

The disciples question Jesus, and I, too, have questions of my own. The first one is simply, why does Jesus stop? The woman has been healed, and Jairus' daughter is deathly ill. So why take time to identify this anonymous woman?

There may be several answers. Maybe he stops to correct her misguided superstition (it was Jesus, not some mystical experience that made her whole). Maybe it is to bring her to the point of verbal confession (he wants to see her fall at his feet and tell him the whole truth). Maybe he wants to use her as a witness to everyone present of what faith can accomplish (letting the crowd know both the power of Jesus and the cleanliness of the woman). Maybe he wants to let her know that he cares for her (she is a person of worth, she is worth stopping for, she is worth talking to, she matters). But, once again, the answer is in the dialogue. Jesus wants to say to her, "Daughter, your faith has healed you. Go in peace and be freed from your suffering" (5:34).

It is worth noting that the word "healed" (*sōzō*) is not just the word for physical healing, but also of salvation. This is also apparent in the phrase, "Go in peace" (5:34). Jesus doesn't dismiss her, he uses the Greek translation (*eirē*) of the Hebrew word "Shalom"—signifying wholeness, well-being, security, friendship, and salvation.

We might also ask and answer the question: Why is she so afraid? Again, there might be several reasons. She has made unlawful contact, illegitimately stolen Christ's power, and made him ceremonially unclean. She might have expected a scolding, but receives a blessing instead. Jesus' healing doesn't come free—he forces her to step out on faith and be identified. He does not bankrupt her (like the doctors before him)—but he wants her to publicly acknowledge him.

That brings us to the end of story two and back to our original story.

Story One: The Synagogue Ruler, Continued (Mark 5:35–43)

> While Jesus was still speaking, some men came from the house of Jairus, the synagogue ruler. "Your daughter is dead," they said. "Why bother the teacher any more?" Ignoring what they said, Jesus told the synagogue ruler, "Don't be afraid; just believe." He did not let anyone follow him except Peter, James and John the

> brother of James. When they came to the home of the synagogue ruler, Jesus saw a commotion, with people crying and wailing loudly. He went in and said to them, "Why all this commotion and wailing? The child is not dead but asleep." But they laughed at him. After he put them all out, he took the child's father and mother and the disciples who were with him, and went in where the child was. He took her by the hand and said to her, "Talitha Koum!" (which means, "Little girl, I say to you, get up!"). Immediately the girl stood up and walked around (she was twelve years old). At this they were completely astonished. He gave strict orders not to let anyone know about this, and told them to give her something to eat. (Mark 5:35–43)

Through all of this, what must Jairus be thinking? I know what I'd be thinking: "My daughter is at the point of death, this woman has been sick for twelve years, she can wait a little longer. I was in line first." The interruption, so profitable to the woman, cost the life of Jairus' daughter.

When the servants come they don't mince words: "Your daughter is dead" (5:39). Then they make an interesting comment. It shows what they believe about Jesus, and maybe signifies what Jairus has himself told them about Jesus: "Why bother the teacher any more?" (5:35). They believe he is a good teacher. He might even be a prophet. They know he can work miracles. But the girl is dead. The teacher is no longer of any use. This is beyond his pay grade.

But Jesus now asks Jairus to do something incredible: "Don't be afraid; just believe" (5:36). The NIV actually adds a word I don't like. The word "just" or "only" does not appear in this passage. "Don't be afraid, believe." Jesus is asking Jairus to believe the impossible. "Will you believe only in what circumstances allow, or will you believe in the God that makes all things possible? "Don't be afraid, believe." It's a question we should all ask—will we only believe in what circumstances allow, or will we believe in the God who makes all things possible?

Then Jesus utters the unbelievable: "The child is not dead, but is asleep" (5:39). When he says it, the crowd laughs. They know what "dead" is. If this girl is sleeping, she's not waking up. Her pulse has faded, her body is limp, her spirit is gone. They, however, fail to recognize who Jesus is. He can calm the storm, cast out the demon, cure disease and raise the dead. He's the one who gives life to begin with. He can turn tragedy into joy. Unlike the woman who sought Jesus, unlike the ruler who came to Jesus, their laughter puts them on the outside. Jesus responds only to those who have faith. He dismisses the crowd.

Jesus takes mother and father, along with three disciples inside. Why three? These are probably the inner circle. Three would serve as legal witnesses. Besides, the others were back doing crowd control (5:37). Once on the inside, Jesus says in Aramaic, *"Talitha koum!"*[5] Aramaic was the language of Jesus. Koine Greek, or common Greek, was the language of commerce. Mark translates it for a Roman audience, and for us. "Little girl, I say to you, get up!" Why give us the Aramaic? Possibly for emphasis. It creates a dramatic effect for the listeners (and for us). Some have suggested that these words had been often repeated and were viewed by some as magical statement (an incantation). Mark clarifies that they are not some mysterious mumbo jumbo, but an ordinary phrase from an extraordinary person: "Little girl, get up."

The girl gets up, and immediately Jesus offers her food. Again, I want to know why. There may be several reasons. Just as Jesus ate after his resurrection, this demonstrates that she is not a vision or a spirit. Clearly it shows that she is fully recovered—she has regained her appetite and is able to eat. One thing is certain—she is not dead.

Two stories: Actually, we'd be hard-pressed to find two stories much different. A wealthy man in good standing in the community—a respected leader; a woman shunned by all—an outcast. A named man, Jairus; the unnamed woman. A man who parades in, expecting to gain an audience; a woman who sneaks in, hoping only to touch a robe. One with servants and a home; the other homeless. But they share one thing. The commonality? The hopelessness of their situation and their willingness to believe that Jesus has the answer to their problems. And Jesus does! They are willing to trust in the midst of their hopelessness.

Our stories are but one piece to answering Mark's overriding question—Who is Jesus? Jesus is the one who can calm a sea; the one who can exorcize a demon from a man no one could control; the one who can heal a woman no physician could cure; and the one who can restore life to a girl when all hope was gone.

Our passage answers this basic question for us: Where is trust best placed in the midst of hopelessness? Not in fear, but in the power of Jesus.

---

5. In the everyday language of Jewish Palestine, this was an expression of affection and tenderness and literally means "Arise, lamb."

Study Questions

1. How do you tend to respond in desperate times?
2. Describe a time when you were at the end of your rope. What did you do?
3. Why did Jairus fall at Jesus' feet and beg? Why did Jesus go with Jairus?
4. Have you ever spent a day in the emergency room with a son/daughter or loved one in critical condition? How did you feel? To what lengths would you have gone to remedy the situation?
5. If Jesus knew that Jairus' daughter would die, why did he not prevent it? What lessons would he be trying to teach?
6. If Jesus was able to raise people from the dead, why didn't he raise more?
7. If you could raise anyone from the dead, who would it be and why?
8. What do we know about the unnamed woman (25–34)?
    a. To what lengths did she go to try to solve the problem on her own?
    b. What situation did this leave her in?
    c. Was she wrong in doing so?
9. What is your typical response when things get difficult (hopeless)? Do you resonate with the unnamed woman?
10. How did she respond to Jesus when he asked, "Who touched me" (31–33)? Why was she so afraid? Why was she so honest?
11. According to Jesus, what healed the sick woman (34)?
12. What did Jesus mean when he said, "Don't be afraid; just believe" (36)? How does faith drive out fear?
13. Of all the people pressing for Jesus' attention, two get through to him. Why?
14. At what costs did Jairus and the bleeding woman come to Jesus (personal, cultural, religious)?

15. Do these stories imply that Jesus is going to fix your every problem? Does God guarantee healing from every disease?

16. How does this chapter show Christ as greater than mere man?

17. Jairus fell at Jesus' feet and begged him to heal his twelve-year-old daughter. When is the last time you fell at Jesus' feet to worship?

For Further Study

18. See Matthew 9:18–26; Luke 8:40–56.

12

Local Yokel

Mark 6:1–6a

AN OLD ADAGE STATES that the expert is the one carrying a briefcase who comes the farthest. In more recent years, the briefcase has been replaced by the laptop. The saying has survived the test of time, because there is much truth in it. We seem to attach a sense of importance to someone who comes from the outside. Unfortunately, we often overlook the true experts in our very midst because of their familiarity. We are confronted with this problem as Jesus returns to his hometown.

> Jesus left there and went to his hometown, accompanied by his disciples. When the Sabbath came, he began to teach in the synagogue, and many who heard him were amazed. "Where did this man get these things?" they asked. "What's this wisdom that has been given him, that he even does miracles! Isn't this the carpenter? Isn't this Mary's son and the brother of James, Joseph, Judas and Simon? Aren't his sisters here with us?" And they took offense at him. Jesus said to them, "Only in his hometown, among his relatives and in his own house is a prophet without honor." He could not do any miracles there, except lay his hands on a few sick people and heal them. And he was amazed at their lack of faith. (Mark 6:1–6)

As we begin, we need to address a couple of difficulties found in this text. First, there are some who suggest a contradiction between the accounts of Matthew 13:53–58, Mark 6:1–6, and Luke 4:16–28. A casual comparison certainly reveals differences with these stories in a number of areas: the number of people involved, the level of intensity of the opposition, and Luke's account that the town people wanted to throw Jesus off a cliff but he walked right through the crowd—are the most notable examples.

While some are troubled by these differences, the explanation for these differences is that these are two different accounts. We have different people, different reactions, and a different conclusion because Jesus returned home twice. Luke records a visit home which occurs very early in the ministry of Jesus. During the first visit, the opposition against Jesus is so strong that Luke records that the people want to throw him off a cliff. Matthew and Mark record a second trip which happens at least a year later. By this time, Jesus' popularity is widespread and his budding reputation earns him an opportunity to speak at the local synagogue. People are still skeptical of the local boy who has returned home.

A second difficulty stems from the belief that Jesus is unable to perform miracles in Nazareth. Actually, this commonly-held belief is not quite accurate. Read the passage again carefully and you will note that Jesus does do some miracles (laying on hands and healing the sick), he just does not do many. The question is, why? Why is Jesus rejected by his hometown, relatives, and family? In our passage we find several reasons.

They Are Perplexed with Jesus (Mark 6:1–2)

In verse 2, we find those listening asking several questions. "Where did this man get these things?" (Where did he get his ideas?) Certainly not from his local upbringing. We've never heard someone like this. "What is the wisdom that has been given to Him?" (He not only has the ability to teach, but does so with wisdom and clarity.) These two questions imply that the people recognize the skill and the authority of Jesus, but cannot explain it. The third response can also be properly formed as a question and concerns the powerful works he does. "He does miracles." The underlying question is: "How does he do them?"

They have undoubtedly heard about the miracles he has performed; maybe they have even seen a few (or maybe not). Clearly Jesus has developed a reputation, but they don't have an explanation for it.

Interestingly enough, there has been a similar progression in the book of Mark. Early in chapter 1 we found a synagogue gathering asking about Jesus: "What is this? A new teaching—and with authority" (1:27). Then we saw the teachers of the law asking, "How can he talk like this?" (2:7), and later still the disciples asking, "Who is this?" (4:41). Now we see the people of Nazareth asking their own question: "From where does this teaching and this power come?" (6:2).

We also find another interesting progression. Note the alternating demonic and then human response throughout the Gospel of Mark.

Demonic response	Human response
You are the Holy One of God (1:24)	Who is this? (1:27)
They knew who he was (1:34)	Why does he talk like this? (2:7)
You are the Son of God (3:11)	Who is this? (4:41)
Jesus, Son of the Most High (5:7)	Isn't this Mary's son? (6:3)

The very ones who should recognize him, don't. The teachers of the law, the Pharisees, the Scribes, his family and relatives, his home town—the ones we might expect to accept him deny him, and the ones we would expect to deny him acknowledge him. Jesus' friends and family can't explain him, they are perplexed and their animosity rises.

They Are Put Off with Jesus (Mark 6:3)

In verse 3, we are confronted with another series of questions: "Isn't this the carpenter? Isn't this Mary's son and the brother of James, Joseph, Judas and Simon? Aren't his sisters here with us?" They took offense with Jesus for several reasons.

First, they were put off with Jesus because of familiarity—they knew Jesus, he grew up in their midst. We remember that after Jesus was born in Bethlehem, his family fled from Herod, from Bethlehem to Egypt. After living near what we would call Cairo for two years, Joseph and Mary returned to Nazareth where Jesus lived from age two until he was thirty. And the people knew his family well. They knew his brothers and sisters—they were ordinary enough. Four brothers are named, and we can conclude that Jesus had at least two sisters.

This understanding is contrary to those who suggest that Mary was perpetually a virgin. Those who hold this view suggest the words "brothers" (*adelphos*) and "sisters" (*adelphē*) here should be translated "cousins" (*anepsios*). The only problem with this view is that this would be the only case where these words are translated this way—not only in the Bible, but in all ancient Greek literature.

Not only did the town folk not accept Jesus—at first, Jesus' brothers didn't believe in him either. Early in the book of Mark we saw them wanting to come and take Jesus by force, because they thought he was crazy (3:21). John records for us: "For even his own brothers did not believe in him" (John 7:5). This all changes after the resurrection. James and Jude become leaders in the church, and write two of our Epistles which bear their names.

Not only did they know Jesus' family, they knew Jesus—and he, too, was ordinary enough. This too, is contrary to apocryphal stories that some teach about Jesus' childhood—those sandbox stories where we read about Jesus raising a dead bird or bringing a dead boy back to life. Jesus lived a normal childhood and young adult life. Our Bibles tell us that he grew in wisdom, stature, and favor with God and man (Luke 2:52) and that his first miracle was in Cana (John 2:11).

Second, they were put off with Jesus because of his carpentry (*tektōn*). Don't misunderstand—there was nothing wrong with being a carpenter—they were much needed and respected members of society. First-century carpenters not only worked with wood, but also metal, and stone. Like many of our carpenters today, they could make or fix most anything. Carpenters were technically skilled and physically strong (not at all like many of the portraits of Jesus which depict him as a weakling).

The people were not mocking carpenters, they were questioning Jesus' ability as a teacher. "He's not a trained scribe. He's not a Rabbi." They knew Jesus. They went to school together. They studied Torah together. Neither were accepted to Rabbinical school. Their point: "He isn't trained to be a Rabbi. He is not a scholar. He's a carpenter." Actually it is a valid criticism—if Jesus were just an ordinary man. We might make this criticism too, if we saw an unskilled, untrained lay person leading a movement.

Third, they were put off with Jesus because of his perceived illegitimacy. Notice the statement, "Isn't this Mary's son?" (6:3). Some simply take this phrase to mean that Joseph had died early and was no longer in the picture. And while there is some evidence of Joseph's early death, even if he was dead, Jesus would not normally have been referred to in this way. Sons would have been referred to by their father's name, even after their passing, unless the people didn't believe Joseph was Jesus' father. People believed the worst about Jesus. They did not believe in the virgin birth, but that Jesus was an illegitimate son, "The son of Mary."

They underestimated Jesus. He did not meet their expectations. They discounted him—he was over-reaching his bounds. Jesus did not fit the bill. And so their feelings for him intensified.

They Took Offense at Jesus (Mark 6:3–6)

As the people studied Jesus, "They took offense at him" (6:3). The word used here (*skandalizō*) is used of bait and a trap. More specifically, it refers to the lever that springs the trap. From this Greek word, we get two English words: "scandal" and "slander." The people think they have Jesus pegged. The people believe they know all there is to know about him and his background.

Then Jesus utters the well-known proverb: "Only in his hometown, among relatives, and in his own house—a prophet is without honor" (6:4). Notice the progression from town, to relatives, to his own house. Notice also that this is the first use of the word "prophet" in the book of Mark.

This brings us to the most difficult section of this passage. The response of Jesus to the people of his hometown, and the phrase, "He could not do any miracles there, except . . ." (6:5).

How is one to understand this verse? Many explanations have been put forward. Some suggest, first, that Jesus is unable to do miracles where there is no faith. There are several problems with this view, including the fact that it seems to limit omnipotence (all-powerfulness) and it ignores the fact that Jesus often does miracles even among unbelieving people in Scripture.

A second explanation suggests that Jesus chose not to do any miracles. This is not the same as the first suggestion, but merely affirms that Jesus chooses to work with people who do have faith. While I believe Jesus does work with those people who have faith, the problem with this view is that it is not what the text says.

How does one reconcile this? A third view suggests that the people won't let him work any miracles. We know that Jesus will not go where he is unwanted. He remains a gentleman. When the Gadarenes ask him to leave, he goes. When people are unconvinced, he doesn't force himself. When people reject him, he complies. When people do not come to him, he stays away.

One simple analogy might be that of a TV with "rabbit-ears" for an antenna. We have all tried to "dial in" good reception by twisting and turning the antenna to a better position. The truth, however, is that the antenna doesn't limit the power of the broadcast no matter what direction it is facing. The signal is unaffected by the antenna. The TV's reception can be changed (made fuzzy or clear) but the signal has remained constant. In a similar manner, people's faith determines the receptivity to the power of Jesus—it doesn't limit his power. Many people simply did not come to Jesus because they didn't believe. Others were not candidates because they didn't seek out Jesus. Ben Wittherington writes, "Lack of faith limits the reception of help readily available from Jesus."[1] Jesus did not perform any miracles because few came to him for help.

Up to this point, we have been looking at the people's response to Jesus. But notice also how Jesus responds to them. It is interesting that in our passage, the synagogue rejects Jesus, and in the book of Mark, Jesus never enters this synagogue again. It is also of interest to note that Jesus is amazed at their lack of faith. We should point out that a different word is used in verse 6 than was used in verse 2. When the people are amazed (*ekplēssō*) at Jesus, they are curious, puzzled, and perplexed. When Jesus is amazed (*thaumazō*), he is astonished. This does not suggest that he is caught off guard, but that he stands in wonderment of how they do not get it. Jesus is amazed that they are amazed.

As I look at this passage, several applications certainly ring true. First, we need to understand that people will reject Jesus. It happened in the first century, it will happen in the twenty-first century. It should not surprise us. Second, people often reject Jesus based on incomplete knowledge of him. Their rejection is based on what they think they know about Christ, their impression of the church, or their impression of Christianity. Their rejection, in part, is due to an incomplete or inadequate view of Jesus. Still, Jesus is amazed at their lack of faith. Again, this is a word of wonder, not surprise. Jesus is not startled, but has jaw-dropping marvel. How could they not believe? Jesus says, "I cannot believe that they cannot believe."

Dr. Dinesh D'Souza recently came to Eagle Christian Church and lectured on "The New Atheists." During one of his lectures he told a story about a debate he had with one of America's leading atheists. During that debate, he asked his sparring partner, "If I'm right, and you are

---

1. Ben Wittherington, *The Gospel of Mark*, 195.

wrong, and you find yourself standing in front of God, what will you say to him about why you didn't believe?" The response was simply, "Why didn't you give me more evidence?" Here we find what might be Jesus' response to that question. It might sound something like this: "You fool. I can't believe that you can't believe!" We should ask, at what does Jesus marvel most? Jesus marvels most at the non-faith of, and the rejection by those closest to him!

I hope I never hear those words: "I can't believe you can't believe."

Study Questions

1. Where did you grow up? Do you enjoy going back to visit?
2. What childhood escapade of yours do you hear about most often when you visit family?
3. Do you find that you are treated differently at home than away from home? How so? Why?
4. Why do we say of Christ, "Jesus of Nazareth"? Where was Jesus born? When did he live in Nazareth? Where else did Jesus live?
5. Many who heard Jesus were "amazed" (6:2). What amazed them as they listened to Jesus in the synagogue (See also 1:21–22)?
6. What are the proper answers to the questions the people pose in verse 2?
7. Verse 3 gives us several more questions asked by the people of Nazareth. What were they suggesting by asking each of these questions?
    a. Isn't this the carpenter?
    b. Isn't this Mary's son?
    c. [Isn't he] the brother of James, Joseph, Judas and Simon? Aren't his sisters here with us?
8. When it comes to the people in Nazareth, they thought they knew Jesus, but their preconceived notions about him made it difficult for them to accept his message.
    a. Have you known people who had preconceived ideas about Jesus which blinded their ability to see him clearly?
    b. What misconceptions/preconceived ideas about Jesus commonly keep people from seeing Jesus clearly today?

9. Read verse 5 carefully. Does this verse tell us that Jesus was unable to do *any* miracles in Nazareth? Why does it say that Jesus "could not do . . . miracles"?

10. What is meant by the statement: "People's faith determines the receptivity to the power of Jesus—it does not diminish the power of Jesus."

    a. Do you agree or disagree?

    b. How does the analogy of a TV antenna (rabbit ears) relate to this statement?

11. Jesus experienced rejection from his hometown, from among his relatives, and even in his own house. Can you relate? If so, how?

12. Read 6:6a again carefully. What amazed Jesus about the people of Nazareth? Why? What does this suggest about those who don't believe in Jesus today?

13. Has familiarity with Jesus blocked you from really seeing who he is? What can you do to get a fresh look?

14. How do your friends and family react to your faith in Christ?

For Further Study

15. See Matthew 13:53–58.

13

Fascinated, but Afraid

Mark 6:6b–31

ON SEVERAL PREVIOUS OCCASIONS we have observed a method employed by Mark called "sandwiching"—a technique by which he weaves two seemingly unrelated stories together to make a single point. This particular sandwich provides more than an interlude between the sending out and return of the disciples—it interprets the halves. What happens to John the Baptist will happen to Jesus in his mission and to the disciples in theirs.

Story One: Jesus Sends the Twelve (Mark 6:6b–11)

> Then Jesus went around teaching from village to village. Calling the Twelve to him, he sent them out two by two and gave them authority over evil spirits. These were his instructions: "Take nothing for the journey except a staff—no bread, no bag, no money in your belts. Wear sandals but not an extra tunic. Whenever you enter a house, stay there until you leave that town. And if any place will not welcome you or listen to you, shake the dust off your feet when you leave as a testimony against them." They went out and preached that people should repent. They drove out many demons and anointed many sick people with oil and healed them. (Mark 6:6b–31)

As I read this passage, once again I have several questions. At times it seems like I have more questions than answers. First, we might ask, why does Jesus send the Twelve out in pairs—two by two? There might be several possible answers to this question (none of which have anything to do with Noah and the ark). Here are some possible explanations:

1. For protection, encouragement, and companionship.

2. To hold each other accountable.

3. To multiply his effectiveness seven fold and cover seven different directions (Jesus being the seventh).

4. Pairs would not overwhelm their hosts (whereas a group of four to six might).

5. To satisfy Jewish witness requirements (Numbers 35:30; Deuteronomy 17:6; 19:15; 1 Corinthians 13:1; 1 Timothy 5:19) and strengthen and confirm the disciples' testimony.

It is possible that Matthew's account of the sending of the Twelve actually gives us the particular pairings of the disciples as they are sent. "These are the names of the twelve apostles: Simon (who is called Peter) and his brother Andrew; James son of Zebedee, and his brother John; Philip and Bartholomew; Thomas and Matthew the tax collector; James son of Alphaeus, and Thaddaeus; Simon the Zealot and Judas Iscariot, who betrayed him" (Matthew 10:2-4).

A second question we might ask is, why these specific instructions? I am especially intrigued with what seems to be the overriding principle: "Take nothing for the journey" (6:8). It seems like more detailed instructions might be given to them. Where should they go? What should they do as they go? What should they preach? These and other details would be helpful to them. Why not detailed operating procedures? Actually, in both Matthew's and Luke's accounts we are given precisely this—instructions on where to preach, to whom to preach, how to preach, and other ministry instructions. Why does Mark leave these details out? Or maybe the more appropriate question is: What is Mark's purpose in recording what he does record? His primary instruction seems to be, "Take nothing on your journey." Again, several answers might be put forward.

1. It expressed urgency (they were not to delay for extensive preparation).

2. They were not to be burdened by needless equipment which might slow them down as well as overwhelm their hosts.

3. They were to expect hospitality from those to whom they preached the gospel.

4. They were to put their trust in God.

5. They were not to create jealousy by moving from one house to another.
6. Their instructions were not meant to express poverty or to make them endure special hardship.

A third question also comes to mind: Why did Jesus send the disciples out so soon? A quick reading through the Gospels seems to suggest that they didn't have a handle on what was going on yet. It seems fairly obvious that the disciples weren't entirely prepared. So why did Jesus send them?

As a professor at a Bible college, it is interesting to watch the freshman class return home after their first year of school. Inevitably, many of them return back to their home churches thinking they are going to solve all church problems. They are going to do church as it ought to be done and save the world from its monstrosities. While it is great to see their passion and enthusiasm, the first summer is often an eye-opening experience that teaches them how little they really know. There is a reason we call them "sophomores"—the word literally means "wise fools." Even as graduating seniors, it is all too easy to have an "ivory tower" mentality that lacks real-world experience. Knowledge and experience must go hand in hand.

This is certainly part of the answer to our question. Jesus is providing the disciples with an opportunity to have real ministry experience, while doing so with a safety net in place—Jesus is still in the area. All too soon that safety net will be gone. This is a reality which Mark turns his attention to shortly.

I need to ask one final question before moving on: Why are the disciples told to shake the dust off their feet when they are not welcome? We might even need to ask a follow-up question: Is this descriptive or prescriptive?

Pious Jews shook the dust off their feet after passing through Gentile cities to show their separation from Gentile influences and practices. In a similar way, when the disciples shook the dust off their feet, it was a vivid sign to the Jews that the people had rejected Jesus and his message. Jesus made it clear that the people were responsible for how they responded to the gospel. The disciples were not to blame if the message was rejected—as long as they had faithfully and carefully presented it. We, too, are not to take it personally when others reject Christ. However, we do have the responsibility to share faithfully with others.

Is this statement meant to be prescriptive for us, or simply descriptive of the disciples and the first century? Let me ask this another way: Are we also to quickly move on every time we experience difficulty in sharing the gospel, or flee when the message of Christ goes unheeded? Understand, the disciples had only a very limited window of opportunity to spread the gospel while Jesus was with them. Time was of the essence. Today, the fact that the gospel has gone forth to much of the earth allows us at least some opportunity to dig in and work the trenches. Wisdom must still dictate when it is time to move on, but we should not always let opposition and rejection force us from needed ministry.

At this point, Mark's narrative changes abruptly as we are confronted with a second story.

Story Two: Herod and John the Baptist (Mark 6:12–29)

I want to divide this story into three parts. The first segment gives us Herod's response to the sending out of the disciples.

> King Herod heard about this, for Jesus' name had become well known. Some were saying, "John the Baptist has been raised from the dead, and that is why miraculous powers are at work in him." Others said, "He is Elijah." And still others claimed, "He is a prophet, like one of the prophets of long ago." But when Herod heard this, he said, "John, the man I beheaded, has been raised from the dead!" (Mark 6:14–16)

Again, I want to ask and answer a question: Why does King Herod concern himself with this? Before I attempt to answer that question, I must address the issue of the word "king" (*basileus*). Both Matthew and Luke more accurately describe Herod as "tetrarch" (*tetraarchēs*) of the region (Matthew 14:1; Luke 9:7). In the first century, Palestine was divided into four territories, each with a different ruler called a tetrarch. This included not only Herod Antipas (called Herod in all four Gospels), but also Herod's brother, Philip. As a ruler, Herod is not satisfied with merely a fourth of the region. He wants power, prestige, position, and control. That being the case, Herod actually takes the name "king" for himself, and even makes an official request of Rome, only to have it denied him. Herod's sister-in-law, Herodias,[1] leaves her husband Philip

---

1. Herodias was the daughter of Aristobulus and niece of Antipas.

Fascinated, but Afraid 117

and marries Herod precisely because she believes he is on the better career path and wants to ride the coattails of his success. This unique marriage creates a number of problems, as we will see later. Ultimately, it is precisely Herod's desire to be king and his very use of this title which result in his demise. Mark is aware of this unfolding drama, and with a hint of sarcasm, points this out to us. More importantly, Mark also uses the word "king" because he wants to provide a deliberate contrast in his Gospel between this so-called king and Jesus himself.

So, back to our original question: Why does King Herod concern himself with Jesus and the disciples? The answer, in part, lies in the fact that Jesus has moved from a small blip on the radar screen to the main attraction. His ministry has grown from a one-man show, to a group of several evangelists roaming throughout the region of Galilee. Jesus is a "back-water prophet" or "local yokel" from Nazareth no longer.

Herod's primary concern obviously stems from what is being said about Jesus. Some were claiming Jesus to be "a prophet of long ago," some were calling him "Elijah"[2] (6:15), and others were calling him "John the Baptist raised from the dead" (6:14). It is this statement that gets Herod's full attention. "When Herod heard this, he said, 'John, the man I beheaded, has been raised from the dead'" (6:16).

This leads us to segment two of our story with Herod and John the Baptist. This section is a flashback. If this were a cinematic portrayal, we would fade-to-black or simply press rewind to move history back two or three months in the life of Herod. In the life-frames of Herod's past, we are shown the reason for his troubled conscience.

> For Herod himself had given orders to have John arrested, and he had him bound and put in prison. He did this because of Herodias, his brother Philip's wife, whom he had married. For John had been saying to Herod, 'It is not lawful for you to have your brother's wife.' So Herodias nursed a grudge against John and wanted to kill him. But she was not able to, because Herod feared John and protected him, knowing him to be a righteous and holy man. When Herod heard John, he was greatly puzzled; yet he liked to listen to him. (Mark 6:17–20)

---

2. Elijah is considered one of the greatest figures in the Old Testament. On the basis of Malachi 4:5, some ancient Jews expected Elijah, or someone like him to come to prepare Israel for God's judgment and salvation. His story can be found in part in 1 Kings 17—19; 2 Kings 1:1—2:12.

The facts pour in quickly: Herod had married his brother's wife; John the Baptist had personally confronted Herod with his immorality; Herod's wife had taken offense and wasn't in a forgiving mood. Then we find an interesting detail—Herod had actually put John the Baptist in prison to protect him from Herodias.

Why? The imprisonment of John the Baptist is not typical. Prisons in the first century were only meant to be temporary holding areas until judgment could be doled out. Once found guilty, a prisoner could be beaten, flogged, forced to do hard labor, banished, enslaved, or even killed. John the Baptist seems to be indefinitely imprisoned. Why? Herod was in a predicament. He enjoyed listening to John the Baptist and considered him to be a righteous and holy man (6:20). An ethical man could not kill an innocent man, much less one who might be a prophet. But how do you do what you want to do and yet satisfy the wrath of your wife? (I think I will leave the answer to that question to one much wiser and braver than I.) For Herod, the answer is to put John the Baptist in prison—John would be protected from Herodias and maybe his imprisonment will appease her.

When thinking about Herod and the fact that he took pleasure in listening to John the Baptist preach, I am startled with this revelation—Herod was probably the first and only man in history who regularly listened to sermons preached by a capable preacher, but was not changed by them! Herod could listen to sermons with fascination, and be unmoved to obey.

The third section takes place on Herod's birthday.

> Finally the opportune time came. On his birthday Herod gave a banquet for his high officials and military commanders and the leading men of Galilee. When the daughter of Herodias came in and danced, she pleased Herod and his dinner guests. The king said to the girl, "Ask me for anything you want, and I'll give it to you." And he promised her with an oath. "Whatever you ask I will give you, up to half my kingdom." She went out and said to her mother, "What shall I ask for?" "The head of John the Baptist," she answered. At once the girl hurried in to the king with the request: "I want you to give me right now the head of John the Baptist on a platter." The king was greatly distressed, but because of his oaths and his dinner guests, he did not want to refuse her. So he immediately sent an executioner with orders to bring John's head. The man went, beheaded John in the prison,

and brought back his head on a platter. He presented it to the girl, and she gave it to her mother. On hearing of this, John's disciples came and took his body and laid it in a tomb. (Mark 6:21–29)

Notice that Herod was distressed at the request. He knew the right thing to do, but he did not want to refuse the request in front of his dinner guests. Ultimately, he was more concerned with saving face than saving his soul. He realized that doing the right thing would have cost him dearly—he might have to give up his wife, his dancing parties, and his power. Then as quickly as the story started, it ends. We are brought full circle back to our original drama.

Jesus Gathers the Twelve (Mark 6:30–31)

The apostles gathered around Jesus and reported to him all they had done and taught. Then, because so many people were coming and going that they did not even have a chance to eat, he said to them, "Come with me by yourselves to a quiet place and get some rest." (Mark 6:30–31)

We are not given much detail. Why? Detail is not needed. We simply learn that the disciples return—tired and hungry, but successful. We learn what Mark wants us to know—the disciples went and kept busy doing Christ's will.

Then we are confronted with the biggest question of all: How in the world do these two stories go together? Why did Mark sandwich these together?

These stories were put together to make this point: What happens to John as he goes out to preach (1:4) foreshadows what will happen to Jesus when he goes out to preach (1:14). Just as John is "handed over" (1:14—put in prison), so Jesus will be handed over (3:19; 9:31; 10:33—betrayed). Just as John is executed by a reluctant political ruler—a puppet of a plot (6:14–29), so Jesus will be sentenced to death by a reluctant political ruler and a plot (14:1–2; 15:1–2, 11). Just as Herodias seizes an opportune time (6:21), Judas will seek an opportunity to betray Jesus (14:11). Just as Herod is caught off guard (6:23–26) so Pilate will be surprised (15:6–15). The violent and shameful death of John serves as prelude to the violent and shameful death of Jesus. Just as John's disciples bury John, Joseph of Arimathea will bury Jesus.

Mark has turned the corner in his Gospel, which now directs Jesus toward the cross. Just as the disciples are rejected, and John the Baptist is rejected, so too will Jesus Christ be rejected. But the true disciple is faithful, no matter what.

It is interesting that Herod sought power, prestige, kingship, popularity, and appeasement. In contrast the disciples chose servanthood, hard work, fatigue, and even martyrdom.

My friend, that is the choice of everyone. The passage is not about how to do missions, but about the character of the disciples' mission.

In the end, a fearless prophet is undone by a cowardly king who saves his face, but loses his soul. Søren Kierkegaard puts it this way, "The tyrant dies and his rule ends, the martyr dies and his rule begins."[3]

Study Questions

1. Who in your family over-packs for a trip?
2. If you were granted one wish for your next birthday, what would it be?
3. What three tasks did Jesus send his disciples to do (6:12–13)?
4. Why did Jesus send out the disciples in pairs (2x2)?
5. Why did Jesus say to take nothing (6:8)?
6. Why were the disciples told to shake the dust off their feet (6:11)?
7. What were people saying about Jesus (6:15–16)?
8. What description of Jesus bothered Herod the most? Why (6:16)?
9. If you were giving a movie rating to the story of Herod and John the Baptist, what would that rating be?
10. Why did Herod's wife want John killed (6:17–19)?
11. Why did King Herod have John the Baptist arrested?
12. Of the people involved in John the Baptist's death, who do you hold the most responsible? Why?
13. Why is the story of John the Baptist sandwiched between Jesus' sending and gathering of the disciples?

---

3. Søren Kierkegaard, ed. Alexander Dru, *The Soul of Kierkegaard*, 151.

14. How is the story of John the Baptist a foreshadowing of what is going to happen to Jesus?
15. Herod had a choice to do the right thing or cave in to peer pressure. How are we given similar choices today? Give some examples.
16. Should ministers/missionaries today do as the disciples did and "shake the dust from their sandals" when they encounter opposition? Why or why not?
17. Should this passage be used as a precedent that ministries should be without regular support? (New Testament churches were actually encouraged to support those ministering to them. See Phil 4:14; 1 Tim 5:17–18; 3 John 5–8.)

For Further Study

18. See Matthew 10:1–16; 14:1–12; Luke 9:1–9.

14

Loaves & Fishes

Mark 6:30–44

THIS PASSAGE IS ONE of the most well-known miracles of Jesus—the feeding of the five thousand. It is interesting how many liberal scholars try to explain it away by dismissing the supernatural. Some of the ill-fated attempts include the following:

1. Jesus has a secret stash hidden in a cave.
2. Jesus has arranged for a number of women to go ahead of him and prepare a meal.
3. Everybody present has food, but is unwilling to share, until the small boy gives his lunch as an example, thereby shaming everyone else into sharing their food.
4. The oral tradition has been exaggerated from what was originally a small crowd, and minimal food, to a miraculous feeding of five thousand.
5. The dinner is simply a sacramental meal where each person receives only a fragment or token.
6. Or, in the words of William Barclay: "This is a miracle of the birth of love in men's souls; it is a miracle of the awakening of fellowship . . . it is the eternal miracle of Christianity, whereby a miscellaneous crowd of men and women becomes a family in Christ."

Can I tell you what I think of Barclay's statement? Fish-sticks! (Am I allowed to write that in a Christian commentary?)

Of all the wonderful miracles recorded in the Bible (a man with a shriveled hand, a paralyzed man and his friends, turning water into wine), this is the only miracle recorded by all four Gospel writers. Those who deny this historical event go against four witnesses. That's dangerous footing.

I need to tell you, from the outset, I believe in miracles. I believe that Jesus healed the blind man, I believe he cast out demons, I believe he walked on the water, I believe he fed five thousand with five loaves and two fish, and I certainly believe the greatest miracle of all: Jesus Christ rose from the dead.

As a Christian, I believe that miracles are at the heart of the gospel and I believe that Jesus still works miracles. I believe in the miracles of answered prayer, of healing, and the transformation of the lives of those people who truly trust him. I also believe there is a great miracle still to come—a day when Jesus will come and take his people home and present to them a new heaven and a new earth. I believe in the miracle of eternal life.

Actually, as far as miracles are concerned, the miracle of the feeding of five thousand seems to be a rather simple one. If God can speak the entire world into existence, if God can hold the galaxy in place by the word of his mouth, if God can listen to and answer the prayers of mankind simultaneously—multiplying a few fish and loaves seems (from God's perspective) a little lightweight.

Let me put it another way: If God can't do this—what can he do? This would make him a little impotent. But I believe God is omnipotent!

Read the account closely.

> The apostles gathered around Jesus and reported to him all they had done and taught. Then, because so many people were coming and going that they did not even have a chance to eat, he said to them, "Come with me by yourselves to a quiet place and get some rest." So they went away by themselves in a boat to a solitary place. But many who saw them leaving recognized them and ran on foot from all the towns and got there ahead of them. When Jesus landed and saw a large crowd, he had compassion on them, because they were like sheep without a shepherd. So he began teaching them many things. By this time it was late in the day, so his disciples came to him. "This is a remote place," they said, "and it's already very late. Send the people away so they can go to the surrounding countryside and villages and buy themselves

something to eat." But he answered, "You give them something to eat." They said to him, "That would take eight months of a man's wages! Are we to go and spend that much on bread and give it to them to eat?" "How many loaves do you have?" he asked. "Go and see." When they found out, they said, "Five—and two fish." Then Jesus directed them to have all the people sit down in groups on the green grass. So they sat down in groups of hundreds and fifties. Taking the five loaves and the two fish and looking up to heaven, he gave thanks and broke the loaves. Then he gave them to his disciples to set before the people. He also divided the two fish among them all. They all ate and were satisfied, and the disciples picked up twelve basketfuls of broken pieces of bread and fish. The number of the men who had eaten was five thousand. (Mark 6:30–44)

The Situation—Departures and Arrivals (Mark 6:30–36)

After the Twelve return from the preaching mission, Jesus invites them to go away to a place where they can get some rest. Notice the language Jesus uses with the disciples. Come "by yourselves (6:31); to a quiet place (6:31); get some rest (6:31); to a solitary place (6:32)."

Sounds good, doesn't it? Jesus' practice throughout the Gospels is that after a busy time of ministry he seeks out solitude. I like the thought—after a busy day of ministry, what you need to do is get in the boat and sail away. This would be a great passage to use as a proof text that every minister needs a boat—or at least one of his elders should have one! Seriously, there is a lesson to be learned about getting away to debrief and seeking solitude. But, if that is what the disciples expect, they are sorely disappointed.

A careful reading reveals that the boat in which they travel is close enough to the shore for the people to observe (6:33). Apparently, the boat does not travel very quickly, nor does it travel very far (from Capernaum to Bethsaida)—for the crowd is waiting when the boat lands.

The crowd is not there by accident. The swelling throng that races ahead to meet them has gathered in response to the disciples' preaching mission. Their mission has been phenomenally successful, which Mark underscores twice when he says that the people see them and recognize them (6:33).

The Disciples' Reaction

These verses give us the disciples' reaction to the situation. "This is a remote place," they said, "and it's already very late. Send the people away so they can go to the surrounding countryside and villages and buy themselves something to eat" (6:35–36).

We can take this one of two ways. First, the disciples could have been genuinely concerned with the affairs of these people. It was a remote place, the people had not eaten, they had gotten plenty of exercise, it was getting late—"Jesus, they *need* something to eat." Their statement could be a sympathetic and pragmatic response based on the legitimate needs of the people. It is possible that the disciples could be genuinely concerned.

But their statement could also have a ring of selfishness to it. Honestly, after a long and tiring preaching tour with multitudes of people—so demanding that it has not even afforded an opportunity to eat (6:31), I know what my reaction would have been. "Jesus, send them away . . . it's very late . . . tell them to go and get something to eat—we need to get something to eat!" You could easily read into their statement, "Jesus, I thought you said we were going to get away. Those pesky people are never satisfied. It's time for some 'me' time. After all, that is what you promised!"

Or, possibly, it could also contain an element of both. If there is a hint of selfishness in the disciples' response, we know that Jesus does not share their sentiment.

Jesus' Reaction

"He had compassion on them, because they were like sheep without a shepherd" (6:34). Jesus doesn't show irritation, but compassion. Jesus does not view them as an inconvenience, but opportunity. The word used here for "compassion" (*splanchnizomai*) is used in our New Testaments only of Jesus (though its cognate *splanchnon* is used of others). It is used to express the divine mercy of Jesus. It is more than mere pity, or simply compassion for physical needs; when it is used it emphasizes lostness (Matthew 9:36; 14:14; 15:32; 18:27; 20:34; Mark 1:41; 6:34; 8:2; 9:22; Luke 7:13; 10:33; 15:20).

The words "sheep" and "shepherd" would generate all kinds of imagery from the Old Testament in the mind of the first-century hearer. Mark is painting the picture of a shepherd for us. Notice the language of green grass and countryside.

The Interaction—A Strange Request
(Mark 6:37-38)

This is the most curious, most intriguing, and most detailed part of the story. It receives more attention than the miracle itself. When the disciples suggest to Jesus that he send the people away so they can eat, Jesus says to them, "You give them something to eat" (6:37). You feed them. My question is, why? Why does Jesus give them this command? There are several possible reasons.

First, does he want them to go and buy provisions? Not likely. The Apostles point out, "That would take eight months of a man's wages"—literally, it would take two hundred denarii. Besides, Jesus has previously told them to "take nothing—no bread, no bag, no money in your belts" (6:9).

Second, maybe he expects them to do a miracle. They have been preaching, casting out demons, and healing many sick people (6:13). Maybe, through the power of God, they would be able to do this miracle as well.

In all likelihood, he wants to push them forward in their ability to minister. Do none of the Twelve even think, "We are with Jesus, maybe with his help, *we* can do it?" or "We are with Jesus, he is able to raise the dead, certainly *he* can do it?" Instead, all of the Apostles think about what they cannot do, rather than what they can do with God's help.

That's a common issue among Christians and churches. We think about what we cannot do, rather than imagining what we might be able to do with God's help. Jesus says, "What is impossible with men is possible with God" (Luke 8:27).

The Culminating Miracle—Jesus Acts
(Mark 6:39-44)

Jesus directs the disciples to have all the people sit down in groups of hundreds and fifties. Statements like this always lead me to ask, why? There might be several possible reasons. Purely from a pragmatic standpoint this makes several aspects of the story more doable. The disciples can easily serve people systematically if they are sitting like this in groups. It would certainly prevent the long lines, pushing and shoving, and jumping the queue that might result if five thousand people were all to line up for a buffet. It would facilitate fast service, ensure that everyone got fed, and would certainly make counting easier. It is interesting that all four Gospels record for us the same number of people served.

After having the people sit down in the grass, Jesus takes the five loaves and two fish and says a quick prayer. These loaves are probably small barley loaves and the two fish are probably little bony, dried fish that would have survived intact in a boy's lunch sack. As Jesus prays, he takes the fish and the loaves and looks up to heaven (which is not the normal position for Jewish prayers—they were usually said with heads lowered) and probably recites the common Jewish dinner prayer, "Blessed art Thou, O Lord our God, king of the world, who bringest forth bread from the earth."

And then we get the miracle. "He broke (*kataklaō*, to break in pieces) the loaves . . . and divided (*merizō*, to divide) the two fish among them all" (6:41–42). Can you say this more succinctly? More attention is given to how to serve the food than the miracle itself. And just in case some might want to suggest a sacramental meal where each only receives a fragment or token piece—a fish scale and a crumb—Mark tells us, "They all ate and were satisfied (*chortazō*, to eat one's fill)" (6:42).

That's the story. As I read the story, I find several interesting insights. The first is actually a troubling observation. This is the first miracle that Jesus performs where there is no comment in Mark's gospel about awe, surprise, or astonishment. We get no reaction from the crowd. Does the audience even know initially where the food is coming from? They are getting bread and being fed; how many know where it's coming from? The disciples are certainly privy to the information. The small child is certainly aware. But do all the people know from the onset what is happening? The purpose of the miracle does not initially seem to be to impress the multitudes (although John tells us they find out and want to make him king). I know the crowds receive the benefit of the miracle, but who is this miracle for? The answer seems to be: It was for the ones closest to Jesus—it was for the disciples. Jesus is trying to teach them, and stretch them—it is primarily for their benefit.

After the feeding of the five thousand, Mark tells us that immediately Jesus makes the disciples get in the boat. He remains behind to dismiss the crowds, and then spends some time in solitary prayer. During this time, there is a windstorm on the lake, and Jesus comes walking on the water—he almost passes them by—and they are terrified. Then we read this line: "They were completely amazed, for they had not understood about the loaves; their hearts were hardened" (6:51–52).

The disciples fail to perceive something crucial in the feeding of the five thousand. Jesus is the Messiah. He is the Good Shepherd. He is the Bread of Life. He is Lord of Lords and King of Kings. Jesus is the Son of God—the miracle worker. They should have picked up on this, but they still miss it.

As Mark tells this story, there are certain elements that the first-century hearer should have understood, that we might have missed. There are several items of prophetic significance.

First, Mark repeatedly uses the phrase "deserted" place (6:31, 32, 35). He has used this phrase often in the Gospel and we have mentioned the parallels to the children of Israel, manna, and Moses in the wilderness. Mark is alluding to Exodus chapter 16. We also see the groupings of fifties and hundreds, which again allude to Moses' own organization of Israel. The phrase, "sheep without a shepherd" is an allusion to Moses praying for God to supply a leader after him (Numbers 27:17). It also brings to mind God's promise to feed his sheep by sending one like David as a shepherd (Ezekiel 34:23).

There is also a deliberate contrast between Herod's banquet and the meager lunch of a peasant's diet. Herod has placed himself on a pedestal as king, seeking popularity and power. Jesus has compassion on the people and presents himself as a shepherd.

One more observation. Why twelve baskets? The disciples pick up the baskets, each one taking his own, and they place them in the boat to set sail. They are visible reminders of what has just happened; and a visible picture of who Jesus is. He is the Bread of Life. Here is the answer to the question: "What kind of king is Jesus?" He is not the kind of king they expect. He's not a military ruler, or a political king, but he is the compassionate shepherd-king. And as a shepherd-king, he responds to the needs of the people around him: he leads, he organizes, he teaches, he cares for, he protects, and he feeds his flock.

That's who Jesus is. The disciples still have not figured it out. But what about you?

Study Questions

1. Where do you go (or what do you do) to find rest?
2. What is the longest you have ever gone without eating (31)?
3. Why does Jesus want to get away with his disciples (30–31)? Can you relate? How?
4. Read verse 31. If you were one of Jesus' disciples, after listening to Jesus, what would you expect was going to happen?
5. Surprise! There are 5,000 men (plus women and children), waiting on the shore.
    a. How do you feel?
    b. With this understanding, how might you interpret the disciples' words in 35–36?
6. How does Jesus respond to the crowds of people (34)?
7. According to verse 34, what is the first thing Jesus' compassion led him to do?
    a. When we think of compassion, is that our typical response?
    b. How was this being compassionate?
8. "You give them something to eat" (37). What was Jesus asking the disciples to do? Was he asking them to buy meals for everyone (37)? If not, what did he expect?
9. What possible reasons might Jesus have for directing the disciples to have the people sit in groups?
10. After organizing the people (41), and before doing the miracle, what does Jesus do?
    a. How often do you pray before meals?
    b. Is it important? Why or why not?
11. According to verse 42, how much food was available?
12. What is the significance of twelve baskets of leftovers? What do you imagine the disciples were thinking as they picked up the extra loaves and fish?

13. Describe a time when God has more than taken care of your needs.

14. In what areas of your life do you have the hardest time trusting Jesus to care for your needs?

15. Read 6:51–52. What lesson had the disciples failed to learn about Jesus?

16. Is it important for believers to cease from work from time to time and seek spiritual solitude and rest? Does this apply to Christian leaders? When would such practices be appropriate?

17. In what area of life do you need to experience Jesus' compassion?

18. In what area of life do you need to demonstrate Jesus' compassion?

19. How does this chapter show that Christ is greater than a mere man?

For Further Study

20. See Matthew 14:13–21; Luke 9:10–17; and John 6:5–13.

15

The Near Transcendent

Mark 6:45–56

Immediately Jesus made his disciples get into the boat and go on ahead of him to Bethsaida, while he dismissed the crowd. After leaving them, he went up on a mountainside to pray. When evening came, the boat was in the middle of the lake, and he was alone on land. He saw the disciples straining at the oars, because the wind was against them. About the fourth watch of the night he went out to them, walking on the lake. He was about to pass by them, but when they saw him walking on the lake, they thought he was a ghost. They cried out, because they all saw him and were terrified. Immediately he spoke to them and said, "Take courage! It is I. Don't be afraid." Then he climbed into the boat with them, and the wind died down. They were completely amazed, for they had not understood about the loaves; their hearts were hardened. When they had crossed over, they landed at Gennesaret and anchored there. As soon as they got out of the boat, people recognized Jesus. They ran throughout that whole region and carried the sick on mats to wherever they heard he was. And wherever he went—into villages, towns or countryside—they placed the sick in the marketplaces. They begged him to let them touch even the edge of his cloak, and all who touched him were healed. (Mark 6:45–56)

OFTEN WE WILL READ a good novel, or watch a movie where the identity of the main character is known to us (the audience), but the supporting cast members don't know who the main character really is. Take, for example, Superman (Clark Kent), or Spiderman (Peter Parker), or even those who-done-it mysteries where we watch a detective unfold the clues to a storyline we already saw happen in the opening scene.

In a sense, that's what is happening in the Gospel of Mark. We know who Jesus is—Mark told us back in chapter 1, but we are watching as the disciples learn bit-by-bit who Jesus really is. The sad fact is, they still don't have Jesus figured out.

In fact, we learn that they have missed something along the way. Our passage reads, "They had not understood about the loaves; their hearts were hardened" (6:52). What did they fail to grasp about Jesus? What were their hearts hardened about? With this passage, I want to ask a similar question: What lesson are the disciples supposed to learn from this event? I might ask this last question another way: Does Jesus walk on water simply as an amazing gimmick, or is something greater in play here?

Once again, many so-called scholars try to downplay this miracle. One can find all kinds of ill-fated attempts to explain away this miracle: the lake is frozen; Jesus is stepping on stones; he is not walking on water, but on the nearby shore. There is one major problem with all these explanations, however. They fail to answer this question: How did Jesus pull all this off without his disciples (including experienced fishermen) recognizing his ploy?

The Sending Away (Mark 6:45–46)

As we begin our story, we see Jesus dismissing both his disciples and the crowds (6:45). We might ask the question, why? The answer comes in the next verse: "After leaving them, he went up on a mountainside to pray" (6:46).

Three times in the book of Mark we see Jesus going off alone to a mountain in the dark to pray. All three of these retreats occur at significant times in his ministry. One might even say they come at "make or break" times in Jesus' ministry (this is not to suggest these are the only times Jesus prays, but these are the only instances Mark chooses to record Jesus praying for us).

Prayer Retreat #1.

Journey back with me in the book of Mark to the first chapter. After Jesus heals the demon-possessed man and Peter's mother-in-law, "The whole town gathered at the door wanting to be healed" (1:33). This healing service goes on late into the evening. After it is over, while it is still dark, Jesus goes off by himself to pray (1:35). The next morning, the disciples come in a panic and say to him, "Everyone is looking for you" (1:37). They want him to start where he has left off—healing people. But Jesus has spent the night refocusing. Rather than staying and appeasing both his disciples and the crowd—he decides to press on with his ministry—he will go elsewhere to preach.

Prayer Retreat #2.

Now, in our passage, we find a second withdrawal. Jesus has just fed thousands. No doubt the disciples are excited. They have seen Jesus work yet another miracle. They've drawn conclusions about Jesus—he attracts crowds of people. They've even got an idea for Jesus—he could be king! In fact, in John's account, that's exactly what the people want to do with Jesus—take him by force and make him king (John 6:15). Refusing these demands, Jesus sends his disciples away and dismisses the crowd and retreats to the mountains to refocus (4:45–46).

Prayer Retreat #3.

The third retreat of Jesus to pray in the book of Mark comes in chapter 14 as Jesus retreats up the hillside to the Garden of Gethsemane. His prayer is "Abba, Father . . . everything is possible for you. Take this cup from me. Yet not what I will, but what you will" (14:36). Faced with the reality of the cross, Jesus is at a crossroads.

In every case, Jesus prays to gain strength over very real temptations and is seeking to get proper direction about how to handle the situation. There are no people around him to observe how to pray, nor audience to observe his techniques. Jesus is praying, because he needs to be praying.

The Straining of Oars (Mark 6:47–48a)

While Jesus has been praying, the disciples have been struggling. Jesus has witnessed their difficulty (6:48). The phrase, "straining at the oars" (*basanizō*) is an interesting one. It literally means being tortured or tormented in the rowing. When the storm comes up, the disciples take down their sails and begin rowing. They have been working feverishly for hours. We would do well to remember that they start out the journey tired and exhausted after their preaching tour. They are given the promise of rest (6:31). Now it is late into the evening. Notice the timeline we are given. Verse 47 says "when evening came." Verse 48 says "about the fourth watch of the night." That's sometime between 3 a.m. and 6 a.m. Even if one might suggest that evening lasts well beyond sunset (even as late as midnight), and they were also to suggest the earliest possible rendering of "the fourth watch" (3 a.m.), the disciples have been struggling for several hours.

The disciples are undergoing a very real ordeal. They have been fighting diligently against the wind and the waves. The storm may not be endangering their lives as we saw earlier (4:35), but the storm is a formidable foe. This, however, has not yet thrown the experienced fishermen into a panic. Tormented? Yes. Terrified? Not yet. However, the sight of Jesus passing by on the water accomplishes what the storm does not. The disciples think they see a phantom—a ghost (6:49). What would you think was happening if you experienced this at 3 a.m., in the middle of the storm, in the middle of the lake?

The Miraculous Crossing (Mark 6:48b–53)

As Jesus walks on the water, I believe we find four clues that help us identify the true identity of Jesus. While the disciples have been tormented by the storm, the wind poses no obstacle to Jesus and the waves provide firm footing as he marches across the sea. This is something only God can do (Psalm 77:19; Isaiah 43:16; 51:10). Here we get our first clue as to the real purpose of this passage.

Clue #1. Jesus walks as only God can—on water.

The Book of Job says of God,

> "He alone stretches out the heavens and treads on the waves of the sea . . . he performs wonders that cannot be fathomed, miracles that cannot be counted. When he passes me, I cannot see him; when he goes by, I cannot perceive him." (Job 9:8, 10–11)

When Jesus comes strolling across the water, he shares in the unlimited power of the Creator. He comes in God-like fashion.

On a side note: It often seems that paintings of Jesus walking on the water occur with a glassy sea, and a windless night. Is it more difficult to walk on turbulent water, or glassy water? Tuck that away in your mind for a moment. I am confident that only God can walk on water.

The Near Transcendent   137

Our narrative builds as we come to the second half of verse 48. The NIV reads at this point, "He [Jesus] was about to pass by them" (6:48). Literally, this verse can be translated, "Jesus wanted to pass by them"—a phrase that is recorded for us only in Mark. It is a phrase that has caused considerable confusion. Some have suggested:

1. Jesus is playfully racing them (he *wants* to pass them by). This would suggest that Jesus wants to leave them floundering and frightened in a race across the lake. He is gleeful that they are burdened by the wind, while he is free to walk.

2. Others suggest that while Jesus wants to pass them by—he doesn't do so because he sees them struggling. His compassion wins out over his competitive nature. He wants to race, but his compassion gets the best of him. The problem is, this doesn't fit what Mark says. Verse 48 tells us that Jesus sees them struggling before he goes out to them.

3. Others have speculated that this is written from the vantage point of the disciples. The disciples mistakenly think that Jesus intends to pass them by, but have misunderstood his purpose. Again, this explanation doesn't fit with the context.

4. Still others try to modify the language and explain that Jesus simply wants to go "beside them" to encourage them in their struggle—not really "pass them by." They suggest that Jesus wants simply to parallel the course of the disciples and let them know he is aware of their circumstance.

The problem with each of these views is that they fail to take into account what the text literally says. These interpretations also likely miss what the original hearers actually heard. The terminology used would have been recognized by Mark's readers as expressing a theophany (a God appearing), because the very same Greek wording used in Mark 6 is used in the Septuagint (LXX, the Greek translation of the Old Testament) to do just that.

Our phrase from Mark 6:48 is used in only two other locations, both in the Greek translation of the Old Testament. The first is Exodus 33 when Moses sees the glory of God.

> Then Moses said, "Now show me your glory." And the Lord said, "I will cause all my goodness to pass in front of you, and I will proclaim my name, the Lord, in your presence. I will have mercy on whom I will have mercy, and I will have compassion on whom I will have compassion. But," he said, "you cannot see my face, for no one may see me and live." Then the Lord said, "There is a place near me where you may stand on a rock. When my glory passes by, I will put you in a cleft in the rock and cover you with my hand until I have passed by. Then I will remove my hand and you will see my back; but my face must not be seen . . . Then the Lord came down in the cloud and stood there with him and proclaimed his name, the Lord. And he passed in front of Moses, proclaiming, "The Lord, the Lord, the compassionate and glorious God, slow to anger, abounding in love and faithfulness, maintaining love to thousands, and forgiving wickedness, rebellion and sin . . ." (Ex 33:19–34:7)

It is also used as God tells Elijah to stand on the mountain, "For the Lord is about to pass by" (1 Kings 19:11–12).

> The Lord said, "Go out and stand on the mountain in the presence of the Lord, for the Lord is about to pass by." Then a great and powerful wind tore the mountains apart and shattered the rocks before the Lord, but the Lord was not in the wind. After the wind there was an earthquake, but the Lord was not in the earthquake. After the earthquake came a fire, but the Lord was not in the fire. And after the fire came a gentle whisper. When Elijah heard it, he pulled his cloak over his face and went out and stood at the mouth of the cave." (1 Kings 19:11–13)

One can conclude from these passages that when Jesus wants to pass by his disciples, he wants them to see his transcendent majesty as a divine being and to give them reassurance. The disciples up until this point have put Jesus in a category of "almost God." This event is intended to shock them wide awake into the reality of Jesus' true identity. Stepping out on the water and walking into the wind, Jesus points them to who he really is. Here we find our second clue.

Clue #2. Jesus moves in God-like fashion—passing by.

Jesus can walk on water, and does so to give the disciples a glimpse of who he really is.

When the disciples see Jesus they are terrified. "Immediately he spoke to them and said, 'Take courage! It is I. Don't be afraid'" (6:50). Here, he actually gives them the third clue to his identity. Did you miss it? Look closely at the verse again. Unfortunately, our modern versions veil Jesus' statement. When Jesus greets the disciples, he doesn't simply give them a hello, but he greets them with the divine formula of self-revelation—he uses the phrase "I am." Literally, "Be of good cheer, I am (*egō eimi*), do not be afraid."

Some rightly propose that Jesus might simply be saying, "Don't be afraid—It is I" in emphatic fashion, but remember where Jesus is standing as he utters this phrase, and hear it with first-century ears. Jesus, as he is standing on the surface of the waters has said, "I AM."

Isaiah 43:1–13 is significant as a backdrop for interpreting this passage. The disciples have been summoned by Jesus to pass through the waters, and Jesus is with them.

> "You are my witnesses," declares the Lord, "and my servant whom I have chosen, so that you may know and believe me and understand that I am he. Before me no god was formed, nor will there be one after me. I, even I, am the Lord, and apart from me there is no Savior." (Isaiah 43:10–11)

Here is the answer to the disciples' question in 4:41: "Who is this? Even the wind and the waves obey him!" Jesus gives the answer: "I am."

Clue #3. Jesus echoes the title of God—the I Am.

Jesus displays his divine power further when he gets into the boat. His mere presence causes the wind to cease howling. In language reminiscent of the calming of the storm in chapter 4—Jesus' mere presence, once again, calms the sea. Here we get our fourth clue to the identity of Jesus.

Clue #4. Jesus controls what only God can—calming the sea.

The disciples were frazzled with fatigue and fear, but became "completely amazed" (6:51). An emphatic statement to say the least—literally exceedingly, extraordinarily beyond measure with themselves. Or another attempt might read, "And they were greatly amazed in themselves beyond measure and marveled." Mark can hardly contain himself.

That's who Jesus is. He is the one who can walk on water. He is the one who can move in God-like fashion and reveal God to us. He is the one who echoes the very title of God. He is the one who can control what only God can. This is Jesus.

Conclusion (Mark 6:54–56)

The disciples have been struggling to understand who Jesus is. In fact, their hearts have been hardened. They think he is a good teacher, a prophet, he certainly can work miracles, he is possibly the Messiah, and they want to make him king. But their understanding is still too limited and they are blinded by their own preconceived ideas to his true identity. The disciples are not alone. It is interesting that people from all over the countryside are coming to see Jesus (6:56). They, too, have plans for Jesus—a Jesus of their own making.

Jesus is stretching their understanding of him. Mark wants us to see clearly who Jesus is. Jesus is standing right with the disciples. The point is clearly being made—this man standing with you is transcendent. Jesus is not just a mere man, not just a good teacher or miracle worker, he is the Son of God. For the disciples the lesson is simply: in your closeness to him, make sure you don't miss his transcendent majesty.

For us, the inverse may sometimes be true. We think of Christ as far removed, distant, and even transcendent—because he is. Maybe we need to remember that the transcendent one came near. He is readily near to help and intercede for us. Jesus is both near and transcendent—the God Man.

Study Questions

1. You have probably heard the expression: "He/She walks on water." What does it mean? Who would you say "walks on water?" Why?

2. In verse 45, Jesus dismisses both his disciples and the crowd.

    a. Why (see verse 46)?

    b. Why does Jesus need to pray?

3. Can you estimate approximately how much time has passed between verse 47 (Jesus alone on land) and when he went out to them in verse 48? (Remember the fourth watch of the night was between 3 a.m. and 6 a.m.)

The Near Transcendent 141

4. The word "straining" at the oars (48), is literally the word "tormented." Have you ever felt like you were "straining at the oars" of life and going nowhere? Explain.

5. Jesus comes walking on the water. Read Psalm 77:19 and Job 9:8. Who walks on water? Is Jesus trying to communicate something to his disciples by walking on water?

6. The phrase "to pass by" (48) is the same phrase used in Exodus 33:19–23 and 1 Kings 19:11. Why is this significant?

7. When the disciples saw Jesus they were terrified (50). Why? What would you have thought if you saw Jesus walking on the water?

8. How does Jesus put their fears at ease (50)? What did you learn about the phrase "It is I"? Who is usually ascribed that title?

9. A second miracle happens as Jesus gets into the boat with the disciples. What is it? How does this story relate to Mark 4:35–41? How does our present passage answer the question asked in 4:41?

10. How well do you understand who Jesus is?

11. What would you say if asked the question: "Who is Jesus?"

12. If the disciples had grasped the true identity of Jesus (52), would they have been shocked to see him walking on the water?

13. How does this passage show that Jesus is greater than a mere man?

For Further Study

14. See Matthew 14:22–32; John 6:15–21. Compare our passage with these accounts. What parts of the account are we missing in Mark?

16

When Rite Is Wrong

Mark 7:1–23

IMAGINE WHAT IT WOULD be like if we were holding church services and a group of ministers barged in, interrupted our service, and began to accuse us of improper worship. Imagine them saying, "Why don't you pray properly? Why do you bow your heads and close your eyes? Don't you know that you must kneel down and raise your eyes and hands toward heaven? God will never hear your prayers unless you pray correctly! When will you ever learn what living the Christian life is all about?" How would you respond?

Or maybe you should turn the tables. What would it be like to walk into another congregation and say to them, "Why do you kneel and raise your eyes and hands toward heaven? God won't hear your prayers if you pray like that." Now, imagine doing that very type of thing to Jesus and his disciples. Essentially, it is this very type of thing that happens in our passage.

> The Pharisees and some of the teachers of the law who had come from Jerusalem gathered around Jesus and saw some of his disciples eating food with hands that were "unclean," that is, unwashed. (The Pharisees and all the Jews do not eat unless they give their hands a ceremonial washing, holding to the tradition of the elders. When they come from the marketplace they do not eat unless they wash. And they observe many other traditions, such as the washing of cups, pitchers and kettles.) So the Pharisees and teachers of the law asked Jesus, "Why don't your disciples live according to the traditions of the elders instead of eating their food with 'unclean' hands?" (Mark 7:1–5)

The Pharisees Accuse the Disciples (Mark 7:1–5)

In our passage, we find another delegation of fact-finding (or fault-finding) theologians coming down from Jerusalem (3:22) to investigate the Galilean activities of Jesus. This nit-picking bunch of Pharisees and teachers of the law are wanting to find reason to accuse Jesus. Worse, ever since Mark 3:6, we know that they are looking for a reason to kill him. Their attitudes are so soured by their disdain for Jesus, that even in his presence they fail to see the Messiah. They are unaware that the very son of God is standing among them. They are blind to the miracles, the teaching, and the wonder of Jesus. They see instead, unwashed hands.

Let me ask you a question: Haven't you known people like that?

Understand, the complaint is not against the disciples' lack of hygiene. The critique focused on the disciples' apparent disregard for tradition. They are being accused of ceremonial defilement. We need to remember that the Pharisees have built a hedge around the law—man-made regulations originally set in place to help make certain people kept the law. They are so intent on keeping the law, they have built laws around the law in order not to break the law.

The tradition finds its origin in a biblical mandate about ceremonial washing in the Old Testament. According to the law, if you are a priest (from the tribe of Levi), you are required to wash your hands in a ceremonial way before entering the Tabernacle and performing religious duties (Exodus 30:19; 40:13).

When performing this ritual, the priest holds out his hands, palms up with his hands slightly cupped. Water is then poured over his hands and with the back of one hand he ceremonially scrubs the other with his fist and then reverses the practice with the other hand.[1] Finally, he turns both hands over and water is poured to remove the dirty water. His hands are now viewed as ceremonially (not hygienically) clean.

For the priest, this is meant to be a symbolic act demonstrating separation literally between the "common" and "uncommon" (clean and unclean) things. But what was originally prescribed for the priests and the Tabernacle, the Pharisees expanded to include all Jewish people and various circumstances (including meals). They had expanded the law: requiring far more than the law required, extending the law to situations beyond the original, and included people to whom the law was

---

1. Literally, the passage speaks of the Jews washing their hands with the fist (*pygmē*).

not intended. So important was this tradition to the Pharisees, that one whole division of the Mishnah (a collection of Jewish interpretations of scriptural ordinances compiled by the Rabbis) was devoted to this one subject of cleanliness. Interestingly enough, the Mishnah is contained in the Halakah (the body of law regulating all aspects of Jewish life). Halakah literally means "the walk." Literally, our passage tells us that the Pharisees ask Jesus, "Why don't your disciples 'walk' (NIV translates it "live") according to the traditions of the elders (this body of literature would later be known as "the walk")?" In other words, "Why aren't the disciples walking the walk—the accepted tradition?"

Here is the point. The teachers of the law are attacking Jesus and the disciples, not for breaking Old Testament law, but for breaking their man-made regulations which they had attached to the law. Understand, there is nothing inherently wrong with tradition, rites, and customs—unless tradition becomes inflexible obedience and scrupulous observance to a man-made standard. This is precisely what has happened. One preacher of yesteryear said, "Tradition was the most constant, the most persistent, the most dogged, the most utterly devilish opposition the master encountered. It openly attacked him on every hand and silently repulsed his teaching."[2]

Before we are too hard on the Pharisees, we need to realize that we can become keepers of tradition ourselves. In fact, we can readily find two kinds of "tradition snobs" among us (at times I have probably been both). The first are those who look at others and say, "Where are your robes, your carved pulpits, and your choir? Where are the hymns, the creeds and doxologies? Where is the stained glass?" They look down their noses on others because they don't keep the "proper" traditions. It is easy to recognize them.

But there is a second type of tradition snob. There are those who look at those keepers of tradition and say, "Those poor tradition-bound souls." Both can be equally repulsive.

We all keep certain types of traditions. The problem is when we no longer keep tradition—but the tradition keeps us. There is nothing inherently wrong with traditions, rites, and customs—nor are they inherently good. Good and bad are determined by the intentions of the heart. Communion, for example can become stale and void if separated from its rightful purpose. The frequency (or infrequency) and the way

---

2. Thomas Dickson as quoted by Ray Stedman, *The Servant Who Rules*, 201.

communion is served can also reek with tradition if one loses sight of its original meaning. Tradition is not inherently good or evil, but its application serves as the determining factor.

At this point, our story takes a strange twist.

Jesus Accuses the Pharisees (Mark 7:6–13)

In response to the Pharisees, Jesus sternly attacks their hypocrisy, even calling the Word of God as witness against them. Two witnesses come to his aid. The first is the prophet Isaiah.

> He replied, "Isaiah was right when he prophesied about you hypocrites; as it is written: 'These people honor me with their lips, but their hearts are far from me. They worship me in vain; their teachings are but rules taught by men.' You have let go of the commands of God and are holding on to the teachings of men." (Mark 7:6–8)

Using Isaiah as a witness, Jesus attacks the Pharisees. This is the first and only time in the book of Mark that we find the word "hypocrite" (*hypokritēs*). We know the word literally means "false face." It describes a person who acts one way on the outside, but the outside is only a facade. In one sense or another, we are all at times hypocrites—we are something different than what we portray. But true hypocrisy runs deeper. Hypocrisy, at its core, is claiming something you never intend to be. The Pharisees wanted to convey an attitude of piety, but it was only a religious show, a religious system. With highly structured and sophisticated ceremony they feigned worship to God and exchanged and elevated their traditions above that of the Word of God. And herein lies the problem. They elevated their traditions to a divine status.

The Pharisees came to attack Jesus, but he has turned the tables on them, not only with Isaiah as a witness, but also with Moses (the giver of the law):

> And he said to them: "You have a fine way of setting aside the commands of God in order to observe your own traditions! For Moses said, 'Honor your father and your mother,' and 'Anyone who curses his father or mother must be put to death.' But you say that if a man says to his father or mother: 'Whatever help you might otherwise have received from me is Corban' (that is, a gift devoted to God), then you no longer let him do anything for his father or mother. Thus you nullify the word of God by your traditions that you have handed down. And you do many things like that." (Mark 7:9–13)

Jesus gives them a clear example of how their own tradition is used to set aside God's clear commands. He quotes Exodus 21:17 ("Anyone who curses father or mother must be put to death"), as well as from the Ten Commandments in Exodus 20:12 ("Honor your father and your mother"). We normally quote the fifth commandment to our young children along with its promise, "That your days will be long on this earth." My mom had her own paraphrase of this last phrase—I can only assume she borrowed it from Bill Cosby: "I brought you into this world, and I can take you out of it."

Actually, this commandment to honor parents, so often applied to young children, was intended for adults. It was intended to require adult children to provide care for their parents when they became elderly. But rather than caring for parents (like the law required), tradition had provided a legal loophole to easily circumvent this command. A son need only to declare that what he intended to give his father and mother were to be considered "Corban"[3] (that is a gift devoted to God) and therefore couldn't be designated for use by the parents. The strange rub was that by devoting assets as a gift to God, a son did not necessarily promise it to the temple, nor did he prevent its use for himself. All he did was to legally exclude his parents from benefitting from it (7:12). It was a religious-sounding way to violate God's law.

The very purpose of the fifth commandment was set aside by the tradition. It nullified (*akyroō*, to make invalid, cancel) the word of God. Their tradition was violating the clear instruction of scripture. Jesus not only gives this clear example, but says that they did "many things like that" (7:13).

To this point in our story, Jesus has been responding directly to the Pharisees and the teachers of the law who so rudely interrupted him. Now he turns again to his original audience and gives the crux of his teaching about what is clean. He then gathers his disciples and takes them into a house (maybe back to Peter's house in Capernaum) and teaches them about what truly defiles a person.

---

3. For the Old Testament commands about vows, see Deuteronomy 23:21–23 and Numbers 30:1–16).

Jesus' Teaching on True Defilement (Mark 7:14–23)[4]

> Again Jesus called the crowd to him and said, "Listen to me, everyone, and understand this. Nothing outside a man can make him 'unclean' by going into him. Rather, it is what comes out of a man that makes him 'unclean.'" After he had left the crowd and entered the house, his disciples asked him about the parable. "Are you so dull?" he asked. "Don't you see that nothing that enters a man from the outside can make him 'unclean'? For it doesn't go into his heart but into his stomach, and then out of his body." (In saying this, Jesus declared all foods "clean.") He went on: "What comes out of a man is what makes him 'unclean.' For from within, out of men's hearts, come evil thoughts, sexual immorality, theft, murder, adultery, greed, malice, deceit, lewdness, envy, slander, arrogance and folly. All these evils come from inside and make a man 'unclean.'" (Mark 7:14–23)

Jesus states clearly what does and does not make a person unclean (7:15). Food, for example, cannot do this—not even if it is eaten with hands that are ceremonially unclean or even if it is declared to be unclean by kosher food laws. Jesus actually uses graphic language suggesting food simply goes in and then is purged out the drain. It doesn't defile a man. What really makes a person "unclean" is what comes from within—what comes from a person's heart, not what goes through the stomach. What a person thinks, desires, and does—are the real cause of uncleanliness.

This must have come as a shock to all the Jewish listeners. It certainly catches the disciples off guard. They even question him about it. Jesus expresses his surprise and says, "Are you so dull?" (7:13). After all the time they have spent with him, they still don't get it. Then he explains again: The heart, not the stomach, defiles a man. What is going on in the heart determines the true issues in life. This first-century expression might be best understood by our word "mind"—the center of human personality that determines man's actions and inactions, as reflected in Isaiah, "These people come near to me with their mouth and honor me with their lips, but their hearts are far from me" (Isaiah 29:13).

What is important is not the tradition. Ceremonially unclean hands will not defile a person; what comes out of a person's heart defiles a person.

---

4. Some early manuscripts add verse 16: "If anyone has ears to hear, let him hear." This probably was a gloss (scribal addition) of an early scribe.

So what does the authentic life look like? Jesus gets very specific. Jesus clarifies with a list that seems to move from overt sins to attitudes. Evil thoughts serve as an overriding principle, followed by sexual immorality (*porneia*), theft, murder, adultery, greed, malice, deceit, lewdness (unrestrained, shameless behavior), envy (evil eye—which was a Semitic term for stinginess), slander, arrogance, and folly.

Man can not achieve holiness through legalistic observances (or non-observances). Tradition is powerless to cleanse the heart. Keeping the outside of the cup clean (ritual) is not nearly as important as keeping the inside of the cup (the heart) clean.

When it comes to the condition of the heart, the Scribes and Pharisees failed. What about you?

Study Questions

1. Religious traditions are not inherently good or bad. They can be useful (if they remind us of what is important) or detrimental (if we allow them to overrule God's eternal principles). Think back on your upbringing. What religious traditions were part of your life?
2. What religious traditions or rituals do you practice today?
3. Why were the Scribes and Pharisees upset with Jesus and his disciples (1–4)?
4. Are the Pharisees concerned with the disciples' lack of hygiene? If not, what is in view?
5. Why was ceremonial washing so important to the Pharisees and teachers of the law?
6. What is hypocrisy (6)? How can one avoid hypocrisy in life?
7. Something declared "Corban" meant it was dedicated to God and no longer able to be given away.
    a. How does this illustrate how tradition can be twisted and abused?
    b. Why does Jesus bring up the fifth commandment and the issue of Corban?
    c. What does it mean to "Honor your father and your mother?"

8. How can empty ritual strip worship of its meaning and power?

    a. When is worship in vain?

    b. What makes worship genuine?

9. Have you ever felt like you were just going through the motions in regards to your faith? Explain.

10. How do you focus your heart on God?

11. What is Jesus' point in verses 14–23?

12. Are you more concerned with things that enter your stomach or things that enter your heart? Why? How would others know that about you?

13. Jesus listed many things that can come out of someone's heart that indicate uncleanliness (21–23).

    a. Which of these things do you struggle with the most?

    b. How do you guard yourself against these evils?

14. What is it that makes a person clean or unclean?

15. Jesus told the Pharisees that fulfilling human traditions can interfere with obeying the commands of God. Have you ever felt like a victim of human or religious tradition in your efforts to obey God?

16. Can you think of any modern-day examples of religious-sounding ways people violate God's law?

For Further Study

17. See Matthew 15:1–20.

17

Table Scraps

Mark 7:24–30

ONE OF MY STRONGEST memories as a new arrival at college was when two upperclassmen invited me to go out to dinner with them. We went to a local pizza joint, sat down at a booth, and waited. It seemed fairly obvious to me that all we needed to do was walk up to the counter, place an order, pay, and wait—we shouldn't expect someone to come and take our order. But, I was the newbie, the underclassman, the freshman, and I didn't want to overstep my bounds.

After waiting for some time, I asked a question I thought would get at the heart of the issue without being pushy: "Do you come here often?" It was obvious in my mind that they had never been there before. But they responded that they came to this particular establishment regularly. That left me puzzled.

And then it happened. An older couple seated in the booth right behind me got up and left, leaving their uneaten pizza behind. Immediately, my comrades grabbed the pizza scraps and made quick work of the leftovers. I sat stunned and embarrassed. Only moments later, one of the guys got up and approached two businessmen who were obviously through eating and said, "We were wondering if we could finish your pizza." My face grew redder than even the pizza sauce. They were begging for table scraps and I was more than surprised.

We find both table scraps and surprise in our passage.

> Jesus left that place and went to the vicinity of Tyre. He entered a house and did not want anyone to know it; yet he could not keep his presence secret. In fact, as soon as she heard about him, a woman whose little daughter was possessed by an evil spirit

came and fell at his feet. The woman was a Greek, born in Syrian Phoenicia. She begged Jesus to drive the demon out of her daughter. "First let the children eat all they want," he told her, "for it is not right to take the children's bread and toss it to their dogs." "Yes, Lord," she replied, "but even the dogs under the table eat the children's crumbs." Then he told her, "For such a reply, you may go; the demon has left your daughter." She went home and found her child lying on the bed, and the demon gone. (Mark 7:24–30)

As our drama unfolds, we find surprises at every turn. I want to look specifically at four.

Surprise #1—That Jesus Would Go to this Area. (Mark 7:24)

"Jesus left that place and went to the vicinity of Tyre" (7:24).

Tyre was a port city on the Mediterranean Sea north of Israel. It was also a Canaanite city located in what we would call Lebanon. It is, therefore, no small surprise when Jesus goes to this pagan area that is "unclean." The question is, why would he go?

After the miraculous feeding of the five thousand in chapter 6, chapter 7 opens with the Pharisees rebuking the disciples for eating with ceremonially unwashed, and therefore unclean, hands. Jesus rebukes them, saying, "Nothing outside a man can make him 'unclean' by going into him. Rather, it is what comes out of a man that makes him 'unclean'" (7:14). In the eyes of the Pharisees, even the disciples were too unclean to eat at their table. The Pharisees attack Jesus by using man-made rules and regulations.

It is not a coincidence, that immediately following this incident, Jesus goes directly from Israel into "unclean" Gentile territory, where a Gentile woman locates him and pleads with him on behalf of her daughter. From here, Jesus will continue on his journey into Sidon, and then down to the Gentile Decapolis where he will heal a deaf and mute man (7:31–36). He then proceeds into a Gentile desert where he will perform a second miraculous feeding of four thousand Gentiles (8:1–10).

I may not always be a quick study, but it seems apparent that Jesus is making a statement. We might miss it, but Mark's original audience would not. First-century readers were being challenged not to set limits on the universality of the good news—it encompasses all people, including the Gentiles.

Actually, Mark uses a three-step progression to get readers to notice something clearly. He says, "The woman was a Greek (Gentile), born in

Syrian Phoenicia" (7:26). Mark starts with the general and moves to the very specific. She was: 1) a woman, 2) a Gentile, and, 3) a Syrophoenician. Expanding on these descriptions, F. F. Bruce writes that she was, "A Greek in religion, a Syrian in tongue, and a Phoenician in race."[1]

We were given a fourth clue earlier: "Jesus left that place and went to the vicinity of Tyre" (7:24). First-century readers knew immediately what probably escapes us. The City of Tyre (although located on a beautiful portion of Mediterranean sea) was not a favorite vacation destination for first-century Jews. The Old Testament deems Tyre as both a wealthy and godless oppressor. Except for a brief treaty with King David, Tyre was a city that had always been an enemy of Israel. Residents of Tyre even rejoiced when Jerusalem was besieged.[2] This city was considered defiled and unclean. They were not just enemies, they were archenemies.

A quick comparison between Matthew and Mark is interesting at this point. When writing to a Roman audience, Mark uses the terminology of a Syrophoenician woman. They would clearly understand the political and racial divisions that this describes. To a Jewish audience, Matthew writes, "A Canaanite woman." To a Jew, that represented thousands of years of conflict. The point was abundantly clear to both audiences—Jesus was in enemy territory.

In the minds of a first-century reader, this would spur many questions, all centering around one issue: "Why does Jesus go here?" It would be akin to an American saying, "I want to vacation in Northern Korea, or the hills of Afghanistan." It would cause some to utter the words "traitor" under their breath. The major difference being that our antagonism with Korea or Kabul is fairly recent, while the conflict between the Jews and the Canaanites had lasted several millennia.

The historian Josephus wrote that the people of Tyre are "our bitterest enemies." It is no small surprise that Jesus goes to this region. It's also a shocker to find that this woman comes to Jesus.

---

1. KJV *Parallel Bible Commentary*, Logos Bible Software electronic edition. Nashville: Thomas Nelson, 1997.

2. See Isaiah 23; Jeremiah 47:4; Ezekiel 26–28; Joel 3:4; Amos 1:9; and Zechariah 9:2.

Surprise #2—That This Woman Would Come to Jesus. (Mark 7:25-26)

"As soon as she heard about him . . . [she] came and fell at his feet" (7:25).

The animosity runs both ways. But we quickly find the reason why this woman comes to Jesus. She has heard about the miracles he has performed, and her daughter is suffering. Any animosity directed toward the Jews or their Messiah was overcome by her personal plight. She comes and prostrates herself at the feet of Jesus. In Matthew's account we read, "A Canaanite woman from that vicinity came to him, crying out, 'Lord, Son of David, have mercy on me! My daughter is suffering terribly from demon-possession'" (15:22).

The fact that she approaches "The Son of David" is curious. The fact that she calls him Lord and falls at his feet is remarkable. Once again, we see a familiar theme depicted for us in this narrative. In the Gospel of Mark, the people we might expect to recognize Jesus (the Jews, Scribes, Pharisees, Teachers of the Law), don't. The ones we might expect to reject Jesus (the demon-possessed and the Gentiles), recognize him for who he is. Said another way, the expected don't make it, the unacceptable do!

That is not unlike today. Sometimes the hardest people to reach with the gospel are the good, upright, law-abiding citizens. They live by a moral law, and often make statements like, "I am just as good as those people down at church." It is also not unusual to see someone who has been raised in the church left unchanged or transformed by the blood of Jesus. It is often the ones who have wandered greatly from the truth who ultimately see Jesus for who he really is.

The righteously upright look down their noses at the seemingly unacceptable, while the seemingly unacceptable come transparently to Jesus. It reminds me of the prayer of the publican: "'God, I thank you that I am not like other men—robbers, evildoers, adulterers—or even like this tax collector' . . . But the tax collector stood at a distance. He would not even look up to heaven, but beat his breast and said, "God, have mercy on me, a sinner." Jesus said it was the tax collector who went home justified (Luke 18:11–14).

As we continue with our story, we are confronted with a third surprise contained in the very words of Jesus.

Surprise #3—That Jesus Would Dismiss Her So Sharply. (Mark 7:27)

"'First let the children eat all they want,' he told her, 'for it is not right to take the children's bread and toss it to their dogs'" (7:27).

At this point we are confronted with a troubling question: "Why does Jesus seem so rude to this woman when she is earnestly pleading for her little daughter?" We don't mind Jesus being rude to the Scribes and Pharisees (who we believe deserve it). But how can Jesus be so callous to a forlorn mother?

In dealing with this question, there have been several explanations given. First, some point to the fact that Jesus obviously doesn't want to be bothered. It says so right in the text (7:24). He especially doesn't want to be bothered by a Canaanite woman. Some even go as far as suggesting that he himself is struggling with the inclusion of the Gentiles. The problem with this explanation is that it simply is not in keeping with the character of Jesus. In previous encounters, he has no trepidation about reaching out to women (5:25–34), or Gentiles (5:1–20). He deals kindly and compassionately with them. Specifically with Gentiles, Jesus does not reject them; they reject him and asked him to leave their region (5:17). He will return there in the very next section (7:31).

Others suggest that Jesus speaks harsh words (words that would be expected from a Jew to a Gentile), only to see how this woman would react. She has called him "Lord" and "the Son of David"—does she really believe it? They suggest that Jesus temporarily withholds his help and compassion to test the woman's faith and resolve to see what she believes and why. His desire is to grow and stretch her faith. When Jesus sees her faith, he grants her request. John Calvin took this view when he said that Jesus wanted, "To whet her zeal and inflame her ardor." Jesus has certainly acted like this before with the hemorrhaging woman (although she is cured before he asks her to step forward).

A third view suggests that Jesus says the words the woman probably expects, but does so with a twinkle in his eye and in a playful manner, which would ease the obvious tension. While his words are harsh, they are in jest. Proponents suggest that the use of the diminutive form of "dog" (a playmate of children and not the word used for a feral pack of dogs that prowls the dump) takes the bite (no pun intended) out of what Jesus says; although, I doubt anyone would take the word "dog" as a term of endearment. There is certainly merit in both the second and third views.

A fourth view may also give insight. It suggests that Jesus' comments are directed as much at the disciples as they are the Syrophoenician woman. In Matthew's account, the disciples are encouraging Jesus to send this woman away and may have been the first to use this terminology. Jesus, by using their words in addressing the woman, wants to ultimately lead them to the understanding that he has compassion on all, including a Gentile woman.

But as Jesus speaks these words we are confronted with a fourth surprise.

Surprise #4—That the Woman Accepts Jesus' Premise. (Mark 7:28-30)

The woman is not put off, but reacts with quick wit. "'Yes, Lord,' she replied, 'but even the dogs under the table eat the children's crumbs'" (7:28).

She understands Jesus' riddle readily, while most of the time, in various circumstances, even the disciples don't. Sometimes, even after explanation, the disciples still don't have a clue. The woman understands. The children who must eat first—are the children of Israel. The dogs represent the Gentiles. This is not unlike Paul's statement about the gospel: "I am not ashamed of the gospel, because it is the power of God for the salvation of everyone who believes: first for the Jew, then for the Gentile" (Romans 1:16).

In other words, Jesus is saying, "This banquet is by invitation only. I don't believe you have a reservation." But Jesus' answer does not embitter her, she understands that she has no right to demand anything from Jesus—and yet, she is unwilling to take "no" for an answer. She understands what Jesus is saying, and agrees with him. "Yes, Lord, I understand that I have no right to demand to dine at the table, but I am not looking for a full-course meal, I'm requesting only a few crumbs." She uses a play on words. Jesus has talked about "little dogs" (*kynarion*), she is requesting "little crumbs" or "children's crumbs" (*paidion psichion*). She understands this fundamental point: She knows she cannot insist on the mercy of Jesus, but she comes like a beggar who will gladly accept even a scrap of food.

How different from the entitlement attitude that is so prevalent today. You owe me. I deserve it. I demand my rights. Understand, each one of us comes before Jesus as a beggar who should rejoice at even a crumb from the Master's table.

When Jesus sees her attitude, coupled with her faith he says, "For such a reply, you may go; the demon has left your daughter" (7:29). She goes home and finds her daughter has been delivered just as Jesus promised. This, by the way, is the only miracle Jesus performs in absentia in the Gospel of Mark.

This story describes for us the proper attitude toward Jesus. We need to have an attitude of humility which accurately reflects a position of beggar before the Master. We have no right to demand our "rights"—we have none.

I have always said that when we get to heaven there will be a few surprises. I think there will be some people there whom we never expected. It may also be true that some of the expected won't be there. There are many who have practiced religion, whose seat in the assembly is never vacant, who live with every appearance as a Godly person, but whose heart is far from God. They will be disappointed.

There may also be those present who have come clinging to the grace and mercy of Jesus Christ, seeking only crumbs from his table, who will experience the full-meal-deal; they will dine at the wedding feast of the Lamb.

Study Questions

1. Share a time when you purposefully went to a place where you knew you would not fit in.
2. Have you known churches/Christians who have been wrongfully unaccepting of others?
3. Locate Tyre on a Bible map. How far was it from Capernaum to Tyre?
4. Why does Jesus try to enter a house without anyone knowing it?
5. Why couldn't Jesus keep his presence a secret?
6. Besides trying to get a little respite, what is Jesus' point in going to Tyre (a Gentile area) after his discussion in 7:1–23?

7. Why does Mark include the background information about this woman? Explain why each of the following is an obstacle presented to us in this story.

    a. A woman

    b. A Gentile

    c. A Syrophoenician

    d. From Tyre

8. Was Jesus rude to the Syrophoenician woman, or did he have something he wanted to bring out in his discussion with her? What would that have been?

9. Was Jesus resisting helping the woman? Or was there a point?

10. What does Jesus' response mean in verse 27? Who are the children? Who are the dogs? Is Jesus' purpose to reject the Gentile people?

11. Read Romans 1:16. How does this passage clarify what is being said in our passage?

12. The woman's persistence indicates she sensed something from Jesus that encouraged her to continue asking—perhaps a twinkle in his eye or a warmth in his tone of voice. What else does the woman's response tell you about her?

13. Jesus tells the woman, "Go; the demon has left your daughter." In the Gospel of Mark, can you find another "absentee" miracle where Jesus is not present when the miracle occurs?

14. The Greek woman from Syrian Phoenicia was a religious outsider. Have you ever felt like a religious outsider? What was it like? What can you do to reach out to someone who might feel like they are outside of God's love?

15. Read the following passages to discover the nature of the conflict between Israel and Tyre. Isaiah 23; Jeremiah 47:4; Ezekiel 26–28; Joel 3:4; Amos 1:9; Zechariah 9:2.

For Further Study

16. See Matthew 15:21–28.

18

Overwhelmed with Amazement

Mark 7:31–37

About every two years, I lead tours throughout the Holy Land. We normally travel through Israel, but often include other areas such as Jordan, Egypt, Turkey, and Greece. These trips are life-changing adventures for most as we experience the lands of the Bible and walk where Jesus walked. It is hard to remain unmoved as you walk up the Mount of Olives or sail across the Sea of Galilee. Over the years, I have taken thousand of pictures of the places we have visited. On these trips, however, there is often one person who is so intent on capturing the event on video, that they only see "The Promised Land" through the half-inch lens on the back of their camera or the two-inch view finder on their camcorder. I guess they don't want to forget what they missed seeing. In a similar way, it's remarkable how many people in the first century missed seeing Jesus because they were looking at him through the wrong lens.

The very ones who should have seen Jesus for who he was, didn't recognize him. The Scribes, the Pharisees, the experts in the Old Testament saw Jesus through a lens of their own making and did not recognize him for who he really was. This led them to reject him and accuse Jesus and the disciples of breaking the law. In actuality, neither Jesus nor the disciples broke the law, they simply did not keep the man-made traditions which had been built around the law. As a result of the scorn and ridicule, Jesus left Israel and headed north and west along the Mediterranean Sea. As we take up the story in chapter 7, Jesus is in the midst of a prolonged preaching tour traveling from Tyre (7:24) north to

Sidon (in modern Lebanon), returning south (in modern Syria) along the eastern coast of the Sea of Galilee (7:31), down to the hills of the Decapolis (in modern Jordan). All this time, Jesus has placed himself squarely in someone else's territory for a period of what most scholars believe to be about eight months. Jesus has circumvented Israel. This would be the equivalent of traveling from Ontario, Oregon, to Boise, Idaho, by way of McCall (for those of you who are not familiar with "God's Country," i.e., the Northwest, it might be like traveling from San Francisco to Los Angeles via Las Vegas). As Jesus reaches the area of the Decapolis, we find a miracle that is recorded for us only in the Gospel of Mark.

> Then Jesus left the vicinity of Tyre and went through Sidon, down to the Sea of Galilee and into the region of the Decapolis. There some people brought to him a man who was deaf and could hardly talk, and they begged him to place his hand on the man. After he took him aside, away from the crowd, Jesus put his fingers into the man's ears. Then he spit and touched the man's tongue. He looked up to heaven and with a deep sigh said to him, "Ephphatha!" (which means, "Be opened!"). At this, the man's ears were opened, his tongue was loosened and he began to speak plainly. Jesus commanded them not to tell anyone. But the more he did so, the more they kept talking about it. People were overwhelmed with amazement. "He has done everything well," they said. "He even makes the deaf hear and the mute speak." (Mark 7:31–37)

In our passage there are five key phrases which will help us unlock what is happening in our text, most of which we might simply overlook if we are not careful. The first describes the people of the Decapolis as they come seeking Jesus.

Phrase #1—"They begged him to place his hand on the man" (Mark 7:32).

Here we find Jesus returning back to the very area where people had formerly rejected him. Remember the confrontation Jesus had with the demon-possessed man. As Jesus first came to the vicinity of the Decapolis, he was confronted by a man filled with evil spirits who cried, "What do you want with me, Jesus, Son of the Most High God?" (5:7). When asked to give his name, the demon-possessed man replied, "My name is Legion

... for we are many" (5:10). Legion had lived in the tombs and tormented the people day and night for some time—the situation growing steadily worse, until he came into the presence of Jesus. Jesus commanded the demons to come out of the man and even granted the demons' request to enter into a herd of pigs. Upon doing so, they immediately ran off the cliff and drowned. But the townsfolk, rather than being appreciative of what Jesus had done for them, began to plead with Jesus to leave their region (5:17). In contrast, the formerly demon-possessed man begged Jesus to allow him to come with him. But Jesus refused, sending him instead back to his family (5:19).

In our passage, Jesus has returned to the region of the Decapolis, and the very people who begged Jesus to leave are now begging him to heal. It is a remarkable turn of events. How do you account for the change in the attitude of the people?

Jesus had given the formerly demon-possessed man these instructions: "Go . . . and tell" (5:19) and we can say with confidence that the man went and told with due diligence how much Jesus had done for him. Mark ended chapter 5 with this commentary: "And all the people were amazed" (5:20). Due in part to this one man's testimony, when Jesus returns to the Decapolis, the pump is primed for Jesus' ministry there. We find the people still begging, but their request has changed. Rather than begging Jesus to leave, they want Jesus to help "a man who was deaf and could hardly talk" (7:32). As they plead with Jesus we encounter a second interesting phrase.

Phrase #2—"After he took him aside, away from the crowd" (Mark 7:33).

Before dismissing this phrase as insignificant, understand that Mark gives emphasis to this very point. The NIV fails to translate one word that at first glance may seem redundant. Literally, our passage reads, "After he took him aside, away from the crowd *by himself*." Mark notes that Jesus took the man aside *privately* in order to deal with the man on a personal level. He took the man away from the crowds, possibly away from his friends, maybe even away from the disciples. We are not told the rationale for this separation, but there could certainly be several possibilities.

First, Jesus might have done this for practical reasons—the man couldn't hear or communicate well. A one-on-one approach away from the crowd would aid in the communication process between Jesus and this man. It would limit the number of distractions and allow Jesus to personally deal with the man in the appropriate manner, without the interruptions of the crowd.

Second, Jesus might have done it for compassionate reasons—Jesus did not want to make a spectacle of a man who had already suffered greatly and had undoubtedly been excluded from much of society because of his ailments. Jesus did not want to place more undue attention on him.

Finally, Jesus also might have separated the man from the crowd for personal reasons—Jesus did not want to be known simply as a miracle worker. He was trying to avoid the appearance of being the leader of a three-ring circus. Jesus has consistently and repeatedly withdrawn every time the people have pressed him to become this type of leader (see 2:35; 3:7; 3:13; 5:21; 6:45; etc.).

Jesus, in a very private way, concentrates entirely on the sufferer's needs and desires. He does not want the man to become part of some miracle show, nor does he want to add to his own personal glory. He wants to make the sufferer hear and speak. Far from promoting his miracles, he will actually command the people "not to tell anyone" (7:36).

How different this is from those so-called faith healers of today who intentionally assemble crowds, clamor for the spotlight, and seek personal glory and revenue. I have often wondered if their intent is to glorify God or self.

But it is not just faith healers who clamor for attention and glory. Many people serve with selfish ambition and ulterior motives. They serve, labor, or give to be seen by men, rather than to please God. I'm reminded of the story of Jesus as he sat near the temple treasury. "Many rich people threw in large amounts. But a poor widow came and put in two very small copper coins, worth only a fraction of a penny" (12:41–42). The rich gave out of their surplus to be seen by men, but the widow gave sacrificially from the heart.

We, too, are guilty of serving out of selfish ambition or ulterior motives whenever we do ministry or acts of service for our own personal benefit. We should always ask ourselves whether our intentions are to make ourselves look good or if we are truly serving for the sake of others. Serving Christ is not about making "self" look good—our motivation should be to make God look good.

After Jesus takes the man off by himself, we come across another interesting phrase.

Phrase #3—"Jesus put his fingers into the man's ears. Then he spit and touched the man's tongue. He looked up to heaven and with a deep sigh said to him, '*Ephphatha!*' (which means, 'Be opened!')" (Mark 7:33–34).

After a quick glance at this verse, my initial response was, "Jesus gave the man a wet-willy!" A careful reading, however, shows this is not exactly what happened. Still, Jesus' actions seem to us a bit strange. Why does Jesus go through these shenanigans? There is no question that Jesus could have merely spoken the word and the deaf man would have left hearing and speaking plainly. What, then, is the significance of Jesus' actions in our passage?

I believe that a cursory review of these actions makes it quite clear that before Jesus actually healed this man, he instructed him using a rough form of sign language. By touching the man's ears, by touching his tongue, by looking to heaven and giving a deep sigh, he acted out what was about to take place. Jesus wanted to communicate to this man clearly and precisely what was about to happen. Jesus was using this as a teaching moment—as he often does. Jesus takes people where they are, meets their needs, but also desires to move and help them grow in their faith. In this story, Jesus acts out the drama that is about to unfold, not simply because he is going to heal the deaf man's ears and tongue, but because Jesus is concerned about the whole man. Jesus wants to perform more than a magic trick. When Jesus speaks the words, "Ephphatha! Be opened," he is concerned with more than just the ears and the mouth. He wants the man to know the *how* and the *who* of the miracle.

Jesus touches the man's ears to show that he is going to bring back the man's hearing. Jesus touches his tongue to demonstrate that his speech will be restored. He looks to heaven and with a deep sigh utters words to heaven to show the man where the power comes from. Jesus communicates clearly his intentions. Still, we might wonder, why does Jesus spit? What may seem crude or even unsanitary to us, might have actually instilled faith in the deaf and mute man. Several Roman writers as well as Jewish rabbis considered saliva to be a valid medical treatment. Jesus likely recognized the man's need for increased faith and offered this physical action to help strengthen him. We will see this again when Jesus restores sight to the blind man (8:22).

But even with everything that we have learned so far, there is still more going on in this text that we dare not miss. The most important element may be one that we might dismiss as unimportant if we are not careful. It is actually found in the description of the man who has been brought to Jesus.

Phrase #4—"A man was deaf and could hardly talk" (Mark 7:32).

The phrase "could hardly talk" (*mogilalos*) is a rare word in Greek. It is actually a word that is used only once in our New Testament—in this passage. It literally means, "speaking with difficulty or impaired in speech." While it is used only here in our New Testament, we do find it in just one other place in our Bible. The very same word is used in the Septuagint (LXX)—which is the Greek translation of the Old Testament—the Bible of Jesus and the disciples. We find this word used in a passage that predicts the coming of the Messiah. Isaiah the prophet writes,

> The desert and the parched land will be glad; the wilderness will rejoice and blossom. Like the crocus, it will burst into bloom; it will rejoice greatly and shout for joy . . . they will see the glory of the Lord, the splendor of our God . . . Be strong, do not fear; your God will come, he will come with vengeance; with divine retribution he will come to save you. Then will the eyes of the blind be opened and the ears of the deaf unstopped. Then will the lame leap like a deer, and the mute tongue shout for joy. (Isaiah 35:1–6)

When one interprets Jesus' miracles from a biblical landscape, we see what is truly going on. Jesus is the fulfillment of Old Testament prophecy. Jesus is the one who reveals the glory of the Lord and the splendor of God. Jesus is the fulfillment of the words, "Your God will come." The healing of the deaf and mute man by Jesus is actually a fulfillment of prophecy.

I am reminded of another incident in the life of Moses. Moses was giving excuses to God about why he was incapable of leading the children of Israel out of Egypt. God responded to those excuses with these words: "Who gave man his mouth? Who makes him deaf or mute? Who gives him sight or makes him blind? Is it not I, the Lord?" (Exodus 4:11). Restoring sight, hearing, or granting the ability to speak is a prerogative of God. Once again, Jesus' actions here show his true identity. Jesus does what only God can do. But somehow, many miss the ramifications of this, both in the first century and the twenty-first century.

Phrase #5—"People were overwhelmed with amazement" (Mark 7:37).

We have seen Jesus command storms, demons, and illness. As he makes the deaf hear and the mute speak, the people are amazed. Literally, "They were astounded most exceedingly" (7:37). But while the people are excited by what happens, they still do not fully understand. While many jabber excitedly about what Jesus has done, the magnitude of what it signifies escapes them. They do not have all the pieces of the puzzle to see a completed picture. This is why Jesus tells them to remain quiet. He is more than a miracle worker. The secrecy motif underlines the fact that it is only those who believe in the risen Lord who can understand the full significance of what is taking place in Jesus' ministry. The command to go and tell comes clearly to all after the resurrection (Matthew 28:19–20).

The people are dazzled. They are shocked and amazed. They say, "He has done everything well . . . He even makes the deaf hear and the mute speak" (7:37). But while they are excited about Jesus, they don't really know Jesus. They are looking through the wrong lens.

I often use the phrase, what you are won by, you are won to. The problem with spiritual emotionalism is simply this: What happens when the emotion fades? If your whole belief system is wound up in the emotional, crisis looms when emotion wanders. Many people have mountain-top experiences where they have encountered a significant "miracle" in their life or they have experienced a spiritual high. In that moment they vow obedience to Jesus. But as they come off the mountain and the scenery changes, they no longer feel God's presence and their Christianity faces crises. Dazzled people don't always comprehend who Jesus really is.

Mark does not want to dazzle you or overwhelm you with amazement, he simply wants to convince you of this one fact: Jesus is the Christ, the son of the living God and you need him as your Lord and Savior. Nothing else short of this matters.

Study Questions

1. Which would you miss most if it was taken from you, your hearing or your sight?
2. If you were to become deaf, what sound would you miss hearing most?
3. The people who brought the deaf and mute man to Jesus, begged Jesus to heal him. Earlier, in Mark 5:17, these same people begged Jesus to leave their region. How do you explain their change in attitude toward Jesus? (See Mark 5:20)
4. Have you ever sent someone away or denied their service, only to find they were the person you really needed? When?
5. Have you ever treated God in a similar fashion as the people of the Decapolis? When?
6. Why does Jesus take the deaf and mute man away from the crowds?
7. What might be the reasoning behind Jesus' actions before healing the deaf and mute man (why did Jesus touch the man's ears and tongue)?
8. What is significant about the language Mark uses to describe the deaf and mute man? How does this relate to Isaiah 35:5–6? How are we to understand Jesus in light of this passage?
9. Why does Jesus command those who witness the miracle not to tell anyone?
10. What are you doing in your life right now that requires faith?
11. How has Jesus' power been demonstrated in your life?
12. How often do you talk about the things Jesus has done or is doing in your life? Why or why not?
13. What is it that God wants you to hear, that you have not been hearing?
14. What is it that God wants you to say, that you have not been saying?
15. When was the last time you were "overwhelmed with amazement" at the work of Jesus?

16. The multitudes were filled with emotion and excitement over the miracles Jesus performed. Unfortunately, they seem to be blinded to the authority behind those very miracles. How are people blinded by emotion to Jesus today?

17. How has your view and grasp of Jesus changed as we have studied the Gospel of Mark?

For Further Study

18. See Matthew 15:21–28.

19

Much Ado About Bread

Mark 8:1–21

During those days another large crowd gathered. Since they had nothing to eat, Jesus called his disciples to him and said, "I have compassion for these people; they have already been with me three days and have nothing to eat. If I send them home hungry, they will collapse on the way, because some of them have come a long distance." His disciples answered, "But where in this remote place can anyone get enough bread to feed them?" "How many loaves do you have?" Jesus asked. "Seven," they replied. He told the crowd to sit down on the ground. When he had taken the seven loaves and given thanks, he broke them and gave them to his disciples to set before the people, and they did so. They had a few small fish as well; he gave thanks for them also and told the disciples to distribute them. The people ate and were satisfied. Afterward the disciples picked up seven basketfuls of broken pieces that were left over. About four thousand men were present. And having sent them away, he got into the boat with his disciples and went to the region of Dalmanutha. (Mark 8:1–10)

Four Thousand Fed (Mark 8:1–10)

As I read this passage, several questions immediately come to my mind. The first one is simply this (and I imagine you have asked it yourself): Haven't we heard this story before? At first blush it might appear so. Mark records both a feeding of the five thousand (6:30–44) along with a feeding of the four thousand (8:1–9).

As mentioned previously, critics have worked overtime to discredit the miraculous feedings and explain away anything supernatural. When it comes to the feeding of the four thousand, they employ a further tactic. Critics try to merge the two into one single story. They suggest that oral tradition morphed the original account into two epic stories.

While it is true that there are many similarities between these two accounts, there are even more differences. The similarities include the thousands of people fed, the shortage of food in the area, the people's hunger, the disciples' lack of understanding, the loaves and the fish, and leftovers. But there are also significant differences: a different location (Bethsaida and the Decapolis); a different crowd (Jews and Gentiles); different circumstances of the feeding; a different timing for the miracle, a different number of people; a different provision (the number of loaves and fish); a different number of prayers, a different amount of leftovers; a different challenge from Jesus; and a different manner of leaving (with or without the disciples) just to name a few.

Besides these differences (which cannot be readily reconciled), the critic still faces three other rather large obstacles. First is the simple fact that Mark records two separate accounts for us. He does so, not after years of oral tradition like the skeptics would have us believe, but he writes a very early account based on an eye witness. Remember, Mark worked closely with Peter, who participated in the event. In effect, the Gospel of Mark is the Gospel of Peter because Mark wrote as Peter spoke. Second, Matthew also records both events. Matthew, too, was an eyewitness of both feedings and is not relying on some oral tradition. Third, Jesus clearly refers to both the feeding of the five thousand and the feeding of the four thousand later in our passage as he teaches the disciples—asking specific questions about both. Skip ahead momentarily and hear the words of Jesus: "And don't you remember? When I broke the five loaves for the five thousand, how many basketfuls of pieces did you pick up? . . . And when I broke the seven loaves for the four thousand, how many basketfuls of pieces did you pick up?" (8:18–20). The disciples give the correct corresponding answers of twelve and seven. When dealing with these facts we must conclude that there were indeed two separate miraculous feedings.

But this understanding raises a second troubling question: If this is the second of two miraculous feedings, how do you account for the disciples' response? The disciples ask Jesus, "But where in this remote place can anyone get enough bread to feed them?" (8:4). If Jesus has already fed five thousand, is it possible that the disciples have actually forgotten the miraculous feeding? I think there are at least three possible answers to that question. The first would be: Yes, the disciples are that forgetful. There is certainly evidence for this answer in the text itself. Previously, Jesus himself has actually said, "Are you so dull?" (7:18). Later, Jesus will say again, "Do you still not understand?" (8:21). We might forget that at least eight months have passed between chapter 6 and chapter 8. One might postulate that it is possible (although, I think unlikely) that the disciples have forgotten.

A second possible answer is that the disciples have not forgotten about the previous miracle, but they have learned that Jesus doesn't want to be known simply as a miracle worker. They don't ask directly for a miracle, because they don't want to impose on Jesus. They do ask where they might find enough food in a deserted area, hoping Jesus will volunteer a miracle. Again, there is certainly evidence that might lead one to believe the disciples don't want to ask for a miracle even in our immediate text. Skipping ahead just a few verses in our passage, the Pharisees are going to ask Jesus for a sign, and Jesus is not pleased (8:11). Again, this is a legitimate possibility which would explain the disciples' response.

But there is also a third explanation worthy of consideration. Remember where Jesus is, and who this specific crowd entails. Jesus is in the area of the Decapolis and this is a predominantly Gentile crowd. The disciples may still be struggling with Jesus' ministry outside of Israel. They may assume that Jesus would not do this type of miracle for such an extremely large group of pagan people. They don't mind a token miracle for the Gentiles here or there—they can have a few crumbs from the table (7:28). It is not big deal if he casts a demon out of a little girl without even visiting her (7:29), or if he heals a man who was deaf and mute after he has taken him away from the crowd (7:35). They are willing to give Jesus a little latitude among the Gentiles, but surely Jesus is not going to publically feed thousands of non-Jews in such dramatic fashion. Or is he?

Which really brings me to a third question. Mark is normally fast-paced and doesn't give a lot of detail—he only gives the bare essentials—he only gives enough detail to make his case. So what is Mark's point? We know Jesus can feed the multitudes. Why would Mark choose to record for us a second miracle that is so similar to one he has already recorded?

We might have actually stumbled upon our answer. Jesus is going to feed the Gentile audience in the same way he fed the Jewish audience earlier. That is the point! Actually, it is interesting that every type of miracle Jesus performs in Gentile country, he has already done in Israel. He has now amazed the crowds, cast out demons, healed the sick, raised a little girl, and performed a miraculous feeding among both Jews and Gentiles. Why? He is demonstrating that he is the Messiah of all people. Remember Paul's statement: "To the Jew first and also to the Greek" (Romans 1:16)? I am also reminded of the story of a Gentile named Cornelius in the book of Acts. He was a devout and God-fearing man (Acts 10:2). Peter came and visited him and his family, and during his stay the Holy Spirit came upon them. Peter then said, "I now realize how true it is that God does not show favoritism but accepts men from every nation who fear him and do what is right. You know the message God sent to the people of Israel, telling the good news of peace through Jesus Christ, who is Lord of all" (Acts 10:34–36). Peter says to all present that they cannot refuse Cornelius and his household, who had received the Holy Spirit just as the Apostles had. In Mark, Jesus performs his miracles for both Jews and Gentiles.

After the miracle concludes, Jesus gets into the boat with the disciples and sails to the region of Dalmanutha. We do not know the precise location of Dalmanutha, but fortunately, in Matthew's account he narrows it down for us. Matthew says, "He got into the boat and went to the vicinity of Magadan" (Matthew 15:39). This takes Jesus and the disciples back into Israel on the midwest side of the Sea of Galilee. Here we find the Pharisees waiting for Jesus' return.

A Deliberate Trap (Mark 8:11–12)

> The Pharisees came and began to question Jesus. To test him, they asked him for a sign from heaven. He sighed deeply and said, "Why does this generation ask for a miraculous sign? I tell you the truth, no sign will be given to it." (Mark 8:11–12)

Since chapter 3, the Pharisees have been plotting with the Herodians how they might kill Jesus (3:6). Here we find them, "Wanting to test him" (8:11). We find two words that might be of interest. The word translated "question" (*syzēteō*) is literally the word to debate or argue.[1] They don't

---

1. There have been many points of conflict already mentioned between them (2:6–12, 16–17, 18–22, 23–38; 7:1–23).

accept Jesus or his teaching. The second word, translated "test" (*peirazō*) is the word "tempt." It is the very same word used of Satan's temptations of Jesus in the wilderness (1:12). The point is clear. The Pharisees do not want Jesus to pass this test, they want him to fail miserably. They want to find fault with Jesus. The purpose of asking for "a sign from heaven" (8:11) is to discredit him. Think back for a moment about everything Jesus has already done in the book of Mark. They are aware of these and many were actually done in their presence. Jesus has taught with authority and cast out demons (1:27; 5:13). He has healed Peter's mother-in-law and cured various diseases (1:30, 34). He has healed a man with leprosy (1:40), raised the paralytic (2:11) and restored a man's hand (3:5). He has calmed the storm (4:39) and walked on water (6:49). He has healed a bleeding woman (5:30) and raised a girl from the dead (5:34). He has fed five thousand (6:41) and most recently, the four thousand (8:8). What is it that Jesus can do to prove his identity to them? Even the most convincing sign will not change their mind. Actually, rather than convincing them, previous signs had just the opposite effect. "The teachers of the law who came down from Jerusalem said, 'He is possessed by Beelzebub! By the prince of demons he is driving out demons'" (3:22).

I might speculate on two things that could possibly win their approval. They might like Jesus to apologize to them and ask their forgiveness for not submitting to their authority. Or Jesus could pledge to be Israel's military conqueror and denounce the Gentiles.[2] This second response is what they are likely looking for by asking for a sign. Neither response would be appropriate for Jesus and both would discredit everything he has accomplished to this point in his ministry. Short of this, no sign will satisfy. Jesus is faced with a conundrum: He can perform another miraculous sign which would undoubtedly bring further criticism from them, or he can refuse them a sign and have them dismiss him completely. Jesus, "Sighed deeply and said, 'Why does this generation ask for a miraculous sign? I tell you the truth, no sign will be given to it'" (8:12).

Jesus answers them with a groan[3] and an oath-like statement which is made in prophetic fashion—I swear I will not do it. Following this, Jesus gets back into the boat with the disciples and heads north to Bethsaida.

---

2. The Pharisees are likely asking Jesus to do something that would signal Israel's deliverance by crushing the Gentiles.

3. The Greek term for "sighed deeply" (*anastenazō*, used only here in the New Testament) reflects weariness and even impatience. It is interesting to compare the various references to Jesus' emotion in Mark (1:41; 3:5; 6:6; 10:14; 14:34).

A Firm Warning (Mark 8:13-21)

> Then he left them, got back into the boat and crossed to the other side. The disciples had forgotten to bring bread, except for one loaf they had with them in the boat. "Be careful," Jesus warned them. "Watch out for the yeast of the Pharisees and that of Herod." They discussed this with one another and said, "It is because we have no bread." Aware of their discussion, Jesus asked them: "Why are you talking about having no bread? Do you still not see or understand? Are your hearts hardened? Do you have eyes but fail to see, and ears but fail to hear? And don't you remember? When I broke the five loaves for the five thousand, how many basketfuls of pieces did you pick up?" "Twelve," they replied. "And when I broke the seven loaves for the four thousand, how many basketfuls of pieces did you pick up?" They answered, "Seven." He said to them, "Do you still not understand?" (Mark 8:13-21)

Our last scene opens awkwardly with a phrase telling us that the disciples had forgotten to bring bread, "Except for one loaf they had with them in the boat" (8:14). Jesus listens to them and responds with a warning: "Watch out for the yeast of the Pharisees and that of Herod" (8:15). The word translated "yeast" here in our passage might more accurately be translated "leaven" (*zymē*). Leaven was produced by keeping back a piece of the previous week's dough, storing it, and adding juices to it to promote the process of fermentation. This homemade rising agent was fraught with health hazards—if it became tainted, it would infect the next batch. In the Old Testament and in Jewish writings, leaven is always used in a negative sense. This negative image is not reflected in our word "yeast" which connotes to us a fresh and wholesome ingredient that makes dough rise and gives bread a pleasing, light texture.

The disciples in typical fashion do not understand what Jesus is saying. They say to each other, "It is because we have no bread" (8:16). The disciples don't understand, but do we? What does Jesus mean by the leaven of the Pharisees? Again, there may be several possible answers. It might be their stubborn, selfish attitude that prevents them from listening to Jesus. It may be their arrogance and lack of compassion for others. It might include their nationalistic pride and rejection of everyone else. It might include all of the above. Whatever the case, it certainly includes their belligerent attempt to discredit Jesus no matter what. We are certainly guilty of being infected with the yeast of the Pharisees when we possess these kind of attitudes.

We might also ask, why does Jesus link Herod with the Pharisees? Jesus does not explicitly identify what the common toxic flaw is, but the context points to both parties' obstinate refusal to believe in spite of the evidence. Neither will admit the truth or embrace it. We have certainly seen this in the lives of the Pharisees. We also saw it in Herod's treatment of John the Baptist (6:14–29) and will see it again as Herod plays a further role in the passion of Jesus (Luke 23:7–12). It is interesting that as Jesus stands before Herod, Herod wants Jesus to perform some miracle. "He plied him with many questions, but Jesus gave him no answer" (Luke 23:9). "Then Herod and his soldiers ridiculed and mocked him. Dressing him in an elegant robe, they sent him back to Pilate. That day Herod and Pilate became friends—before this they had been enemies" (Luke 23:11–12).

Jesus is clearly predicting what is about to happen. We have noted before, the Gospel of Mark is ready to take a turn toward the crucifixion, where the Pharisees and Herod will play a part in ushering Jesus to the cross.

Jesus is aware of the disciples' lack of understanding. "Why are you talking about having no bread? Do you still not see or understand? Are your hearts hardened? Do you have eyes but fail to see, and ears but fail to hear? And don't you remember?" (8:17–18). The disciples have been with Jesus and yet they do not understand about the bread. The disciples do not yet recognize that they have "The Bread Maker" with them in the boat! Jesus is the compassionate, bread-giving Messiah to all—both Jews and Gentiles, but they still do not yet understand.

Do you? Jesus is not a trickster or the sign-producing Messiah of only Israel, but the compassionate, bread-giving Savior of all.

Study Questions

1. How did your parents complete this sentence when you were young: "How many times do I have to tell you to . . ."?
2. Jesus showed compassion on the crowds (8:2). When was the last time you were the recipient of an act of compassion? When was the last time you had compassion on someone else?

3. Jesus had previously fed five thousand people in a similar situation (6:30–44). Why was it important for Mark to include the feeding of the four thousand?

4. In light of the feeding of the five thousand, what is curious about the disciples' question (4)? Did the disciples simply forget Jesus' previous miracle, or was something else in play?

5. When Jesus returns to Israel, the Pharisees begin to question (debate) Jesus and test (tempt) him (11). Do the Pharisees really want to be convinced that Jesus is the Messiah, or do they want him to fail?

6. Look back through the Gospel of Mark. How many miracles can you find recorded for us so far? After all these, what "sign" from heaven could possibly convince the Pharisees that Jesus was the Messiah (11)?

7. What does Jesus' response tell us about his perspective regarding the Pharisees' request (12)?

8. From what you have seen so far about the Pharisees and Herod, what does Jesus mean by his warning (15)?

    a. What is the "yeast of the Pharisees?"

    b. How does the "yeast of the Pharisees" manifest itself in our world today?

9. What does "hardness of heart" mean to you (17)? How do we sometimes have "eyes but fail to see, and ears but fail to hear" (18)?

10. What is it that Jesus wants the disciples to understand (21)?

For Further Study

11. See Matthew's account in Matthew 15:32–39.

12. Compare the similarities and differences between the feeding of the five thousand (6:32–44) and the feeding of the four thousand (8:1–21).

13. Trace Jesus' route on a map from the Decapolis (7:31), to Dalmanutha/Magadan (8:10, cf. Matthew 15:39), to Bethsaida (8:22).

20

Seeing and Not Perceiving

Mark 8:22–30

THE GOSPEL OF MARK can be simply outlined as answering two basic questions: Who is Jesus (1:1—8:30); and what did he come to do (8:31—16:20)? Mark provides this structure for us in the opening sentence of his narrative: "The beginning of the gospel about Jesus Christ" (1:1). Since that time, we have been overwhelmed with clues to help us answer that first question.

Here is what we have been privy to so far. We have seen Jesus as he taught with authority and demonstrated that authority by casting out demons (1:27; 5:13). He has healed Peter's mother-in-law and cured various diseases (1:30–34). He has cleansed the leper (1:40), raised the paralytic (2:11), restored a man's hand (3:5), healed a bleeding woman (5:30), and even raised a girl from the dead (5:34). Along with his obvious ability to teach and physically restore mankind, he has demonstrated power over nature itself: by multiplying scanty provisions to feed five thousand (6:41), by calming the storm (4:39), and by walking on the water (6:49). Most recently, we have seen Jesus reach out to all people of all backgrounds by feeding a predominantly Gentile audience of four thousand (8:1–10). These all help answer the question: "Who is this?" (4:41).

But after this last miracle, Jesus gives the disciples a severe reprimand: "Do you still not understand?" (8:21). Jesus expects the disciples to have learned a lesson that they have not yet comprehended. And in the midst of that reprimand, we find a statement of Jesus that would be easy to simply pass by without notice: "Do you still not see or understand? . . . Do you have eyes but fail to see, and ears but fail to hear?"

(8:17–18). More than just a fleshing out of the question, "Do you still not understand?" it also serves as its own type of outline. Look again at the words Jesus uses—seeing and hearing, or inversely hearing and seeing. Then notice that the miracle of the feeding of the four thousand is itself flanked by two miracles: the healing of the deaf-mute (7:31–36), and now the passage before us, the healing of the blind man (8:22–25). Is this a strange coincidence, or is it another of Jesus' masterful teaching techniques?

An Intriguing Miracle (Mark 8:22–26)

> They came to Bethsaida,[1] and some people brought a blind man and begged Jesus to touch him. He took the blind man by the hand and led him outside the village. When he had spit on the man's eyes and put his hands on him, Jesus asked, "Do you see anything?" He looked up and said, "I see people; they look like trees walking around." Once more Jesus put his hands on the man's eyes. Then his eyes were opened, his sight was restored, and he saw everything clearly. Jesus sent him home, saying, "Don't go into the village." (Mark 8:22–26)

It is an intriguing miracle for many reasons. First, it is the only miracle in scripture where the healing is accomplished in stages. The blind man sees partially, and then after a second touch, he is healed completely. Tuck that away for a moment. It will become important for us later. It is also intriguing because it parallels the story of the deaf-mute in many ways. In both stories we see crowds bring two men to Jesus without comment about their individual desires. In both cases, Jesus takes the individual aside, away from their friends, the crowd, and possibly even the disciples. In both cases Jesus spits, and then commands the one who has been healed not to tell (the command not to tell, however, has nothing to do with the fact that Jesus spits). It is also interesting that both these miracles are only recorded for us in the Gospel of Mark. All those details make this story intriguing!

The most important parallel between these two accounts is one we dare not miss. Both of these miracle narratives are a fulfillment of Old Testament prophecy. We mentioned this before when we looked at the story of the deaf-mute. Isaiah records these words:

---

1. A few ancient manuscripts read "Bethany," but the strongest evidence is in support of the reading "Bethsaida." Mark calls it a village (8:23, 26), but it was a town of a few thousand people at the time of Jesus.

> They will see the glory of the Lord, the splendor of our God . . . Then will the eyes of the blind be opened and the ears of the deaf unstopped. Then will the lame leap like a deer, and the mute tongue shout for joy. (Isaiah 35:2, 5–6).

These two miracle accounts are juxtaposed in such a way as to clearly demonstrate who Jesus is. He is the one of whom Isaiah speaks. Sandwiched between the two miracles we find the question of Jesus to the disciples: "Do you have eyes but fail to see, and ears but fail to hear?" (8:18).

More than just a fulfillment of Isaiah's prophecy, the story of the healing of the blind man serves as an introduction and an interpretive tool for our next section.

An Intriguing Conversation (Mark 8:27–30)

Jesus leaves and takes his disciples on yet another road trip. They had just gotten home, were once again rejected by the Pharisees (8:11), and now they get as far away from Jerusalem as possible while remaining in Israel.[2]

> Jesus and his disciples went on to the village around Caesarea Philippi. On the way he asked them, "Who do people say I am?" They replied, "Some say John the Baptist; others say Elijah; and still others, one of the prophets." "But what about you?" he asked. "Who do you say I am?" Peter answered, "You are the Christ." Jesus warned them not to tell anyone about him. (Mark 8:27–30)

As they are traveling, Jesus asks the disciples a question: "Who do people say I am?" (8:27). What have you heard? It may have been awkward for them to answer this question. What should they say and what shouldn't they say? They offer a positive response. "Jesus, you have a favorable rating among likely voters. The man on the street holds a good opinion of you." The disciples answer, "Some say John the Baptist; others say Elijah; and still others, one of the prophets" (8:28). The opinion polls haven't moved much since King Herod first heard about Jesus—the same answers were given to him (6:14). It is curious, however, that the disciples don't answer the question completely. Jesus asks the question,

---

2. Caesarea Philippi was located near the uppermost part of Galilee. Herod Philip ruled the city in Jesus' time as part of his territory. It was named both for Caesar (Tiberius) and Philip. The population was largely non-Jewish.

who do people say that I am, and they respond by giving safe answers. The disciples don't offer the response of the Pharisees or the teachers of the law (3:22), nor do they report the response of the demons who have also testified about him (1:23; 5:7). The given answers may be safe, but they are inadequate. Jesus is more than just a herald like John the Baptist. Jesus is not "Elijah *redivivus*"—Elijah returned.[3] Jesus is not simply another in a long list of prophets like Jeremiah, Ezekiel or Daniel. These are all low and inadequate views of who Jesus really is. They all blur his true identity.

Not only have the answers not changed since Herod first asked about Jesus, they haven't changed much today. Many people, when asked about Jesus, believe him to simply be a good teacher, a moral leader, a philosopher, or even a prophet—but Jesus' true identity runs much deeper.

Jesus isn't surprised by the answers of the populace. He has asked this question, not because he doesn't know what people think of him, but because he wants to ask a second and more probing question of the disciples: "But what about you? . . . Who do you say I am?" (8:29). In the Greek, the "you" is emphatic. This is the all-important question—"What do *you* think?"

If the disciples weren't uncomfortable before, they are certainly uncomfortable now. If there was a moment of awkward silence, it doesn't last long. Who else but Peter would you expect to break the silence? Peter is always the first out of the boat, among the first to the tomb, the first to pull out a sword to take off an ear, the first to make prideful boasts—"Not me, Lord." Peter, true-to-form, responds with an unrehearsed, unplanned, spontaneous blurt: "You are the Christ" (8:29). Peter's answer is immediate and definite. Matthew gives us a fuller account: "You are the Christ, the Son of the living God" (Matthew 16:16).

We need to stop for a moment and analyze exactly what Peter means when he says, "You are the Christ." Many think of the term "Christ" simply as Jesus' surname. After all, isn't his full name Jesus Christ (as if it were akin to Steve Crane)? Actually, the term Christ is not a name, but a title. Christ is the Greek form of the Hebrew word *Messiah*. Jesus is his name, Christ is his office. In both Hebrew and Greek, it means "Anointed One." In the Old Testament, two offices required anointing—the positions of priest and king. Both are in play when it comes to Jesus.

---

3. Orthodox Jewish ceremonies still include a chair for Elijah at the Passover feast.

He is the anointed one, the king, and our high priest. Toward the end of the Old Testament period, the word "anointed" assumed an even higher position than king or priest. It denoted the one who would be anointed and empowered by God to deliver his people and establish his righteous kingdom. This ruler is spoken of as restoring David's kingdom to its former prosperity and greatness. Israel expected the Messiah to be political and national in nature. When he utters, "Jesus is the Christ!" Peter, for the first time, has acknowledged that Jesus is the predicted one of old who would come to rule over the people of God and over the nations of the earth.

The next observation might shock you. This is the first usage of the word "Christ" or "Messiah" since the first verse of the Gospel of Mark. Mark set forth his purpose clearly for us, "The beginning of the gospel of Jesus Christ" (1:1). This title has been strangely absent up till this point.[4] Finally, it re-emerges from the lips of Peter. Here is the long-awaited answer to the question that has been looming so large: "Who is this?" (4:41). Jesus is the Christ.

Peter has just had a monumental breakthrough in his declaration about Jesus—He is the promised Messiah. But then our story takes an interesting turn. "Jesus warned them not to tell anyone about him" (8:30). The question is, why does Jesus ask his disciples to remain silent?

We have stumbled over this type of question before. The Messianic secret seems to contain several elements. Sometimes Jesus commands people not to speak because he doesn't want certain types of character witnesses (i.e., the testimony of demons). Sometimes he tells people not to speak because he doesn't want to simply be known as a miracle worker. Sometimes he doesn't want people to speak because the crowds are too overwhelming and the pressure from opposition has become too great. Sometimes he commands people not to speak because they have an incomplete or improper view of who he is. I believe this last reason is in play in our passage.[5]

Peter has the right answer, but an improper understanding of who Jesus is. Jesus is the Christ. He is the promised Messiah. But Jesus is not Messiah in the sense in which Peter believes. The Jewish people thought the Messiah would be a military commander, a conquering general, and a reigning monarch. The Jews thought that the Messiah would expel the Romans, drive out the Gentiles, and establish a politically-independent

---

4. It will be used five more times in the Gospel of Mark.
5. Jesus will again give a prohibition to speak in 9:9.

Israel. But this is not Jesus' purpose. He is Christ, but not in the sense they understand.

Actually, this becomes the hinge in the Gospel of Mark. Mark has been leading us to answer this question: Who is this man? We now have our answer, but Mark will begin defining for us what Jesus came to do—and it's not what the disciples expect. In fact, in our very next passage, immediately after Peter gives his confession, Jesus will say these words: "Get behind me, Satan! . . . You do not have in mind the things of God, but the things of men" (8:33). Peter has the right answer (Messiah), but the wrong understanding (political leader). He is beginning to see who Jesus is, but not clearly.

Which actually brings me back to the miracle of restoring sight to the blind man. We previously stated that it is the only miracle recorded for us in scripture where the healing is not complete. Jesus touches the man, but his sight is blurry. He sees men walking around like trees. Let me ask you this question. Why? Why is the man not healed completely the first time? Why is his healing gradual? Is Jesus incapable of healing this man completely in one attempt? Is his problem so bad that it takes two treatments to accomplish the necessary results? Is it the man's lack of faith that prevents Jesus' power from working? No! Jesus' power is not limited by the circumstances or the man's faith. Jesus is using the blind man as an illustration of the disciples' sight. Achieving spiritual insight is normally a gradual process rather than a dramatic event. They are beginning to see Jesus—but not clearly. Their view of Jesus is still clouded and fuzzy. Jesus is saying to them, "You are not completely blind, but you don't yet see fully. You are seeing, but not perceiving." The disciples have witnessed the glory and greatness of Jesus, but do not yet understand fully why he came. That comes with the second touch—the second half of Mark.

In the first half of Mark, Jesus' power is prominent. In the second half, Jesus' weakness will take center stage. In the last half of the gospel of Mark we find that the "Son of Man did not come to be served, but to serve, and to give his life as a ransom for many" (10:45). Jesus is the Christ who came to reconcile people to God.

In the first century, the Scribes and the Pharisees were blind to who Jesus was. When the disciples begin to catch on to the identity of Jesus, their vision is blurred. But the real question, the all-important question is, "What about you?"

Study Questions

1. Share an "eye-opening" life experience.
2. What oddities do you find in the healing of the blind man?
3. What other miracles did Jesus perform that involved spittle? Why?
4. Why does Jesus heal the blind man in stages? Was Jesus incapable of curing the man instantly?
5. How is the healing of the blind man an illustration of the disciples' understanding of who Jesus was?
6. Who did the people of Jesus' day say he was (28)?
7. Who do people today say Jesus is?
8. What about you?
    a. Has your answer changed over time? How?
    b. When did you first begin to recognize Christ for who he really is?
9. Why is the question, "Who do you say I am?" (29) so important?
10. Why does Jesus command the disciples not to tell anyone (30)?
11. As for your understanding of Jesus, are you: almost blind, seeing with blurred vision, or enjoying 20/20 sight? Explain.
12. When we see Jesus clearly, who is he, what should he look like, what are some of his characteristics?
13. How can we improve our perception of who Jesus is?

For Further Study

14. See Matthew 16:13–20 and Luke 9:18–20.
15. Compare the healing of the deaf-mute man and the blind man. How are they similar? How are they different?
16. Locate Bethsaida and Caesarea Philippi on a map.

Part Two

What Did He Come to Do?
Mark 8:31—16:20

"For even the Son of Man did not come to be served, but to serve, and to give his life as a ransom for many."

Mark 10:45

21

Finders Weepers, Losers Keepers

Mark 8:31—9:1

I HAVE LONG TRIED to teach my children to reject the old saying, "Finders keepers, losers weepers,"[1] because I believe it is akin to stealing. My reasoning goes as follows: If you find something that does not belong to you, by definition it must belong to someone else. If you knowingly keep something for yourself that does not belong to you and don't try to find its rightful owner—it is no different than stealing. I ask my children, "How would you feel if you lost your Nintendo DSI and someone else found it only to have them say, 'Finders keepers, losers weepers'?"

In our passage, Jesus seems to have his own twist on our popular childhood saying. Jesus says, "For whoever wants to save his life will lose it, but whoever loses his life for me and for the gospel will save it" (8:35). Those who think they have found life, haven't. But those who lose life will gain it. In a profound allusion to coming events, Jesus also says, "If anyone would come after me, he must deny himself and take up his cross and follow me" (8:34). Following Jesus means giving up all rights to run our own lives and submitting ourselves to him for his leadership and lordship. Jesus is calling all disciples to exchange all that they are, for all that he is. We need to exchange self for Savior.

As we come to our passage, we have come to the second half of the Gospel of Mark. In part one, Mark answered the question, "Who is Jesus?" and after many amazing stories and miracles we found our

---

1. The old adage comes from an English proverb, "losers weepers, finders keepers." Songs by Elvis Presley (1963), the Beach Boys (1963), and Murray Kellum and Pearly Mitchell (1979) reversed the saying to its modern version of "finders keepers, losers weepers."

answer formed for us in the words of Peter's confession: "You are the Christ" (8:29). In the second half of the Gospel of Mark, Jesus' role as Messiah will now be defined. Mark is now answering the question: "What did Jesus Christ come to do?" Mark is not content in telling us about Jesus (1:1—8:30), but wants to demonstrate what Jesus came to accomplish (8:31—16:20).

As we read, we quickly find that while the disciples have stumbled across the right answer ("You are the Christ") to Mark's first question, they have a faulty understanding of what "Messiah" is all about. The disciples (as well as others) are looking for a conquering general, a military leader, and the establishment of a theocratic kingdom. Jesus makes it clear that a true disciple must do more than simply get Jesus' title right—that's only the first step. A true disciple must also understand what "Messiah" really means. The second half of Mark's Gospel spells out clearly what Jesus came to accomplish and lays out plainly what following Jesus requires. This new revelation and interpretation of Messiah comes as a great surprise to the disciples and serves as the turning point for the book. From this point on, Mark's purpose changes, as does the direction of Jesus. Jesus is on his way to Jerusalem, plotting his way toward Gethsemane and ultimately Golgotha.[2]

Interestingly enough, the first half of the Gospel of Mark moves rapidly, covering nearly three years of Jesus' ministry and showcasing the word "immediately." The second half of the Gospel of Mark slows remarkably, covering only the journey to Jerusalem and the final passion week of Christ. As I have previously stated, when Mark slows his pace, pay attention! Here we find Jesus headed to the cross and the true purpose of Messiah.

Steps to the Cross (Mark 8:31–33)

> He then began to teach them that the Son of Man must suffer many things and be rejected by the elders, chief priests and the teachers of the law, and that he must be killed and after three days rise again. He spoke plainly about this, and Peter took him aside and began to rebuke him. But when Jesus turned and looked at his disciples, he rebuked Peter. "Get behind me, Satan!" he said. "You do not have in mind the things of God, but the things of men." (Mark 8:31–33)

---

2. We will read several accounts as Jesus and the disciples pass through Galilee (9:30) and even stay in Capernaum (9:33), but Jesus' focus has clearly changed and has the events of Jerusalem in view.

As Jesus begins to tell the disciples about his coming suffering and death, the disciples are not merely shocked; what they hear from Jesus is perceived as inconceivable. Jesus had demonstrated his power as he commanded both the wind and the waves. He had demonstrated authority as he healed many and cast out demons. He had fed thousands and even raised the dead—how could any human authority take him prisoner, much less make him suffer, or put him to death? They cannot comprehend how the Messiah could possibly die. They do not appreciate what Jesus is telling them!

It is not that Jesus had given them no teaching about the cross—there were some allusions to what was going to happen. He had hinted about it earlier when he said, "But the time will come when the bridegroom will be taken away from them, and on that day they will fast" (2:20). In the Gospel of John, Jesus said, "Destroy this temple, and I will raise it again in three days" (John 2:19). Of course the building of which he spoke—the temple that would be destroyed and rebuilt—was his own body (John 3:21). Jesus had also said to Nicodemus, "Just as Moses lifted up the snake in the desert, so the Son of Man must be lifted up" (John 3:14). This too, was a foreshadowing of the cross. But these were riddles and allusions that the disciples did not comprehend or understand.

But now, Jesus "spoke plainly" to them (8:32). Jesus had put away the parables and the metaphors and plainly foretold his suffering and death. Jesus said, "He must suffer many things and be rejected . . . and that he must be killed" (8:31). Other gospel accounts warn of the impending beatings, scourging, and rejection that is going to happen. Mark says that Jesus, "Began to teach them that the Son of Man must suffer many things" (8:31). Jesus starts and continues speaking plainly about what is going to happen in the very near future. In fact, we find in our passage the first of three major predictions of Christ's passion (8:31; 9:31; 10:33–34). In these verses we learn that Jesus will suffer, be mocked, be spit upon, be beaten and scourged, be rejected, be killed, and rise again.

As Jesus speaks, his words do not sit well with Peter. Speaking once again on behalf of all the disciples, Peter takes Jesus aside and rebukes Him (8:32). The word "rebuke" (*epitimaō*, to rebuke, warn, or censure) is the same word that Jesus used when casting out demons. Jesus rebuked the demon-possessed man by saying: "Be quiet . . . Come out of him" (1:25). Can you imagine—Peter rebuking Jesus? In essence Peter is saying, "Jesus, you just be quiet. Don't talk like a fool. Nothing like what you are describing is possible." Matthew records Peter's actual words for us: "Never Lord . . . This shall never happen to you!" (Matthew 16:22).

As Peter chides, Jesus responds in amazing harshness with a rebuke of his own: "Get behind me, Satan" (8:33). Jesus utters here the very same phrase he used when being tempted by Satan in the wilderness: "Away from me, Satan" (Matthew 4:10). Jesus is not calling Peter Satan. But he is equating Peter's intentions with those of the prince of darkness. Jesus is essentially saying to his errant disciple, "I recognize those sentiments. They are the very type of words that came from Satan himself as he tried to tempt me in the wilderness. Peter, just like Satan, you are trying to tempt me away from God's purpose in my life." Peter is serving as Satan's mouthpiece. So are all who try to subvert God's purposes.

It is interesting that Peter is the first of many who will stumble over the cross. Paul writes:

> But we preach Christ crucified: a stumbling block to Jews and foolishness to Gentiles, but to those whom God has called, both Jews and Greeks, Christ the power of God and the wisdom of God. For the foolishness of God is wiser than man's wisdom, and the weakness of God is stronger than man's strength. (1 Corinthians 1:23–25)

Neither Peter, nor the disciples can comprehend what lies ahead for Jesus. They have their own understanding of what the Christ is supposed to accomplish and their plan does not include these difficult steps to the cross. Because of their misunderstanding of the role of Messiah, Jesus looks directly at the disciples as he rebukes Peter and says, "You do not have in mind the things of God, but the things of men" (8:33).

Make no mistake about it: Jesus is headed toward the cross. As shocking as those words must sound to the disciples, Jesus is not finished with his hard sayings. He now turns his attention to what a true disciple looks like. He has spoken plainly about what the Messiah must do, now he turns his attention to what a follower of the Messiah must do.

Steps of Discipleship (Mark 8:34—9:1)

I mentioned earlier that our passage is the first of three major predictions of Christ's passion (8:31; 9:31; 10:33–34). It is also interesting that with each major prediction of Christ's suffering we find a discussion of what it means to be a follower of Jesus (8:34–38; 9:35; 10:29–39). When Jesus tells the disciples that he will suffer and be killed (8:34–38), he challenges them to deny themselves and take up his cross (8:34–38). When he reminds them of his arrest and betrayal (9:31), he teaches them that the first must be last and the greatest must become a servant (9:35). When Jesus warns the disciples that he will be mocked, condemned and killed (10:33–34), he asks them if they can drink the cup with him (10:29–39).

> Then he called the crowd to him along with his disciples and said: "If anyone would come after me, he must deny himself and take up his cross and follow me. For whoever wants to save his life will lose it, but whoever loses his life for me and for the gospel will save it. What good is it for a man to gain the whole world, yet forfeit his soul? Or what can a man give in exchange for his soul? If anyone is ashamed of me and my words in this adulterous and sinful generation, the Son of Man will be ashamed of him when he comes in his Father's glory with the holy angels." And he said to them, "I tell you the truth, some who are standing here will not taste death before they see the kingdom of God come with power." (Mark 8:34—9:1)

Here we find three qualifications of following Christ. First, a Christ follower must deny himself (8:34). Self-denial is not a popular subject. It was not a popular idea then, nor is it now. In fact, this statement goes against the tide of American thought. The very idea of denying oneself is counterculture. The only phrase we are used to hearing that contains the word "deny" may be the phrase "deny yourself nothing." We are told to take what we can get, grab what we can, and always demand respect. We are all looking to gain something for nothing. We want a deal—we think that everyone owes us something, but we are not willing to work to get it. We want the easy way out, we want a shortcut, we want something for nothing. Most of us have bought into a good portion of the world's ideology—we live for things of the world and are consumed with the cares of this age. Our chief pursuits are our careers, our homes, our cars, our hobbies, and even our wardrobe.

Denying yourself is a difficult concept. It would have been a much easier sentence if Jesus had said, "Deny yourself . . ." and then put a noun at the end of the sentence. He could have said, "Deny yourself coffee," or tasty food, or money, or fame, or just about anything, and we could work towards that goal. The problem is that we can deny ourselves each of these items and still be left with ourselves. Jesus wants to dismantle our very selves. We are to renounce self and reorient the principles of life around Christ. You might ask, "To what extent?" Jesus answers that question for us.

The second qualification of a follower of Christ is that we are to take up a cross. Here Jesus uses vivid imagery. The idea of taking up a cross was not a novelty. The cross was an instrument of death, and criminals were expected to carry their own cross or at least the cross-beam. For the Jew, the very concept was repugnant. The Old Testament clearly spells out that:

If a man guilty of a capital offense is put to death and his body is hung on a tree, you must not leave his body on the tree overnight. Be sure to bury him that same day, because anyone who is hung on a tree is under God's curse (Deuteronomy 21:21–22).

The New Testament echoes that sentiment: "Cursed is everyone who is hung on a tree" (Galatians 3:13). Because of this, crucifixion carried an unparalleled stigma.

The Romans (remember Mark was written to Romans) were even more familiar with public execution than the Jews. While Roman citizens themselves were actually exempt from this type of death, crucifixion was a method of torture they had perfected. Crucifixion was for the death of a slave or reserved for those who committed treason; who deserted in the face of an enemy; who committed piracy, assassination, or led sedition and revolt. It was not only a painful death, but a public disgrace and mockery. The common Roman colloquialism was: "Crucifixion is dying a thousand deaths." Cicero, a Roman philosopher and statesman, is attributed as saying, "Let the very name of the cross be far away not only from the body of a Roman citizen, but even from his thoughts, his eyes, his ears."

Jesus takes this disgraceful imagery of the cross—the instrument reserved for political criminals and radicals—and thrusts it right to the very forefront, right in front of the disciples' eyes and ears and lets them see and hear it vividly. Jesus is calling them to put "self" to death. Like a criminal bearing the crossbar, a disciple is to take up his cross. But where is a disciple to go?

The third qualification of a disciple is that he is to follow Christ's way. Just as Jesus denied himself and took up his cross, we are to do the same. Jesus is not asking you to do something he hasn't done. He is asking you to follow what he has already accomplished. He is calling you to walk in the steps he has already walked. We often have misunderstood Jesus' intentions. Jesus is not asking us to follow him, while maintaining a semblance of our own lifestyle. Jesus is asking us to follow him completely. Following him requires that we do so in every area of our lives. The formula of discipleship is not: "Your way + Jesus' way = the right way." The correct formula is: "Jesus' way = your way."

To drive home this message, Jesus asks several rhetorical questions and uses the literary device of restatement. He first starts with a paradoxical statement: "For whoever wants to save his life will lose it, but whoever loses his life for me and for the gospel will save it. What good is it for a man to gain the whole world, yet forfeit his soul? Or what can a man give in exchange for his soul?" (8:35-37). The point seems clear enough. We must exchange all we are for all he is. We are to trade self for Savior. We probably should stop and answer Jesus' question. What good is it to gain the whole word yet lose your soul? What can a man give in exchange for his very soul?

In case we still have not caught the point, Jesus makes this statement: "If anyone is ashamed of me and my words in this adulterous and sinful generation, the Son of Man will be ashamed of him when he comes in his Father's glory with the holy angels" (8:38). A true disciple is one who follows completely, continually, and unashamedly.

At this point Jesus makes a curious statement. "I tell you the truth, some who are standing here will not taste death before they see the kingdom of God come with power" (9:1). Of course the question that needs to be answered is this: Of what does this speak? There are essentially four possible answers to this question. First, some have suggested that this verse refers to Christ's second coming. The obvious objection comes with Jesus' phrase, "Some who are standing here will not taste death" (9:1). This answer would require either a very old apostle or a previous second coming which most of us missed. Actually, both of these solutions have been postulated by those who hold to this answer!

A second answer given is that Jesus is specifically referring to the transfiguration, which takes place in the very next section of the Gospel of Mark (9:2-13). Context makes this answer very attractive—along with the fact that during the transfiguration, Peter, James and John undoubtedly see Jesus' glory, identity, and power as the Son of God. This event certainly meets with the "power" motif that Jesus describes and is at least partially in view. I don't, however, believe it was solely in view—it seems a little awkward for Jesus to emphatically tell his disciples that "some standing here will not taste death," when the transfiguration occurs only six days later (9:2). Was Jesus concerned that a disciple would die within the week?

Not unlike answer two, a third solution points to one of any number of specific events that occur in the life of Christ (or the church) which demonstrates the power of Jesus. Many such events have been targeted. Some point to the death, burial, and resurrection of Jesus; others to his ascension. Some suggest that this refers to the Day of Pentecost with the coming of the Holy Spirit and the establishment of the church. Still others suggest that the destruction of the temple in Jerusalem is in view. Again most, if not all, of these suggestions are a possibility.

The fourth answer runs in the same vein, but suggests that our answer should not be limited to one single event. The answer might include all of the above mentioned: the transfiguration; the death, burial, and resurrection; the ascension; the Day of Pentecost and the establishment of the church; and the destruction of the temple in Jerusalem in AD 70, and possibly others as well. Actually, the key to understanding this passage rests not in the particular event to which it describes, but in the fact that the Kingdom of God will be undeniably visible and will come with great power even though Jesus will suffer persecution and death. Yes, Jesus will be killed, but after three days he will rise again (8:32) and his kingdom will be established with power.

Understandably, it was a shock to the disciples to learn that Jesus was going to suffer and die. Similarly, it is also shocking for the follower of Christ to realize that Jesus calls us to follow in his footsteps. We are to deny ourselves, to take up his cross, and follow. Many today still don't understand.

It is interesting that in the first century, the disciples expected Jesus to be a political ruler and king. If that were his objective, it would be understandable for the disciples to request a position of authority on the right or left of his throne. They could envision themselves as officials and political statesmen. The problem, however, was that their understanding of Messiah was wrong. A wrong view of Messiahship leads to a wrong view of Discipleship. Jesus came not to be served, but to serve and give his life a ransom for many (10:45). As his disciples, he expects us to do the same.

We must understand that those who think they have found life, will lose it; but those who lose life, will keep it. The old adage had it wrong. Finders will be weepers, while losers will be keepers.

Study Questions

1. We have all heard the childhood phrase, "finders keepers, losers weepers." Do you agree with its basic premise? Why or why not?
2. What four things does Jesus prophesy about himself in verses 31–32?
3. How does Peter go from being the "star pupil" (8:29) to being in the doghouse (8:33)?
4. Why does Peter feel the need to rebuke Jesus (8:32)?
5. Why did Jesus call Peter Satan (8:33)?
6. How did Peter have in mind the things of men rather than the things of God (8:33)?
7. What differentiates the things of God from the things of men? What happens when we focus our attention on the things of men rather than the things of God?
8. According to verses 34–38, what is involved in being a Christ-follower?
9. What does it mean to deny yourself (8:34)? What does this look like in everyday life? Where do you need to improve?
10. Why is self-denial a prerequisite for being a Christian (8:34)?
11. What does it mean to "take up his cross" (8:34)? What does this look like in everyday life? In what areas do you need to improve?
12. What does it mean to truly follow Jesus (8:34)? How well have you been following?
13. How would you explain the paradox contained in verse 35 (finders weepers, losers keepers)? What does it mean to lose your life in order to save it?
14. What is the answer to the questions Jesus poses in verses 36 and 37?

15. Why the warning against being ashamed of Christ and his words (8:38)? How are we sometimes ashamed of Jesus?

For Further Study

16. See Matthew 16:21–28; Luke 9:21–27.

22

Resplendent Glory

Mark 9:2–13

OUR PASSAGE IS AMONG the most enlightening, intriguing, and important scriptures recorded for us in the Gospel of Mark—and yet, to my recollection, I have never heard it preached. While it finds its way into an occasional Sunday School lesson, it is not included in what we normally teach as salvific[1] history. Yet almost every student of the Bible would rank it among the highlights in the life of Christ: the baptism of Jesus; the death, burial, and resurrection; and the transfiguration.[2] Why then the discrepancy between its level of importance and its prominence? The answer, in part, comes with its difficulty. It is a hard passage to apply and understand.

Much of our angst for preaching this passage stems from the fact that it is rampant with Old Testament allusions and themes which first-century readers would have understood, but that we often miss. To understand what is at stake, a reader needs to be a student of the Old Testament.

> After six days Jesus took Peter, James and John with him and led them up a high mountain, where they were all alone. There he was transfigured before them. His clothes became dazzling white, whiter than anyone in the world could bleach them. And there appeared before them Elijah and Moses, who were talking with Jesus. Peter said to Jesus, "Rabbi, it is good for us to be here. Let us put up three shelters—one for you, one for Moses and one for Elijah." (He did not know what to say, they were so frightened.) Then a cloud appeared and enveloped them, and a

---

1. Having the intention or power to bring about salvation or redemption.
2. Some might include the ascension in this list.

voice came from the cloud: "This is my Son, whom I love. Listen to him!" Suddenly, when they looked around, they no longer saw anyone with them except Jesus. As they were coming down the mountain, Jesus gave them orders not to tell anyone what they had seen until the Son of Man had risen from the dead. They kept the matter to themselves, discussing what "rising from the dead" meant. And they asked him "Why do the teachers of the law say that Elijah must come first?" Jesus replied, "To be sure, Elijah does come first, and restores all things. Why then is it written that the Son of Man must suffer much and be rejected? But I tell you, Elijah has come, and they have done to him everything they wished, just as it is written about him." (Mark 9:2–13)

This disclosure of Jesus' true significance as the Son of God, comes right on the heels of Jesus' teaching on his impending death.

Background

Jesus has taken the disciples to Caesarea Philippi (the northernmost point of Israel) where he has plainly told them that he will suffer many things, be rejected, and killed (8:31–32). Jesus is headed toward Jerusalem, Gethsemane, and Golgotha,[3] and his focus is squarely on the cross. In view of this, Jesus takes the disciples up on a mountain to pray (Luke 9:28).

That Jesus chooses to pray should not surprise us. He has carved out time to pray at every major juncture during his ministry: the selection of the disciples (Luke 6:12); when he is tempted by the crowds to become a popular Messiah (1:35); and later, as he faces crucifixion (14:32).

The fact that Jesus goes to the mountainside to pray shouldn't surprise us either—mountains are often associated with closeness to God and readiness to receive his words, and this is in keeping with Jesus' *modus operandi*. Which mountain he chooses to ascend is up for discussion. The traditional site for this event[4] is Mount Tabor—a hill that stands 1,932 feet high and is located about 20 miles to the southwest of the Sea of Galilee. Mount Tabor, while on the way from Caesarea Philippi to Jerusalem, is probably not regarded as a "high mountain"[5] (9:2). Others

---

3. His path will take him through Galilee and Capernaum one more time.
4. As established by Saint Helena in the early fourth century.
5. The city of Jerusalem itself stands almost six hundred feet higher than Mount Tabor at 2,500 feet above sea level.

have suggested that Jesus traveled with his disciples to Caesarea Philippi (8:27) with Mount Hermon as his ultimate destination. Mount Hermon is about twelve miles to the north of Caesarea Philippi and in contrast to Mount Tabor, reaches skyward 9,232 feet—it probably qualifies! Ultimately, the specific mountain is not as important in our story as the events that unfold on the mountain. What happens is extraordinary— Jesus is transfigured.

Climbing the Hill (Mark 9:2-8)

"After six days Jesus took Peter, James and John with him and led them up a high mountain, where they were all alone. There he was transfigured before them" (9:2). For obvious reasons, our event is referred to as the transfiguration. To understand this passage, I believe there are several questions we must ask and answer. The first is simply, what exactly is transfiguration?

The word "transfiguration" (*metamorphoō*) is the word from which we get our English word "metamorphosis." It literally means to be changed in form or transformed. It is commonly pictured as the caterpillar changing to the butterfly or the tadpole becoming a frog—their very forms change. Cartoons depict this as well. A Saturday morning TV highlight used to be the *Mighty Morphin' Power Rangers* whose catch phrase was, "It's morphin' time." More recently we find the Transformers movies with Optimus Prime—he looks like a truck, but he is much more. Optimus is really an alien robot—there is more than meets the eye. This is true of Jesus as well. With Jesus, however, we have no fictional cartoon character. Here we get a glimpse into the very essence of Jesus' being. Jesus is the very Son of God who morphed into man (concealing his true identity). But we get a glimpse of that identity during the transfiguration. This is the greatest of Immanuel moments. Philippians chapter 2 sketches the picture for us:

> Who, being in very nature [*morphē*] God, did not consider equality with God something to be grasped, but made himself nothing, taking the very nature [*morphē*] of a servant, being made in human likeness. And being found in appearance as a man, he humbled himself and became obedient to death—even death on a cross! (Philippians 2:6–8)

Jesus is God who emptied his God *morphē* and took the *morphē* of a slave. In our passage, the original *morphē* forces its way back into our world momentarily. In a sense, for Jesus, this is a re-transfiguration!

Jesus is portrayed as clothed in dazzling white: "Whiter than anyone in the world could bleach them" (9:3). This is certainly an allusion to the prophecy of Daniel: "His clothing was as white as snow; the hair of his head was white like wool. His throne was flaming with fire" (Daniel 7:9), and brings to mind the description of Jesus in Revelation as:

> Someone "like a son of man," dressed in a robe . . . His head and hair were white like wool, as white as snow, and his eyes were like blazing fire . . . His face was like the sun shining in all its brilliance. (Revelation 1:13–16)

When God chooses to reveal himself, amazing things happen. On the mountain, the disciples got a glimpse of Jesus' true *morphē*.

When the disciples see Jesus with Moses and Elijah, they don't know how to respond. In typical fashion Peter breaks the silence: "Rabbi, it is good for us to be here. Let us put up three shelters—one for you, one for Moses and one for Elijah" (9:5). A second question we should answer is: Why does Peter suggest tents?

Various reasons are given to explain Peter's response. Some believe Peter is suggesting the need to spend some more time at this spot: "Let's camp out." Others have suggested that Peter wants to build a monument on the mountain to commemorate the occasion—a new tabernacle or temple—something to remember the moment by. Still others point to the specific word used here for tent (*skēnē*), and conclude that Peter has in mind either the Festival of Tents (which celebrate God's protection and guidance in the desert) or the Tent of Meeting upon which the cloud of God's presence would descend (Exodus 40:34) and signified Moses' Sinai experience. No matter what Peter was thinking, he wasn't thinking clearly, because we get this commentary: "He did not know what to say, they were so frightened" (9:6).

But a more pressing question looms large. Why do we have the appearance of Moses and Elijah? The simple Sunday School answer is: "Moses represents the Law, and Elijah represents the prophets." This is true. However, I believe the answer runs much deeper. We probably need to be reminded of the stories of these two men.

Moses was the leader of God's chosen people and the one to whom God gave the law. God called to Moses and said, "Come up to the Lord, you and Aaron, Nadab and Abihu . . . You are to worship at a distance, but Moses alone is to approach the Lord; the others must not come near" (Exodus 24:1–2). Moses went up the mountain and a cloud covered the mountain. Moses was required to wait for six days. Finally, Moses was allowed to enter the cloud and he remained there for forty days and forty nights (Exodus 24:15–18).

When Moses descended the mountain with the Ten Commandments God had given him, he discovered that the people had rebelled against God and had built for themselves a golden calf to worship (Exodus 32). "When Moses approached the camp and saw the calf and the dancing, his anger burned and he threw the tablets out of his hands, breaking them to pieces at the foot of the mountain" (Exodus 32:19).

Moses was surrounded by a stubborn, obstinate, and wicked people. He began complaining to God and finally says to God, "Now show me your glory" (Exodus 33:18). God, in Jack Nicholson fashion, essentially tells him, "You can't handle my glory!" But God calls Moses to the mountain, hides him in the cleft of a rock, covers his eyes while his *Shekinah* passes by, and then removes his hand, allowing Moses to see his back (Exodus 33:23). When Moses returns to the Israelites, "His face was radiant because he had spoken with the Lord . . . and they were afraid to come near to him" (Exodus 34:29–30). Moses had gotten too close to the nuclear reactor of the universe.

Notice all the parallels of our story with that of Moses: a mountaintop experience, taking three witnesses to the mountain, being engulfed by an overshadowing cloud, the mention of six days, objects glowing brilliantly, a voice speaking from heaven, and all those who witness the events are alarmed. There is no doubt Mark wants us to pick up this imagery.

Moses, who met face to face with God on a mountain, now meets with Jesus. It is this very same Moses who said, "The Lord your God will raise up for you a prophet like me from among your own brothers. You must listen to him" (Deuteronomy 18:15). Notice, it is those last three words which make their way into our passage (9:7).

Our second story is of Elijah the prophet. Elijah is not a writing prophet, like many others, but a verbal prophet. We know the story of Elijah as he fights the prophets of Baal—challenging them to a duel on Mount Carmel. Two altars are prepared, and the lines clearly demarcated: "Call on the name of your god, and I will call on the name of the

Lord. The god who answers by fire—he is God" (1 Kings 18:24). Elijah not only taunts the prophets of Baal, he ups the ante by digging a trench and pouring water around his own altar. The gods of the false prophets remain strangely quiet, but when Elijah calls on God, "The fire of the Lord fell and burned up the sacrifices, the wood, the stones and the soil, and also licked up the water on the trench" (1 Kings 18:38). Following the sacrifice, four hundred and fifty prophets of Baal are killed in the Kishon Valley.

But then things get rough for Elijah. Ahab and Jezebel make a threat to kill Elijah within twenty-four hours (1 Kings 19:2). Elijah is afraid and runs for his life. After running a great distance, he holds a pity-party and even prays that his own life be taken (1 Kings 19:4). God, however, sends an angel to strengthen and feed him. God then calls him to travel for forty days to Mount Horeb (also known as Mount Sinai) where God meets him—first powerfully through wind, earthquake, and fire; then through a still, small voice. "When Elijah heard it, he pulled his cloak over his face" (1 Kings 19:13).

The comparisons between what happens on Mount Sinai with Moses and Elijah are undeniable. Both men meet God on a mountain. Both speak, and are the only men who speak with God on Mount Sinai. Both men face rejection at the hands of their people. Both come to the mountain for encouragement. Both are vindicated by God. Both make statements about the coming Messiah. The only two men who ever converse with God on Sinai, now meet with Jesus on the mountain.

Coming Down the Hill (Mark 9:9-13)

Elijah and Moses vanish as quickly as they appear, leaving the disciples frightened. Jesus has been re-figured as the Jesus they are accustomed to seeing. Together they leave that place and travel down the mountain and we see familiar language: "Jesus gave them orders not to tell anyone" (9:9). This is the last time this prohibition to speak is given in the Gospel of Mark. It is also the first time we find a stated reason—they are to wait until the Son of Man has risen from the dead.

> It is only in the light of the crucifixion and resurrection that Jesus' true person can be understood, for he is not just a wonderful visitor from heaven or an especially favored man given mystic glory but the one called to "give his life as a ransom for many" (10:45).[6]

---

6. Hurtado, p. 146.

But the disciples are confused. As they walk, they are discussing the resurrection of the dead, and they ask this question: "Why do the teachers of the law say that Elijah must come first?" (9:11). The whole incident is based on the last words recorded for us in our Old Testaments: "Remember the law of my servant Moses, the decrees and laws I gave him at Horeb for all Israel. See, I will send you the prophet Elijah before that great and dreadful day of the Lord comes" (Malachi 4:4–5). The Scribes and Pharisees were denying that Jesus was the Messiah because Elijah hadn't yet come. But if Elijah had just now appeared—to which the disciples were witnesses—how could Jesus be the Messiah, having preceded him?

At this point Jesus actually agrees with the teachers of the law: "Elijah does come first" (9:12). Matthew's account helps clarify this for us: "Then the disciples understood that he was talking to them about John the Baptist" (Matthew 17:13). Then Jesus adds, what about the "Great and dreadful day of the Lord?" (Malachi 4:5). This is a prophecy about the Suffering Servant: "The Son of Man must suffer much and be rejected" (9:12). Jesus is the Messiah, but as Messiah he is headed for the cross.

Setting Out for a Second Hill (Mark 9:12)

As we have pointed out previously, Jesus is headed for Jerusalem, Gethsemane, and Golgotha. There he will face the hill called Mount Calvary. This forces me to answer one last question: Why the transfiguration? This might seem similar to a question we answered earlier. The earlier question, however, was "what," not "why." Why the transfiguration? Why Moses and Elijah? Why here? Why now? Why this?

It was for Jesus' benefit! Jesus is headed to the cross where he will be rejected, suffer, and die. Jesus will be rejected and abandoned. Jesus will sweat what appear to be drops of blood in the Garden and pray, "Father, take this cup from me" (14:36). The transfiguration is a "pep rally" of sorts for Jesus. Elijah and Moses can come and say, "We've been there! We have been ridiculed and rejected, but we were vindicated by God. You can do this." Jesus goes to the mountain top to pray—he has been seeking God's will. And God sends Moses and Elijah to strengthen him and prepare him for what is soon to happen. Luke summarizes their conversation for us: "They spoke of his departure, which he was to accomplish in Jerusalem" (Luke 9:31). Elijah and Moses prepped Jesus for "trial."

The transfiguration is also for the disciples' benefit. They were being called to take up their own cross and follow Jesus. They had in mind a different type of Messiah, but they receive a glimpse of the Son of God. Peter writes for us:

> We did not follow cleverly invented stories when we told you about the power and coming of our Lord Jesus Christ, but we were eyewitnesses of his majesty. For he received honor and glory from God the Father when the voice came to him from the Majestic Glory, saying, "This is my Son, whom I love; with him I am well pleased." We ourselves heard this voice that came from heaven when we were with him on the sacred mountain. (2 Peter 1:16–18)

It is interesting that Elijah and Moses spoke with God on the mountain. But Jesus is much greater. More than a law giver, more than a prophet. It is Jesus of whom God said, "This is my Son, whom I love. Listen to him" (9:7). Elijah and Moses listened to God, but God tells the disciples to listen to Jesus. Jesus alone of the three on the mountain is clothed in glory, majesty, power, and splendor. Jesus is Immanuel—God incarnate.

Study Questions

1. If you could take three people up a mountain to meet God, who would you take and why?

2. What does it mean to be "transfigured?" How does Jesus' appearance change (2–3)?

3. Why was Jesus transfigured?

4. What is significant about Elijah and Moses appearing on the mountain with Jesus (4)? Why these two?

5. How might Peter, James and John recognize Elijah and Moses (4)?

6. Why did Peter feel compelled to build three shelters (5)?

7. What would the appearance of the cloud communicate to Peter, James, and John (7)?

8. Why does Jesus command Peter, James, and John not to tell anyone what they have seen until after he has risen from the dead (9)?

9. What questions did Peter, James, and John have as they came down the mountain (11)? What questions would you have been asking?

10. How did Jesus answer their question about Elijah (12-13)? How does Elijah's experience foreshadow Jesus' experience?

11. How would the transfiguration be an encouragement to Jesus as he drew nearer to Jerusalem and his time of death?

12. How would the transfiguration be an encouragement to the disciples? See 2 Peter 1:16-21.

13. How would you describe your relationship with God right now: In the valley? On the mountaintop? Climbing? Other?

14. Where have you grasped a bit of Jesus' glory in a special way?

For Further Study

15. Matthew 17:1-9; Luke 9:28-36.

16. Moses on Sinai: Exodus 24:1—32:18; 33:12—34:35. Elijah on Sinai: 1 Kings 19:1-21.

17. Read Deuteronomy 18:15 and Malachi 4:4-6.

18. Locate these three mountains on a map: Mount Sinai (Horeb), Mount Tabor, and Mount Hermon.

23

Misplaced Confidence

Mark 9:14–29

Life is hard and some battles are not easily won, especially when it comes to our spiritual life! Ebbs and flows and highs and lows are not uncommon and certain aspects of faith are far more difficult than others. If you have ever experienced spiritual failure, or have been overcome by doubt, this passage will bring help and encouragement.

> When they came to the other disciples, they saw a large crowd around them and the teachers of the law arguing with them. As soon as all the people saw Jesus, they were overwhelmed with wonder and ran to greet him. "What are you arguing with them about?" he asked. A man in the crowd answered, "Teacher, I brought you my son, who is possessed by a spirit that has robbed him of speech. Whenever it seizes him, it throws him to the ground. He foams at the mouth, gnashes his teeth and becomes rigid. I asked your disciples to drive out the spirit, but they could not." "O unbelieving generation," Jesus replied, "how long shall I stay with you? How long shall I put up with you? Bring the boy to me." So they brought him. When the spirit saw Jesus, it immediately threw the boy into a convulsion. He fell to the ground and rolled around, foaming at the mouth. Jesus asked the boy's father, "How long has he been like this?" "From childhood," he answered. "It has often thrown him into fire or water to kill him. But if you can do anything, take pity on us and help us." "'If you can'?" said Jesus. "Everything is possible for him who believes." Immediately the boy's father exclaimed, "I do believe; help me overcome my unbelief!" When Jesus saw that a crowd was running to the scene, he rebuked the evil spirit. "You deaf and mute spirit," he said, "I command you, come out of him and never enter him again." The spirit shrieked, convulsed him violently and

came out. The boy looked so much like a corpse that many said, "He's dead." But Jesus took him by the hand and lifted him to his feet, and he stood up. After Jesus had gone indoors, his disciples asked him privately, "Why couldn't we drive it out?" He replied, "This kind can come out only by prayer." (Mark 9:14–29)

For purposes of evaluation, I would like to divide our passage into four scenes.

Helpless Disciples (Mark 9:14–19)

Our story begins as Jesus, Peter, James, and John come down the mountain only to find the other nine disciples struggling—things have not gone as they have planned. It is worth noting that this particular event follows immediately on the heels of the transfiguration account in all the Synoptic gospels.[1] Here we find one more similarity between the transfiguration of Jesus on the mountain and Moses on Mount Sinai—when Moses descended the mountain, he found a faithless, faltering Israel.

Jesus finds the disciples in the midst of a large crowd, arguing with the teachers of law (9:14). We are not specifically told what they are arguing about, but the context suggests it revolves around the disciples' inability to deliver a demon-possessed boy from his unwelcome occupant. The boy's father has sought out Jesus, but finds the disciples instead. It is likely that the teachers of the law are using the disciples' failure as one more reason, amongst many, to reject Jesus. Not only have the disciples failed in their attempt to help the distraught father, they are unable to answer the vocal objections of their detractors.

At this point, we are confronted with a very real question: Why were the disciples unable to cast out this demon? The disciples had certainly been commissioned to do so (3:14–15), and they had previously been successful (6:13) in their endeavors. The answer to our question is not given immediately, but comes later, after more details unfold.

Mark's focus rests primarily on the disciples' immediate circumstances, and we get the impression that they are receiving a tongue-lashing from the teachers of the law when Jesus suddenly appears from his descent down the mountain. As Jesus enters the crowd, the people are "overwhelmed with wonder" (15). The phrase, as it is translated for us, is one we are accustomed to seeing in Mark. We have been "Marveling

---

1. It is also interesting to note that Mark's account is actually the longest recorded for us.

with Mark" throughout his gospel. In fact, as we come to our passage, Mark has now used five different words for being amazed: *ekthambeō, ekplēssō, thaumazō, thambeō, and existēmi*). He will later add two more: *ekthaumazō* and *thaumastos*.

There are several explanations given for the people's awed reaction. Some suggest that Jesus, like Moses, experienced residual effects from his transfiguration experience—his face might have been glowing like that of Moses (Exodus 34:29). This seems unlikely, however, in view of Jesus' instructions to the disciples to keep the event a secret (9:9)—a difficult task if he was still radiating a divine glory. Others suggest that Jesus' very presence provoked wonder and astonishment much like people today would respond to a celebrity. This view certainly holds merit and is in keeping with how crowds have previously responded to Jesus' presence.

Something else might also be in play, however. The specific word used here for wonder (*ekthambeō*) is slightly different than what we have previously seen, and is the first of three times it is used in the Gospel of Mark (9:15; 14:33; 16:5). It has the nuance, not only of amazement, but of shock and alarm. Imagine a scene where the teachers of the law are arguing with the disciples (presumably about the Christ), when none other than Jesus himself appears. The critics who were minimizing Jesus in his absence will now have to deal with him directly.

We have presumably all had the awkward experience of talking about someone (either positively or negatively), only to realize they are standing behind us and have heard every word we said. It is a startling and uncomfortable experience. This may be at play in our passage—Jesus has appeared on the scene at the very moment when he is the topic of discussion. For the disciples, Jesus has appeared at an opportune time!

As Jesus arrives, he asks a probing question that shifts the hostilities away from his disciples. Jesus simply asks about the nature of their argument: "What are you arguing with them about?" (9:16). It is curious that neither the disciples, nor their detractors, answer Jesus' question. Rather, a man in the crowd responds, "Teacher, I brought you my son, who is possessed by a spirit" (9:17). We then are given a graphic description of the symptoms his son has experienced at the hand of the evil spirit: "Whenever it seizes him, it throws him to the ground. He foams at the mouth, gnashes his teeth and becomes rigid" (9:18).

Jesus' response is unexpected: "O unbelieving generation"[2] (9:19). It might be helpful to stop for a moment and ask to whom this comment is directed. The crowds? Possibly. The teachers of the law? This certainly seems to apply. The father? Perhaps. But notice the next two phrases of Jesus: "How long shall I stay with you? How long shall I put up with you?" (9:19). These sentiments seem to be specifically directed at the disciples. Jesus has already been with them nearly three years—do they still not understand? When will they get it? Jesus has only a few more short weeks. In Matthew's account Jesus says to the disciples, "You have so little faith" (Matthew 17:20). The disciples have walked with him so long, and still they don't believe.

The cry of Jesus reveals his bitter disappointment with them. In a crucial moment they have failed because of their lack of faith. Jesus rebukes them, but does not abandon them. He then says, "Bring the boy to me" (9:19). Jesus then turns his attention to the boy and his father.

A Desperate Father (Mark 9:20–24)

As the disciples bring the boy to Jesus, the demonic spirit throws the boy into a convulsion. Jesus then asks a question, not because he needs to know, but to illicit a response from the forlorn father: "How long has he been like this?" (9:21). The question causes the father to reflect upon the situation and realize how desperate the picture really is: "From childhood . . . It has often thrown him into fire or water to kill him" (9:21–22).

The father initially brings his son to Jesus for healing, but in his absence the disciples have failed—will Jesus also be impotent? Is this man's faith misplaced? What little faith the man once possessed has been shaken. "But if you can do anything, take pity on us and help us" (9:22).

Jesus turns the man's words around and sends them back with some force, correcting the "if" clause.[3] The question is not "if" Jesus is capable, but whether one believes—the deficiency is not with Jesus. "Everything is possible for him who believes" (9:23). Jesus' response should not be used to suggest that believing will magically produce anything we desire, only that Jesus' power is available by faith to meet any need that arises

---

2. The term for "generation" (*genea*) is used in 8:12 and 8:38 with reference to those who deny and oppose Jesus.

3. The Greek literally reads, "The if you can." Jesus repeats the doubt expressed by the father and challenges it.

in the course of ministering in his name. We are not promised that faith can accomplish anything, but that those who have faith will not set limits on the power of God.

At this point the man utters a phrase which is one of the most remarkable statements made by any man in the Gospel of Mark. It makes my top ten list of favorite sayings in this book. It resonates with anyone who has struggled with the issue of doubt: "I believe, help me overcome my unbelief" (9:24). In the midst of anguish and fear, the man is pleading for help to trust more completely.

Remarkably, Jesus accepts the man in his sincerity. How can this be? To the analytical among us, the statement seems contradictory and even mutually exclusive. How can one believe yet doubt? Actually, we need to understand that faith and doubt are not opposites but run along the same continuum. Faith is not the absence of doubt, nor is doubting necessarily the same as disbelief. Belief and disbelief are opposites while doubt resides in varying degrees between the two. Faith and doubt are varying degrees of certainty. It is helpful to know that a person can believe in God and still have real doubts. Through the years, I have verbalized many: "Why is life so unfair? Why does God allow suffering? Why doesn't God answer my prayers? Why does evil seem to prosper? How can God be three and one?" I daresay that we have all had doubts of some variety, to varying degrees, at one time or another. The person who has never experienced doubt has likely never thought critically. What a comfort to know that a person can believe while retaining some areas of doubt. But we need to ask: What divides the one who believes from the one who denies? One person chooses to believe through their doubts while the other chooses to let their doubts lead them to disbelief.

The third scene presents Jesus doing battle with an evil spirit.

A Reluctant Demon (Mark 9:25–27)

As we come to this section of the story we find the last exorcism recorded for us in the book of Mark. In some ways, this demon seems to show a heightened sense of resistance. Early demons testified about who Jesus was (1:24) or begged Jesus not to torture them (5:7), but here the demon defiantly resists, even as Jesus gives him a double rebuke: "I command you, come out of him and never enter him again" (9:25). The evil spirit will not go quietly, but "shrieked, convulsed . . . violently and came out. The boy looked so much like a corpse that many said, 'He's dead'" (9:26).

I love the different emphasis that each of the Synoptic writers puts on this story. Matthew records for us that "He was healed from that moment" (Matthew 17:18). Luke tells us that Jesus "Healed the boy and gave him back to his father" (Luke 9:42). Mark says, "Jesus took him by the hand and lifted him to his feet" (9:27). Literally, this passage reads that Jesus raised him (*egeirō*). Mark uses the very same language that would be used of Jesus just weeks later.[4]

Before moving on, take note of the demonic intentions for the little boy—from them we can learn about Satan's true intentions. Satan's purpose is to distort and destroy the image of God in man. He longs to hurt, harm, maim, destroy and kill. Satan's desire is to separate a child from his father. Each of these runs directly contrary to what Jesus wants to accomplish in us. Jesus wants to restore in us the image of God and plans to reunite Father and child.

Insufficient Prayer (Mark 9:28–29)

As we come to our last two verses, we finally arrive at the answer to the question that has been taunting us since verse 18. Why couldn't the disciples expel the demon from the young boy? The disciples ask Jesus this question specifically (9:28) to which Jesus simply responds, "This kind can come out only by prayer"[5] (9:29).

It is interesting that Jesus is not recorded as having said a prayer before driving out the demon. So how can it be said that this kind of demon can only come out in this way? I would suggest that Jesus is not talking about a single prayer, but a lifestyle of prayer. Jesus is not suggesting the formulation of a few words. The prayer Jesus talks about is not a magic formula. Prayer is not reciting the right incantation. Prayerful communion is not simply stopping at a given situation and trying to force God's hand or convince him to act. A committed prayer life is a lifestyle of ultimate dependence upon God. It is to be a constant, persistent, ongoing relationship with him. A committed prayer life shows that our ultimate dependence rests upon God and not ourselves. Jesus is

---

4. The word "raised him" is the same term used to describe the action of God in raising Jesus from the dead in Mark 14:28. It is also used in Acts 3:15; 4:10; and 5:30.

5. Some add "and fasting." This has weak manuscript support and was likely added because fasting was of interest to the early church (Acts 13:2; 14:23). "Fasting" was likely added to prayer in other texts as well: Acts 10:30 and 1 Corinthians 7:5.

asserting that only this type of prayer life—a persistent, prayerful communion with God—can and will be effective.

William Lane writes,

> The disciples had been tempted to believe that the gift they had received from Jesus (6:7) was in their control and could be exercised at their disposal. This was a subtle form of unbelief, for it encouraged them to trust in themselves rather than in God.[6]

The disciples suffered from misplaced confidence. They too struggled with unbelief.

As we look at this passage, it would be easy to make application for the non-Christian. "Non-Christian, you need to understand that you should not place your confidence in self. You need to repent—change who you are living for, and confess—acknowledge that there is a God and you are not him; acknowledge that there is a God and you need him." And while this is certainly true, I must remind you that this is not the purpose of this passage.

This story does not focus on the non-Christian or even the nominal Christian. In our passage, the disciples take center stage. The disciples—the ones who had left everything to follow Jesus—had misplaced their confidence and in so doing had failed miserably. They had trusted in their own abilities rather than in the power of God.

We are not any different. We often trust in self rather than God. We have convinced ourselves that by our own efforts we can prevail. We are sons and daughters of enlightenment, thinking we can solve not only our own problems, but the problems of the world. We have been told, "If you put your mind to it, you can do anything." But we need to quickly come to the realization that if our confidence is in ourselves, our confidence is misplaced.

Let me spiritualize our story for a moment with the understanding that I fully believe that this man's son was literally demon possessed. Allow me, however, to take our application up the ladder of abstraction. We all have our own demons: problems with anger, addictions to narcotics, greed, laziness, lust, etc. Some of our demons are of a different kind: health problems, financial problems, or relationships. Some we are able

---

6. William Lane, *The Gospel According to Mark*, *The New International Commentary of the New Testament*, 335–336.

to control, but others are particularly stubborn. Am I right? We need to hear the words of Jesus: "This kind can come out only by prayer."

Isn't it time that we commit ourselves to a prayerful life which shows ultimate dependence upon God? A faithful life, a life that unleashes the power of God, is one that is lived in prayerful communion and total dependence upon him and him alone. Don't be deluded by misplaced confidence!

Study Questions

1. When you were younger, what issues were most likely to trigger an argument within your family?
2. While the three disciples were up on the mountain, what problem were the other nine having?
3. What do you think the argument was about in verse 14?
4. As the boy's father, how would you feel during the argument?
5. How do you think the disciples' inability to heal the boy affected the father?
6. Read verse 19 carefully.
    a. What was Jesus' reaction to the situation?
    b. Who was Jesus specifically speaking to?
7. Why were the people amazed at seeing Jesus (15)?
8. What do we learn from the father who brought to Christ his demon-possessed son?
    a. Can you relate to him?
    b. Are most believers this honest about their faith?
9. When have you felt like the father of the boy, one moment saying, "I do believe," and the next, "Help me overcome my unbelief"?
10. Is it wrong to have doubts? What is the difference between doubt and disbelief?
11. What is the hardest aspect of Christianity for you to believe? What doubts have you experienced in your faith? Which hit you the hardest?

12. What would help you silence the doubts you feel? Does the father's statement in verse 24 help you? How?

13. Does this passage promise that if we believe, all our prayers will be answered (9:23)? See also: 1 John 5:14–15; James 4:3; Luke 11:8–10; 18:14.

14. Jesus tells the disciples they could not drive out the evil spirit because some come out only by prayer (29). What does this tell us about prayer? Do you ever take prayer for granted?

For Further Study

15. See Matthew 17:14–23; Luke 9:37–45.

24

Redefining Greatness

Mark 9:30–50

There is so much to be studied in this passage, it is difficult to even know where to begin. Maybe the best introduction to this passage is simply to assert that Jesus takes the norms of the day and turns them on their head. Jesus reverses normal protocol and turns everything upside down. His sayings were so counterculture that they were misunderstood by his own disciples; and, if we are going to understand this passage, we may also have to modify some of our own values and beliefs. Jesus redefines greatness.

> They left that place and passed through Galilee. Jesus did not want anyone to know where they were, because he was teaching his disciples. He said to them, "The Son of Man is going to be betrayed into the hands of men. They will kill him, and after three days he will rise." But they did not understand what he meant and were afraid to ask him about it. They came to Capernaum. When he was in the house, he asked them, "What were you arguing about on the road?" But they kept quiet because on the way they had argued about who was the greatest. Sitting down, Jesus called the Twelve and said, "If anyone wants to be first, he must be the very last, and the servant of all." He took a little child and had him stand among them. Taking him in his arms, he said to them, "Whoever welcomes one of these little children in my name welcomes me; and whoever welcomes me does not welcome me but the one who sent me." "Teacher," said John, "we saw a man driving out demons in your name and we told him to stop, because he was not one of us." "Don't stop him," Jesus said, "No one who does a miracle in my name can in the next moment say anything bad about me, for whoever is not against us is for

us. I tell you the truth, anyone who gives you a cup of water in my name because you belong to Christ will certainly not lose his reward. And if anyone causes one of these little ones who believe in me to sin, it would be better for him to be thrown into the sea with a large millstone tied around his neck. If your hand causes you to sin, cut it off. It is better for you to enter life maimed than with two hands to go into hell, where the fire never goes out. And if your foot causes you to sin, cut it off. It is better for you to enter life crippled than to have two feet and be thrown into hell. And if your eye causes you to sin, pluck it out. It is better for you to enter the kingdom of God with one eye than to have two eyes and be thrown into hell, where 'their worm does not die, and the fire is not quenched.' Everyone will be salted with fire. Salt is good, but if it loses its saltiness, how can you make it salty again? Have salt in yourselves, and be at peace with each other." (Mark 9:30–50)

Greatness Exemplified (Mark 9:30–32)

Our account is the second of three passages (8:31; 9:31; 10:33–34) in which Jesus prepares his disciples for his upcoming passion. In each instance, Jesus not only predicts his death and resurrection, but he also uses the events surrounding his own death to teach the disciples the meaning of true discipleship. In the first instance, Jesus plainly said that he would suffer many things and be killed (8:31). He then made application to them: "If anyone would come after me, he must deny himself and take up his cross and follow me. For whoever wants to save his life will lose it, but whoever loses his life for me and for the gospel will save it" (8:35–36).

In the first passion prediction, Jesus taught the disciples with the crowds present (8:34). But as the cross looms ever nearer, Jesus isolates himself from the crowds in order to focus his attention solely on equipping the Twelve. His second prediction contains the previous language of being killed and rising again, but also includes a new element: "The Son of Man is going to be betrayed into the hands of men" (9:31).

The disciples "did not understand what he meant" (9:31) and would not comprehend fully until after the resurrection. It is interesting, however, that in their confusion they were afraid to ask for clarification (9:32). Several explanations have been proposed to suggest why. Some assert that the disciples were afraid to ask for fear of receiving a rebuke. Peter certainly experienced this when the topic last surfaced (8:33), although in that instance it was Peter who first attempted to rebuke Jesus.

Others suggest that the disciples feared not a rebuke, but Jesus' answer—they didn't want to hear Jesus promulgate his impending death. In either case, they remained silent, confused and troubled.

Actually, there are several elements of Jesus' statement that would have been puzzling and difficult for the disciples to reconcile. First, they were still blinded by their wrong understanding of what the Messiah was to accomplish. They were looking for a political leader who would restore Israel and drive out the Romans and remove the Gentiles. The very thought that the Son of Man[1] would die was inconceivable.

Second, there is a wordplay in Greek between the phrases, "the Son of Man" and "hands of men" (*ho huios tou anthrōpou . . . eis cheiras anthrōpōn*). This phrase gives Jesus' words a riddle-like characteristic—as if Jesus was speaking in parables. The disciples may have been trying to find the hidden meaning behind the teaching.

Finally, the NIV's use of the word "betrayed" (*paradidōmi*), while not inaccurate, may be misleading. Our passage literally reads that the Son of Man will be "handed over" or "delivered." At first glance this might appear benign, but it makes a theological presupposition that might be unwarranted. Let me illustrate. When you read the phrase that Jesus was "betrayed into the hands of men," chances are you immediately think of Judas and the role he played—a human agent who betrayed Jesus. While historically accurate, this view insinuates that Judas, a mere man, delivered Jesus into the hands of men. The wording is not only a little redundant (man betraying into the hands of men), but it puts Judas in the driver's seat. The phrase literally reads: "the Son of Man was handed over into the hands of men." The question is: Who allowed such a thing to happen? Ultimately, it was not Judas, but God who delivered Jesus over, and it was Jesus who willingly consented. The renderings of other translations like the NASB or RSV are to be preferred here: "The Son of Man is to be delivered into the hands of men." The point is not that man will take Jesus by force, but that Jesus came to give his life as a ransom for many. Jesus gave himself freely and willingly to suffer rejection and death and in so doing, we find "greatness exemplified."

After Jesus predicts his own sacrifice, he uses this to teach the disciples about discipleship.

---

1. The phrase "the Son of Man" comes from Daniel 7:13 which depicts one who is given authority, glory and sovereign power from all people and nations.

Greatness Redefined (Mark 9:33–41)

As Jesus and the disciples traveled from Caesarea Philippi[2] to Capernaum, an argument arose among the disciples about who was the greatest (9:34). Actually, it is easy to speculate why this might have happened (and no, the argument did not center around Muhammad Ali). Jesus had just taken three of the disciples up the mountain where they experienced the transfiguration and witnessed Jesus talking with Moses and Elijah. As they returned down the mountain, "Jesus gave them orders not to tell anyone" (9:9). Upon reaching the base of the mountain, the backpacking foursome found that the other nine disciples had failed to expel a demon from a young boy. With human nature in play, can you imagine the possible ensuing discussions among them? One of the nine simply needed to ask, "What happened on the mountain?" How might Peter, James, and John reply? "Sorry, we can't tell you!" or "It's for us to know and you to find out!" It would be easy for the three to have an attitude of smugness over their being chosen for the elite field trip—they were the honor society, the gifted and talented.

The discussion could have just as easily gone a different direction. One of the three could have simply asked the question: "What went wrong casting out that demon?" Did any of the three possibly think or even verbalize, "If I had been there, it wouldn't have been a problem"? Either way, you can see how the conversation could quickly lead to a heated argument about greatness.

Whatever the conversation entailed, Jesus asks a simple question that shames them all: "What were you arguing about on the road?" (9:33). The mere fact that Jesus was aware of their conversation gives rise to their embarrassment. (I wonder how many of our conversations and activities would bring us pause if we realized Jesus' presence?)

Seizing upon a teachable moment, Jesus calls the Twelve to himself, sits down in Rabbinic fashion and redefines greatness. "If anyone wants to be first, he must be the very last, and the servant of all" (9:35). In one simple statement, Jesus reverses normal protocol and turns everything upside down.

Taking a child in his arms he says to them, "Whoever welcomes one of these little children in my name welcomes me; and whoever welcomes me does not welcome me but the one who sent me" (9:37). Jesus teaches

---

2. It is my opinion that the transfiguration occurred on the high mountain of Hermon rather than the traditional location of Mount Tabor. See previous chapter.

the disciples to welcome children. Again, a reversal of cultural values. On a sliding scale of prominence in first century, a child[3] (*paidion*) was near the bottom in terms of importance. At the top of the "Who's Who" list were the adult males—especially those with wealth, power, or appointed positions. Of course, as chosen Apostles to the Messiah of Israel, the disciples consider themselves to be at the pinnacle of Christ's top-ten list.[4] But as the disciples listen to Jesus, I'm sure they nod their heads in agreement.

It is important to recognize the repeated use of the phrase, "in the name" (9:37, 38, 39, 41). It becomes an important catchword and serves a pivotal purpose. In the first century, this phrase was used in a royal sense for one speaking on behalf of a king. This kingship principle regarded the words spoken on behalf of a king by his representative as binding as the words of the king himself. So when the disciples hear these words, they are likely thinking, "Okay Jesus, as your ambassadors, your chosen elite, we will welcome children in your name—we will carry out your orders."

But then John speaks up: "We saw a man driving out demons in your name and we told him to stop, because he was not one of us" (9:38). Notice his thinking: "Jesus! A non-chosen, non-appointed one was speaking 'in your name.'" Understand, John was confident that Jesus would commend him for what they had just done. John was expecting a pat on the back and an "atta-boy" for his efforts. The disciples had this understanding: "If you are not with us, you have no place among us." Again, Jesus turns their thinking upside down and says, "For whoever is not against us is for us" (9:40). Jesus values the people whom the disciples consider to be beneath them. Jesus' principle for valuing people is not based on what they have achieved, or accumulated, or invented, or inherited. The value of each person is established by the value God sets on them—every person is of worth, no matter how great or small.

Jesus also says that every good deed done in his name, no matter how small, will not go unnoticed. Even the smallest sacrifice of service done in the name of Christ is significant (9:40).

Jesus certainly does redefine greatness. But as Jesus continues, he almost seems a trifle miffed at the disciples and utters some rather strong language.

---

3. This Greek word refers to a very small child or infant. Interestingly enough, in Aramaic (the language Jesus was likely speaking), the term for child and servant is the same.

4. I know there were twelve, but they were arguing about who was the greatest.

The Cost of True Greatness (Mark 9:42–48).

"If anyone causes one of these little ones who believe in me to sin, it would be better for him to be thrown into the sea with a large millstone tied around his neck" (9:42).

The common understanding of this passage pictures Jesus, still with a little child in his arms saying, "Don't you dare cause one of these precious little children to sin." I need to stop at this point and say that this certainly is an appropriate application. But there are two words in our text that I would like to point out for you.

The first is the word rendered "sin" by the NIV. It is actually the word *skandalizō*: which means to offend, to stumble, or even cause to fall away. It is the very word from which we get our term scandal or scandalous. The second word is translated as "little one" (9:42). Take note that it is not the word "child" like we often suppose. Jesus has actually changed terminology. When Jesus first spoke, he used the word "infant" or "small child" (*paidion*). Now he uses a different word. The word used here (*mikros*) can mean small, humble, or of lesser importance. Jesus' point may not focus only on the small child in his arms, but may also refer to the man the disciples have deemed insignificant. "If you cause anyone to stumble or turn from me (even one whom you deem less important), it would be better for you to be equipped with concrete boots and thrown into the Hudson River."

Jesus then tumbles the tables once more. Rather than judging others (i.e., the man driving out demons), you need to take a closer look at yourselves. With four "it is better" statements (9:42, 43, 45, 47), Jesus pictures the seriousness and eternal consequences of sin in our lives. "If your hand causes you to sin, cut it off . . . if your foot causes you to sin, cut it off . . . if your eye causes you to sin, pluck it out. It is better for you to enter the kingdom of God with one eye than to have two eyes and be thrown into hell"[5] (42–47).

Is this just hyperbole? Probably. But the point is clear: anything that keeps you from becoming what God wants you to be is sin, and anything that might prevent your ongoing, eternal relationship with him requires radical surgery.

---

5. The Greek word *geenna* comes from the Hebrew term which originally refers to a ravine south of Jerusalem, *gē-hinnom*. By the time of Jesus, the term had acquired a metaphorical usage denoting the fiery judgment that would be inflicted upon the wicked at the last judgment.

Conclusion (Mark 9:49–50)

As we come to the end of our passage, we find what may be the most difficult sentence in the Gospel of Mark. I have found no less than a dozen different interpretations of what is meant by the phrase: "Everyone will be salted with fire" (9:49). Two seem worthy of consideration. Some suggest that the imagery here comes from Leviticus[6] and suggests that we are to offer our very selves as offerings (salt) on the altar (fire).[7] Others suggest that salt was used as a preservative (to keep things pure) and that fire represents persecution.[8] Both seem to make sense in context.

The next verse, while not difficult, has critics. Some are opposed to Jesus saying that salt is good.[9] Others argue that salt cannot lose its saltiness.[10] The point Jesus is making, however, is that Christians are to be salt. Jesus verbalizes this in the Sermon on the Mount. "You are the salt of the earth . . . You are the light of the world" (Matthew 5:13–14). Jesus makes it clear that as Christians, we too, are to be counterculture. We are to reverse normal protocol and turn everything upside down.

If you are truly salt, you will realize that your job description is that of servant. If you are salt, you will value the least among us. If you are salt, you will not cause anyone to stumble nor will you scandalize the name of Christ. If you are salt, you will be more concerned with your own shortcomings than the shortcomings of others. If you are salt, you will strive for peace. "Have salt in yourselves, and be at peace with each other" (9:50).

Study Questions

1. Who is the "greatest" person you have ever met?

2. What do you consider to be characteristics of a great person?

3. What lesson of Jesus was so important that he didn't want any distractions (30–31)?

---

6. "Season all your grain offerings with salt. Do not leave the salt of the covenant of your God out of your grain offerings; add salt to all your offerings" (Leviticus 2:13).

7. Early scribal glosses tie this passage directly to the sacrificial system.

8. This would seem to be particularly helpful to a Roman audience suffering persecution.

9. I would concur that salt tastes good, even if its health properties are debated by some.

10. Salt from around the area of the Dead Sea was mixed with impurities and often acquired a stale, flat taste.

4. Why were the disciples concerned about which of them was the greatest (33)? What events could have fueled the disciples' discussion?

5. As a disciple, how would you feel when Jesus asked about the argument?

6. Why does Jesus use a little child as an object lesson about true greatness in his kingdom (36)?

7. How does Jesus define greatness? How does Jesus' idea of greatness differ from what is portrayed by television or pursued by most people (35)?

    a. In this context, what does it mean to be last?

    b. What does it mean to be the servant of all?

8. What is significant about doing acts of service in the name of Christ (37, 38, 39, 41)?

9. What should be our response/attitude to those with whom we differ on doctrine, but who are still preaching the clear message of salvation in Christ (38–41)?

10. What do verses 42–48 have to say about the seriousness of sin or causing someone to stumble?

11. If you had to give up a hand, a foot, or an eye, which would you give up (43)?

12. What four things does Jesus say are "better" (42–47)?

13. Short of cutting off body parts, what do you need to cut out of your life in order to avoid sin or cause someone else to stumble?

14. How does the command to be at peace (50) relate to verses 42–49?

15. Are you at peace with others? What can you do to "salt" your relationships with peace this week (50)?

For Further Study

16. See Matthew 17:22–23; 18:1–9; Luke 9:44–50.

17. Notice the catchwords: "in the name" (9:37, 38, 39, 41); "to cause to sin" [stumble] (9:42, 43, 45, 47); "fire" (9:43, 48, 49); and, "salt" (9:49, 50).

25

It's Just a Piece of Paper Anyway!

Mark 10:1–12

Jesus then left that place and went into the region of Judea and across the Jordan. Again crowds of people came to him, and as was his custom, he taught them. Some Pharisees came and tested him by asking, "Is it lawful for a man to divorce his wife?" What did Moses command you?" he replied. They said, "Moses permitted a man to write a certificate of divorce and send her away." "It was because your hearts were hard that Moses wrote you this law," Jesus replied. "But at the beginning of creation God 'made them male and female.' 'For this reason a man will leave his father and mother and be united to his wife, and the two will become one flesh.' So they are no longer two, but one. Therefore what God has joined together, let man not separate." When they were in the house again, the disciples asked Jesus about this. He answered, "Anyone who divorces his wife and marries another woman commits adultery against her. And if she divorces her husband and marries another man, she commits adultery." (Mark 10:1–12)

ONE OLDER COUPLE WAS known for their happy and successful marriage. One day a friend asked the wife if she and her husband had ever considered divorce. "Divorce!" she replied, laughing. "Oh, no, never! But murder, often!" Most who have been married any length of time can probably identify with that statement.

I know that divorce is a sensitive topic. It makes people uncomfortable. Though this passage makes us ill at ease, we all know its importance. In America alone each year there are over one million divorces. By definition, that means two million adults will be directly involved. Add the collateral damage of children involved as a result of those marriages and the number easily multiplies into the millions. Even in so-called "amiable divorces," no one escapes the suffering.

But the harmful consequences swell well beyond those immediately entangled. I daresay there is not a single adult left in our society who has not heard a child, parent, friend, or acquaintance describe the agony of divorce. One need not be a victim of divorce to sense the hurt, hate, and animosity of those involved. So while the topic of divorce is sensitive, it is also relevant.

Ours is a difficult passage. In these verses, Jesus once again makes radical demands on his disciples that were counterculture. We shouldn't expect the teaching to be easy. Jesus' words weren't easy to swallow in the first century, nor are they in the twenty-first century.

The Background of the Pharisees' Trap (Mark 10:1–2)

As we pick up the story, Jesus has left Capernaum and is headed south toward Jerusalem. This signals the close of Jesus' ministry in the area that has been his center of operation. He would never return again. His journey takes him through the region of Judea, beyond the Jordan.[1] This area is often called Perea, which simply means beyond. Although Jesus tried to remain incognito (9:30), the crowds found him and, as usual, he began to teach them. As he taught, the Pharisees came forward to test him.[2] Mark makes a point in telling us that they weren't seeking the truth, but were setting a trap. The Pharisees asked Jesus a legal question which was designed to place Jesus in a predicament:[3] "Is it lawful for a man to divorce his wife?" (10:2).

---

1. Judea was the southern Roman province in Palestine, in which the chief city was Jerusalem. The Jordan River, which runs south from Lake Galilee to the Dead Sea, formed the eastern border of both Galilee and Judea. In order to avoid going through Samaria (which laid between Galilee and Judea), Jews would cross over to the eastern shore of the Jordan and travel southward to cross back into Judea near Jericho. Mark here alerts his readers that Jesus is indeed heading toward Jerusalem for the final stage of his ministry.

2. To put to the test (*peirazō*). The same word appears in 8:11 and 12:15, where other hostile questions are directed at Jesus.

3. The Pharisees have been plotting to destroy him since 3:6. They hope not only to derail him, discredit him in the eyes of the people, and cause him to lose popularity; but also seek to have him killed.

At this point, I want to stop and make the first of three observations from our passage.

Observation One: Jesus is responding to hostile questioners who are bent on trapping him.

The Pharisees are not seeking truth, they are deliberately testing Jesus to find fault with him. They want to trap him. We should not expect to find pastoral help for divorced persons here. The Pharisees are using a controversial topic of the day to place Jesus in an impossible situation in order to find reason to bring accusations against him. That is their purpose. Jesus' response targets their intentions. To understand this passage, you must understand that the purpose of this passage is not to console those who are going through difficult times in their marriages, or struggling through divorce,[4] but to correct those who have evil intentions toward Jesus.

With that in mind, we should ask: What is the trap the Pharisees are setting? It comes in the form of a well-thought-out and carefully calculated question that they hope will place Jesus at odds with the majority of people, as well as at odds with Moses—the great giver of God's law. For centuries divorce had been a volatile issue of debate—a bed of hot coals—with two opposite schools of thought. The Pharisees took a very liberal position toward divorce, following the teachings of Rabbi Hillel. According to this position, a man could divorce a woman for just about any reason whatsoever: taking her hair down in public, talking to other men, burning the toast, taking command of the remote control, or too much salt in the falafel.[5] Women were treated almost like merchandise to be bought, sold, or traded. In fact, history demonstrates that the Pharisees were among the leading practitioners of easy divorce— divorcing their wives for any cause at all. Some Pharisees actually taught that the practice was not only permissible, but sometimes mandatory.

At the other extreme were the less influential faction of rabbis who maintained that divorce was never permissible.[6] The narrow-minded,

---

4. We can look to other passages to see the pastoral nature of Jesus. For example, see John 4:15–35 where Jesus deals with a woman who has been married five times, and the person she is currently living with is not her husband.

5. A patty of ground chickpeas and other vegetables and spices, deep-fried and usually served in a pita.

6. Some held that divorce was only permissible in the case of infidelity, but they

hard-line view of Rabbi Shammai was not only unpopular, but, like the liberal position of the Pharisees, was also unscriptural.

The Pharisees had heard Jesus speak before and knew that he did not hold to the liberalized view of divorce (Matthew 5:32). They expected Jesus to reject divorce and therefore associate himself by default with the narrow-minded and intolerant view. Not only would he be risking his own popularity, but he would seemingly be placing himself against the law of Moses—for Moses himself had allowed divorce.

But that was only part of their trap. Remember also that Mark intentionally places this incident in the region of Judea. This was the region of Herod Antipas, who we have encountered before. Herod had originally married a Nabatean princess for political purposes, but had divorced her to marry Herodias—the wife of his half-brother, Philip. John the Baptist had condemned Herod's marriage, and ultimately lost his head because of it (6:14–29). The Pharisees were not only expecting Jesus to take an unpopular view by opposing divorce, they were secretly hoping that Jesus might suffer the same fate as John the Baptist before him.

But Jesus is wise to their plans and quickly turns the tables on them by directing them to the words of Moses.

The Background of the Law of Moses (Mark 10:3–5)

The way Jesus responds is interesting for a variety of reasons. First, he turns the argument around. They want to trap him by asking a question, but he asks a question in return. "What did Moses command you?" (10:3). Rather than giving his opinion (which they would not accept anyway), he directed them back to Moses and therefore Scripture.[7]

The Pharisees answer, "Moses permitted a man to write a certificate of divorce and send her away" (10:4). Notice that Jesus' answer to the question of the legality of divorce is phrased as a question about what Moses *commanded*. The Pharisees respond by saying that Moses *allowed* the writing of a certificate of divorce. They cite Scripture to justify their actions—specifically Deuteronomy 24:1: "Moses permitted a man to write a certificate of divorce and send her away." But while the Deuteronomy passage does assume the practice of divorce by a written

---

were only a fraction of the minority.

7. This should be our approach as well. Too often people are quick to give opinions and remiss in turning to Scripture as the ultimate authority.

certificate, in context, it is actually a prohibition. It prohibited a husband remarrying a woman he had divorced, after being remarried and divorced again.

Men would divorce for a couple of reasons: one was financial (for the dowry); one was physical (they had something else in mind). In both cases a man would marry a woman, but then be attracted to another. He would divorce the first, marry the second to have as his wife, but as soon as he got what he wanted, he would divorce her and remarry the first (or yet another). Some of these marriages lasted only minutes or hours,[8] but the men's actions were, nonetheless, deemed legal.

The purpose of the law of Moses was to place restrictions on this practice in an attempt to curb the divorce rate. First, rather than simply uttering a few words (I divorce you), a man was required to provide a written certificate of divorce, making it a matter of public record and providing some legal protection for the woman. Second, a man was not able to divorce, remarry, divorce and take back his original wife—it was forbidden by the law. Also, the law required that the woman be found guilty of some form of indecency.[9]

Here we need to state a second principle to clarify the situation.

Observation Two: Divorce was frivolous and rampant.

We tend to think of divorce as a uniquely twenty-first century problem—and while America's divorce rate has reached pandemic proportions,[10] it is not uniquely a modern problem. It was a serious problem in the fifteenth century BC, and continued to be a problem in the first century AD as well.

The Pharisees are correct in saying that the Law of Moses allowed for divorce. Divorce was tolerated. But notice why Moses allowed divorce. Jesus says, "It was because your hearts were hard that Moses wrote you this law" (10:5). Divorce always is due to the hardness of heart on the part of one or both individuals. Moses allowed divorce, but only be-

---

8. There is some scarce evidence that time limits were imposed on those who wanted to divorce within only minutes.

9. The Rabbis argued over what constituted indecency.

10. In America, forty-three percent (43%) of marriages end in divorce in the first fifteen years. Second marriages fare far worse with a failure rate of sixty-three percent (63%). Third marriages fail seventy-three percent (73%) of the time.

cause of sin in the world.[11] God's plan has always been for faithfulness. In fact, God's will is recorded for us in Malachi: "Has not the Lord made them one? In flesh and spirit they are his. And why one? Because he was seeking godly offspring. So guard yourself in your spirit, and do not break faith with the wife of your youth. 'I hate divorce,' says the Lord God . . ." (Malachi 2:15–16).

Jesus then takes the conversation back farther in time. Not just to the law of Moses, but to the writings of Moses—Genesis chapters 1 and 2. Jesus takes the issue of marriage and divorce back to the very beginning.

The Background of Marriage (Mark 10:6–9)

While it is true that Moses gave laws to regulate divorce, divorce was not and is not God's will for marriage. Jesus wanted the Pharisees to discover what God commanded, not just what Moses permitted, in contrast to the Pharisees, who were looking at the procedures for ending marriage. Jesus took them back to God's intended purpose for marriage by looking at the creation account. One does not find God's intentions by looking at Deuteronomy 24:1–4, but at Genesis chapters 1 and 2.

> But at the beginning of creation God 'made them male and female.' 'For this reason a man will leave his father and mother and be united to his wife, and the two will become one flesh.' So they are no longer two, but one. Therefore what God has joined together, let man not separate. (Mark 10:6–9)

The word translated "joined" (*syzeugnymi*)[12] is literally the word "glued together." Most couples married in a church heard these words at their wedding. And here we find the heart of the matter concerning marriage and divorce. Marriage is not just a festive ceremony or a simple piece of paper.[13] Marriage is a God-created union between a male and female.[14] Marriage is not about a sexual act, or a civil service; nor is divorce simply the ending of some wedding vows. Divorce is wrong because it

---

11. Jesus' response to the Pharisees shows that we cannot simply search Scripture for proof-text escape clauses, but we must look for God's true desires.

12. Used only here and Matthew 19:6.

13. These sentiments about marriage are all too often voiced.

14. Many who would like to redefine marriage should take up their argument with God himself who defines marriage for us.

separates two individuals whom God has joined together. In the act of marriage, two people somehow become one in the eyes of God. This is the mystery of marriage and is what makes marriage unique. Marriage is not just a legal contract or civil procedure, it is a "God event." The bond of marriage is a bonding that God performs—therefore what God yokes together, Jesus commands that a man should not separate. Those are not my words, they are the words of Jesus. So important is the marriage bond that when the Bible speaks about the union between Jesus and the church he uses this as the illustration.[15]

We must be very careful in our teaching that we do not start to substitute our assumptions of what is right and wrong, or our opinions about marriage for the intention of God, which is clear in Scripture.

The disciples are shocked about what Jesus says, because his words go against the very values of the age in which they live. So when they are alone, they ask him about it (10:10). Jesus responds with two statements that are foreign to the ears of the first-century audience—and likely to ours. First, "Anyone who divorces his wife and marries another woman commits adultery against her" (10:11). In the first century, a man could never commit adultery against a woman, only against another man. And second, "If she divorces her husband and marries another man, she commits adultery" (10:12). This was even more of a shock, because a Jewish woman could not initiate a divorce.[16]

Jesus reverses the values of Jewish society. A man who divorces (contrary to God's intention in creation) and remarries, commits adultery against his first wife. A woman who divorces (contrary to God's intention in creation and Jewish culture) and remarries, also commits adultery. There is no way to minimize or rationalize this to avoid Jesus' explicit teaching on this subject. Jesus corrects society's lax view of divorce by saying that one who divorces and marries again commits adultery. The adultery is against the first partner, not the new partner. Other texts teach us that the only exceptions are sexual immorality, or if an unbelieving partner desires/initiates the divorce.

They are understandably shocking words! They are meant to be! I believe Jesus says these words precisely because of the shock value.

---

15. See Ephesians 5:22–33.

16. Mark's audience was Roman. In a Roman environment a woman could divorce her husband, but Jesus' words were to the Pharisees, who would have been shocked by such a statement.

Jesus is making radical demands of his disciples. Anyone who is seeking justification for his wrong action is not fully following Jesus. When we start asking, "How much can I deviate from God's will for my life?" we have stopped becoming the kind of person Christ longs for us to be. Jesus is calling us to radical transformation. He has done this before when he says:

> If anyone would come after me, he must deny himself and take up his cross and follow me. For whoever wants to save his life will lose it, but whoever loses his life for me and for the gospel will save it. What good is it for a man to gain the whole world, yet forfeit his soul? Or what can a man give in exchange for his soul? (Mark 8:34–36)

Here we find our third and final insight.

Observation Three: Jesus proclaims that God's reign is to break into our world and our lives.

This has direct implications for how we are to live, how we are to talk, and even how we are to marry. We are to make decisions not just based on what Moses may have "permitted" or what the law "allows," but on what God desires. God's will is to invade what is culturally accepted and legally allowed. It should not surprise us that when society holds a low view of marriage, there is always a high rate of divorce.

Let me conclude by saying, divorce happens. Sometimes divorce is justified. Other times it may even be warranted (especially in the case of spousal[17] abuse, or worse, child abuse). Even then, divorce saddens the heart of God. We need to understand that in most cases (all cases from the vantage point of one individual), divorce is a sin. But we also need to understand that divorce is not the unforgivable sin, and it need not forever carry the stigma that it so often does. Divorce is a sin, but fortunately, Jesus is in the sin-forgiving business. Above all, we need to remember that marriage is not just a piece of paper—it is a God-purposed, God-given, God-designed, God-implemented God-event. It is not primarily a civil affair, it is not only a legal affair, it is a miracle of God. "Therefore, what God has joined together, let man not separate" (10:9).

---

17. Literally, this should read espousal, but the correct usage has become rare.

Study Questions

1. Who has the best marriage you have ever seen? Why is it so special?
2. What was your mom's advice to you about marriage? What was your dad's?
3. What was God's intention for marriage?
4. What causes so much divorce today?
5. How were the Pharisees trying to test Jesus by their question?
6. What was their view on divorce (Deuteronomy 24:1–3)?
7. Was Moses' original intention in giving the law on divorce to encourage or hinder divorce? How?
8. The Pharisees seem to be using scripture to justify their own behavior. Have you known people who used scripture that way? Have you ever been guilty of doing this?
9. What reason does Jesus give for Moses allowing divorce (5)?
10. What is the relationship between hardness of heart and divorce?
11. What do the words, "What God has joined together, let man not separate" (9) mean?
12. In what sense do two become one in marriage?
13. Jesus is responding to people who are trying to trap him in his words. Do you think Jesus would respond the same way to someone in a troubled marriage who was sincerely asking the question in verse 2? Why or why not?
14. How would you respond to someone who said of marriage, "It's just a piece of paper anyway"?

For Further Study

15. See Matthew 19:1–2; 1 Corinthians 12:12–13; Ephesians 5:21–33; Romans 7:1–3.

26

Camels & Needles

Mark 10:13–31

People were bringing little children to Jesus to have him touch them, but the disciples rebuked them. When Jesus saw this, he was indignant. He said to them, "Let the little children come to me, and do not hinder them, for the kingdom of God belongs to such as these. I tell you the truth, anyone who will not receive the kingdom of God like a little child will never enter it." And he took the children in his arms, put his hands on them and blessed them. As Jesus started on his way, a man ran up to him and fell on his knees before him. "Good teacher," he asked, "what must I do to inherit eternal life?" "Why do you call me good?" Jesus answered. "No one is good—except God alone. You know the commandments: 'Do not murder, do not commit adultery, do not steal, do not give false testimony, do not defraud, honor your father and mother.'" "Teacher," he declared, "all these I have kept since I was a boy." Jesus looked at him and loved him. "One thing you lack," he said. "Go, sell everything you have and give to the poor, and you will have treasure in heaven. Then come, follow me." At this the man's face fell. He went away sad, because he had great wealth. Jesus looked around and said to his disciples, "How hard it is for the rich to enter the kingdom of God!" The disciples were amazed at his words. But Jesus said again, "Children, how hard it is to enter the kingdom of God! It is easier for a camel to go through the eye of a needle than for a rich man to enter the kingdom of God." The disciples were even more amazed, and said to each other, "Who then can be saved?" Jesus looked at them and said, "With man this is impossible, but not with God; all things are possible with God." Peter said to him, "We have left everything to follow you!" "I tell you the truth," Jesus replied, "no one who has left home or brothers or sisters or mother or father or children or fields for me and the gospel will fail to receive a hundred times as much in this present age (homes, brothers, sisters, mothers, children and fields—and with them, persecutions) and in the age to come, eternal life. But many who are first will be last, and the last first." (Mark 10:13–31)

HERE WE FIND TWO stories that are often told separately. Although they are both well-known, they are often misunderstood. I believe these two stories should not only be tied together, but they share a common theme.[1]

Story One—Jesus Blesses the Children (Mark 10:13–16)

This well-loved story is the inspiration for our childhood songs "Jesus Loves Me, This I Know" and "Jesus Loves the Little Children." It is also the basis of the many famous pictures that show Jesus surrounded by little children, usually with one small child sitting on his lap. I must admit, with a three-year-old child, I sing "Jesus Loves Me" almost every night; and few would argue that the story provides the backdrop for a beautiful painting.

This passage, however, with all its beauty and meaning has often been misapplied and misunderstood. Let me briefly highlight a few misconceptions:

Misconception #1

Some have used this passage to promote and proof-text the doctrine of infant baptism, suggesting that the words "Let the little children come to me, and do not hinder them" (10:14) refer specifically to infant baptism. Most who hold this view base their argument on the wording of the King James Version. They point specifically to the phrase, "Whosoever shall not receive the kingdom of God as a little child, he shall not enter

---

1. This can be demonstrated by the inclusio between "receive the kingdom like a little child" (10:15) and the instruction that the "first will be last, and the last first" (10:31). There may also be a chiastic structure (A-B-C-D-C-B-A):
  A. Take a low position in life (13–16),
    B. Question about eternal life (17),
      C. Rich Man cannot leave possession to follow (22),
        D. Jesus' explanation and disciples' reaction (2x, 23–25),
      C. Disciples have left possessions to follow (28),
    B. Answer to question about eternal life (30),
  A. Take a low position in life (31).

therein" (10:15, KJV). They concentrate on the phrase "as" and use it to create a "time stamp"—unless you receive Christ (i.e. through baptism) as a child (i.e. infant), you cannot be saved. This is an obvious, although not infrequent, misuse of the text. Modern versions do well in translating the phrase "like a child"[2] instead of "as a child."

Misconception #2

Others use our passage to argue against the theology of human depravity and original sin. The point is usually made through the use of a question: "How can children be sinners, if Jesus is telling us to become like a little child?" This too, is a misuse of Mark 10:14–15 and is not the primary point of this passage. No matter what you think about these two theological issues, neither are the intended point of our narrative and should not be its focus.

Misconception #3

Most commonly, this passage is preached as follows: The preacher quotes verse 15, "I tell you the truth, anyone who will not receive the kingdom of God like a little child will never enter it," and then speculates about all the wonderful qualities in children that Christians must emulate. Here is an outline by way of example:

1. Children were drawn to Jesus and wanted to be in his presence—We should be drawn towards Jesus and desire to be in his presence.
2. Children have a simple, uncomplicated approach to life (they go right to the heart of things)—We need to have an uncomplicated view of spiritual things.
3. Children have a marvelous sense of wonder and mystery and are not only teachable, but open and malleable—We need to marvel at God and be open to his leading.[3]

Really? Although this might preach well, is this the purpose of this narrative? If so, why stop with just these few? One can speculate about all the good characteristics of children that Christians should model in

---

2. Although, as you will see in a moment, this terminology brings with it another set of problems.

3. This is an actual sermon outline from a respected preacher who will remain unnamed.

their lives and simply insert them into this story as well. An expanded list might include the following commendable characteristics of a child: humility, trustfulness, transparency, hopefulness, willingness to believe, naivety, obedience, etc. As long as we are inserting characteristics into the text, what prevents us from also inserting other observable traits of children? In my experience children are also: disobedient, demanding, short-tempered, stubborn, thankless, and selfish. Are we to be child-like in these areas as well? We must always be careful not to substitute our assumptions into scripture rather than asking what is really at hand.

In our passage, Jesus does not have in mind inherent childlike qualities (of any kind) when he talks about being like little children. He has in mind the status of children rather than any specific quality they might posses. The children were a nuisance and bother precisely because they had no rank or standing. The disciples have been acting like kingdom bouncers and body guards—determining who could and could not see Jesus. They deemed their own position as important and the children's standing unimportant. This was in keeping with the first century mindset that placed children on the low rung on the totem pole, and for this very reason, the disciples prevented them from coming to Jesus. The disciples were self-appointed gate keepers, and the children an intolerable annoyance. But Jesus, in a strange turn of events, says the disciples need to become "like a child."[4] Once again, he is not talking about a specific character trait of a child, he is talking about status. Skip down to the last verse for a moment where Jesus says, "But many who are first will be last, and the last first" (10:31). This is not new teaching—we have seen it before. Previously, in chapter 9, the disciples had been arguing about who was the greatest. In that instance, Jesus took a child[5] in his arms and said, "If anyone wants to be first, he must be the very last, and the servant of all" (9:35).

In both cases, Jesus is saying to the disciples, "adopt an attitude of littleness." Children had no status, and for this very reason Jesus holds them up as examples. The unimportance of children contrasts sharply with the overreaching attitude the disciples had of themselves. The dis-

---

4. The phrase is literally, "of such a kind as this," and is always used as a classification: kinds, types, or classes. It is not a quality, or a particular attribute that the children hold, but to what class they belong.

5. We have talked previously about how in Aramaic, the word "child" and "slave" are the same word.

ciples continued to hold themselves above others and wielded power and influence over others. Again, this is not new. Earlier the disciples had reported to Jesus, "Teacher . . . we saw a man driving out demons in your name and we told him to stop, because he was not one of us" (9:38). They had determined for themselves who should and should not be included in Jesus' circle. Now the issue resurfaces as: "People were bringing little children to Jesus to have him touch them, but the disciples rebuked them" (10:13).[6]

The disciples had defined themselves in terms of power, authority, status and position—as people of prominence; while Jesus wanted them to define themselves as servants. The disciples had an attitude of bigness while Jesus wanted them to have an attitude of littleness.

Story Two—The Rich Young Ruler (Mark 10:17-31)

This story, too, is one of the most recognizable stories found in the Gospels. The account is recorded for us by all three Synoptic Gospels.[7] The story we are familiar with is usually a compilation of all three accounts. Even the story title borrows elements from each account. All three accounts tell us that he was wealthy. It is Matthew who tells us he was young (Matthew 19:20). Luke calls him a ruler (Luke 18:18). Mark includes the details that Jesus loved him (10:21).[8]

Most are familiar with the man and his question. "Good teacher . . . what must I do to inherit eternal life?" (10:17). We also recognize Jesus' response: "Why do you call me good? . . . No one is good—except God alone" (10:18). Even though we are familiar with the story, once again elements are often misunderstood.

Misconception #1

Liberal commentators and atheists[9] alike have seized on Jesus' reply and suggest that he denies any claim to deity. Their argument paraphrases

---

6. The word "rebuked" (*epitimaō*) is the same word that is used in 4:39 and 8:32-33.

7. Matthew 19:16-30; Luke 18:18-30.

8. This is the only place in the Book of Mark where Jesus explicitly loves someone.

9. Several years ago I had the opportunity to meet with several self-proclaimed atheists about the nature of Jesus. Unable to deny his historicity, they focused on the idea that Jesus never claimed to be divine. Those who make such an uninformed claim need to "Marvel with Mark" about the nature of Jesus.

Jesus this way: "Don't call me good. I'm not good. Only God is good, and I'm not God." The problem with this view is that in many other passages, Jesus does identify himself with God. For example, Jesus says, "I and the father are one" (John 10:30). Later, when the high priest asks Jesus under oath if he is the Christ, the Son of God, Jesus responds, "Yes, it is as you say" (Matthew 26:63–66).[10] In our passage, Jesus is not denying his own goodness or God-ness, but is probing the young man to see what he believes about Jesus—why would you call me good, if you know God alone is good?

Through Jesus' probing (10:19), we find out that the man claims to have lived an exemplary life (10:20). While we might object to this man's elevated opinion of himself, Jesus seems satisfied that the man had indeed lived a respectable life. In fact we read: "He looked at him and loved him" (10:21).

While the man had seemingly lived a righteous life, Jesus knew that his wealth defined him and understood that the man's financial assets would keep him from following fully. Because of this, Jesus hits him where it hurts most—his pocketbook. "One thing you lack . . . Go, sell everything you have . . . Then come follow me"[11] (10:21).

From the demand of Jesus to sell everything, we find a second misconception.

Misconception #2

Many, through the years, have taken this passage to mean that Jesus requires everyone to sell everything in order to follow him. The church has not only preached that wealth is bad, but that virtuous followers should take vows of poverty. It should be pointed out, however, that in many other instances, Jesus makes no such demands: Mark's own mother was wealthy, as was Joseph of Arimathea.[12]

Jesus asks the rich young ruler to give up his wealth, because it was his wealth that defined him. This young man was so overly attached to his

---

10. Remember, the first half of the Gospel of Mark seeks to answer the very question: "Who is this Man?"

11. It is telling of this man's character that Jesus offers the same invitation he had given to the rest of the disciples.

12. It could be pointed out that Zacchaeus did give half of his possessions to the poor and offered to reimburse four-fold those he had cheated. But this appears to be volunteered by Zacchaeus himself, rather than a requirement of Jesus.

possessions that Jesus challenged him to sacrifice in the one crucial area that kept him from following fully. The rich young ruler's self-opinion was "big" and Jesus wanted it to be "little." Unfortunately, the rich young ruler is not the only one who has been lured away from Christ by riches. Jesus warns, "How hard it is for the rich to enter the kingdom of God" (10:23). But he does not isolate only the rich: "Children,[13] how hard it is to enter the kingdom of God" (10:24).

Misconception #3

The third misconception revolves specifically about Jesus' phrase, "It is easier for a camel to go through the eye of a needle than for a rich man to enter the kingdom of God" (10:25).

Some Bible commentators have attempted to soften this metaphor by explaining that the eye of a needle referred to a tiny gate, about four feet high, located in the wall of Jerusalem. The reasoning goes that if a camel was to unloaded his burden, he could then, by squirming and wiggling, squeeze through the tiny gate. While most have us have heard this explanation, it should be relegated to the category of folklore and old-wives' tales.

There are two words used for "needle" in scripture: *rhaphis*,[14] used here in our text and Matthew's account; and, *belonē*[15] used in Luke 18:25. The first simply is the common word for sewing needle. The second word used by Doctor Luke is more specific and refers to a surgical needle. If Jesus were referring to a literal gate, we would first expect him to mention the word "gate" and associate it with either one of these words. Second, if this were a fact of history, we would expect to find such a gate in archaeology, or at least find some mention of at least one such gate. The truth is, although this is a widely-held opinion, no such gate or mention of such gate has ever been found in Jerusalem or elsewhere. This relatively modern explanation did not surface until the eleventh century[16] and was not made popular until the nineteenth century.

Other so-called scholars have tried to explain away Jesus' teaching by suggesting a variant spelling to the Greek word "camel" which would

---

13. This is the only time the disciples are called "children" in the gospels.
14. Matthew 19:24; Mark 10:25.
15. Luke 18:25.
16. Theophylact first suggested this interpretation in the eleventh century.

change its meaning to "ship cable." Try as I might, I don't know how this helps their cause. Jesus is taking the largest animal from their culture and trying to put it through the smallest visible hole of which they are familiar.[17]

I would warn you to be suspicious of exegesis that softens the radical demands of Jesus. Jesus takes the largest known animal from the area and tries to squeeze it through the smallest, commonly known hole. If Jesus' command to the rich young ruler to leave everything in order to follow him seems totally unreasonable—understand, that is exactly the point. Jesus is calling each and every one of us to radically follow him. He wants us to divest ourselves of what provides our security, and place our dependence totally upon him. Mark Twain is purported to have said, "It ain't those parts of the Bible that I can't understand that bother me, it is the parts that I do understand."

The disciples are shocked at Jesus' teaching and say, "Who then can be saved?" The commonly-held view was that the rich had been blessed by God. Then we finally find the answer to the rich young ruler's earlier question: "What must I do to inherit eternal life?" (10:17) "With man this is impossible, but not with God; all things are possible with God" (10:27).

Peter, hearing Jesus only partially, says, "We have left everything to follow you!" (10:28). Jesus acknowledges that any sacrifice for his name will be duly noted (10:30), but then gives us the common thread that has been running throughout this passage. "But many who are first will be last, and the last first" (10:31). There are several parts of this passage that have been misunderstood, and we have looked at those. But one thing is perfectly clear—Jesus is calling us to radical discipleship.

As we began our story, we saw the disciples who were allowing their position to define them. They thought that with their title came power, position, and prestige. They thought that their status gave them the right to decide who could and could not approach Jesus. They thought they had achieved prominence and position. Jesus tells them—I want you to have the status of a little child—whoever is first, will be last.

The rich young ruler defined himself by his wealth, his rule, his morality, and his possessions. Jesus asks him to redefine himself, saying essentially, "I don't want you to be defined by who you are, or what you

---

17. Later Rabbinical writings do change the word "camel" to "elephant."

have, or what you think you have accomplished—abandon it all. The first will be last, and the last first."

People today define themselves in terms of their careers, their portfolio, their beauty, their education, their homes, their cars, their athletic ability, their wit, their pedigree, or their political position. In each case, it would probably be helpful to ask the question: What would Jesus demand them to give up in order to follow him fully? I believe that Jesus would ask them to relinquish the very thing by which they define themselves.

Most importantly, it would be helpful for us to do our own self-evaluation. If Jesus were to evaluate your life, what would he say is holding you back from being totally committed to him? What is keeping you from following Jesus completely? Maybe it would be helpful for you to ask, "What defines me?"

Study Questions

1. If your house was on fire, what three items would you try to save?
2. What would you say "defines you"? How would other people answer that question for you?
3. What are your top priorities in life right now?
4. Why are parents bringing their children to Jesus?
5. Why would the disciples want to keep the children away from Jesus (10:13)?
6. Why was Jesus upset with his disciples?
7. How should adults act like children (10:14–15)?
8. What does the man believe about how to obtain eternal life (10:20)?
9. How would you respond to the man's question in verse 17?
10. Does Jesus require Christians today to sell everything they have (10:21)?
11. Jesus hit this man where it hurt—in his wallet. If Jesus were to address you where it hurts, what would be his hot topic?
12. Why is it so difficult for the rich to enter the kingdom of heaven (10:23–25)?

13. On what basis is it possible for anyone (rich or poor) to enter the kingdom of heaven? How does verse 27 answer this question?

14. Does Jesus suggest that salvation comes by obeying the commandments (10:19)?

15. What have you given up to follow Jesus? How is your life different as a result?

16. If Jesus were to evaluate your life, what would he say holds you back from being totally committed to God? What is keeping you from following Jesus as you should?

17. What are the implications of verse 31?

For Further Study

18. Matthew 19:13–30; Luke 18:15–30.

27

Blind Entitlement

Mark 10:32–52

> They were on their way up to Jerusalem, with Jesus leading the way, and the disciples were astonished, while those who followed were afraid. Again he took the Twelve aside and told them what was going to happen to him. "We are going up to Jerusalem," he said, "and the Son of Man will be betrayed to the chief priests and teachers of the law. They will condemn him to death and will hand him over to the Gentiles, who will mock him and spit on him, flog him and kill him. Three days later he will rise." (Mark 10:32–34)

What Did Jesus See Ahead? (Mark 10:32–34)

As we pick up our story, Jesus and the disciples are on their way up[1] to Jerusalem. Footsteps bring him closer and closer to the cross. Jesus is leading the way (*proagō*, 14:28; 16:7) and as he draws ever nearer, he predicts his death for the third time.[2] Each time Jesus has warned of coming events, he has done so with increasing detail of what the way of the cross will entail. Each time he has included not only the betrayal and his death, but the promise of the resurrection. Either his disciples don't believe him, or they don't want to believe him—either way they are blind to his message.

---

1. Jerusalem is situated on a rocky plateau at an elevation of 2,550 feet. It rises 3,800 feet above the level of the Dead Sea. No matter what direction one travels, approaching Jerusalem is always up. The Bible always rightly identifies travelers as moving up to, or down from Jerusalem.

2. Mark 8:31—9:1; 9:30–32.

As they walk together, the atmosphere is tense among the disciples and other followers as they walk the road. Mark carefully sets the scene for us. The disciples marveled[3] while the others were afraid. There is a strange sense of impending doom as the entourage nears what is perceived to be an approaching crisis.

We would do well to ask what astonished the disciples and made the crowds fearful. The hostilities of the Jewish religious leaders towards Jesus were well known and Jerusalem was the hotbed of this animosity. Jesus' attitude toward the religious leaders was equally known—everyone knew Jesus was going into danger and yet, Jesus had a tough, resolute determination to go. He was adamant, and no one could dissuade him.

What Jesus tells his disciples has remarkable precision: "The Son of Man will be betrayed to the chief priests and teachers of the law. They will condemn him to death and will hand him over to the Gentiles, who will mock him and spit on him, flog him and kill him. Three days later he will rise" (10:33–34). Jesus adds four details that are new to our understanding: the involvement of the Gentiles (Romans—their involvement is necessary because the Jewish were not allowed the right of capital punishment); the mocking; the spitting; and the scourging.

One might ask how Jesus knew these things. While they certainly could have been revealed to him, every one of these events is predicted by the Old Testament prophets (Luke 18:31). It did not require any supernatural insight to know what was about to happen. What Jesus predicted could have been learned by studying Isaiah 53, Psalm 22, and other Old Testament passages.

One thing is clear—Jesus knew what was coming and he resolutely focused on the way of the cross.

What Did James and John See Ahead? (Mark 10:35–40)

> Then James and John, the sons of Zebedee, came to him. "Teacher," they said, "we want you to do for us whatever we ask." "What do you want me to do for you?" he asked. They replied, "Let one of us sit at your right and the other at your left in your glory." (Mark 10:35–37)

Although the disciples also are drawing closer to Jerusalem, they are coming no closer to understanding. Contrast Jesus' goal with the goal

---

3. Once again we are marveling with Mark. Also translated amazed (*thambeō ekthaumazō*).

of James and John. Jesus has set his face toward Jerusalem and the cross. But these brothers are looking toward a different goal. They have set their sights on personal glory. They want position, power, honor, authority, and a throne. They want, not just to be next to Jesus, but to be crowned princes. They want co-thrones when Jesus comes into his kingdom.[4] Their perception of what Jesus came to accomplish has colored their request. The first two "called" want to be the first two "crowned."

Matthew tells us that it is the mother of James and John who made this request of Jesus (Matthew 20:20), suggesting that either the brothers had talked her into asking for them, or the reverse is true. Mark shows that whatever role their mother played, these two disciples were eager participants and Jesus answers them.

> "You don't know what you are asking," Jesus said. "Can you drink the cup I drink or be baptized with the baptism I am baptized with?" "We can," they answered. Jesus said to them, "You will drink the cup I drink and be baptized with the baptism I am baptized with, but to sit at my right or left is not for me to grant. These places belong to those for whom they have been prepared." (Mark 10:38–40)

Jesus, through the use of his question, highlights the fact that the disciples do not know what they are asking for, nor do they understand what is involved—they have not looked at the price tag. The term "cup" is simply a metaphor for whatever life brings you—it can be good or bad.[5] The cup the disciples desire is not the cup of which Jesus speaks. When Jesus speaks of the cup that he must drink, he is speaking about his impending death. Later, in the Garden of Gethsemane, Jesus will pray: "Abba, Father . . . everything is possible for you. Take this cup from me. Yet not what I will, but what you will" (14:36). Jesus is speaking of the events surrounding the cross: the rejection, the torture, the mocking, the ridicule, the scourging, the spitting, the nails. But most of all, his cup was the burden of the sin of the world, the lonely separation from the Father, and the darkness of death. This is the cup the Father has handed him to drink.

---

4. While the request of James and John is seemingly outlandish and their timing is terrible, their request does not come out of thin air. After the discussion with the rich young ruler, Jesus had told the disciples, "I tell you the truth, at the renewal of all things, when the Son of Man sits on his glorious throne, you who have followed me will also sit on twelve thrones, judging the twelve tribes of Israel" (Matthew 19:28).

5. When the Psalmist uses the phrase, "My cup overflows" (Psalm 23:5), he has good things in view. Other Old Testament writers, however, speak of the cup of God's wrath (Isaiah 51:17; Jeremiah 25:15–17).

When Jesus uses the metaphor of baptism, he again uses imagery that is common to Scripture. To baptize means to dip or submerge a person. We see this in Christian baptism. In some places it is used figuratively to show that people are totally submerged in an event. The Israelites were baptized into Moses as they crossed the Red Sea.[6] Here, Jesus will be baptized into death—which is so fitting because that is the very image baptism now portrays.[7]

With this insight into the meaning of the cup and the baptism, we now have a sense of what he is saying to James and John when he asks, "Are you willing to pay it?" He is really asking if they can bear the reproach, shame, anguish, suffering, and death. Did the disciples know what they were asking for? They didn't have a clue. It is interesting that James and John want positions on the left and the right of Jesus. The next and only time this language is used in the Gospel of Mark, it is used of the thieves on the cross next to Jesus (15:27).

As it turned out, the disciples were willing to drink this cup. The Apostle James was the first of the Apostles to die, as recorded for us in Acts 22. He was arrested and beheaded by Herod. The Apostle John, while not martyred, was banished to the island of Patmos for his testimony about Jesus.

While James and John saw thrones ahead of them, Jesus answers that "These places belong to those for whom they have been prepared" (10:40).

What Did the Other Disciples See? (Mark 10:41–45)

"When the ten heard about this, they became indignant with James and John" (10:41).

Picture the scene again, Jesus walking on the road to Jerusalem. Jesus looks ahead and sees a cross waiting for him. James and John look ahead and see two thrones waiting for them. And what do the other ten see? They see James and John. They are angry and upset, but not because

---

6. Paul writes that the Israelites who fled Egypt "were all baptized into Moses in the cloud and in the sea" (1 Corinthians 10:2). They were surrounded by water, even though they walked on dry land. Thus they were "baptized into Moses."

7. "Or don't you know that all of us who were baptized into Christ Jesus were baptized into his death? We were therefore buried with him through baptism into death in order that, just as Christ was raised from the dead through the glory of the Father, we too may live a new life" (Romans 6:3–6).

James and John have been so calloused in their questioning. They are not upset because the Sons of Thunder have asked the worst possible question at the worst possible time—but because they want the same things that James and John want.

If I were Jesus, I would have been more than disappointed—I would have been furious! Not only has he bared his soul and told of his impending death, but he has told them repeatedly—the first will be last and the last will be first. Sound familiar? He's already done this at Caesarea Philippi when he said, "If anyone would come after me, he must deny himself and take up his cross and follow me" (8:34). He did this again as they came to Capernaum: "If anyone wants to be first, he must be the very last, and the servant of all" (9:35). He said it again in the region of Judea: "But many who are first will be last, and the last first" (10:31). How many times does it take? At least one more time.

> Jesus called them together and said, "You know that those who are regarded as rulers of the Gentiles lord it over them, and their high officials exercise authority over them. Not so with you. Instead, whoever wants to become great among you must be your servant, and whoever wants to be first must be slave of all. For even the Son of Man did not come to be served, but to serve, and to give his life as a ransom for many." (Mark 10:42–45)

Here Jesus gives us a kingdom principle. True authority arises out of service. True greatness requires giving. Those who have true authority are those who have emptied themselves and therefore have earned the respect of others. While there are bosses in the unbelieving world, Jesus says, "Not so with you" (10:43). Then Jesus offers himself as the ultimate example of greatness in what is the central verse of the Gospel of Mark: "For even the Son of Man did not come to be served, but to serve, and to give his life as a ransom for many" (10:45). This is how we are to function in the kingdom of God.

Jesus has often told his disciples *what* he must do; here is the only place in the Gospel of Mark where we are given the *why*. Jesus will give his life as a ransom. A ransom (*lytron*) is the purchasing price of freedom. It is translated in various ways including the use of such words as redeeming, setting free, releasing, and rescuing. While the disciples were blinded by their own selfish desires, Jesus was giving his final instructions to them about true discipleship by selflessly walking toward Jerusalem.

What Did the Blind Man See? (Mark 10:46–52)

> Then they came to Jericho. As Jesus and his disciples, together with a large crowd, were leaving the city, a blind man, Bartimaeus (that is, the Son of Timaeus), was sitting by the roadside begging. When he heard that it was Jesus of Nazareth, he began to shout, "Jesus, Son of David, have mercy on me!" Many rebuked him and told him to be quiet, but he shouted all the more, "Son of David, have mercy on me!" Jesus stopped and said, "Call him." So they called to the blind man, "Cheer up! On your feet! He's calling you." Throwing his cloak aside, he jumped to his feet and came to Jesus. "What do you want me to do for you?" Jesus asked him. The blind man said, "Rabbi, I want to see." "Go," said Jesus, "your faith has healed you." Immediately he received his sight and followed Jesus along the road. (Mark 10:46–52)

As Jesus and the disciples come[8] to the city of Jericho they encounter a blind man. The inclusion of this story seems at first like an abrupt change. A closer inspection, however, shows a unique tie with what has gone before. This can be demonstrated by looking at a couple of phrases.

First, there is an unusual repetition involved when Mark gives us the name of this blind man. His name is Bartimaeus, a blind beggar, the son of Timaeus. At first glance this may seem trivial and unimportant until you realize that the name Bartimaeus means, "Bar (son of) Timaeus." It is, therefore, redundant for Mark to say, "Bartimaeus, the son of Timaeus" (10:46). Let me say it again: it is redundant for Mark to say, "Bartimaeus, the son of Timaeus"—it means the same thing! Mark underscores the blind man's name for a reason. Look up the meaning of Timaeus and the purpose becomes clear. Timaeus means honor. The beggar was named, "the son of honor." On one hand, James and John were seeking positions of honor. Now we find the story of the son of honor. Coincidence or divine appointment?

Second, notice the question that Jesus poses to Bartimaeus: "What do you want me to do for you?" (10:51). That is word for word the question Jesus put to James and John when they came to him with their request (10:36). Coincidence or divine appointment? (Sorry about

---

8. Matthew records this event as taking place as they leave Jericho (Matthew 20:29). The simplest explanation asserts the fact of two Jerichos—the ancient city and the city of Jesus' day. This event took place as he left one and came to the other.

being redundant.) A close examination shows that these stories do go together.

Let me ask you a question. What was the problem with the disciples? They were blind to what Jesus was trying to tell them. They were blind to who he was and what he came to accomplish. Because of their own preconceptions, they could not see what was involved. Physically, they could see, but spiritually, they were blind.

Now, we find a man who was blind physically, but who saw Jesus clearly. One man was conscious of his blindness, while the others were not conscious of theirs. When the blind man came to Jesus, he came as a beggar asking for mercy, rather than asking for a position of authority. "When he heard that it was Jesus of Nazareth, he began to shout, 'Jesus, Son of David,'[9] have mercy on me'" (10:47). The fact that Bartimaeus addressed Jesus in such a way showed that he recognized Jesus as the Messiah. His faith in Jesus brought about his healing.

As I compare the difference in approach of the disciples and Bartimaeus, I am confronted with this question: What would we look like if our prayers were made public? Would we look like shameless gold-diggers asking only for promotions, new jobs, homes, cars, or thrones? Or would we be recognized as approaching God with humbleness and mercy coming as beggars before him?

We live in a world where many or most come to God with an attitude of entitlement and our requests betray us. How can we shamefully seek glory, honor, and position for ourselves when Jesus gave his life in shameful death? I hope our approach more closely resembles that of Bartimaeus (Lord have mercy on me!), than that of the disciples (do for me whatever I ask).

Study Questions

1. If Jesus asked you, "What do you want me to do for you?" how would you answer?

2. How do you think the disciples felt when Jesus described what was going to happen to him in Jerusalem (10:33–34)?

3. What do James and John ask of Jesus (35–37)?

4. What view of "kingdom" are James and John still clinging to?

---

9. This is the first use of the phrase, "Son of David" in Mark.

5. How should they have responded in light of verses 33–34?
6. What did Jesus mean when he said, "You don't know what you are asking" (38)?
7. What does Jesus mean when he asks, "Can you drink the cup . . . or be baptized with the baptism I am baptized with" (38)?
8. Why are the other disciples indignant (41)?
9. How are the attitudes of true disciples to be different from the world in which they live (42–44)? How does Jesus redefine greatness?
10. Jesus defines greatness, not by how many people serve you, but by how many you serve. How do you feel about following the servant's path to greatness?
11. What does being the servant of all mean to you?
12. Who has been the greatest example of Christlike servanthood to you in your life?
13. How often do you ask God for something without really knowing what you are asking for? Why are we so prone to doing this?
14. What does the name Bartimaeus mean?
15. Compare Bartimaeus' request (47) with the request of James and John.
16. What would we look like if our prayers were made public? Would we look more like shameless gold-diggers, or humble beggars seeking mercy?
17. In what areas of your life would you like Jesus to open your eyes so you can "see" more clearly?
18. How can you model servanthood this week?

For Further Study

19. See Matthew 20:17–34; Luke 18:31–43.
20. Many Old Testament writers foretold of the events surrounding the crucifixion. For Christ's betrayal, see Psalm 41:5–9. The crucifixion is foretold in Psalm 22:16–18 and Isaiah 53:4–7. The resurrection is foretold in Psalm 16:10.

28

Not a Gentle Jesus

Mark 11:1–26

ONE TEENAGE BOY WAS angered by his father's insistence that he cut his hair. So adamant was the father about his son's appearance that he laid down this law: "Until you cut your hair, you cannot drive the car." The boy was rather discouraged until he saw a painting of a bearded Jesus. He ran to his father and exclaimed in triumph, "Jesus had long hair!" To which his father responded, "Yes, and he walked everywhere he went."

We find in our passage today, the only instance where Jesus is said to have ridden an animal.[1] With the exception of a few boat rides on the Sea of Galilee, Jesus walked everywhere he went—sometimes lake included.

As we come to Mark chapter 11, we have come to the last week of Jesus' life, often called the passion week. Unfortunately, many people hear sermons on Palm Sunday about Jesus marching triumphantly into Jerusalem, only to go home and then return the following week to hear a message about the triumph of Easter Sunday. In doing so, they hear very little about Jesus during the week (both theirs and his). This limited focus is so unlike the Gospel of Mark. Nearly forty percent of Mark's gospel is dedicated to the passion week of Jesus. It seems only fitting that if Mark deems it necessary to concentrate on the events of this one week in the life of Christ, we too, should make it a priority.

In the passage at hand, Jesus demonstrates his knowledge, his identity, and his purpose.

---

1. The book of Revelation gives the future picture of Jesus riding a horse!

The Triumphal Entry (Mark 11:1–11)

> As they approached Jerusalem and came to Bethphage and Bethany at the Mount of Olives, Jesus sent two of his disciples, saying to them, "Go to the village ahead of you, and just as you enter it, you will find a colt tied there, which no one has ever ridden. Untie it and bring it here. If anyone asks you, 'Why are you doing this?' tell him, 'The Lord needs it and will send it back here shortly.'" They went and found a colt outside in the street, tied at a doorway. As they untied it, some people standing there asked, "What are you doing, untying that colt?" They answered as Jesus had told them to, and the people let them go. When they brought the colt to Jesus and threw their cloaks over it, he sat on it. Many people spread their cloaks on the road, while others spread branches they had cut in the fields. Those who went ahead and those who followed shouted, "Hosanna!" "Blessed is he who comes in the name of the Lord!" "Blessed is the coming kingdom of our father David!" "Hosanna in the highest!" Jesus entered Jerusalem and went to the temple. He looked around at everything, but since it was already late, he went out to Bethany with the Twelve. (Mark 11:1–11)

As Jesus and the disciples walk toward Jerusalem,[2] they travel by the smaller towns of Bethphage[3] and Bethany.[4] In so doing, they encounter an ever-growing crowd of pilgrims who are also heading toward the Holy City. As they approach the Mount of Olives,[5] Jesus sends two of his disciples ahead with these instructions: "Go to the village ahead of you, and just as you enter it, you will find a colt tied there, which no one has

---

2. Jerusalem was the chief city of Palestine and the religious center of ancient Judaism.

3. It is uncertain where Bethphage was located. It is traditionally believed to have been slightly west of Bethany on the eastern slope of the Mount of Olives and about a mile from the eastern wall of Jerusalem. Bethphage means, "house of unripe figs" and refers to a specific type of fig that appears late and never seems ripe—even when it is ready to eat.

4. Bethany was about two miles east of Jerusalem. Its name may mean "house of affliction or suffering." It is telling that Jesus chooses to stay here on visits to Jerusalem. John 12:1 seems to indicate that Jesus may have even spent the night with Mary, Martha, and Lazarus in Bethany on the way by.

5. The Mount of Olives is a ridge about two-and-a half miles long lying east of Jerusalem across a small valley. From the top (about 2,900 feet), you can see the entire city as well as look back to the Dead Sea. This is not only how Jesus arrives in Jerusalem, but where he will also be led out to be crucified.

ever ridden. Untie it and bring it here." (11:2). The term "colt" (*pōlos*) can simply mean a young animal of several species, such as an elephant, camel, donkey, or horse. Matthew clarifies it for us, however, when he specifically uses the word "donkey" (Matthew 21:2)[6] and thus, gives us a direct fulfillment of the Messianic prophecy of Zechariah: "See, your king comes to you, righteous and having salvation, gentle and riding on a donkey, on a colt, the foal of a donkey" (Zechariah 9:9). The fact that this colt has never been ridden may be significant in light of the ancient rule that only animals that had not been put to ordinary use could be used for sacred purposes (cf. Numbers 19:2; Deuteronomy 21:3; 1 Samuel 6:7).

Obviously, taking someone's personal colt might be met with some opposition (akin to driving off in someone else's car), and so Jesus tells them, "If anyone asks . . . tell him, 'The Lord needs it and will send it back here shortly'" (11:3).

As I read this passage, immediately several questions begin spinning around in my head. First, what kind of person would be satisfied with the answer the disciples are supposed to give? The response: "The Lord needs it," even if they promise to return it shortly (11:3), seems weak at best.[7] These people, at a minimum, must have been aware of Jesus' public ministry, and it is likely they were even numbered among his followers. This would explain how the disciples could take the animal without making a donkey[8] of themselves.

A second question also needs to be asked. How exactly did Jesus know where the colt would be and that the owners would allow the disciples to take it? Several answers could be put forward: (a1 Jesus is the Son of God, which would certainly make him capable of knowing such things—although I personally believe that Jesus emptied himself of his omniscience during the incarnation; (2) the circumstances could have been revealed to him by his Father—this certainly is not without precedent; or, (3) it is also possible that the events could have been prearranged by Jesus himself. While Mark does not record the event for us, John shows

---

6. Matthew uses the word "*onos*."

7. Some have suggested that borrowing another's possessions was a common practice during festival times, but they fail to substantiate their claims. Others suggest that the word "Lord" (*kyrios*) is best translated "Master." Neither of these satisfy my longing to know "who" would allow such a thing?

8. I obviously understand that I don't have the euphemism quite right.

a previous trip by Jesus to Jerusalem a couple of months earlier at the Feast of Dedication (John 10:22). It is also quite possible that Jesus stayed the night in Bethany at the house of Lazarus (John 12:1) on this current journey. In either case, Jesus could have prearranged the encounter.

No matter how you account for Jesus knowing the circumstances surrounding the commandeering of the donkey, this passage clearly demonstrates that Jesus knew about predictive history, accepted the Messianic implications of his actions, and rode into town on a beast of burden. In so doing, his triumphal entry stands in stark contrast with a typical coronation. For a first-century king's processional, one would expect a royal stallion or at least a chariot. Today, we'd expect a limo—not a Jerusalem Jeep. But Jesus comes making a statement—he's not that kind of Messiah—a point he has been trying to make to his disciples.

Which brings me to my third question. It centers around a colt that has never been ridden. I need to ask, does that bit of information bother anyone? I understand the Old Testament guidelines for animals used for sacred purposes (i.e. sacrifice)—that they should not have been put to common use. But circumstances seem a little different when one expects to ride an animal that has never been ridden before, at least if you plan on doing so for more than eight seconds. Personally, I would prefer my mount to be well-ridden.

I want to postulate two opinions about the triumphal entry. The first idea is fun, but probably sacrilege—it might even be blasphemous in some circles. Could it be that Jesus mounts an unbroken colt[9] (and it behaves as we might expect) to mock the whole idea of status, prestige, royalty, and honor? Simply riding on a donkey rather than a stallion would certainly fit this motif, but riding a donkey that is braying and kicking would buck this point home with some force. Picture (if you can) the scene with the disciples running—their robes flapping in the wind, the donkey giving Jesus the "what for," and the people waving branches and crying, "Hosanna."[10] It's probably not the picture you've seen on your Palm Sunday bulletin or the account taught to you in Sunday School.

---

9. One animal trainer reported to me that donkeys are four times more difficult to break than horses.

10. The term "Hosanna" comes from the Hebrew expression meaning "save now." It became the cry of acclamation used by pilgrims coming to Jerusalem for festivals. It comes from Psalm 118:25, a portion of the Hallel Psalms (113—118), which were chanted liturgically during certain festivals. Placing coats and branches on the roadway was a customary way for a crowd to welcome a triumphant king (See 2 Kings 9:13).

Not a Gentle Jesus 257

It is, however, what we would expect. Actually, it fits quite well with Jesus' theme of position, honor, and authority—about the "first being the last, the last first." It also explains the crowd's excitement on the way to Jerusalem. I must admit, it fits well with my depiction of Jesus—not the mild-mannered, even-tempered, emasculated male that he is often portrayed to be. Rather it depicts a strong manly-man who can not only hold his own when confronted, but who can overturn tables and drive out moneychangers.

It might not, however, fit very well with Zechariah's prophecy about coming "gently" on a donkey. Or does it? The Hebrew word for "gently" actually means lowly, or with great humiliation. Okay, maybe this is still a stretch. I bring it up only to suggest—this is exactly what we should expect from a man riding on a donkey colt that has never been ridden. Unless . . . unless something else is in play.

The second idea is not as fun, but it is even more impressive. Let me ask you again, how is Jesus able to ride gently into Jerusalem on a donkey that has never been ridden?[11] How is this humanly possible? It's not! We must either adopt view number one (and buck the trend), or understand that here we have yet another miracle of Jesus. Jesus is the "Donkey Whisperer." I've never seen this listed among his miracles, but how can it be anything less? Jesus once again demonstrates his power over nature. He establishes his authority as Creator over creation. Jesus rides an unbroken colt—it demonstrates who he is.

But lest we miss the point, don't miss three facts: (1) Jesus is knowingly fulfilling prophesy; (2) Jesus, by knowingly fulfilling prophesy is declaring himself to be Israel's king and Messiah; and, (3) Jesus is deliberately riding into Jerusalem, challenging the religious leaders of Jerusalem.[12]

By the time Jesus arrives at the temple, evening is fast approaching. Mark is the only gospel writer who notes that it is late. Jesus merely looks around the temple area and then departs with the Twelve—a somewhat anti-climatic ending, if this was indeed the end of what he came to do. Actually, Jesus went to the temple area to assess the situation before publicly presenting himself there the following day.

---

11. Matthew's account tells us that the disciples find a donkey with her colt (Matthew 21:2). Some have suggested that the presence of the mother keeps the colt calm. I would simply suggest these scholars do some research at a local dude ranch.

12. The Pharisees initially decide not to arrest Jesus until after the Passover—but Jesus makes sure it does indeed happen this way because he is the Lamb of God.

The Lesson of the Fig Tree—Part One
(Mark 11:12–14)

> The next day as they were leaving Bethany, Jesus was hungry. Seeing in the distance a fig tree in leaf, he went to find out if it had any fruit. When he reached it, he found nothing but leaves, because it was not the season for figs. Then he said to the tree, "May no one ever eat fruit from you again." And his disciples heard him say it. (Mark 11:12–14)

The following morning, as Jesus and the disciples were on their way back to Jerusalem, Jesus notices a leafing fig tree in the distance. We are told that he became hungry, and so, he approached the fig tree to see if perhaps he would find anything on it. Unfortunately, the fig tree was not producing figs, "for it was not the season for figs" (11:13). At this point, Jesus did something that might seem somewhat out of character for him—if you hold to a gentle Jesus. He not only spoke to the tree, but cursed it: "May no one ever eat fruit from you again" (11:14).

While I don't claim to be a fig expert (unless we are talking Fig Newtons), I have learned that fig trees produce both an early, edible bud (spring) and a late fig (fall).[13] A fully-leafed fig tree advertised the fact that the early bud was ripe. It was likely these buds that Jesus was expecting on the tree. A fully-leafed fig tree without early buds meant that the tree would not bear the more valuable fruit (figs) that would come during the months of August to October. In our passage, Jesus expected to find something to satisfy his hunger. Finding no fruit on the tree meant not only that his hunger would not be satisfied, but that this tree would not produce any fruit at all this season. Jesus cursed the tree and continued on his journey. But we are not done with the fig tree. Mark employs this as a sandwich technique for the story that follows. The story of the fig tree becomes a living parable.

Interestingly, in prophetic writings, the fig tree was used as a symbol of judgement (Isaiah 34:4; Jeremiah 29:17; Hosea 2:12; 9:10; Joel 1:7; Micah 7:1). In the judgment against Judah, the prophet Jeremiah writes, "There will be no figs on the tree, and their leaves wither" (8:13). Jesus gives this same parable with the same point—it dramatizes what is going to take place at the temple. The temple was spiritually deceptive. It was supposed to be a center of worship, but had become a center for religious

---

13. Some trees yield fruit twice a year, in late spring and early autumn.

commercialism and a place of outlaws (10:17). The cursing of the fig tree was a symbolic act of God's judgment on the temple, on Israel, and on all who are spiritually deceptive.

The Cleansing of the Temple
(Mark 11:15–19)

> On reaching Jerusalem, Jesus entered the temple area and began driving out those who were buying and selling there. He overturned the tables of the money changers and the benches of those selling doves, and would not allow anyone to carry merchandise through the temple courts. And as he taught them, he said, "Is it not written: 'My house will be called a house of prayer for all nations'? But you have made it 'a den of robbers.'" The chief priests and the teachers of the law heard this and began looking for a way to kill him, for they feared him, because the whole crowd was amazed at his teaching. When evening came, they went out of the city. (Mark 11:15–19)

Once again we find a picture that does not sit well with those who regard Christ as a "gentle Jesus." Those who are troubled do not understand the holy indignation that made him act as he did here. Theirs is a Jesus of love without righteousness.

People from all regions of the world had approached Jerusalem for the Passover. From a distance, everything appeared great. But as one approached the temple, it soon became apparent that the outer court (the Court of the Gentiles) had been turned into an oriental bazaar and a marketplace for sacrificial animals. Gentiles who had become proselytes not only had no place to worship, but worse, the court had become the center of illegitimate enterprise. Merchants were selling animals as a so-called service to the people;[14] money changers had set up shop to exchange currency for people at exorbitant rates; and unclean utensils were being carried through temple precincts.[15] Here we find preacher turned bouncer! Jesus goes into the temple and immediately begins throwing out those selling and buying, overturning the tables of the money changers, and then turning over the seats of those selling doves. Jesus quotes a

---

14. In AD 30, the temple hierarchy authorized sales in the temple courtyard in exchange for a cut of the profits. It appears that the high priest Caiaphas himself instituted this practice in the Court of the Gentiles.

15. Apparently people were irreverently using the temple as a shortcut.

couple of Old Testament passages. The first describes those whose sacrifices God will honor:

> Let no foreigner who has bound himself to the Lord say, "The Lord will surely exclude me from his people." And let not any eunuch complain, "I am only a dry tree" . . . All who keep the Sabbath without desecrating it and who hold fast to my covenant—these I will bring to my holy mountain and give them joy in my house of prayer. Their burnt offerings and sacrifices will be accepted on my altar; for my house will be called a house of prayer for all nations. (Isaiah 56:3, 6–7)

Jesus also quotes Jeremiah:

> Hear the word of the Lord, all you people of Judah who come through these gates to worship the Lord. This is what the Lord Almighty, the God of Israel, says: "Reform your ways and your actions . . . Will you steal and murder, commit adultery and perjury, burn incense to Baal and follow other gods you have not known, and then come and stand before me in this house, which bears my Name, and say, 'We are safe'—safe to do all these detestable things? Has this house, which bears my Name, become a den of robbers to you? But I have been watching!" declares the Lord. (Jeremiah 7:2–11)

There should be no doubt in regards to what Jesus meant. Like the fig tree, the Temple was all leaves and no fruit.

The Lesson of the Fig Tree—Part Two
(Mark 11:20–26)

> In the morning, as they went along, they saw the fig tree withered from the roots. Peter remembered and said to Jesus, "Rabbi, look! The fig tree you cursed has withered!" "Have faith in God," Jesus answered. "I tell you the truth, if anyone says to this mountain, 'Go, throw yourself into the sea,' and does not doubt in his heart but believes that what he says will happen, it will be done for him. Therefore I tell you, whatever you ask for in prayer, believe that you have received it, and it will be yours. And when you stand praying, if you hold anything against anyone, forgive him, so that your Father in heaven may forgive you your sins." (Mark 11:20–26)

The next morning, Jesus and his disciples again head for Jerusalem and the temple. No doubt they take the same path they had taken the day before. When they come to the fig tree they notice that it has withered from the roots up. In typical fashion, as a spokesman for the group, Peter blurts out the obvious: "The fig tree you cursed has withered" (11:22). In Matthew's account, Peter asks a question: "How did the fig tree wither so quickly?" (Matthew 21:20).

Jesus seems to give a strange answer: "Have faith in God" (11:22). Some have used this passage (neglecting to read it in context) as a formula for how to work miracles. They suggest that Jesus is saying, "You too can curse fig trees and make them wither if you have enough faith in God." But read Jesus' words in connection with the events of this passage and the meaning becomes clear. It is significant that the story of the cursed fig tree is sandwiched (or should we say, "Fig-Newtoned?") around and encapsulates the story of the cleansing of the temple. This is a deliberate technique of Mark. They are not two stories but one.

Jesus is not telling us the secret of how to curse fig trees; he is telling us the secret of how to live so that we will not be cursed. The fig tree was cursed because it showed the outward appearance of fruit, but it bore no fruit. The temple and therefore the nation was cursed because it showed the outward signs of religion, but showed no fruit. People had substituted empty rituals and meaningless performance for a true, loving, obedient worship of God. Israel's religion was one that went through the motions, but was empty and hypocritical. The corrupt priests were in collusion with the moneychangers and the merchants who were milking people out of their money in the name of God. The worship that was once green and fruitful was now dried up and withered. And then the question: "How did it happen so quickly?"

We need to hear Jesus' answer. When a nation begins to dry up and wither, when it ceases to become fruitful, the only answer is to have faith in God. Whether the nation is Israel of the first century, or the United States of the twenty-first century—the only answer is to have faith in God. And what is true of a nation is true of an individual. If you feel dried up, wasted, withered, and dead inside, have faith in God.

Using the description of the Temple as the house of prayer (11:17), Jesus ends with these simple words. Believe. Pray. Forgive. Be forgiven.

> "Have faith in God . . . I tell you the truth, if anyone says to this mountain, 'Go throw yourself into the sea,' and does not doubt in his heart but believes that what he says will happen, it will be done for him. Therefore I tell you, whatever you ask for in prayer, believe that you have received it, and it will be yours. And when you stand praying, if you hold anything against anyone, forgive him, so that your Father in heaven may forgive you your sins." (Mark 11:22–25)

Sometimes we don't like to think in terms of Jesus overthrowing tables and cursing fig trees. We certainly don't like to think of Jesus riding a bucking bronco. As I read through this passage, I am reminded that ours is not a gentle Jesus, nor does he make simple requests. Jesus expects us to radically follow him. Jesus does not want token followers or feigned allegiance. Jesus wants fruit-producing disciples. Understand, Jesus never has a kind word for those who play religion, or pretend to be something they are not—they are hypocrites and whitewashed tombs. Those who live lives of compromise will experience anything but a gentle Jesus.

In C. S. Lewis', *The Chronicles of Narnia*, we are introduced to Aslan the Lion by the Beavers. "If there's anyone who can appear before Aslan without their knees knocking, they're either braver than me or else just silly." Then Lucy asks, "Then he isn't safe?" To which Mr. Beaver responds, "Safe? . . . Who said anything about safe? Course he isn't safe. But he's good."[16]

Jesus is not gentle, but he's good.

Study Questions

1. Have you ever experienced an inauguration or an inaugural parade? What types of festivities were involved?

2. How might you expect a first-century king or conquering hero to enter a city? How does Jesus' entry into Jerusalem compare?

3. Why did Jesus ride into Jerusalem on a colt? Read Zechariah 9:9. What is the significance of this verse?

4. What does the way Jesus enters Jerusalem say about who he is and what he has come to do?

---

16. C.S. Lewis, *The Chronicles of Narnia: the Lion, the Witch, and the Wardrobe*, revised ed. New York: MacMillan Publishing, 1982. p 86.

5. If you were in charge of Jesus' entry into Jerusalem, how would you have done things differently?
6. Does the Lord have need of us (11:3)? Why or why not?
7. In your own words, explain why Jesus cursed the fig tree.
8. What does the fig tree typify?
9. What was going on in the temple area that angered Jesus?
10. If Jesus visited our modern-day churches, do you think he would be pleased or disgusted? Why?
11. If Jesus came to clean up your community, where would he start?
12. Does your life contain the appearance of Christianity, but without the proof? In what ways do you need Jesus to revive and renew you?

For Further Study

13. Matthew 21:1–22; Luke 19:28–48; John 12:12–19.
14. Read Psalm 118. How does this Psalm enhance your sense of the scene described in Mark 11?

29

Q & A, Part One

Mark 11:27—12:17

AFTER THE TRIUMPHAL ENTRY of Jesus into Jerusalem and his cleansing of the temple, we read: "The chief priests and the teachers of the law . . . began looking for a way to kill him" (11:18). The religious leaders clearly understood the implications of Jesus' actions the previous day, and now join with the Pharisees and Herodians who have been bent on killing Jesus since 3:6. The intent is clear—kill Jesus. The only question that remains is how to accomplish it. They must create the right set of circumstances in order to accomplish their purpose and reach their desired goal. Their strategy unfolds as they confront Jesus with a series of questions designed to trap him in his words.

As the pace in the Gospel of Mark slows during the passion week of Jesus, we have now reached Tuesday—the day of questions. It is called the day of questions because, one by one, different groups come and ask, "Are you smarter than a religious leader?" They think they can outwit the carpenter's son, but they are sadly mistaken.

In round one, we find the chief priests,[1] the teachers of the law,[2] and the elders[3] questioning Jesus' authority (11:27–33). In round two, we find

---

1. The chief priests were made up of former High Priests and priests with permanent duties in the temple.
2. The teachers of the law were the learned legal experts who emphasized tradition. Many teachers of the law were Pharisees. They denied Jesus' authority to reinterpret the law.
3. The elders were made up of wealthy laymen.

the Pharisees[4] and Herodians[5] with a question about taxes (12:13–17). Then, the Sadducees[6] take a turn in round three with a question about marriage (12:18–27). This is followed by another teacher of the law with a fourth question about the greatest commandment (12:28–35). Finally, in the bonus round, Jesus ends the day by asking yet another question of his own—if David calls Christ, "Lord," how can he be his son? (12:35–37).

In this section, we will focus on the first two questions, which flank a parable of Jesus.

Question #1—By Whose Authority?
(Mark 11:27–33)

> They arrived again in Jerusalem, and while Jesus was walking in the temple courts, the chief priests, the teachers of the law and the elders came to him. "By what authority are you doing these things?" they asked. "And who gave you authority to do this?" Jesus replied, "I will ask you one question. Answer me, and I will tell you by what authority I am doing these things. John's baptism—was it from heaven, or from men? Tell me!" They discussed it among themselves and said, "If we say, 'From heaven,' he will ask, 'Then why didn't you believe him?' But if we say, 'From men' . . . ." (They feared the people, for everyone held that John really was a prophet.) So they answered Jesus, "We don't know." Jesus said, "Neither will I tell you by what authority I am doing these things." (Mark 11:27–30)

With the first question, the religious leaders are essentially saying to Jesus, present your credentials, prove your legitimacy. "Who gave you authority to do this?" (11:28). They are not sincerely asking, nor will they be convinced—no matter how Jesus answers. They have already made up

---

4. The Pharisees were primarily a religious group concerned with ritual purity. They advocated minute obedience to the Jewish laws and traditions. They saw themselves as righteous and everyone else as sinners. They rejected Jesus because he did not follow all their traditions and he associated with notoriously wicked people.

5. The Herodians were a Jewish political party made up of wealthy aristocrats. They approved of Herod and supported his compromises with Rome. They were afraid that Jesus would cause political instability and was therefore a threat to their political future.

6. The Sadducees were a wealthy, upper-class Jewish party. They rejected the authority of the Bible beyond the first five books of Moses. They profited from business in the temple. They denied the resurrection of the dead.

their minds about him. They have previously questioned Jesus' authority to forgive sins (2:6–7), and have rejected his authority to cleanse the temple (11:18). Their trap lies in how they think Jesus will answer. If he claims that his authority[7] comes from God, or even if he claims to have authority in his own right (as the Son of God)—they will accuse him of blasphemy. If he cannot provide someone to authenticate his ministry (and only their blessing will do), they will dismiss him as unimportant.

It is interesting that the religious leaders ask Jesus a direct question, but he does not answer them directly (11:28). In the Gospel of Mark, those who approach Jesus with hostility never receive direct answers or incontrovertible proof. Jesus typically asks a question of his own, uses a pithy illustration, or directs them back to scripture as the ultimate authority. When accused of eating with tax collectors and sinners, Jesus responds, "It is not the healthy who need a doctor, but the sick. I have not come to call the righteous, but sinners" (2:17). When the disciples are criticized for not fasting, Jesus says, "How can the guests of the bridegroom fast while he is with them? They cannot, so long as they have him with them. But the time will come when the bridegroom will be taken from them, and on that day they will fast" (2:19–20). When the disciples are found picking grain on the Sabbath, Jesus tells of David eating the consecrated bread (2:25; cf. 2 Samuel 21:1–9). To those who try to trap him for healing on the Sabbath, Jesus asks a question: "Which is lawful . . . to do good or to do evil, to save a life or to kill?" (3:4). When the teachers of the law accuse him of driving out demons by the prince of demons, he responds yet again with a question: "How can Satan drive out Satan?" (3:23). When his disciples are accused of eating with unclean hands he quotes Isaiah 29:13: "These people honor me with their lips, but their hearts are far from me. They worship me in vain; their teachings are but rules taught by men" (7:6–7). When the Pharisees ask for a sign from heaven, Jesus again asks a question: "Why does this generation ask for a miraculous sign?" (8:11) When asked if it is lawful to divorce, Jesus takes them to scripture by way of a question: "What did Moses command you?" (10:3).

It should not surprise us then, as the religious leaders try to trap Jesus, he fends them off with his own question, and then twice demands

---

7. The term "authority" is used twice in 11:28, again in 11:29 and 11:33. It is also found in 1:22, 27; 2:10; 3:15; and 6:7. Its frequent usage in Mark makes it an important theological term. See also 13:34.

they answer: "I will ask you one question. Answer me, and I will tell you by what authority I am doing these things. John's baptism—was it from heaven, or from men? Tell me!" (11:29–30).

One might ask why Jesus uses John the Baptist as his point of reference. I think there are several possibilities to account for this. John the Baptist was called the greatest prophet and foretold by Isaiah (1:2). John came preaching a baptism of repentance for the forgiveness of sins (1:4) outside of the restraints of the temple and without sacrifice. John the Baptist gave clear testimony to who Jesus was and spoke of Jesus' authority (1:7), and John the Baptist certainly was held in high esteem by the people (11:32). His popularity as a prophet swelled even after his death.

In this game of chess, Jesus has placed the religious leaders in a fork—either move the opponent makes will cause him to lose a game piece (I am not a chess master, but I've certainly often put myself in this position in life). If the religious leaders answer that John's baptism was from heaven, Jesus can respond, "Then why didn't you believe him" (11:31), but if they say from men, they will be discredited among the people (11:32). After discussing[8] this among themselves, they answer, "We don't know" (11:33). Their question directed at Jesus was meant to subvert his authority, but he has turned the tables on them and they have undermined their own.

The refusal of the religious leaders to answer Jesus' question, not only frees him from answering, but demonstrates the religious leaders have no understanding of God's working. Jesus then uses the opportunity to tell a parable.

A Parable—The Wicked Tenants
(Mark 12:1–12)

> He then began to speak to them in parables: "A man planted a vineyard. He put a wall around it, dug a pit for the winepress and built a watchtower. Then he rented the vineyard to some farmers and went away on a journey. At harvest time he sent a servant to the tenants to collect from them some of the fruit of the vineyard. But they seized him, beat him and sent him away empty-handed. Then he sent another servant to them; they struck this man on

---

8. The word "discussed" (*dialogizomai*) is the word from which we get our word "dialogue." It literally means to argue or reason among themselves and is used seven times in the Gospel of Mark.

the head and treated him shamefully. He sent still another, and that one they killed. He sent many others; some of them they beat, others they killed. "He had one left to send, a son, whom he loved. He sent him last of all, saying, 'They will respect my son.' "But the tenants said to one another, 'This is the heir. Come, let's kill him, and the inheritance will be ours.' So they took him and killed him, and threw him out of the vineyard. "What then will the owner of the vineyard do? He will come and kill those tenants and give the vineyard to others. Haven't you read this scripture: "'The stone the builders rejected has become the capstone; the Lord has done this, and it is marvelous in our eyes'?" Then they looked for a way to arrest him because they knew he had spoken the parable against them. But they were afraid of the crowd; so they left him and went away. (Mark 12:1-12)

Using the framework of the fifth chapter of Isaiah,[9] Jesus tells a parable. With close examination, it is not difficult to identify the parties involved in the story: the owner[10] of the vineyard is undoubtedly God; the vineyard is Israel;[11] the tenants are the religious leaders; the servants are the prophets (including John the Baptist); and the son[12] is none other than Jesus himself.

As the story unfolds, the tenants have willfully subverted the authority of the owner. Not only do they reject the master's messengers, but they eventually kill the son—dragging his body outside the vineyard without burial. Then we are given the focal point of the parable in the form of yet another question and answer: "What then will the owner of the vineyard do? He will come and kill those tenants and give the vineyard to others" (12:9).

Like the tenants of the parable, the priests and teachers of the law are asserting their own authority and claiming ownership of the vineyard, thereby superceding the authority and ownership of God. In no uncertain language, Jesus renounces the religious leaders. Jesus then quotes from Psalm 118—the very Psalm we just studied in connection with the triumphal entry. "The stone the builders rejected has become

---

9. The wording he uses reflects the Septuagint.

10. "Owner" (*kurios*) can mean "master" but was used as the title for God (the Lord). The term is a deliberate play on words that shows that this landowner represents God.

11. A comparison with the writings of Isaiah shows the relationship of the vineyard and watchtower with the temple and altar.

12. The description of the son here is literally, "beloved son" (*agapēton*) and reflects 1:11 and 9:7.

the capstone" (12:10). Although Jesus has been rejected by the Jewish leaders, it is Jesus himself who has ultimate authority—he is the Son and the capstone.

"Then they looked for a way to arrest him because they knew he had spoken the parable against them" (12:12).

Question #2—Should We Pay Taxes or Not? (Mark 12:13–17)

> Later they sent some of the Pharisees and Herodians to Jesus to catch him in his words. They came to him and said, "Teacher, we know you are a man of integrity. You aren't swayed by men, because you pay no attention to who they are; but you teach the way of God in accordance with the truth. Is it right to pay taxes to Caesar or not? Should we pay or shouldn't we?" But Jesus knew their hypocrisy. "Why are you trying to trap me?" he asked. "Bring me a denarius and let me look at it." They brought the coin, and he asked them, "Whose portrait is this? And whose inscription?" "Caesar's," they replied. Then Jesus said to them, "Give to Caesar what is Caesar's and to God what is God's." And they were amazed at him. (Mark 12:13–17)

Having not fared well with the first question, the religious leaders are not deterred—they send in reinforcements by way of the Pharisees and the Herodians. Normally, these two groups had nothing to do with each other, but in this situation, they rallied together against a common enemy.[13] They come trying to "catch him in his words" (12:13). The term translated "catch" (*agreuō*) is used only here in the New Testament. It is literally the word for catching a wild animal. It means to trap or ensnare. Once again, their intentions are clear to Jesus who asks, "Why are you trying to trap me?" (12:15).

The whole encounter is framed in the same manner as the previous episode: (1) the approach of the religious leaders, (2) the use of flattery, (3) the subversive question designed to challenge Jesus' authority, (4) Jesus poses a counter question to capture what his opponents really value, (5) the opponents respond and reveal something significant about themselves, and (6) Jesus answers.

The question they ask revolves around paying taxes: "Is it right to pay taxes to Caesar or not?" (12:14). With Roman soldiers presum-

---

13. The enemy of my enemy is my friend.

ably standing within eyesight around the temple mount, the question takes on a new level of intensity. Anyone who avoided paying taxes[14] faced harsh penalties. Anyone who enticed a riot faced death. If Jesus denounced paying taxes to Rome, it would likely bring accusations of treason and rebellion, and could lead to death—the ultimate goal of the religious leaders.

But the Roman taxes were used by these oppressors of Israel to maintain the pagan temples and luxurious lifestyles of the upper class. The Jewish people hated paying taxes. If Jesus commanded them to fulfill their duty (pay taxes), he would be supporting Rome, which would turn the Jewish people against him.

"Jesus knew their hypocrisy" (12:15), and not having a coin of his own, he asked them to bring him a denarius.[15] After examining the coin, Jesus asked them, "Whose portrait is this? And whose inscription?" (12:16). This coin carried on the front a picture of Caesar Tiberius and the inscription, "Son of the Divine Augustus." On the back of the coin was an eagle with the words, "Most High Prince."

In Greek, Jesus' question is even more revealing. Literally, Jesus asks whose "image" (*eikōn*) was stamped upon it. Of course, it bore the image of Caesar. In contrast, we need to remember whose image is stamped upon us: "God created man in his own image, in the image of God he created him; male and female he created them" (Genesis 1:27). Jesus makes it clear that those things that bear the emperor's image should be given to the emperor. But our lives, which bear God's image, belong to God. In the modern vernacular we might say, "Give to Barack, what is Barack's, and give to God what is God's."

I have often heard this passage preached as a tithing passage: "Pay your taxes and pay God." Let me state emphatically, this passage is not about tithing! The point is actually much bigger. You are to give God all that is rightfully his—including your very being, because you bear his image.

Early on I suggested that these passages have a common theme. The first question could be rephrased to ask: Where does the authority

---

14. This particular tax was the tribute paid to the emperor. Caesar at this time was Tiberius (AD 14–37).

15. A denarius was the usual day's wage for a laborer. The coin was minted by the emperor and was considered his property even when in circulation. It was the only currency in which the tax could be paid.

of Jesus come from? Of course the answer is that Jesus is the Christ the Son of the Living God. His authority derives from who he is. The second question asks: Where does your allegiance lie? With Rome or God? Does your allegiance lie with this world or another?

Right in the middle of these two questions about authority, we are given a story about those people who were granted authority by the owner of the vineyard, only to try to revolt against him and usurp his authority. The parable serves as an accurate picture of most lives. Although God is the one who designed us and made us, we often knowingly forget him. We then knowingly reject him, and finally, we attempt to usurp his authority over our lives. Maybe we should ask the question: What then will the owner of the vineyard do? (12:9). The point becomes clear. We must show our allegiance to the one who has true authority.

Personally, I know that everything I have ultimately belongs to God. I never want it to be said of me, that I was a poor steward of what God has given me. I pray that when that day comes, I will hear the words, "Well done, good and faithful servant . . . Come and share your master's happiness" (Matthew 25:21).

Study Questions

1. Whose picture appears on a five dollar bill? Ten? Twenty? Fifty? Hundred?
2. What subject is guaranteed to spark a debate in your family?
3. Why were the religious leaders questioning Jesus' authority?
4. What "things" are the Jewish leaders referring to in verse 28?
5. How is the question about authority a trap for Jesus (11:28)?
6. How could Jesus have answered the question (11:28)?
7. Why doesn't Jesus answer the religious leaders directly? How does he turn the tables on them?
8. How was Jesus' authority linked to John the Baptist?
9. Who do the various characters in the parable of the wicked tenants represent?
    a. The owner
    b. The vineyard

c. The tenants
   d. The servants
   e. The son
10. What real event corresponds to the son's death in the parable?
11. Who are "the others" (12:9) that the owner will give the vineyard to?
12. What was so dangerous about the trap in 12:14–15? What would be the consequences if Jesus simply said, "Pay Caesar"? What would be the consequences if Jesus simply said, "Don't pay Caesar"?
13. How can you "render to Caesar the things that are Caesar's"? What would that mean for us today?
14. Is Jesus the capstone in your life (12:9)?
15. In giving yourself to God, are you in the 15, 28, 45, or 100 percent tax bracket? Why or why not?

For Further Study

16. See Matthew 21:23–46; 22:15–22; Luke 20:1–26.

30

Q & A, Part Two

Mark 12:18–44

AS WE COME TO our passage, we continue with the Day of Questions. Throughout the day, we see people questioning Jesus. No sooner is one group of religious leaders dismissed, than another arises to take their place. First, the Sanhedrin came with a question about the source of Jesus' authority (11:27–33); then the Pharisees and the Herodians came to Jesus with a political question about paying taxes (12:13–17); now, in this passage, the Sadducees try to trap Jesus with a controversial, theological question (12:18–27). One way or another, the religious leaders are bound and determined to eliminate Jesus.

The Sadducees and the Resurrection
(Mark 12:18–27)

> Then the Sadducees, who say there is no resurrection, came to him with a question. "Teacher," they said, "Moses wrote for us that if a man's brother dies and leaves a wife but no children, the man must marry the widow and have children for his brother. Now there were seven brothers. The first one married and died without leaving any children. The second one married the widow, but he also died, leaving no child. It was the same with the third. In fact, none of the seven left any children. Last of all, the woman died too. At the resurrection whose wife will she be, since the seven were married to her?" Jesus replied, "Are you not in error because you do not know the Scriptures or the power of God? When the dead rise, they will neither marry nor be given in marriage; they will be like the angels in heaven. Now about the dead rising—have you not read in the book of Moses, in the account of the bush, how

God said to him, 'I am the God of Abraham, the God of Isaac, and the God of Jacob'? He is not the God of the dead, but of the living. You are badly mistaken!" (Mark 12:18–27)

The appearance of the Sadducees on the scene may reveal one of two things. Either Jesus' opponents were running out of ammunition,[1] or the Sadducees saw an opportunity to put Jesus and the Pharisees in their proper place. In any event, the Sadducees came asking the very question that signifies the division between Pharisees and Sadducees.

The Sadducees' question recorded for us in 12:20–23, is over the top and ridiculous—and intentionally so. They are mocking the Pharisees, who have been unable to answer the specific objection; and now are mocking Jesus, who has spoken on three previous occasions about his own resurrection (8:31; 9:31; 10:34). The Sadducees think that Jesus will fail their test just as the Pharisees before him—but Jesus is about to prove otherwise. Their question centers around the resurrection and Levirate marriage.[2] But to understand their question, we must first understand the background.

This is the first and only mention of the Sadducees in the Gospel of Mark. They are referenced only fourteen times in the entire New Testament[3] compared with over one hundred references to the Pharisees. We actually know very little about the Sadducees, because no documents that are clearly Sadducean have been preserved.[4] Here is what we do know.

The word "Sadducee" likely comes from the name Zadok (*Saddouk* in Greek) who was a High Priest during the time of David.[5] Annas, the high priest (who later questions Peter and John), may have been a Sadducee as well.[6] In any case, the Sadducees were a well-educated bunch and part of the urban, wealthy, sophisticated class who were centralized in Jerusalem. They were a small group numerically (compared

---

1. If, like the others, they are sent by the Pharisees, the Pharisees were desperate enough to send their own opposition to try to trap Jesus, maybe affording the opportunity to come up with another question of their own.

2. Explained later in this chapter.

3. Matthew 3:7; 16:1, 6, 11, 12; 22:23, 24; Mark 12:18; Luke 20:27; Acts 4:1; 5:17; 23:6, 7, 8.

4. When Jerusalem was destroyed in AD 70, they disappeared from history.

5. 2 Samuel 8:17; 15:24–36; 17:15; 18:19–27; 20:25; 1 Kings 1:8–45; etc.

6. Acts 4:1–6.

to the Pharisees), but they wielded great political and religious influence. While they were powerful, they were not popular among the populace.

As mentioned before, they were opponents of the Pharisees. The great rub between the Pharisees and the Sadducees was due to the fact that the Sadducees accepted only the Pentateuch (the first five books of the Old Testament), and rejected all beliefs not found there (the resurrection, angels, spirits),[7] along with all religious innovation. The Pharisees accepted other Old Testament Scripture, along with oral tradition, and were the innovators of much of the religious practices of the day. One question in particular became illustrative of the division between the two groups. The question had at its core the issue of resurrection. It is this question that the Sadducees bring to Jesus (12:18–23).

Apparently, the Pharisees had never been able to come up with a convincing argument in favor of the resurrection from within the Pentateuch—so, as good debaters, the Sadducees kept asking the same question again and again. They had probably asked the question so often, it had taken on ridiculous proportions[8] and become a well-known Sadducean joke used for poking fun at the Pharisees and their beliefs. So, as the Sadducees come to Jesus and call him "teacher" (12:19)—their purpose is not to learn from him, they want to mock him and discredit him.

The question itself is based upon a misapplication of Deuteronomy 25:5–6, which required that if a man died without children, his brother would marry his widow. This is often called Levirate marriage (or law), based on a Latin term *levir* which simply means "brother-in-law." The purpose of the law was to protect a widow (who had no viable source of income) and to guarantee the continuance of the family line. The Sadducees' question was simply, if a woman had seven husbands, "At the resurrection whose wife would she be?" (12:23).

Jesus wasted no time in dealing with the Sadducees. He went directly to their underlying assumption about the resurrection. They were wrong about the resurrection because they didn't know the Scriptures (it is clearly found there), and they were ignorant of the power of God (whose omnipotence makes all things possible).

---

7. Acts 23:8.

8. The story likely has its roots in the apocryphal book of Tobit which shows a woman married to seven men successively who all died without having children, though in the Tobit they are not brothers. The Sadducees mockingly use this story, because they do not accept this as scripture, as do the Pharisees.

Jesus addressed the second misconception first. The Sadducees assumed that if there were a resurrection (which they denied), it would simply be a continuation of life as usual. But Jesus said, "When (not if) the dead rise" (12:24), they will experience a life that is dramatically different. Things in heaven are not like things on earth. Even relationships as we know them will change. Jesus uses their example—marriage: "They will neither marry nor be given in marriage; they will be like the angels in heaven" (12:25). Jesus is not promoting the popular, but erroneous view that we will all be angels in heaven—with our own cloud, a halo, and a golden harp. But Jesus is suggesting that in heaven, the specific aspects of marrying and procreating are no longer necessary. Our relationships in this life are limited by time, death, and sin, but in heaven, the same physical and natural rules do not apply. In heaven, things are not the same! I love the words of Revelation 21:

> Then I saw a new heaven and a new earth, for the first heaven and the first earth had passed away, and there was no longer any sea. I saw the Holy City, the new Jerusalem, coming down out of heaven from God, prepared as a bride beautifully dressed for her husband. And I heard a loud voice from the throne saying, "Now the dwelling of God is with men, and he will live with them. They will be his people, and God himself will be with them and be their God. He will wipe every tear from their eyes. There will be no more death or mourning or crying or pain, for the old order of things has passed away." (Revelation 21:1–4)

After correcting the misconception about marriage, Jesus returns to the issue of resurrection. Because the Sadducees accepted only the Pentateuch as the Word of God, Jesus directed them back to the book of Exodus and the story of Moses and the burning bush. He not only answered them from their Scriptures, but employed a grammatical argument that would have been particularly appealing to the Sadducees. The Sadducees loved to focus on word tenses and sentence nuances. As Jesus takes them back to a beloved story, he points out that when God spoke to Moses, he said to him, "I am the God of Abraham, the God of Isaac, and the God of Jacob" (12:26). By the time God spoke these words to Moses, these patriarchs were long dead. And yet, God did not say, "I was" the God of Abraham, Isaac, and Jacob. God spoke of the dead men as though they were still living.[9] God did not speak of a past relation-

---

9. Jesus answers the Sadducees using a chiastic structure.

ship with Abraham, but a continuing relationship in the present. Jesus was saying, "If you believe in Abraham's God, you should believe that Abraham still exists." The Sadducees were "badly mistaken" (12:27).

As Jesus corrected the Sadducees, another Pharisee[10] came to Jesus.

A Teacher and the Greatest Commandment
(Mark 12:28–34)

> One of the teachers of the law came and heard them debating. Noticing that Jesus had given them a good answer, he asked him, "Of all the commandments, which is the most important?" "The most important one," answered Jesus, "is this: 'Hear, O Israel, the Lord our God, the Lord is one. Love the Lord your God with all your heart and with all your soul and with all your mind and with all your strength.' The second is this: 'Love your neighbor as yourself.' There is no commandment greater than these." "Well said, teacher," the man replied. "You are right in saying that God is one and there is no other but him. To love him with all your heart, with all your understanding and with all your strength, and to love your neighbor as yourself is more important than all burnt offerings and sacrifices." When Jesus saw that he had answered wisely, he said to him, "You are not far from the kingdom of God." And from then on no one dared ask him any more questions. (Mark 12:28–34)

Many suggest that the question asked by the teacher of the law stands in contrast to the previous questions asked of Jesus that day. While the others seemed antagonistic, his question seems to be asked with honest sincerity. A close examination of the parallel account in Matthew demonstrates, however, that Mark simply does not record the man's motive for us. Matthew writes, "One of them, an expert in the law, tested him with this question" (Matthew 22:35).

On first blush, his question may seem insignificant. "Of all the commandments, which is the most important?" (12:28). We might mistakenly think, "There are Ten Commandments, right? Pick one and get on

---

    A. You are in error [*planaō*]
        B. You don't know the scriptures
            C. You don't know the power of God
            C. The power that raises the dead
        B. Have you not read Moses (scripture)
    A. You are badly mistaken [*planaō*]

10. Matthew's account points out that this teacher of the law was a Pharisee.

with it!" We would probably even choose the first: "I am the Lord your God . . . you shall have no other gods before me" (Exodus 20:2-3). The teacher's question, however, runs much deeper. The rabbis counted 613 individual commands in the law. Of these specific commands, 365 were negative prohibitions and 248 were positive requirements. The Pharisees had argued among themselves about which of these was the most important. They attempted to categorize all of them into "great" commands and "light" commands. Even more significant was the attempt to formulate all of the commands under one single principle by which all of the commands could be categorized. This last insight is actually the nature of the question to Jesus. "What is the underlying principle on which all of the law rests?" The teacher comes to Jesus asking that he do what no other Rabbi had successfully accomplished[11] before him—determine what law encapsulated all others. Again, Jesus is able to succeed where others have failed.

In answering this question, Jesus quoted two passages from the Old Testament.[12] The first is called the *Shema*.[13] "Hear, O Israel, the Lord our God, the Lord is one" (12:29). "The second is this: 'Love your neighbor as yourself.' There is no commandment greater than these" (12:31). Jesus explained that in loving God and loving others, the Ten Commandments (and all the other Old Testament commands) are fulfilled. After all the debate and wrestling over the law—the answer was amazingly simple.

The man recognizes the wisdom of Jesus' words (12:32-33) and Jesus commends him for his response: "You are not far from the kingdom of God" (12:34). While the man is "close," he is not in! Entrance into God's kingdom requires more than a simple affirmation that Jesus answered well (12:32-33).

If we were to drop the story here, one might get the impression that the religious leaders and Jesus have actually closed the gap of animosity. One might mistakenly think, "Maybe the two groups can be reconciled." Jesus, however, will ask his own question to demonstrate that there are irreconcilable differences.

---

11. Rabbi Hillel concluded that this command summarized the whole law: "What you hate for yourself, do not do to your neighbor."

12. Deuteronomy 6:4-5 and Leviticus 19:18.

13. In Hebrew, the word *Shema* means "hear" and is taken from the first words of Deuteronomy 6:4-5. Pious Jews recited the *Shema* twice daily.

Jesus and the Son of David (Mark 12:35-37)

> While Jesus was teaching in the temple courts, he asked, "How is it that the teachers of the law say that the Christ is the son of David? David himself, speaking by the Holy Spirit, declared: "'The Lord said to my Lord: "Sit at my right hand until I put your enemies under your feet."' David himself calls him 'Lord.' How then can he be his son?" The large crowd listened to him with delight. (Mark 12:35-37)

Up to this point, Jesus was being asked questions. Now Jesus takes the initiative and asks a question of his own. His doing so demonstrates that Jesus is not content with a truce or stalemate with his opponents. Jesus asks how the teachers of the law can say that the Messiah is the son of David.

Jesus again employs a rabbinic debate technique. By using a Psalm of David he asks a question. The question revolves around two issues. First, the Messiah was expected to be from the family line of David[14] and is therefore a "Son of David." It would not be unusual for the son to refer to the father as "Lord." But the second point is this: It would be very unusual for the father to refer to his son as "Lord." And yet, that is exactly what happens in Scripture. Jesus quotes Psalm 110:1 (a clearly Messianic passage which the Pharisees themselves used to describe the coming Messiah), to make his point. David calls the coming Messiah "Lord."[15] Jesus' point is simple: "How can the Christ be at the same time David's son and David's Lord?" (12:37). The answer is that the Christ is indeed a descendant of David, but he is much more than simply a son—he is the divine Son of God.[16] Jesus is lifting the veil of his identity.

As Jesus speaks, the crowd enjoys Jesus' words. They don't fully understand the implications of Jesus' message, but they delight in seeing the Pharisees beaten at their own game. But Jesus pushes the envelope a step further, by using the religious leaders as a negative example.

---

14. Isaiah 9:2-7; 11:1-9; Jeremiah 23:5-6; 30:9; 33:15, 17, 22; Ezekiel 34:23-24; 37:24; Hosea 3:5; Amos 9:11.

15. Hebrews 1:13 uses the same text as proof of Christ's deity.

16. It is interesting that in this passage the first word David uses as Lord is *Yahweh*—the Hebrew name for God the Father. The second word David uses in Hebrew is *Adonai*—and refers to David speaking of the coming Messiah as his Lord.

A Negative Illustration (Mark 12:38-40)

> As he taught, Jesus said, "Watch out for the teachers of the law. They like to walk around in flowing robes and be greeted in the marketplaces, and have the most important seats in the synagogues and the places of honor at banquets. They devour widows' houses and for a show make lengthy prayers. Such men will be punished most severely." (Mark 12:38-40)

Jesus condemns the religious leaders for their hypocrisy. Their worship was a show. They sought positions of authority for themselves. Their prayers were for the ears of men, rather than for God. They preyed on the unsuspecting. And the words of judgment Jesus uses for them are hard to hear: "Such men will be punished most severely" (12:40). The message is clear: "Do not be like them!"

But Jesus also gives a positive example of what to strive for.

A Positive Illustration (Mark 12:41-44)

> Jesus sat down opposite the place where the offerings were put and watched the crowd putting their money into the temple treasury. Many rich people threw in large amounts. But a poor widow came and put in two very small copper coins, worth only a fraction of a penny. Calling his disciples to him, Jesus said, "I tell you the truth, this poor widow has put more into the treasury than all the others. They all gave out of their wealth; but she, out of her poverty, put in everything—all she had to live on." (Mark 12:41-44)

The story shows in vivid detail the contrast between the greed of the teachers of the law and the purity of the widow. It serves as a good summation of what has gone on previously in the Gospel of Mark. Those who hold themselves first (the religious leaders) will be last, and the last (the widow) will be first. It also preludes what will happen in the following chapters, as Jesus, like the widow, gives up everything.

The story takes place in the courtyard[17] where both men and women were allowed to pass. During the Passover, thirteen trumpet-shaped boxes[18] called "sofars" were used to collect the offerings. Stories are told of how the rich could throw in their coinage in such a way as to "sound the trumpets." As many rich people put in their offerings, a poor widow caught Jesus' attention. She placed in the box two widow's mites—cop-

---

17. Called the court of the women.
18. Seven were for collecting the temple tax, six were for free-will offerings.

per coins called *lepta*,[19] or literally, "tiny things." These were the smallest coins in circulation in Palestine. Mark intentionally explains the money to his Roman audience so they don't miss the point. Two mites were the approximate equivalent to the cent (Greek, *kodrantēs*). Two cents equaled a Roman farthing. The farthing was the smallest Roman coin currently in circulation. Sixteen farthings equaled one denarius, which equaled a laborer's daily wage. This woman gave one sixty-fourth (1/64) of a commoner's daily wage. In our vernacular, it is not wrong to think of this as mere pennies—this woman was truly poor. And yet Jesus says, "I tell you the truth, this poor widow has put more into the treasury than all the others. They all gave out of their wealth; but she, out of her poverty, put in everything—all she had to live on" (12:43–44).

When comparing the gifts of the rich and the gifts of the widow, in proportion, the widow gave far more. In context, we clearly see that the giver and the motive are the true measures of generosity. Jesus makes his point abundantly clear. What Jesus wanted the disciples (and us) to see is that she willingly and unresistantly gave all. She did not give to be seen by men, but gave completely to God—a true lesson in total surrender of self, commitment to God, and willingness to trust his provision.

Once again, rather than being a passage about tithing, Jesus is teaching that a true Christ follower is not one who plays at religion, or who wears a God-facade, but is one who gives all that he has, for all that Christ is.

Study Questions

1. Would you rather ask questions, or answer them? What kind of questions would you ask Jesus if you had the chance?
2. What do you hope for in heaven? How does the hope of going to heaven affect your everyday life?
3. What do you know about the Sadducees (12:18)?
4. What makes the question the Sadducees ask Jesus so interesting?
5. If you heard a story about a woman who had outlived seven husbands, what might you conclude (12:22)?
6. How does Jesus answer the Sadducees' question in 12:24?

---

19. Each coin was called a *leptos*. The plural is *lepta*. Each coin was worth 1/128 of a denarius (a commoner's day wage). Two coins would equal 1/64 of a day's wage.

7. Read 12:25. Do you know what Mormons teach on this subject? Is it right?

8. Why did Jesus accuse the Sadducees of not knowing the Scriptures or the power of God (12:24)?

9. How well do you know your Bible?

10. How does Exodus 3:6 (12:26) demonstrate the fact of the resurrection?

11. What are the implications of God being the God of the living, not the dead?

12. While Mark presents the teacher of law in a rather good light, note what Matthew records for us about his question (Matthew 22:35).

13. What makes the teacher's question difficult to answer?

14. Look closely at 12:29–31. Why are these two commandments the greatest?

15. How well are you living out "the Great Commandment" (12:29–30)?

16. In the three possible love relationships (God, neighbors, self), in which area are you the strongest (12:30–31)?

17. In 12:35–37, Jesus asks a question about "the Son of David." What point is Jesus trying to make in verse 37?

18. Notice the warning to religious leaders in 12:38–40. Do some religious leaders today deserve a similar warning?

19. How do people use religion to make themselves look good? Have you ever been guilty of this?

20. Why did the poor widow catch Jesus' eye? What message is Jesus attempting to convey to the disciples through this incident? What is Jesus' point in contrasting the religious leaders with the widow (12:41–44)?

21. In what way did the widow give more than all the others (12:43)? What motivated the widow to give all she had to live on?

22. What needs to change in your life when it comes to giving back to God?

For Further Study

23. See Matthew 22:23–46; 23:1–12 ; Luke 20:27–47; 21:1–4.

31

Keep Watch

Mark 13:1-37

As we begin, I want to acknowledge two things in advance. First, we are covering a large amount of Scripture. In order to cover the entire chapter, I am unable to give extended treatment to many of the details found within these verses. I have, instead, given a rather broad treatment of the passage and have done so intentionally. We often get so caught up in the many interesting details of this text, that we lose sight of its intended purpose. I will note some of the more important details in the footnotes, but on many I simply will not expound.

The second acknowledgment is this: Christianity has divided far too long over many issues that are not salvation issues. As we come to this passage, we come to a major litmus test for many. The question they ask is: "What is your view of the millennium?" Give the wrong answer, and immediately your very faith is brought into question. Personally, I do not believe that one's view of the second coming constitutes a salvation issue, although I do understand that there are significant ramifications for faith depending on how you answer the question. I recognize that mature Christians have argued, and divided, and divided again over this issue.

I want you to know that I believe that Christ will return physically to take his people home—this is an essential. How exactly that will play out, is an issue over which I will not divide. If you disagree with me, it's okay—often times I don't even agree with myself! Honestly, if you have a different opinion, I respect your right to be wrong (just kidding)!

That being said, as we reach Mark 13, we come to the longest, uninterrupted narrative of Jesus found in the Gospel of Mark. Jesus is leaving the temple area never to return again. As he does, conversation arises about the size and beauty of the temple (13:1). Jesus uses this opportunity to predict the destruction of the temple (13:2). That's the immediate focus of this passage—no scholar doubts this. And yet, this remains a source of confusion because Jesus moves beyond the temple's destruction to teaching about his return (13:26). This has led many to debate over the interpretation of this passage. The difficulty arises in part for three reasons. First, we don't know our Old Testaments well, and therefore miss the allusions found in this passage.[1] Second, we read into this passage our presuppositions about the second coming. And finally, we fail to read the passage carefully and in context.

As we begin our endeavor, I don't want to make these mistakes. No matter what your view of the millennium (and it's okay to disagree), my hope is that we can simply wrestle with the text, and seek to determine the overriding principle that Jesus espouses. This is an attempt to look at the passage in its context and let it speak for itself.

> As he was leaving the temple, one of his disciples said to him, "Look, Teacher! What massive stones! What magnificent buildings!" "Do you see all these great buildings?" replied Jesus. "Not one stone here will be left on another; every one will be thrown down." As Jesus was sitting on the Mount of Olives opposite the temple, Peter, James, John and Andrew asked him privately, "Tell us, when will these things happen? And what will be the sign that they are all about to be fulfilled?" Jesus said to them: "Watch out that no one deceives you. Many will come in my name, claiming, 'I am he,' and will deceive many. When you hear of wars and rumors of wars, do not be alarmed. Such things must happen, but the end is still to come. Nation will rise against nation, and kingdom against kingdom. There will be earthquakes in various places, and famines. These are the beginning of birth pains. You must be on your guard. You will be handed over to the local councils and flogged in the synagogues. On account of me you will stand before governors and kings as witnesses to them. And the gospel must first be preached to all nations. Whenever you are arrested and brought to trial, do not worry beforehand about what to say. Just say whatever is given you at the time, for it is not you speaking, but the Holy Spirit. Brother will betray brother to death, and a father his child. Children will rebel against their parents and have them put to death. All men will hate you because

---

1. For example, the language of the abomination that causes desolation is virtually identical to what appears in Daniel 9:27 and 11:31.

of me, but he who stands firm to the end will be saved. When you see 'the abomination that causes desolation' standing where it does not belong—let the reader understand—then let those who are in Judea flee to the mountains. Let no one on the roof of his house go down or enter the house to take anything out. Let no one in the field go back to get his cloak. How dreadful it will be in those days for pregnant women and nursing mothers! Pray that this will not take place in winter, because those will be days of distress unequaled from the beginning, when God created the world, until now—and never to be equaled again. If the Lord had not cut short those days, no one would survive. But for the sake of the elect, whom he has chosen, he has shortened them. At that time if anyone says to you, 'Look, here is the Christ!' or, 'Look, there he is!' do not believe it. For false Christs and false prophets will appear and perform signs and miracles to deceive the elect—if that were possible. So be on your guard; I have told you everything ahead of time. But in those days, following that distress, 'the sun will be darkened, and the moon will not give its light; the stars will fall from the sky, and the heavenly bodies will be shaken.' At that time men will see the Son of Man coming in clouds with great power and glory. And he will send his angels and gather his elect from the four winds, from the ends of the earth to the ends of the heavens. Now learn this lesson from the fig tree: As soon as its twigs get tender and its leaves come out, you know that summer is near. Even so, when you see these things happening, you know that it is near, right at the door. I tell you the truth, this generation will certainly not pass away until all these things have happened. Heaven and earth will pass away, but my words will never pass away. No one knows about that day or hour, not even the angels in heaven, nor the Son, but only the Father. Be on guard! Be alert! You do not know when that time will come. It's like a man going away: He leaves his house and puts his servants in charge, each with his assigned task, and tells the one at the door to keep watch. Therefore keep watch because you do not know when the owner of the house will come back—whether in the evening, or at midnight, or when the rooster crows, or at dawn. If he comes suddenly, do not let him find you sleeping. What I say to you, I say to everyone: 'Watch!'" (Mark 13:1–37)

As Jesus leaves the temple area, the disciples marvel at the magnificent buildings built out of massive stones (13:1),[2] and the temple mount

---

2. Some of the stones measured twenty-five by eight by twelve feet and weighed more than one hundred tons.

whose buildings occupied approximately one-sixth of all Jerusalem.[3] As they marveled (these Galilean boys didn't get out much), Jesus said, "Do you see all these great buildings? . . . Not one stone here will be left on another; every one will be thrown down" (13:2). Jesus left the temple area and journeyed across the valley and up on the Mount of Olives where he would have had an impressive view of the temple and all of Jerusalem.

We need to stop for a moment and make an important observation. This passage contains, not one, but two important events: the signs of the destruction of the temple, and Christ's second coming. It is necessary to bring clarity to this observation because what is said about one, is not necessarily true of the other.

I would outline this text as follows.

1. The destruction of the temple in Jerusalem (13:1–23).

2. The coming of the Son of Man (13:24–27).

3. The story of the fig tree (13:28–31).

4. The story of the watchman (13:32–37).

Allow me to take a moment and present the evidence that two separate events are indeed in view in this passage, and that the first section has the destruction of the temple in view.

First, let me give you a contextual argument. The conversation between Jesus and the disciples initially centers around the temple and its destruction (13:1–4). In response to Jesus' statement about the stones of the temple being scattered (13:2), Peter, James, John, and Andrew ask Jesus a question: "Tell us, when will these things happen? And what will be the sign that they are all about to be fulfilled?" (13:4). Matthew's account gives us the following question: "When will this happen, and what will be the sign of your coming and of the end of the age?" (Matthew 24:3). This is the context of Jesus' narrative. No scholar doubts that the first part of this passage describes the destruction of the temple in Jerusalem. At the same time, it is also readily apparent that part of this passage refers to the second coming. For example, Jesus says, "At that time men will see the Son of Man coming in the clouds with great power and glory. And he will send his angels and gather his elect from the four

---

3. In addition to the temple proper, the temple mount included porches, colonnades, courtyards and other buildings. Solomon's porch alone was 1,562 feet long.

winds from the ends of the earth to the ends of the heavens" (13:26–27). Few would question the fact that Jesus' return is pictured for us in these verses. Therefore, there are two events in view.

Second, there is the grammatical argument. As our passage begins, Jesus says to four of his disciples (Peter, James, John, Andrew) the following: "Watch out that no one deceives you" (13:5); "When you hear of wars" (13:7); "You must be on your guard" (13:9); "You will be handed over to the Sanhedrin" (13:9); "You will stand before governors and kings" (13:9); "When you see the abomination that causes desolation" (13:14); and, "This generation will not pass away until these things happen" (13:30). Tell me, who are these words directed to? The obvious answer is—to Peter, James, John, and Andrew. Many times in this passage, the use of the word "you" is emphatic. It is readily apparent that the first part of this passage relates to something that will happen in their lifetime[4] and speaks directly about the temple. Again, no scholar denies this.

Third, there is the historical argument. When Jesus speaks about "The abomination that causes desolation" (13:14), he is alluding to the Old Testament passage of Daniel 9:27. Daniel predicted the desecration of the temple which occurred as Antiochus IV slaughtered a pig on the temple altar. This abomination took place in 167 BC and would have stirred up an intense reaction in the hearts of the disciples as Jesus described it. Jesus, using this allusion, predicts another abomination—the coming destruction of the temple by the Romans in AD 70. The destruction of the temple is clearly in view in the first part of our narrative. One need only took to Luke's account where he says, "When you see Jerusalem being surrounded by armies, you will know that its desolation is near" (Luke 21:21).

The fourth argument is a pragmatic argument. Jesus makes the following comments to the Apostles in the first part of our passage: "Pray it's not winter" (13:18); "How dreadful it will be . . . for pregnant women and nursing mothers" (3:17); "Let no one on the roof of his house go down or enter the house to take anything out" (3:15); "Let no one in the fields go back to get his cloak" (3:16). If these refer to Christ's second coming, what good are Christ's instructions to them? Even more out of place is the command he gives: "Then let those who are in Judea flee

---

4. Some do define "generation" as race or genealogy. This is not, however, consistent with how Jesus uses the term. Jesus, for example, does not ask, "Why does your race ask for a sign?"

to the mountains" (13:14). These remarks make no sense in regard to Christ's second coming, but make perfect sense in relationship to an invading army bent on capturing Jerusalem and destroying the temple. The first section of this dialogue clearly centers on the destruction of the temple and its warning signs.

The final line of reasoning is the chronological argument. In answering the disciples' questions: "When will these things happen? And what will be the sign that they are all about to be fulfilled?" (13:4), Jesus responds, "So be on your guard; I have told you everything ahead of time" (13:23). At this point, Jesus changes focus. Notice his words: "But in those days, following that distress" (13:24). Following what distress? Clearly, the destruction of the temple—the desolation is in view. The events that Jesus will now describe happen after the previous distress. This brief survey shows that originally, Mark 13:5–23 focused on the destruction of the temple while 13:24–27 centers on the return of Christ. We have identified two separate and distinct events.

Only after we acknowledge this fact, can we realize that the predictive signs given in Mark 13:5–23 served primarily as predictors of the coming destruction of the temple in Jerusalem. To discern this event, the disciples were given many clues. There would be many deceivers (13:6). There would be wars and rumors of war (13:7). There would be earthquakes and famines (13:8). The Apostles would be delivered over to the Sanhedrin[5] and speak before governors and kings (13:9). They would be betrayed, arrested, and put on trial (13:11). All of these predictions came true and served as warning signs. For those who were prepared, the conquest of Jerusalem and destruction of the temple were not a surprise. Those who heeded Jesus' warnings in AD 70, fled to the mountains to safety, while those who remained in Jerusalem were slaughtered and killed.

Do not misunderstand me. I am not suggesting that a "post-AD 70" world will not be inflicted with wars and rumors of wars, or earthquakes, or false prophets. I am suggesting, however, that these signs were initially meant to serve as warning signs for the destruction of Jerusalem, not as commonly suggested, warning signs of the second coming. In fact, if we are studying Mark's narrative, Jesus gives no signs of forewarning that predict his coming. Actually, the point of this passage is that no man knows when Christ's return will occur (13:32).

---

5. The word translated by the NIV as "councils" is literally *synedrion* or Sanhedrin.

When the temple was destroyed, from the perspective of the disciples, it undoubtedly looked like the world had ended, but it had not. Jesus makes it clear that although the temple would be destroyed, the stone the builders rejected would become the capstone for a new temple (God's people), a new era (Christ's kingdom), and a bright future which will culminate in the return of Christ.

According to Jesus' words recorded for us here in Mark, although there are predictive signs preceding the annihilation of the temple, there are not necessarily premonitory signs for Christ's return. It will come unexpectedly, but unmistakably. The events surrounding his return will be cataclysmic.

> But in those days, following that distress, "the sun will be darkened, and the moon will not give its light; the stars will fall from the sky, and the heavenly bodies will be shaken." At that time men will see the Son of Man coming in clouds with great power and glory. And he will send his angels and gather his elect from the four winds, from the ends of the earth to the ends of the heavens. (Mark 13:24–27)

The events of the final day will include the following:

1. The sun will be darkened (13:24).
2. The moon won't give light (13:24).
3. The stars will fall from the sky (13:25).
4. The Son of Man will be visible to all (13:26).
5. He will come with angels (13:27).

This certainly squares with what we read elsewhere in scripture. Peter says, "But the day of the Lord will come like a thief" (2 Peter 3:10). Paul writes:

> For you know very well that the day of the Lord will come like a thief in the night. While people are saying "Peace and safety," destruction will come on them suddenly, as labor pains on a pregnant woman, and they will not escape." (1 Thessalonians 5:2–3)

I am not always the most observant. But of this I am quite aware: thieves generally don't make appointments. One of their critical success factors is not leaving signs of their coming. The second coming will happen at a time when it is not expected.

At this point, Jesus gives two parables.[6] The first relates to the destruction of the temple; the second to his return. We can make this distinction in light of a couple of clear grammatical indicators. The first is the phrasing Jesus uses in the lesson of the fig tree.

> Now learn this lesson from the fig tree: As soon as its twigs get tender and its leaves come out, you know that summer is near. Even so, when you see these things happening, you know that it is near, right at the door. I tell you the truth, this generation will certainly not pass away until all these things have happened. Heaven and earth will pass away, but my words will never pass away. (Mark 13:28–31)

Notice Jesus' words: "Even so when you see these things happening" (13:29) and "Until these things have happened" (13:30). This is a restatement of the disciples' question about the destruction of the temple: "Tell us, when will these things happen?" (13:4). It is also made clear by the phrase, "This generation will certainly not pass away until these things have happened" (13:30). Notice the repeated emphasis on "these things." Jesus directly answers the disciples' question and tells them that they will witness the event Jesus is describing. With these observations in view, there can be no doubt Jesus has returned to the topic of the temple's destruction.

His point is also easily discernable—just as fig leaves signify that summer has come, the predictive signs will forewarn the coming of the destruction of the temple (13:29). But even when it happens, the end has not yet come.

Then Jesus tells a second parable—about the second event. Notice how the language changes from "these things" to "at that time." Earlier Jesus said, "At that time men will see the Son of Man coming in clouds" (13:26). Now Jesus says, "No one knows about that day or hour" (13:32).

> Therefore keep watch because you do not know when the owner of the house will come back—whether in the evening, or at midnight, or when the rooster crows, or at dawn. If he comes suddenly, do not let him find you sleeping. What I say to you, I say to everyone: "Watch!" (Mark 13:35–37)

---

6. The word translated by the NIV as "lesson" is the word "parable" (*parabolē*).

We are given several clear statements regarding the second coming. No one knows: not the angels, nor the Son, but only the Father (13:32). You don't know when that time will come (13:33). It may be evening, or midnight, or daybreak (13:35).

Over the years I have heard people predict when Jesus would return. One man even suggested, "I don't know the day or the hour, but I think I have the month figured out."

Jesus' point is clear. "Be on guard! Be alert" (13:33). "Do not let him find you sleeping" (13:36). "What I say to you, I say to everyone: 'Watch!'" (13:37). We are to keep watch because we do not know when Christ will come. We are to remain faithful expecting his return. We are to remain prepared because we don't know when the owner will come back. But two things are certain: It could happen at any moment—and we must be ready.

As I write this, rescue attempts are being made in Haiti after an extreme earthquake. An estimated 250,000 people may have died in this small country. Immediately, people began to question me: "Is this a sign of his coming?" I remember similar questions after hurricane Katrina swept the shores of New Orleans, or after the Tsunami of 2004 in Indonesia. Of course the second coming was a main topic of discussion after the terrorist attack on the twin towers. But are these signs of Christ's coming? Obviously, Christ's return is closer than ever before, but Christ's return is not dependent upon yet another earthquake, another false prophet, or another war. Jesus could return tomorrow, and no one could claim, "Jesus, your prophecies about your coming were left unfulfilled." Jesus' command to his disciples, as well as his command to us is simply: "Watch!"

Study Questions

1. What prompts Jesus' lesson about the destruction of the temple (13:1–2)?

2. How do you think the disciples felt as Jesus was describing the destruction of Jerusalem/the temple and the persecution of Christians?

3. In AD 70, Jerusalem and the temple were destroyed by the Romans. Why did Jesus warn of this event? Why would this be so terrifying?

4. What made the temple so significant for the disciples?
5. What would the temple's destruction symbolize for them?
6. What should the inhabitants of Judea do (and not do) when they see that the temple is about to be destroyed (13:14–18)?
7. According to Luke 21:20, when will the desolation happen?
8. What questions about this passage would you ask Jesus if you had the opportunity?
9. According to 13:9–13, what types of persecution would the disciples face as they spread the gospel?
10. What comforter and advocate will aid them to endure their trials (13:11)?
11. Have you ever faced persecution for your faith?
12. How does verse 13 apply to believers today?
13. How does verse 32 impact all the end time predictions we tend to hear today?
14. Have you known people/groups who have made predictions about the second coming?
15. Why might God want to keep the time of the second coming secret (13:32)?
16. In light of Christ's second coming, how should we live (13:32–37)?
17. What is the most exciting aspect of the second coming to you? What is the most distressing?
18. How does Jesus describe his second coming in verses 24–27?
19. According to 13:32–37, when will the second coming happen?
20. How do 1 Thessalonians 5:2–3 and 2 Peter 3:10 shed light on Jesus' second coming?
21. What can you do to become better prepared for Christ's return?

For Further Study

22. See Matthew 24:1–25 and Luke 21:5–24.

32

A Beautiful Thing

Mark 14:1-11

As we come to chapter 14, we find ourselves at Thursday in the last week of Jesus' life. While the religious leaders continue to try to find a way to arrest and kill Jesus, not everyone shares their animosity. Mark inserts an earlier account which takes place at the home of Simon the Leper where a woman comes and anoints Jesus with expensive perfume.[1] This beloved story is intentionally sandwiched between two acts of evil. On the top side (14:1-2) are the schemers who desire to kill Jesus and who won't stop until he is arrested, tried, and convicted. On the bottom side (14:10, 11) we read of Judas' treachery as he sells out Jesus to the chief priests.

Mark includes this story in his narrative, to show the contrast between those who live their lives out of selfishness and pettiness, and those who live life out of gratitude and thankfulness. This story not only informs us of a beautiful act that one woman did for Jesus, but is meant to inspire us to rise above the pettiness, the selfishness, and the evil that is very much a part of this world.

> Now the Passover and the Feast of Unleavened Bread were only two days away, and the chief priests and the teachers of the law were looking for some sly way to arrest Jesus and kill him. "But not during the Feast," they said, "or the people may riot." While he was in Bethany, reclining at the table in the home of a man

---

1. The time stamp of 14:1-2 reflects the actions of the chief priests and teachers of the law on Thursday of the Passion week and also applies to 14:10-12. Mark intentionally inserts 14:3-9 at this spot to create a sandwich between those who are hostile towards Jesus and the actions of the woman bringing perfume to anoint Jesus. John 12:1-11 relates that this middle portion occurred six days before Passover.

known as Simon the Leper, a woman came with an alabaster jar of very expensive perfume, made of pure nard. She broke the jar and poured the perfume on his head. Some of those present were saying indignantly to one another, "Why this waste of perfume? It could have been sold for more than a year's wages and the money given to the poor." And they rebuked her harshly. "Leave her alone," said Jesus. "Why are you bothering her? She has done a beautiful thing to me. The poor you will always have with you, and you can help them any time you want. But you will not always have me. She did what she could. She poured perfume on my body beforehand to prepare for my burial. I tell you the truth, wherever the gospel is preached throughout the world, what she has done will also be told, in memory of her." Then Judas Iscariot, one of the Twelve, went to the chief priests to betray Jesus to them. They were delighted to hear this and promised to give him money. So he watched for an opportunity to hand him over. (Mark 14:1–11)

Background

The setting is Bethany, a town about two miles from Jerusalem located just over the hill on the eastern slope of the Mount of Olives. Bethany is the home of Lazarus, Mary and Martha. But the story does not take place there, but rather at the home of Simon the Leper.

We cannot identify Simon anywhere else in scripture, but he is evidently well known to Jesus and his followers. We can probably assume that Simon once had leprosy, but that Jesus had cured him of this highly contagious disease or this event would not be taking place in his home. Jesus is attending a special banquet that is being held in his honor, and is eating at the table when a woman enters,[2] breaks an alabaster jar, and pours perfumed ointment of pure nard on Jesus' head. The woman who anointed Jesus is identified in the Gospel of John as Mary, the sister of Martha and Lazarus (John 12:3).

Jesus says that her act of compassion will be told wherever the gospel is preached. What is it about Mary's gift that is so remarkable? I believe there are at least five characteristics of Mary's gift that we would do well to emulate in our lives.

---

2. Women did not normally enter a dinner setting where men were eating, except to serve them. This detail alone would have raised more than a few eyebrows.

She Gave with a Right Motive (Mark 14:6)

"She has done a beautiful thing" (14:6).

Have you ever had someone befriend you just to get something from you in return; or had someone feign friendship only to find out that they had ulterior motives? A few years ago there was a man who kept offering me assistance under the guise of friendship. I really wasn't interested in what he was offering and told him so. But, he continued to stop by my office—I assumed out of friendship. Finally, I returned the favor—I stopped by his business to say hello. We had what I thought was a friendly visit which lasted for only a couple of minutes. Days later, I received a bill for $175 for "consultation fees," including three sessions which apparently took place in my office—the very days he stopped at the church. I was shocked. Feigned friendship.

A cartoon which appeared in *The New Yorker* magazine shows a group of hogs eagerly assembled for feeding as a farmer is filling their trough to the brim. One pig suspiciously asks the others in the group, "Have you ever wondered *why* he's being so good to us?" Ulterior motives. Someone has said, "There is no hypocrite to rival the man who pretends to like folks in order to exploit them."

We have certainly seen ulterior motives in the lives of the Pharisees and Sadducees as they tried to flatter Jesus before asking their questions (12:14; 19). But there are no ulterior motives or hint of deception in Mary. In fact, in verse 6 Jesus says, "She has done a beautiful thing." Her actions were pure and thoughtful. Mary did not give to get something from Jesus. She didn't act out of false pretenses. There were no surreptitious motives to her gift. She gave out of appreciation. She gave out of thankfulness. She gave out of love.

Jesus had taught her many life lessons. Jesus had been kind and compassionate. Jesus had been a real friend to her and her family. And, most of all, Jesus had even raised her brother Lazarus from the dead. That was her motivation for giving—appreciation, love, and thankfulness.

And those are the reasons we should give. The reason we worship and serve Christ should be—first and foremost—because of who he is and what he has done. He is the living Son of God. It is he who has broken for us the bondage of sin and death. It is he who has opened the door into the presence of God. It is he who died for our sins on the cross. It is he who has taught us how to live and how to love, and provided us hope for the future. Our worship of him should stem from pure motives of appreciation, love and thankfulness for all that he has done. We need to give with right motives.

Jesus said in Matthew 5:8, "Blessed are the pure in heart, for they will see God." And this purity of heart is not limited to our relationship with God, but it also manifests itself in our relationships with others. As Christians, we should be generous and giving; and our motivation for kindness should never stem from the desire to get something in return, but because of thoughtfulness and thankfulness for all that we have been given. As Christians, we need to practice random acts of kindness and do so with the right motives.

She Gave Lavishly (Mark 14:3)

Mark tells us that Mary "... came with an alabaster jar of very expensive perfume, made of pure nard ... broke the jar and poured the perfume on His head" (14:3).

Nard is distilled from a plant that is native to the area around India and the Himalayas. It was an expensive perfume formed from two plants: nadala, imported from Nepal, and spike; and is sometimes called spikenard. Mark makes it clear that many objected because it was very expensive: "Why this waste of perfume? It could have been sold for more than a year's wages" (14:4–5). John tells us that Judas objected the most vehemently (John 12:4–6). We are told that what Mary poured on Jesus represented a year's wages, or three hundred denarii.

To put this in perspective, I want to remind you of the account of the feeding of the five thousand (6:30–44). When Jesus instructed the disciples to feed the crowd, they responded, "That would take eight months of a man's wage" (6:37)! That was two hundred denarii—enough to feed 5,000 people. Based on that formula, Mary's gift would have fed 7,500 people.

As I write, I am reminded of the current Subway sandwich commercials which advertise "Five-dollar footlongs." Give each of the 7,500 people a sub sandwich and it would cost $37,500, even if we made them purchase their own chips and soda. It is no wonder that gift raised eyebrows.

Mary did not save back any of the perfume. Mary spent it all on Jesus. You might ask how Mary came to have this expensive perfume. Maybe it was a family heirloom that was passed on from one generation to another, from mother to daughter. Maybe she had saved money for a very long time to buy it.³ Maybe she herself had been given this expensive gift. Whatever the case, Mary gave it all, and Jesus commends her for it.

It is interesting that throughout Scripture, Jesus always praised the person who made the big commitment. He always honored loyalty and sacrifice. Jesus praised those who gave with abandonment. In chapter 12 he applauds the widow who gave pennies because it was all she had, and now, in chapter 14, we have the story of Mary. These gifts were just a foretaste of the way Jesus himself gave. He gave everything he had—everything he was—he gave his very life.

Take note of this lesson. Love is sometimes extravagant. When ordinary acts do not suffice to express one's feelings, an extraordinary show of love is in order. And it should be true of us, when one has experienced the love and forgiveness of Christ, the natural reaction, for the Christian, is to love back—to love in a big way. To love with lavish abandonment.

She Gave with Originality (Mark 14:8)

There is a very interesting phrase in verse 8. Jesus said of Mary, "She did what she could" (14:8). Some translations say, she gave what she had. Literally, it reads, "What she had, she did." Maybe this was the one possession, the one thing, the one treasure that Mary valued. It was an object of meaning. The language even suggests that this was the only thing that Mary could give. She did what she could!

Do you remember the story from earlier in the gospels where Martha got upset because she was doing all the cooking, and Mary was simply sitting listening to Jesus? Mary and Martha were two different personality types. Martha was always cooking and working around the house. Chances are, even though this wasn't her home, you could have found Martha helping with the preparations. That's what Martha did. But Mary was different. She was more of the artist and inquirer. Preparing a meal suited Martha, but somehow, the perfume represented Mary and was what she treasured, so that's what she gave. She had answered the question: What could I give of value to Jesus and what would be the most meaningful?

---

3. This would have been out of the reach of most women. Some have speculated that Mary's previous lifestyle as a prostitute enabled her to buy this gift.

People criticized and rebuked (*embrimaomai*) Mary. An interesting word is used here. It is literally the word to snort or roar. Its used of angry horses.[4] The people were stomping about and accusing her of being extravagant.

Present at the supper were at least fifteen men. Besides Jesus, there were twelve disciples, Lazarus and Simon the Leper. They were all snorting around claiming that there were better uses for the money. They "spiritualized" their own selfishness and pettiness, and criticized Mary. They gave the "church answer"—let's give it to the poor.[5]

But, if you really think about it, if they were *that* concerned about the needy, they could have fasted from their dinner celebration and given their food to the poor. The people in the room were being picky and petty.

It is interesting that Mary gives to Jesus perfume worth a year's wages, and yet the one who makes the most ruckus about her gift (Judas), sells Jesus to the high priest for the insignificant price of a common slave.

It is telling that Jesus rebukes the disciples and commends Mary for her originality. He says, "Leave her alone, why are you bothering her . . ." (14:6). She will become an example of giving wherever the gospel is preached (14:9).

She Gave to Be Helpful (Mark 14:7–8)

Mark tells us: "She broke the jar and poured perfume on his head" (14:7–8). This is the only gift Jesus receives before his death, except of course, for the kiss of betrayal from Judas.

We don't know exactly what Mary is thinking. She may have been anointing Jesus as the Messiah, but the perfume she uses was often associated with burial. Jesus certainly implies that Mary understands the meaning of the moment. "She poured perfume on my body beforehand to prepare for my burial" (14:8). Jesus was touched deeply by what she did. Jesus had been speaking about his upcoming death, and it appears that out of all the people present—the disciples and others who were

---

4. *Embrimaomai*. To scold or censure. Originally used to describe the snort of a horse. Used only five times in scripture: Mark 1:43; 14:5; Matthew 9:30; John 11:33, 38.

5. The contrast is between the perpetual opportunity to help the poor and the immediate need of Jesus and his impending death. Some twist Jesus' words as a justification for not helping the destitute, but this is a misapplication of this passage.

gathered in this room—Mary is the only one who understands what Jesus has been talking about. Mary, in her thoughtfulness, takes the time to anoint the head of Jesus with perfume while he is still living.

Mary was sensitive to the situation. She was a true friend. While all the others were unresponsive, not really hearing or understanding or caring what was troubling Jesus, Mary listened with her heart to his feelings. She understood that Jesus was concerned and troubled. Jesus' heart was in turmoil and Mary's gift was a needed source of consolation.

Here again we find a valuable truth. In times of struggle, more times than not, what a person really needs is someone who will listen and try to understand and provide comfort. Compassion provides strength. And that's what Mary offered.

There is a story about Sam Rayburn, who was Speaker for The House of Representatives longer than any other man. One of his friends lost a teenage daughter and early the next morning Rayburn knocked on his door. When his friends opened the door, he gave them a big hug and said, "I just came by to see what I could do to help." The father replied that there was nothing he could do. Rayburn said, "Have you had your coffee this morning?" The man replied that they had not taken time for breakfast and so Rayburn went to work in the kitchen. While Rayburn was working, the man came in, and said to his friend, "Mr. Speaker, I thought you were supposed to be having breakfast at the White House with the White House staff this morning." Rayburn responded, "Well, I was, but I called the President and told him I had something more important. I had a friend who was in trouble and I couldn't come."

Jesus was more important than a jar of costly perfume.

She Gave at the Right Time (Mark 14:8)

"She poured perfume on my body beforehand to prepare for my burial" (14:8). Mary gave when it would do the most good: she gave while Jesus was alive. She was different than Nicodemus who anointed Jesus' body after He had died, or Joseph of Arimathea who provided the burial tomb. Mary gave while Jesus was still around to enjoy it.

Timing is so very important. Kind words at a eulogy are nice and comforting, but words of praise and encouragement before death are more helpful. Flowers at a graveside help to express love and appreciation for the one who has died, but small gifts before death are more appreciated. It's amazing how we can always find time to attend a funeral, but rarely have time to visit a living friend.

I have stood at many funerals and heard these, all-too-common words . . . "If only." "If only I had the opportunity to say what needed to be said. If only I had the opportunity to do what needed to be done. If only I had shared Christ. If only I had spent more time. If only . . ." The phrases are as varied as the people who speak them.

Our lives are full of opportunities to show compassion, love, and thankfulness, and yet so often we let those opportunities slip away. Mary challenges us to rise to new levels of compassion as we learn how to give to others and how to give to God, as she gave.

Where is your heart? What are your priorities? What are you waiting for? Life is too short, and time is too precious to waste what has been given us. What can you do this week to show sensitivity and concern for those you love? What is it that you need to do now with your life, that you have been putting off? Don't delay, lead from your heart—it would be a beautiful thing!

Study Questions

1. What is the greatest act of kindness someone has ever done for you?
2. If you had a year's wages to blow on friends, what would you do? Would it be a gift for many, or an extravagant gift for one? What might the gift be?
3. If you had a year's salary (or a year of service) to give to Christ, what would you do? How is your time and money reflected in your budget and priorities now?
4. What do you think motivated Mary's gift to Jesus?
5. How did others view Mary's extravagant display (4–5)? How did Jesus view it (6)?
6. Given the value of the perfume, how would you have reacted as you watched Mary?
7. Is Jesus saying that we shouldn't care for the poor?
8. How would you summarize what Jesus is trying to say in verse 7?

9. Read the first part of verse 8. What strikes you about Jesus' comment "She did what she could"?

10. Could/would Jesus say of you that you have done what you could? Why or why not?

11. What was the significance of Mary's anointing of Jesus?

12. Why did Mary seem to know to prepare Jesus for his burial when the disciples did not?

13. What was Judas's motivation in betraying Christ? How might Mary's gift to Jesus have motivated Judas's actions in verse 10?

14. What stands in the way of you truly worshiping God?

15. What beautiful thing could you do this week for Jesus?

For Further Study

16. See Matthew 26:1–16; Luke 22:1–6; John 12:1–11.

33

No Ordinary Meal

Mark 14:12-26

As our story begins, hundreds of thousands of people are making their pilgrimage toward Jerusalem to celebrate the Passover. Passover was a holiday instituted by God himself. It was designed to celebrate Israel's deliverance from Egypt and to remind the people of what God had done by rescuing them. The celebration was an expression of covenant, and centered around a meal—but it was no ordinary meal—it was done in remembrance. It reminded Israel that through Moses, God performed a series of plagues against Pharaoh and Egypt that culminated in the plague of death against all male first-born children. During the first Passover, in order to be spared from that last plague of death,[1] a lamb with no defects had to be killed and the blood from that sacrifice needed to be placed on the doorframes of each home. The lamb was not only a sacrifice, but a substitute for each person who would have died in the plague. Every year, Passover was reenacted, commemorating the events that freed the children of Israel from the bonds of their slavery in Egypt.

As we read this passage,[2] we need to be thinking with the mind-set of a first-century Hebrew: "This is no ordinary meal! This is the most important meal of the year!"

> On the first day of the Feast of Unleavened Bread, when it was customary to sacrifice the Passover lamb, Jesus' disciples asked him, "Where do you want us to go and make preparations for you

---

1. See Exodus 12 for details about the Passover.

2. This is one of four accounts in N.T. It is also found in Matthew 26:26–29; Luke 22:15–20; and 1 Corinthians 11:23–25.

to eat the Passover?" So he sent two of his disciples, telling them, "Go into the city, and a man carrying a jar of water will meet you. Follow him. Say to the owner of the house he enters, 'The Teacher asks: Where is my guest room, where I may eat the Passover with my disciples?' He will show you a large upper room, furnished and ready. Make preparations for us there." The disciples left, went into the city and found things just as Jesus had told them. So they prepared the Passover. (Mark 14:12–16)

Passover Secretly Prepared (Mark 14:12–16)

This particular Passover was unusual inasmuch as it was secretly prepared. Our passage reads like a covert op. The disciples are excited about the Pascal meal and ask Jesus where they should make preparations (14:12), including specific items that need to be purchased, acquiring a lamb to take to the temple for slaughter, the roasting of the lamb as prescribed by Jewish law, etc.[3] They also need a place inside Jerusalem to have the meal.[4] But instead of disclosing a location, Jesus gives two disciples, Peter and John,[5] veiled instructions: "Go into the city, and a man carrying a jar of water will meet you. Follow him" (14:13). Jesus' instructions are a bit strange. Women carried water jars—not men. This might be akin to someone saying, "Go down to the city center and follow the guy carrying the 'man purse.'"

The obvious question that needs to be answered is: Why the secrecy and cloak-and-dagger methods? John's gospel reveals the answer—there was a warrant out for Jesus' arrest: "But the chief priests and Pharisees had given orders that if anyone found out where Jesus was, he should report it so that they might arrest him" (John 11:57).

To avoid premature arrest, Jesus has made previous arrangements. He has not only prearranged the secret rendevous, and orchestrated a signal the disciples could recognize so they could follow without saying a word; but has arranged accommodations, and likely arranged obtaining the lamb.[6]

---

3. Exodus 12:8–9.

4. Jewish law required that the Passover meal be eaten within Jerusalem, although the boundaries of Jerusalem were extended to accommodate the sheer number of people.

5. Luke 22:8 reveals the identity of the two disciples.

6. The prearranged nature of this event is strikingly similar to the account of the

All this was necessary. Mark refers to this day as "The first day of the Feast of Unleavened Bread" (14:12). Technically speaking, the first day of the feast was the day after Passover, but it had become common to celebrate them together.[7] We can be certain of the timetable because Mark indicates it for us: "When it was customary to sacrifice the Passover lamb" (14:12). Early on this day, a ceremonial search was conducted of every home, trying to remove all leaven from each dwelling. At noon, all work stopped. At three o'clock, lambs were taken to the temple to be slaughtered and their blood sprinkled on the altar at the temple. Jesus and the disciples would be unable to show themselves in the temple area for fear of arrest, so someone else needed to perform this task. But Jesus had arranged everything. "Say to the owner of the house he enters, 'The Teacher asks: Where is my guest room, where I may eat the Passover with my disciples?' He will show you a large upper room, furnished and ready" (14:14-15). Early tradition, as well as biblical nuances, suggest that the upper room was likely the childhood home of John Mark.[8]

This was no ordinary meal, it was a Passover like none other.

Passover Grievously Celebrated (Mark 14:17-21)

> When evening came, Jesus arrived with the Twelve. While they were reclining at the table eating, he said, "I tell you the truth, one of you will betray me—one who is eating with me." They were saddened, and one by one they said to him, "Surely not I?" "It is one of the Twelve," he replied, "one who dips bread into the bowl with me. The Son of Man will go just as it is written about him. But woe to that man who betrays the Son of Man! It would be better for him if he had not been born." (Mark 14:17-21)

The Passover meal began after sunset[9] and usually continued until midnight. We read that the disciples reclined[10] at the table. We should not,

---

Triumphal entry and the acquisition of the colt. In fact, eleven Greek words are identical to the story in Mark 11.

7. 2 Chronicles 35:17.

8. This was the home to which Peter returned when being released from prison (Acts 12:12) and the probable location for the events of Acts 2:1ff. It is speculated that John Mark is the young boy who follows Jesus and the disciples to the garden wearing nothing but a linen garment (12:51).

9. The beginning of Nisan 15. Nisan usually falls somewhere in March or April.

10. The original Passover meal was to be eaten while standing. By the first century,

however, limit this meal to only the disciples—many others were likely present as well. As they were joyously eating, Jesus threw a wrench in the celebration: "I tell you the truth, one of you will betray me" (14:18). This came like a bombshell to the disciples—even though he had predicted his betrayal twice previously.[11] Jesus made the moment painfully awkward. One in their midst had turned "Benedict." The NIV translates the word used to describe the moment as "saddened," but it is actually much stronger. They are grieved (*lypeō*), pained, insulted and offended.

Each disciple examines his own life and motivation, and each in turn responds, "Surely not I?"[12] (14:19). Even Judas chimes in, "Surely not I, Rabbi?" (Matthew 26:25). But Jesus reassures no one. Jesus simply acknowledges that it is, "One who is eating with me"[13] (14:18); "It is one of the Twelve" (14:20a); and, "One who dips bread into the bowl"[14] (14:20b).

It is hard for us to imagine the horror the disciples felt without understanding a principle called "Table Fellowship." To eat a meal with someone around their table signified that you were throwing your hat in with them. This is why Jesus was condemned by the religious leaders when he ate with tax collectors and sinners.[15] Eating with someone morally barred one from hostile actions. It was evidence of peace, trust, brotherhood, and forgiveness. To betray someone whom you had eaten with was a horrendous act. It was considered so terrible that Jesus even says, "Woe to the man who betrays the Son of Man! It would be better for him if he had not been born" (14:21).

This horrendous act, committed by Judas, fulfilled what scripture had said about the Son of Man (14:21): "Even my close friend, whom I trusted, he who shared my bread, has lifted up his heel against me" (Psalm 41:9).

The meal of celebration turned somber, and thus it was no ordinary meal.

---

it had taken on a more formal setting. In Hellenistic fashion, guests reclined on a couch that stretched around three sides of a room. The host took the center seat at a U-shaped series of low tables, surrounded by the most honored guests on either side, with the guests' heads reclining toward the tables and their feet toward the wall.

11. Mark 9:31 and 10:33.
12. More literally, "It is not I, is it?"
13. No definite article is used here.
14. The use of a common bowl provided anonymity even with this statement.
15. Mark 2:15–16.

Passover Redefined (Mark 14:22-26)

> While they were eating, Jesus took bread, gave thanks and broke it, and gave it to his disciples, saying, "Take it; this is my body." Then he took the cup, gave thanks and offered it to them, and they all drank from it. "This is my blood of the covenant, which is poured out for many," he said to them. "I tell you the truth, I will not drink again of the fruit of the vine until that day when I drink it anew in the kingdom of God." When they had sung a hymn, they went out to the Mount of Olives. (Mark 14:22-26)

As mentioned previously, the Passover meal for the Jews symbolized the deliverance of Israel from Egypt and the details of its observance were very specific. Each element had deep significance because God wanted to embed meaning into the mind of the Hebrews. The Pascal lamb, unleavened bread free of yeast, and a hyssop branch dipped in blood and used to paint the doorframe were indelibly fixed in the minds of all participants.

But Jesus takes these elements and gives them new meaning. Rather than looking back to Exodus, he looks forward. Jesus takes the bread and the cup and uses them to illustrate the liberating power of his death on the cross which is imminent. The bread and cup, used to celebrate deliverance from Egyptian slavery, now represents release from the slavery to sin. Jesus liberally redefines the elements. He uses them to give us a living parable and changes the metaphor. Jesus becomes the Pascal Lamb. The bread and cup are connected to his coming suffering and death.

He also alludes to the violent nature of his death. He took the bread and broke it, saying, "Take it; this is my body" (14:22). He then took the cup and they drank from it. Jesus said, "This is my blood of the covenant, which is poured out for many" (14:24). What is so significant is that Jesus uses articles of food so simple and so universal that the disciples can never again recline at a meal, take bread, or drink from the fruit of the vine without thinking about the last night they were together. They were common, everyday reminders of what Jesus would accomplish on the cross—mnemonic devices to aid memory. Far from being rare and infrequent, they were daily reminders of Christ's sacrifice.

The earliest traditions of Christianity indicate that the Lord's Supper was a regular part of church meetings, and the memory of a last supper with the Twelve was a regular part of the story of Jesus (Acts 20:7).

It is also interesting to relate these articles to the ministry of Jesus and what the disciples would have heard. Bread, for example, played a central role in Christ's teaching. Think back to the feeding of the five thousand. When the disciples came to Jesus and expressed concern for hungry people, Jesus responded, "You give them something to eat" (6:37). The disciples responded that it would take eight months' wages to feed so many and then said, "Are we to go and spend that much on bread?" (6:37). Of course, a few loaves and fish were supplied which Jesus would multiply. Jesus divided the people into groups. He then blessed the bread, broke it, and gave it to the disciples to set before the people (6:41–42). Does that language sound familiar? I wonder if the disciples would have connected this language. Mark did! He explains for us in the same chapter, "For they had not understood about the loaves" (6:52).

Later, with the feeding of the four thousand, the same thing happens. Jesus again takes the loaves, and after he had, "given thanks, he broke them and gave them to his disciples to set before the people" (8:6). Mark then makes another interesting comment—the disciples forgot to bring the bread with them, to which Jesus responds, "Why are you talking about having no bread? Do you still not see or understand?" (8:17). Jesus, the bread of life, was with them. Jesus said those very words: "I am the bread of life. He who comes to me will never go hungry, and he who believes in me will never be thirsty" (John 6:35). Now, we read, "Jesus took bread, gave thanks[16] and broke it, and gave it to his disciples, saying, 'Take it; this is my body'" (14:22).

Jesus also took the cup and gave it to the disciples and they drank. It is interesting that he did not comment about its symbolism until after they drank. "This is my blood of the covenant, which is poured out for many" (14:24). Years of taking communion has conditioned us to the point where we hardly blink an eye. How would you respond if you heard Jesus for the first time say, "Whoever eats my flesh and drinks my blood has eternal life" (John 6:54)?

The Old Testament is replete with the command not to drink blood or eat meat that has its lifeblood still in it.[17] Blood was the means of

---

16. Two different words are translated "thanks" in our passage. The first, used of the bread, is the word from which we get "Eulogy" (*eulogeō*). The second is used of the cup and is the word "Eucharist" (*eucharisteō*).

17. See Genesis 9:4; Leviticus 3:17; 7:26; Deuteronomy 12:16, 23–25; 15:23; 1 Samuel 14:32; 1 Chronicles 11:15–19.

atonement in the Old Testament, but it would have been nearly impossible for a Jew to hear the words, "This is my blood," and still drink.

In the Old Testament, the blood of sacrificed animals was poured out by the priests on the altar as a sin offering to atone for the sins of the people.[18] Jesus, with this background and understanding, says to his disciples that his death is a new sacrifice offered to God. No more sacrifice will be needed. Jesus' blood sealed and inaugurated a new covenant. This new meal is certainly no ordinary meal.

The most amazing fact of this story is that Jesus institutes a new covenant for a group of disciples who he knows will betray him. We know that Judas goes from this room to betray Jesus, but Jesus says in the very next verse of Mark, "You will all fall away" (14:27). To me, that makes this passage more than ordinary, it makes it extraordinary!

This first time this meal is taken, it is done secretly and in private. Again, I need to ask why. It is done secretly because Jesus does not want to be betrayed and arrested before he institutes the Lord's Supper. And yet, after instituting the Lord's Supper, he will say to Judas, "What you are about to do, do quickly" (John 13:27). Jesus has accomplished the one last thing he needed to accomplish before he was ready to head to the cross. This demonstrates how important the Lord's Supper was to him.

It is also interesting that after initiating the Lord's Supper, Jesus says, "I tell you the truth, I will not drink again of the fruit of the vine until that day when I drink it anew in the kingdom of God" (14:25). When Jesus returns, we will celebrate Communion with him in perfect fellowship with all his followers. When that day comes, I want to be well practiced! Until that day, as Christians celebrate Communion, we are remembering not only his crucifixion, but also looking ahead to his second coming.

In communion, we gather around the Lord's Table, remembering what he has done. I want to tell you, this is *No Ordinary Meal*. My prayer is that I will never break Table Fellowship.

Study Questions

1. What is your favorite place to eat? How often do you share a meal with others?
2. What is the most shocking news or statement you have ever heard?

---

18. Leviticus 4:17, 18, 25, 30, 34.

3. Why the secrecy in regards to the location of the Passover meal? (See John 11:57).
4. What was "table fellowship?" How does this apply to the Lord's Supper (both then and now)?
5. How would you have felt if you had been sharing this Passover meal with Jesus and heard the news about a betrayer?
6. How do Judas' actions fulfill Mark 14:21? (See Psalm 41:9).
7. What connection is there between the Passover meal and the Lord's Supper?
8. How does Jesus redefine the Passover meal? What profound new meaning does Jesus give to the Passover bread (22)? To the cup (23–24)?
9. Read again verses 22–24. Should we take Jesus' description of his body and blood literally? Did the disciples take the bread and cup literally?
10. How much do you think the disciples understood when Jesus spoke about his body and blood?
11. Why do/should believers continue to observe the Lord's Supper (1 Corinthians 11:23–32)?
12. Why is it important for Christians to observe Communion? How important is Communion to you?
13. What should you reflect on during the Lord's Supper (Communion) at church?
14. How will this message impact your time of Communion?
15. Before you take Communion next, what can you do to make it more spiritually meaningful?

For Further Study

16. See Matthew 26:17–26; Luke 22:7–30; John 13:21–31.

34

Pressed at Gethsemane

Mark 14:26–52

JESUS HAS JUST INSTITUTED the Lord's supper, during which time he dropped a bombshell: "I tell you the truth, one of you will betray me" (14:18). Shocked, each of the disciples responded, "Surely not I" (14:20). Jesus simply responded while reassuring no one, "It is one of the Twelve . . . One who dips bread into the bowl with me" (14:20). We learn from the other gospel accounts that Judas left during this meal to do his dastardly deed. But Judas is not the only one who betrayed Jesus that night. In fact, all the disciples deserted Jesus in the dark hours at Gethsemane. Our passage begins with Jesus predicting that betrayal.

The Betrayal Predicted (Mark 14:26–30)

> When they had sung a hymn, they went out to the Mount of Olives. "You will all fall away," Jesus told them, "for it is written: 'I will strike the shepherd, and the sheep will be scattered.' But after I have risen, I will go ahead of you into Galilee." Peter declared, "Even if all fall away, I will not." "I tell you the truth," Jesus answered, "today—yes, tonight—before the rooster crows twice you yourself will disown me three times." But Peter insisted emphatically, "Even if I have to die with you, I will never disown you." And all the others said the same. (Mark 14:26–31)

Alluding to Zechariah 13:7, Jesus tells the disciples that he (the shepherd) will be struck—and that they (the sheep) will abandon him.[1] Peter (in Peter-like fashion) makes a bold boast. "Even if all fall away, I will

---

1. Luke 22:31–34 and John 13:36–38 give us other information about the denial and desertion of the disciples.

not" (14:29). You can almost visualize Peter (the ever confident, first-out of the boat, first to speak out) saying these words: "Those other guys probably will fall away, but me—never!"

Poor Peter. The last time he spoke up, he protested Jesus' statement that he would undergo suffering (8:31–33) and got chastised for it. Now, Peter boldly announces his willingness to suffer alongside of Jesus, but receives yet another painful correction. "I tell you the truth . . . today—yes, tonight—before the rooster crows twice you yourself will disown me three times" (14:30). Peter can't win for losing.[2] Peter emphatically pledges his loyalty, but he is not the only one to make bold boasts about continued faithfulness that night: "All the others said the same" (14:31).

Peter always takes the blame, but he merely voices what all the others are thinking. Actually, James and John earlier made similar boasts. On the way to Jerusalem, they had asked Jesus for positions of authority when he came into his kingdom. In response Jesus asked them, "Can you drink the cup I drink?" (10:38). Both replied, "We can" (10:39). Every one of the disciples pledge their faithfulness and loyalty—but can they back up their words? Words are cheap! Are they all talk and no game? Or will they stand by Jesus when the going gets tough? Only time will tell—but it won't take long—the pressure will be applied at Gethsemane.

Gethsemane was an olive orchard on the Mount of Olives just east of Jerusalem. Although familiar to most, you might be surprised to find the specific word "Gethsemane" is used only twice in Scripture.[3] Gethsemane literally means "olive press," but it specifically described an olive grove on the Mount of Olives where olive oil was prepared. It was a specific location and a spot you can still visit to this day next to the modern Church of All Nations. But Gethsemane is not only a location, its name is also analogous to what will happen to Jesus there—Jesus will be pressed: physically, emotionally, and spiritually. At Gethsemane, Jesus feels the pressure of Golgotha weighing down upon him.

As we look at our passage, I want to note the reaction of several different characters to the pressure of Gethsemane.

---

2. Jesus chooses an apt time marker for when the betrayal will occur—the rooster. We'll examine Peter's actions more closely at the end of Mark chapter 14.

3. Matthew 26:36; Mark 14:32.

The Disposition of Jesus—Submission
(Mark 14:32-36)

> They went to a place called Gethsemane, and Jesus said to his disciples, "Sit here while I pray." He took Peter, James and John along with him, and he began to be deeply distressed and troubled. "My soul is overwhelmed with sorrow to the point of death," he said to them. "Stay here and keep watch." Going a little farther, he fell to the ground and prayed that if possible the hour might pass from him. "Abba, Father," he said, "everything is possible for you. Take this cup from me. Yet not what I will, but what you will." (Mark 14:32-36)

As we read these words, there may be no clearer statement as to Jesus' humanity. Three words are used in our passage that reflect Jesus' disposition at this moment. The first two are commentary provided by Mark. The third gives us the very words of Jesus. All three are rare words in our New Testaments.

First, we read that Jesus was "deeply distressed" (*ekthambeō*). This word is used only by Mark and only three times.[4] It can have a positive connotation (overwhelmingly amazed), but in context it means to be overwhelmingly disturbed, distressed, or alarmed. The NIV translates the second word as "troubled" (*adēmoneō*). It, too, is used only three times in Scripture,[5] and literally means to be anxious or distressed. These are not pleasant words and are used by Mark to describe Jesus' emotional state as he enters the garden.

The third rare word is verbalized by Jesus himself as he confesses to Peter, James, and John: "My soul is overwhelmed with sorrow to the point of death" (14:34). The English Standard Version reads, "My soul is very sorrowful, even to death." Both are accurate attempts to translate a word that is used only four times in our New Testaments. It literally means to be "exceedingly sad" or "deeply grieved" (*perilypos*). Jesus is so troubled that Luke the physician writes, "His sweat was like drops of blood falling to the ground" (Luke 22:44).[6] There can be no doubt that Jesus is in extreme agony as he is being pressed at Gethsemane.

---

4. Mark 9:15; 14:33; 16:5.
5. Matthew 26:37; Mark 14:33; Philippians 2:26.
6. The word "like" (*hōsei*) may indicate that this is to be understood metaphorically. But both ancient and modern accounts record people sweating blood—a condition known as hematidrosis, where extreme anguish or physical strain causes the blood ves-

This pressure is also reflected in the prayer of Jesus, where we find four remarkable statements. First, Jesus prays "Abba, Father" (14:36). This was a term of both respect and endearment. The claim that "Abba"[7] meant "Daddy" is a little misleading, because it was also used by adults to address their fathers. But it is helpful as long as we use it properly, and understand that it was never a flippant, or casual word—but a word of respect. I have heard the misinformed pray to God as "pops" or "daddy-o" in a manner which borders on sacrilege. Still, what great comfort to know that we can confidently approach our heavenly father with intimacy.

The second remarkable statement needs little comment, but does deserve mention. Jesus prays, "Everything is possible for you" (14:36). This is a statement of God's omnipotence. Taken together with the first description, we understand that we can boldly and intimately approach the very creator of the universe—the one who can do all things.

The third statement comes as a request from the lips of Jesus: "Take this cup from me" (14:36). The cup is the same one Jesus referred to in 10:38–39. It was a metaphor for the wrath of God. It spoke of the upcoming suffering, the isolation from God, the crucifixion he would have to endure on our behalf. Part of Christ's role would be to take the sin of the world upon himself—to become a curse for us. This was a cup that Jesus truly hated to drink. The physical suffering would be hard enough, but the spiritual suffering would be unbearable. Jesus is asking his father the question: "Is there some way to provide salvation other than through the extreme suffering and death that I am about to experience?" Jesus is asking for an acceptable alternative to the cross.

With this in mind, I want to ask this question: Is it proper to pray, asking that God change his mind? The answer is yes, with one condition—we must pray asking that God's will be done. Which takes us to the fourth remarkable statement. Jesus prays, "Yet not what I will, but what you will" (14:36). Jesus asked for the removal of the cup, but he willingly submitted to the will of his Father.

This leads me to ask yet another question. Did God hear Jesus' prayer? A common answer people give when their prayers seem un-

---

sels to dilate and burst, mixing sweat and blood.

7. "Abba" is an Aramaic term. Although Mark wrote in Greek, he used this word because it was far more personal than the Greek word for father. Jews would have never dreamed of addressing God this way.

heeded is that God answered the prayer, but the answer was no. Actually, with the prayer of Jesus, we read an interesting statement in the Gospel of Luke: "An angel from heaven appeared to him and strengthened him" (Luke 22:43). As it turns out, Jesus was not delivered *from* death, but he was delivered *through* death. He was given strength to endure because he had the disposition of submission.

The Disposition of the Disciples—Apathetic (Mark 14:37-42)

> Then he returned to his disciples and found them sleeping. "Simon," he said to Peter, "are you asleep? Could you not keep watch for one hour? Watch and pray so that you will not fall into temptation. The spirit is willing, but the body is weak." Once more he went away and prayed the same thing. When he came back, he again found them sleeping, because their eyes were heavy. They did not know what to say to him. Returning the third time, he said to them, "Are you still sleeping and resting? Enough! The hour has come. Look, the Son of Man is betrayed into the hands of sinners. Rise! Let us go! Here comes my betrayer!" (Mark 14:37-42)

Before we proceed, I want to make a few observations about what is occurring. Consider the following details. Jesus has just told all of the disciples that they will betray him. He has taken them out to the garden where he tells them he is going to pray. (John 18:2 tells us that Jesus took them here often for this purpose. This is why Judas is able to lead them to him.) Jesus is obviously anxious and bares his soul to three disciples. He is deeply distressed, troubled, and overwhelmed. In this context, Jesus asks his disciples to keep watch (14:34). What exactly is he asking?

To my recollection, this is the only place in Scripture where Jesus asks the disciples to do something specifically for him. Jesus has sent them out to gather a donkey, or prepare an upper room, or to retrieve supplies, but this request is personal. He is asking specifically for their support in his hour of need. Imagine the loneliness as Jesus literally awaits death. Jesus asks the disciples to wait (14:32); to watch (14:34); and to pray (14:38). They are to pray not only for him, but for their own benefit—that they will not fall into temptation. In context, the temptation probably includes both their temptation to sleep, and the fact that Jesus has warned that they will betray him. They are to pray for strength.

Rather than praying, three times the disciples are caught snoozing. I find it rather interesting that we actually read very little about Jesus' prayer in Mark's account. We read much more, each time with increasing detail, about what the disciples did—or more specifically, what they did not do. They did not pray. We find several stinging indictments against them. "Could you not keep watch for one hour?" (14:37). "Their eyes were heavy. They did not know what to say to him" (14:40). And a phrase that could be translated either as a question—"Are you still sleeping and resting?" or, more likely, as a statement of fact—"You are still sleeping and resting" (14:41). At the very moment Jesus needed them most—they were napping.

One interesting phrase from this passage is often misquoted: "The spirit is willing, but the body is weak." For some, it should be paraphrased this way: The Spirit is willing, but the body wants the weekend. Have you ever heard the following: "I'd love to go to church and worship with my church family, but the mountains are calling" or, "I work all week, I need to get away"? The weekend trumps the spiritual, hands down.

Others use this phrase as a justification for their wrong actions. "Lord, I really wanted to serve you (my spirit was willing)—but I just couldn't (my body was too weak)." "God, you made me this way and I'm just unable to conquer." I wonder how Jesus will respond to their flimsy excuses. Try them on Jesus, and he may say to you in return, "Enough!" (14:41).

Actually, I would probably prefer that our Bible capitalize the word "Spirit" here in this verse. Jesus does not give us a contrast between man's spirit and man's body, but a contrast between God's spirit and man's spirit. Jesus is likely saying to his disciples, "The Spirit (capital "S", i.e. God) is willing, and wanting, and desiring to help you in your time of need, if you would simply turn to him, but your body is weak." Left to your own merits, you will fail. But with God's help, you can conquer. Paul says this very thing when he writes, "No temptation has seized you except what is common to man. And God is faithful; he will not let you be tempted beyond what you can bear. But when you are tempted, he will also provide a way out so that you can stand up under it" (1 Corinthians 10:13).

Jesus gives us the example of how to resist temptation. Pray, seek the support of friends and loved ones, focus on the purpose God has given us and say, "Lord, not my will, but yours be done" (14:42).

In Jesus' hour of need, the disciples, at best, were insensitive or misinformed about the importance of the moment. At worst, they were simply apathetic. They missed their opportunity. "The hour has come. Look, the Son of Man is betrayed into the hands of sinners. Rise! Let us go! Here comes my betrayer" (14:41-42).

Which brings us to the last character in our drama.

The Disposition of Judas—Rebellious
(Mark 14:43–50)

> Just as he was speaking, Judas, one of the Twelve, appeared. With him was a crowd armed with swords and clubs, sent from the chief priests, the teachers of the law, and the elders. Now the betrayer had arranged a signal with them: "The one I kiss is the man; arrest him and lead him away under guard." Going at once to Jesus, Judas said, "Rabbi!" and kissed him. The men seized Jesus and arrested him. Then one of those standing near drew his sword and struck the servant of the high priest, cutting off his ear. "Am I leading a rebellion," said Jesus, "that you have come out with swords and clubs to capture me? Every day I was with you, teaching in the temple courts, and you did not arrest me. But the Scriptures must be fulfilled." Then everyone deserted him and fled. (Mark 14:43–50)

We know the story well. Judas has sought out the high priests, the chief priests, and the elders and has sold Jesus' whereabouts for thirty pieces of silver. Judas himself leads a crowd out from Jerusalem, down through the valley and up the mountain. It is quite the processional. John records for us that Judas leads a detachment of soldiers and some officials who were carrying torches, lanterns, and weapons (John 18:3). Here, Judas feigns friendship. Judas misuses familiar actions of respect and friendship. First, Judas calls Jesus "Rabbi," which we know means teacher. By the way, there is no record of Judas ever calling Jesus Lord. That's a rather telling point.

Next, Judas greets Jesus with a kiss. This was not only a common first-century greeting in Israel (and remains so to this day), but was an act depicting intimacy, love, affection, and respect. It was expected that the less important initiate the kiss on the cheek or the beard. Judas gives Jesus a kiss that is meant to signify honor, but it is the kiss of betrayal and death. Take these three markers: the betrayal of table fellowship, the betrayal of the term "Rabbi," and a kiss of betrayal, and the actions of

Judas are unfathomable. His was intentional, deliberate, and unrepentant betrayal.

As the high priest and his minions come to arrest Jesus, "Everyone deserted him and fled" (14:50), fulfilling Jesus' words, and the words of Zechariah: "I will strike the shepherd, and the sheep will be scattered" (14:27).

Mark leaves us with what is likely an editorial note about his own participation in the betrayal. "A young man, wearing nothing but a linen garment, was following Jesus. When they seized him, he fled naked, leaving his garment behind" (14:51).

Application

As I look at this passage, it is easy to make application to our lives.

First, I believe we all fit into one of the three categories that are depicted for us in this chapter (especially when under pressure). When it comes to our relationship with Christ we can be rebellious, apathetic, or submissive. The question is: Which one best describes you? The beauty is, you don't need to remain unresponsive or rebellious.

Second, I believe that our success through trials can be directly linked to prayer. Let me demonstrate this for you two ways. Consider the prayers of Jesus. Were Jesus' temptations and fears real? Was his request, "Remove this cup," authentic? Could Jesus have backed out on Golgotha? I think the answer to each of these questions is yes. But Jesus gained strength in the garden through prayer. In the same vein, consider the disciples. What would have happened if they had fervently prayed? Would God have strengthened them and given them courage to follow Jesus? I believe the answer is yes.

Finally, we need to remove a misconception about prayer. Answered prayer does not always mean that God will remove us from turmoil and suffering, but we are promised that God will see us through those trials—if we will diligently seek him.

Jesus, give us the strength to endure our Gethsemanes.

Study Questions

1. How do you cope with difficult situations (where do you go, what do you do)? Do you prefer to be alone or in the company of close friends?

2. Have you ever felt betrayed or deserted? Explain.
3. How does Mark describe Christ's mood in Gethsemane (33)?
4. How does Jesus himself describe his mood in Gethsemane (34)?
5. Why was Jesus so troubled and disturbed?
6. What do you think was the hardest part of the Gethsemane experience for Jesus?
7. What did Jesus ask the disciples to do in the garden?
8. What does Jesus suggest might result from the disciples' failure to pray (38)?
9. If you were to choose three people to support you during a very trying time, who would you choose and why?
10. What does Jesus ask God to do in this passage?
11. Is it okay to ask God to change his mind?
12. What model for our prayers does Jesus provide here?
13. What does Jesus' use of "Abba" say about his relationship with God? What might it imply about how we can approach God?
14. What does this passage reveal about Jesus' humanity?
15. What does the phrase "the spirit is willing, but the body is weak" (38) mean?
16. Judas betrays Jesus with a kiss. Why is this so despicable?
17. What is so significant about verse 50?
18. Have you ever denied Christ when you should have stood up for him? When?

For Further Study

19. See Matthew 26:31–56; Luke 22:39–53; John 18:1–11.

35

Deafening Silence

Mark 14:53–65

IF YOU WERE ASKED to list the most high profile trials in world history, which would you include? Chances are, your list might look similar to mine. I would likely select the following: Socrates, Luther, the Salem Witch Trials, the Scopes Monkey Trial, Nuremberg, Roe versus Wade, O. J. Simpson, Saddam Hussein, and in light of recent events surrounding its location, the future trial of Khalid Sheikh Mohammed. Of course at least one other high profile case has yet to take place—final judgment. All of these were high profile cases and "headline worthy." The most important trial in history, however, was profoundly silent. Most of the people of the day didn't even know it happened—it was the secret trial of Jesus.

> They took Jesus to the high priest, and all the chief priests, elders and teachers of the law came together. Peter followed him at a distance, right into the courtyard of the high priest. There he sat with the guards and warmed himself at the fire. The chief priests and the whole Sanhedrin were looking for evidence against Jesus so that they could put him to death, but they did not find any. Many testified falsely against him, but their statements did not agree. Then some stood up and gave this false testimony against him: "We heard him say, 'I will destroy this man-made temple and in three days will build another, not made by man.'" Yet even then their testimony did not agree. Then the high priest stood up before them and asked Jesus, "Are you not going to answer? What is this testimony that these men are bringing against you?" But Jesus remained silent and gave no answer. Again the high priest asked him, "Are you the Christ, the Son of the Blessed One?" "I am," said Jesus. "And you will see the Son of Man sitting at the

right hand of the Mighty One and coming on the clouds of heaven." The high priest tore his clothes. "Why do we need any more witnesses?" he asked. "You have heard the blasphemy. What do you think?" They all condemned him as worthy of death. Then some began to spit at him; they blindfolded him, struck him with their fists, and said, "Prophesy!" And the guards took him and beat him. (Mark 14:53–65)

It began with a silent arrest.

Silent Arrest (Mark 14:48)

As we pick up Mark's narrative, we find all the trimmings of an action-packed thriller. We find lies and innuendo, frame-ups, and a rigged jury. But we also see great secrecy. His arrest was done in the middle of the night, away from the Temple Mount, outside the city walls, and in a garden area where Jesus was isolated from the masses. This was a deliberate and intentional strategy on the part of the Jewish leaders. We have been well informed of the events that precipitated this moment. Ever since chapter 3, the Pharisees had been plotting "with the Herodians how they might kill Jesus" (3:6). Similar statements are made of the chief priests and the teachers of the law (11:18; 12:12). Then, as we begin chapter 14 we read, "The chief priests and the teachers of the law were looking for some sly way to arrest Jesus and kill him" and we are told the reason for their secrecy—they want Jesus away from the throngs of people for fear that "the people may riot'" (14:1). Judas afforded them the opportunity they had been looking for. "Judas Iscariot, one of the Twelve, went to the chief priests to betray Jesus to them. They were delighted to hear this and promised to give him money. So he watched for an opportunity to hand him over" (14:10–11).

At the opportune time, when Jesus was isolated from the crowds and many of his followers, Judas led them to him in the Garden of Gethsemane. Here, in the middle of the night, with only a handful of witnesses, "The men seized Jesus and arrested him" (14:46).

Jesus points to their adroit actions when he says, "Am I leading a rebellion . . . that you have come out with swords and clubs to capture me? Every day I was with you, teaching in the temple courts, and you did not arrest me" (14:48–49). With the exception of one small skirmish (Peter and a sword), it was for all intents and purposes, a silent arrest—Jesus goes willingly.

This led to a silent trial.

Silent Trial (Mark 14:53-54)

After Jesus' arrest he is taken through a series of secret trials. It should not surprise us that Mark gives us an abbreviated version of these proceedings. In typical fashion, he condenses things for us. The trials of Jesus essentially happen in two stages. In the first stage we find the religious trials, and since the religious leaders do not have the authority to put Jesus to death, we also get the civil trials. Each of these stages also contains three parts.

The religious trials include the preliminary hearing before Annas—a fact gathering or fact generating procedure (Jn 18:12-14, 19-23); the initial trial before daybreak with Caiaphas & the Sanhedrin (14:53-65); and after daybreak, a trial before this same group (15:1).

The civil trials include a hearing before Pilate (15:1-4); a hearing before Herod Antipas (Lk 23:6-12); and a second hearing before Pilate (15:6-15). Once again, Mark condenses these accounts.

The religious trial starts with a preliminary hearing in front of Annas. Annas is the former High Priest (AD 7-14) but was deposed by Pilate's predecessor. Five sons, including his son-in-law Joseph Caiaphas, serve after him, but many of the Jews still consider Annas the High Priest because it was a lifetime appointment. So they go there first to try to trump up some charge to use against Jesus. After the preliminary hearing, Jesus is taken before Caiaphas and the Sanhedrin. The Sanhedrin is made up mostly of Pharisees and Sadducees with the High Priest presiding (70+1). Again, it is essential to realize that this takes place, not in public, but at Caiaphas's house. Interestingly, it was at his home that the original plot was birthed to arrest Jesus (Matthew 26:3-4) and probably the very spot where Judas sold Jesus out. It is here that "Many testified falsely against him, but their statements did not agree" (14:56). Throughout these proceedings, Jesus remains silent.

Today, you can visit the Church of Saint Peter (Gallicantu, cock-crow) erected over the site of Caiaphas' house. Down below the foundations you can observe rock-hewn pits, cisterns and grottos designed specifically for the purpose of detaining and interrogating prisoners. It is likely that at this very spot, Jesus was bound and whipped for the first time. As mentioned previously, it is likely the spot Judas first betrayed Jesus, and is also the spot where Peter denies Jesus.

Silent Truth (Mark 14:55–61a)

We see immediately how rigged the trial of Jesus was. "Many bore false witness against him" (14:56),[1] and yet, they could not agree with each other. According to the law (Numbers 35:30; Deuteronomy 17:6; 19:15) it was necessary to find two witnesses who gave consistent testimony—a feat they could not accomplish. It was also required that false witnesses be punished, a fact they strangely ignore. "If the witness proves to be a liar, giving false testimony against his brother, then do to him as he intended to do to his brother" (Deuteronomy 19:18–19). But the inconsistent testimony didn't dissuade them. They claimed that Jesus said he would destroy the temple (14:58), but Jesus hadn't said this.[2] The closest saying one might find to this is John 2:19, which Jesus uttered two years previous: "Destroy this temple, and in three days I will raise it up." But we are also provided commentary that tells us Jesus was speaking about his body (John 2: 21). As they falsely accuse Jesus, he remains silent, thus fulfilling Psalm 38:13–14 and Isaiah 53:7.[3]

As we read our passage, it becomes readily apparent that the religious leaders are not looking for the truth. The whole process is a sham and is not even conducted by their own rules of law. Consider the following.

1. They have arrested Jesus without charge.
2. The law prohibits them from considering the case on a feast day.
3. The law prohibits them from meeting at night.
4. The law requires them to meet openly within the Chambers of the Sanhedrin.
5. The charge requires unanimous testimony from at least two witnesses that agree.

But perjury, and not truth, pervades. Truth remains silent. With every increasing moment, the tension rises. The religious leaders are infuriated with the silence of Jesus.

---

1. Remember, this took place very early Friday morning (probably 1–2 a.m.), and yet false witnesses were available.

2. The word for "temple" (*naos*) is used only two times by Mark (15:29; 15:38) and depicts the innermost sacred part of the sanctuary. When Jesus predicted the destruction of the temple (13:3), he used the word for the temple complex (*hieron*).

3. It is also referred to in 1 Peter 2:23.

Silence Broken (Mark 14:61b–65)

The trial is illegal on several accounts—the witnesses have discredited themselves; the religious leaders are involved in an evil treacherous act, but throughout the proceedings, they want to maintain an appearance of justice and a pretense of righteousness. The truth is, the whole ordeal is a sham. Finally, Caiaphas, the high priest, who is the president of the Sanhedrin, puts aside his role as judge and assumes the role of prosecutor. He starts by asking leading questions of the accused: "Are you not going to answer? What is this testimony that these men are bringing against you?" (14:60).

Jesus does not need to answer, because no accusation has been leveled which can be used as a legitimate charge against him. They have not proved their case! Their charges are based on confusing and erroneous evidence. Not answering is wiser than trying to clarify the fabricated accusations.

Caiaphas then asks a question which Jesus does answer. For Jesus not to answer could be perceived as a denial of his mission, so Jesus breaks the silence. "Again the high priest asked him, 'Are you the Christ, the Son of the Blessed One?'" (14:61). The question is likely drawn from Jesus' public teaching in the temple[4] and designed to place Jesus in a conundrum. If Jesus answers no, he discredits himself. If Jesus answers yes, he condemns himself. Jesus answers emphatically, *"Ego eimi"*—I AM! This is the first time in the Gospel of Mark that Jesus openly makes this claim. The demons have testified. God himself has testified. Peter has testified. Jesus' miracles have spoken volumes. But here Jesus verbally and openly declares his identity. His time of veiled-ness has passed.

Caiaphas believes he has vindicated himself. The ends justify the means. He tears his clothes to show how right he is and how wrong Jesus is. It is a formal, judicial act. "What further witnesses do we need?" (14:63). Following the High Priests' lead, they all condemn Jesus. They have arrested, arraigned, tried, convicted, passed judgment, and sentenced Jesus within a period of one or two hours. The one option they fatally disregard is that Jesus is indeed speaking the truth.

We should note that the illegal measures continue: the judge has assumed the role of prosecutor; he has asked leading questions; and the trial and sentencing occur on the same day.

---

4. Mark 12:1–12, 35–37.

The soldiers begin to spit on Jesus and strike him. They taunt "prophesy"(14:65). The irony is that as they ask him to prophesy, they are the fulfillment of what he has already predicted. Jesus said earlier, "We are going up to Jerusalem . . . and the Son of Man will be betrayed to the chief priests and teachers of the law. They will condemn him to death and will hand him over to the Gentiles, who will mock him and spit on him, flog him and kill him. Three days later he will rise" (14:33–34).

While the enemies of Christ have blindfolded Jesus, they are the ones who are blind, and he is the only one who sees clearly. From this we learn an important point. Caiaphas is not in control. Even at this moment, as he stands trial in a court of law, it is Jesus who is in control. Jesus has clarified the situation, Jesus has spoken, Jesus has given the religious leaders the mantle on which they can crucify him. Jesus is the "I AM."

But Jesus was not finished with Caiaphas. Jesus said, "And you will see the Son of Man sitting at the right hand of the Mighty One and coming on the clouds of heaven" (14:62). Jesus alludes to an Old Testament passage from the book of Daniel which the religious leaders would have known well. It pictures a scene where God calls down judgment on those who have rejected him. The religious leaders think they have passed judgment on Jesus, when in reality, they have passed judgment upon themselves. While it may appear as if Jesus is on trial, it is actually the other way around.

It is interesting that many today still want to bring judgment down upon Christ. Let us remember, he is not on trial—they are. One day, everyone will stand before Jesus and they will be judged based on what they did with him.

David Garland makes an interesting observation about our text.

> When we read this account, we must see how easily we can become a crafty high priest, a devious Judas, a lying false witness, a cowardly Peter, a wishy-washy governor, a mindless member of a hate-filled crowd, a coarse soldier, and an absent disciple hidden for fear. Then we realize that it is we who are on trial before Jesus and not vice versa.[5]

---

5. *The NIV Application Commentary*, David E. Garland, p. 572.

Study Questions

1. Have you ever been falsely accused? How did you respond?
2. Share an experience from serving on a jury or in a courtroom.
3. How do you react when someone gives you the "fifth degree"?
4. What aspects of Jesus' trial make it illegal?
5. According to verse 55, what evidence did the Sanhedrin have against Jesus?
6. Read Deuteronomy 19:15. How many witnesses/testimonies were required by Jewish law in order to condemn someone?
7. What was the penalty for bearing false witness against someone (Deuteronomy 19:16–21)?
8. Read the charge against Jesus from verse 58. Is this what Jesus said in John 2:19?
9. Why do you think that Jesus, for the most part, remains silent?
10. Why doesn't Jesus defend himself? What about this fact bothers you?
11. Read Isaiah 53:7. How does this verse apply?
12. Why does Jesus finally speak up when he does?
13. What is it about Jesus' response in verse 62 that causes the high priest to tear his clothes?
14. Who is ultimately on trial in this passage: Jesus or the religious leaders?
15. In what ways is Jesus still on trial today?
16. How difficult was it for you to accept that Jesus is the Son of God?
17. How do you deal with someone who rejects Jesus?
18. How would you react to seeing Jesus spit on, blindfolded, struck, and mocked?

For Further Study

19. See Matthew 26:57–68; John 18:12–13, 19–24.

36

The Great In-Between

Mark 14:66–72

Few people are unfamiliar with the story of Peter's denial. But we must not let our familiarity with this passage cause us to look at it casually. This story is one of significant proportions, for if the Apostle Peter can deny Christ—the danger certainly will not escape us. This particular story is one that Mark has been working toward for some time. This moment has not only been alluded to, but Jesus himself has made some striking predictions concerning this event. In order for us to understand properly, we first must take a glance backwards.

Before—The Events Preceding (Mark 14:27–31; 54)

Just following the Last Supper, as Jesus took the disciples toward the Mount of Olives, he predicted the following:

> "You will all fall away," Jesus told them, "for it is written: 'I will strike the shepherd, and the sheep will be scattered.' But after I have risen, I will go ahead of you into Galilee." Peter declared, "Even if all fall away, I will not." "I tell you the truth," Jesus answered, "today—yes, tonight—before the rooster crows twice you yourself will disown me three times." But Peter insisted emphatically, "Even if I have to die with you, I will never disown you." (Mark 14:27–31)

It is interesting that Jesus employs the language of a rooster for the time stamp of Peter's betrayal. He could have used other descriptive language: before the sun rises, before dawn, while the dew is still on the roses. Instead, he chose the rooster. This image just seems to fit, doesn't it. I can picture Peter strutting around, shoulders back, crowing—I will die with you. Notice his language: all the others may betray you, but me, never! Peter is the epitome of cockiness. And this is not his only "rooster" moment. He's always the first one to speak up, he's the first out of the boat, he's the one who believes he has the right to rebuke Jesus. When Peter boasts, he is not out of character. He's a rooster!

At the church where I serve, there are chickens at a farmhouse across the street. Every Sunday, I park away from the building and walk down the street to free up parking spaces for visitors. As I walk by, one rooster will always walk out, crow and carry on—much like an attack dog. He is more than happy to strut his stuff—until you take one step toward him. That one step forward transforms him from rooster to chicken. Again—Peter! While Peter has declared his absolute loyalty to Christ, and even yields a sword in Christ's defense while he is with Jesus (Luke 22:15); when Christ is arrested, Peter (like the others) turns tail and runs—at least initially. But after his initial denial, Peter had a change of heart. We read these words: "Peter followed him at a distance, right into the courtyard of the high priest." (14:54). Peter is at least trying to fulfill his pledge. While Jesus is on trial at the house of Caiaphas, Peter is outside in the courtyard.

Before moving on, I need to point out the structure of our passage. Mark once again uses a sandwiching technique. Before the trial of Jesus, Mark mentions that Peter was in the courtyard of the high priest (15:54). Then Mark proceeds to tell us about the illegal trial of Jesus (14:55–65). Following that trial, we again find this statement: "While Peter was below in the courtyard" (14:66). Mark has intentionally placed these accounts together for emphasis. Not only do Jesus' trial and Peter's denial occur simultaneously, but Mark wants us to vividly understand the contrasts. We will see these more fully in a moment. First, notice our passage.

> While Peter was below in the courtyard, one of the servant girls of the high priest came by. When she saw Peter warming himself, she looked closely at him. "You also were with that Nazarene, Jesus," she said. But he denied it. "I don't know or understand what you're talking about," he said, and went out into the entryway. When the servant girl saw him there, she said again to those standing around, "This fellow is one of them." Again he denied it. After a little while, those standing near said to Peter, "Surely you are one of them, for you are a Galilean." He began to call down curses on himself, and he swore to them, "I don't know this man you're talking about." Immediately the rooster crowed the second

time. Then Peter remembered the word Jesus had spoken to him: "Before the rooster crows twice you will disown me three times." And he broke down and wept. (Mark 14:66–72)

During—The Events Unfolding (Mark 14:66–72)

Peter's three-fold denial is narrated by three escalating encounters. First we see a servant girl's encounter with Peter as he stands warming himself by the fire. Her contempt for Christ is clearly seen in the order of the words she speaks—"That Nazarene, Jesus" (14:67). She has associated Peter with Jesus, but he denies her charge (14:68) by employing a common rabbinical technique we might call plausible deniability. In the first century, it served as a formal, legal denial: "I don't know this man you're talking about" (14:71).[1] Of course, it was a lie.

Peter uncomfortably retreats to the safety of darkness, probably near the gate by which he entered. But the servant girl now shares her insight with others standing nearby—probably guards and employees of the high priest: "This fellow is one of them" (14:69). But Peter denies the accusation a second time. This time his language changes to the imperfect—implying that he repeatedly denied their charge. But the more he protests, the more his Galilean accent betrays him.[2] A Galilean would stick out like a sore thumb in a high priest's courtyard and would sound like a New Zealander in Boise, or a Tennessean leading worship in Idaho.[3] Peter's insistent clamor falls on deaf ears.

Finally, Peter invokes a curse. The NIV takes some liberties here. It reads: "He began to call down curses on himself" (14:71). The verb has no object in the Greek text and doesn't warrant the phrase "on himself." Three main interpretations have been put forward. Some have suggested that Peter used vulgarity and profanity for emphasis. Those holding this view would suggest he said something like this: "Bleepity-bleep, I don't know the man." Others suggest that he may have cursed Jesus. Their interpretation might read like this: "I don't know this bleepity-bleep man."

---

1. The phrase may be a loaded one for Mark. See 4:12–13; 6:52; 8:17–18; 9:32.
2. See Matthew 26:73.
3. Our children's minister comes from New Zealand and our worship minister spawns Tennessean vernacular when it pleases him.

Actually, in support of this view, Pliny records for us that the emperor Trajan required this very thing of Christians. Trajan demanded that Christians either curse Christ or die, believing that a true Christian would never curse their Lord and Savior. This is what Polycarp was asked to do to spare his life—curse Christ. Polycarp replied, "Eighty-six years I have served him, and he has done me no wrong. How can I blaspheme my King who has saved me?"[4]

A third explanation posits that Peter was uttering an oath-like formula: "May I be cursed if I am lying and may you be cursed for suggesting it." This would be akin to our saying on our own behalf, "Cross my heart, hope to die, stick a needle in my eye;" or cursing others, "May the fleas of a thousand camels infest your armpits." Okay, maybe a better example would be, "I swear to tell the truth, the whole truth, and nothing but the truth, so help me, God."

It is important to note that the first two times, Peter denied being "with" Jesus. The third time Peter denied Jesus himself. How far he had fallen.

Here we begin to see the contrasts that Mark is setting before us. Inside, Jesus boldly confesses his identity before the high priest, while outside, Peter denies his identity before a servant girl. While Jesus is under fire, Peter warms himself by the fire (54, 66). As Jesus remains steadfast under immense pressure, Peter capitulates under gentle pressure. As Jesus tells the truth, which costs his life, Peter lies to save his life. The one who previously uttered the words, "You are the Christ" (8:29), now proclaims, "I don't know this man you're talking about" (14:71).

After—The Events Applied (Mark 17:72; 16:7)

"Immediately the rooster crowed the second time. Then Peter remembered the word Jesus had spoken to him: 'Before the rooster crows twice you will disown me three times'" (14:72). It is at this moment (as Peter denies Jesus in the courtyard) that the Gospel of Luke presents a vivid detail: "The Lord turned and looked straight at Peter" (Luke 22:61).

If we were unfamiliar with this story, we might think this was the end for Peter. He had been caught in the very act of denying his Lord and

---

4. See www.Theopedia.com/polycarp.

Savior. How could he possibly be restored? From this moment on in the Gospel of Mark, Peter seemingly drops off the page.[5]

If we are honest with the facts, what Peter did is not unlike the actions of Judas as he betrayed the location of Jesus. But there is one significant difference. While Judas did show some remorse and returned the thirty silver coins to the chief priest (Matthew 27:3-5), he went away and hanged himself (Matthew 27:5). Peter, realizing what he had done, "Broke down and wept" (14:72). This phrase is actually a difficult one in Greek to render to English. It has been translated in sundry ways: "he began to cry;" "he set to and wept;" "he burst into tears;" "he thought on it and wept;" "he covered his head and wept;" "he threw himself on the ground and wept;" "he dashed out and wept." The other gospel writers simply say, "He wept bitterly." All paint for us a clear picture of the remorse of Peter. This, in part, led to Peter's restoration. As we know well, Peter's repudiation of Christ was not the end for Peter. In fact, two words shine brightly later in the Gospel of Mark. You will find them included with the news of Jesus' resurrection. An angel brings the news of Jesus: "He has risen! He is not here. See the place where they laid him." And then we read, "But go, tell his disciples *and Peter*" (16:6-7). These special instructions are left to let everyone know, not only that Jesus is alive, but that even those like Peter are welcomed into the presence of Jesus.

The story would not be complete without mentioning that Peter went on to boldly preach the gospel message of Jesus Christ, for which he ultimately gave his life. Tradition tells us that Peter was given the opportunity to deny Christ and live, or be crucified. Peter's last request was to be hung upside down because he did not want to be compared to his Lord and Savior Jesus Christ.

The words of this passage would have been extremely impacting for the first century church in Rome (where Peter preached) who were undergoing extreme pressure. To them, Peter's story spoke both words of warning and solace. They should speak similar things to us today.

Peter's story provides the warning that denial is possible, even for an Apostle of Jesus Christ. We would be wise to learn from his mistake. If Peter, the spokesman for the Apostles, could within hours move from pledged loyalty to denial, we should not consider ourselves impregnable. I am reminded of the words of the Apostle Paul when he said,

---

5. This is similar to what happens to him after Acts 12:17.

"So, if you think you are standing firm, be careful that you don't fall!" (1 Corinthians 10:12).

The passage also provides great solace. There is great assurance in the realization that there is forgiveness, even for those who have abandoned Christ. Reconciliation is possible, even for those who have denied him. In Christ wrongs can be made right. There is hope for Noah the drunk, Moses the liar, Mary the prostitute, Paul the murderer, and Peter the denier. That means there is hope available for us.

As I reflect on Peter, I wonder what would have happened if Peter had not fled and had stood by Jesus' side through it all? What would have become of him? Instead, Peter found himself in an awkward situation, close enough to Jesus to be identified with him, but far enough away from Jesus to easily reject him. He was caught in-between.

I believe this remains a problem for many professing Christians. Some, although they profess Christ, are standing too far away to even be confused by the world to be disciples. Other true Christians are dangerously exposed—they stand so close to Jesus that their discipleship is not questioned. But for many, maybe even most, they are caught somewhere in the fog of "The Great In-Between"—standing nearby, but not close enough to be standing with Jesus.

The question is simply this: "Where are you standing?"

Study Questions

1. What would you say has been your greatest failure in life? What have you done that you wish you could take back?
2. Peter often gets a bad rap for things. How do you feel about the fact that Peter follows Jesus to the courtyard of the high priest (14:54, 66)?
3. What might we conclude about the servant girl's opinion of Jesus from her words in verse 67?
4. How were the three denials similar? How were they different?
5. What is it about Peter that blows his cover (Matthew 26:73; Mark 14:70)?
6. Have you ever stood out in a crowd as a follower of Christ? When? How?
7. Have you ever shied away from referring to Jesus when conversing with others?

8. What does it mean that Peter called down "curses" and "swore" (71)?
9. Contrast Peter's "trial" and Christ's trial.
10. Why did Peter weep?
11. Just as the rooster's crow would serve as a reminder to Peter of his failure, what is it that serves as a constant reminder of a mistake you made?
12. Have you ever felt that your failures made it impossible for you to serve Christ again? How does this passage apply to those times?
13. In your journey with Christ, which statement best reflects you?
    a. Safely hidden—too far away to be confused as a disciple.
    b. Dangerously exposed—so close that your discipleship is not questioned.
    c. Somewhere in the fog of "The Great In-Between."

For Further Study

14. See Matthew 26:69–75; Luke 22:54–65; John 18:25–27.

37

What to Do with Jesus?

Mark 15:1–20

Very early in the morning, the chief priests, with the elders, the teachers of the law and the whole Sanhedrin, reached a decision. They bound Jesus, led him away and handed him over to Pilate. "Are you the king of the Jews?" asked Pilate. "Yes, it is as you say," Jesus replied. The chief priests accused him of many things. So again Pilate asked him, "Aren't you going to answer? See how many things they are accusing you of." But Jesus still made no reply, and Pilate was amazed. Now it was the custom at the Feast to release a prisoner whom the people requested. A man called Barabbas was in prison with the insurrectionists who had committed murder in the uprising. The crowd came up and asked Pilate to do for them what he usually did. "Do you want me to release to you the king of the Jews?" asked Pilate, knowing it was out of envy that the chief priests had handed Jesus over to him. But the chief priests stirred up the crowd to have Pilate release Barabbas instead. "What shall I do, then, with the one you call the king of the Jews?" Pilate asked them. "Crucify him!" they shouted. "Why? What crime has he committed?" asked Pilate. But they shouted all the louder, "Crucify him!" Wanting to satisfy the crowd, Pilate released Barabbas to them. He had Jesus flogged, and handed him over to be crucified. The soldiers led Jesus away into the palace (that is, the Praetorium) and called together the whole company of soldiers. They put a purple robe on him, then twisted together a crown of thorns and set it on him. And they began to call out to him, "Hail, king of the Jews!" Again and again they struck him on the head with a staff and spit on him. Falling on their knees, they paid homage to him. And when they had mocked him, they took off the purple robe and put his own clothes on him. Then they led him out to crucify him. (Mark 15:1–20)

PREVIOUSLY, WE SAW JESUS on trial before the Jewish religious leaders. They had the power to convict Jesus of violating their own laws, but they could not kill him. In order to accomplish this task, they needed the help of the Roman government. In our passage, the Jewish leaders take Jesus to the Tower of Antonia (a fortress built by Herod the Great) to appear before Pilate. Here, Jesus appears before a Gentile judge, the Roman governor, in an attempt to gain permission to administrate capital punishment. In our passage we are introduced to several different characters and see several troubling responses on the behalf of the religious leaders and Roman people.

Pilate (Mark 15:1–5)

The Jewish leaders had found Jesus guilty of blasphemy, but their accusations would have no sway in this court. The judge would pay no attention to a religious charge. In order to gain a conviction, they needed to accuse Jesus of a crime under Roman law. So, the religious leaders revised the charges to appeal to Pilate.[1] Luke records for us that they brought three charges against Jesus. First, he was charged with "subverting" the nation—that is, creating riots and dissension. They also charged him with revolting against paying taxes to Caesar. Finally, they charged him with attempting to make himself king (Luke 23:2). It was this third charge that caught Pilate's attention. "So Pilate asked Jesus, 'Are you the king of the Jews?'" (23:3). Jesus replied, "Yes, it is as you say" (15:2), but Pilate seemed convinced that Jesus was not after political power. Whatever kind of king Jesus might aspire to be, he obviously was not a revolutionary bent on overthrowing Rome.

"Then Pilate announced . . . 'I find no basis for a charge against this man'" (Luke 23:4). At this, the religious leaders began accusing Jesus of "many things" (15:3). They needed to convince Pilate that Jesus was indeed a dangerous criminal. But Pilate was not persuaded. He knew, "that it was out of envy that the chief priests had handed Jesus over to him" (15:10). As the religious leaders hurled more charges against Jesus, Jesus once again remained silent.

Then we are confronted with an interesting phrase: "Pilate was amazed" (15:5). What was it about Jesus' silence that amazed (*thaumazō*) Pilate? It is actually an interesting question. Pilate was looking for a rea-

---

1. Pilate was the Roman governor of Judea from AD 26–36.

son to release Jesus. Jesus could have easily persuaded Pilate to release him. Pilate's sympathy was with Jesus, not the religious leaders, but the governor could not release someone who refused to answer the charges brought against him. Jesus could have easily saved himself, and yet he chose to go to the cross. Jesus knowingly and willingly rejected release. Jesus' silence not only amazed Pilate—it should amaze us as well.

Barabbas (Mark 15:6–15)

Not wanting to convict Jesus, and yet wanting to appease the people, Pilate apparently uses a custom of the day to maneuver for Christ's release.[2] Pilate brings out a criminal and asks the crowd to choose between Jesus and Barabbas. History provides evidence that Barabbas' full name was Jesus Barabbas.[3] All four gospels mention Barabbas, and from these accounts we learn that he was a revolutionary who committed murder. "The chief priests stirred up the crowd to have Pilate release Barabbas" (15:11). The crowd's choice was rather ironic. They had fallaciously accused Jesus on charges of insurrection and revolt, yet he was innocent of these crimes. Barabbas, a revolutionary who had committed murder, was deserving of death. And yet Barabbas would go free and Jesus would take the cross intended for him.

Pilate releases Barabbas and then asks, "What shall I do, then, with the one you call the king of the Jews?" (15:12). They respond, "Crucify him!" (15:13). Pilate, the consummate politician and people pleaser, makes one more attempt to appease the people—have Jesus beaten (15:15).[4] It was not a normal practice to scourge someone before crucifying them. Pilate ordered this horrible punishment in an attempt to avoid sending him to the cross. This was Pilate's last-ditch effort to spare Jesus' life. He hoped that by beating Jesus nearly to death, the crowd

---

2. The Gospels provide the only evidence for this practice, but it is not disputed that the governor had the privilege to do what he liked. Releasing a prisoner once a year is neither improbable or unlikely.

3. The early biblical scholar Origen records this for us.

4. Literally, "scourged" (*phragelloō*). This is different than a Jewish flogging. The Jews used a leather whip and limited the strokes to thirty-nine lashes. But the scourging mentioned here used a short leather whip (*flagellum*) imbedded with bits of bone, hooks, and metal that was called a "cat of nine tails." Using this device of torture, a Roman soldier would rip away flesh with each blow. This punishment often killed people or permanently maimed the recipient. If a person survived, it would take years to recover.

would say that he had been punished enough. But he was wrong. Jesus was condemned to die by crucifixion.[5]

The choices made that day are striking. The people had the opportunity to choose Jesus, instead they clamored for a murderer. Pilate could have chosen to do the right thing, instead he wanted to satisfy the crowd (15:15). Both chose poorly.

Truth be known, we face the same choices—Jesus or someone/something else? Doing what we know is right, or appeasing others? Unfortunately, we too often choose poorly.

The Soldiers (Mark 15:16-20)

The abuse of Jesus did not stop with the Roman scourging. Jesus was mocked, struck, spat upon, and dressed in purple. This treatment was highly unusual. Roman soldiers were normally highly-disciplined professionals and not sadistic tormentors. And yet they made sport of Jesus. They wove a crown of thorns[6] and placed it on him. They put a reed in his hand as a scepter for him to wield. They dressed him in purple. Why? The answer is revealed in what they said to him: "Hail, king of the Jews!" (15:18).

It really is quite interesting to think about. The religious leaders hated Jesus because he had upset the applecart of their religion. He had played havoc with their ritualistic piety. Jesus exposed their corruption and hypocrisy—so they tried to shut him up. The Roman officials could unfairly protest that Jesus was a rebel leading a revolt. Or more likely (as is the case with Pilate), they simply wanted to appease the crowd. But what reason do the soldiers have to mock Jesus so? It is unjustified, and yet they tortured and tormented Jesus. The question is, why?

The soldiers' ridicule expresses some contempt for the Jewish people. Officially, the Jews had not had a king since Herod the Great. Part of their mockery was directed at the Jewish people, and yet, at the very core we find people mocking Jesus because of who he was—he was king.

I am amazed at the hatred today towards Jesus by those who say they don't believe. People go to all lengths to try to discredit and defame

---

5. Cicero called crucifixion the cruelest and most hideous punishment possible.

6. The thorns likely came from a type of palm tree common to Jerusalem. The thorn palm had formidable spikes that could have easily been woven into a crown. Some suggest a plant called the Thorny Burnet (Sarcopoterium spinosum) was used. It is a shrub that can reach a height of 20 inches whose outer branches end in sharp thorns.

the name of Jesus. I believe we see the same attitude towards Jesus by nonbelievers today as we saw with the soldiers. People hate Jesus because he makes radical claims on their life. They mock Jesus because they don't want someone else to be in charge. They mock Jesus simply because they don't want him to be king.

We have seen all kinds of different responses to Jesus, but the proper question really is: "What will you do with him?"

Study Questions

1. As a child, would you rather have been punished by your mom or your dad?
2. Why do the Jewish leaders bring Jesus before Pilate?
3. What three adjectives would you use to describe Pilate in this story?
4. What is Pilate's overriding concern in this trial?
5. Why was Jesus silent before Pilate?
6. What was Pilate's reaction to Christ's silence?
7. How does the story of Barabbas illustrate what Christ has done for you?
8. Why did the crowd want a notorious criminal to be released instead of Jesus?
9. What thoughts come to mind as you read of the soldier's mockery of Jesus?
10. In what ways is Jesus still mocked today?

For Further Study

11. See Matthew 27:1-2; 11-31; Luke 22:66-71; 23:1-5; 13-25; John 18:28-19:16.
12. How can you show gratitude to God for sending Jesus to die on the cross for your sins?

38

Glimpses from the Cross

Mark 15:21–47

A certain man from Cyrene, Simon, the father of Alexander and Rufus, was passing by on his way in from the country, and they forced him to carry the cross. They brought Jesus to the place called Golgotha (which means The Place of the Skull). Then they offered him wine mixed with myrrh, but he did not take it. And they crucified him. Dividing up his clothes, they cast lots to see what each would get. It was the third hour when they crucified him. The written notice of the charge against him read: the KING OF THE JEWS. They crucified two robbers with him, one on his right and one on his left. Those who passed by hurled insults at him, shaking their heads and saying, "So! You who are going to destroy the temple and build it in three days, come down from the cross and save yourself!" In the same way the chief priests and the teachers of the law mocked him among themselves. "He saved others," they said, "but he can't save himself! Let this Christ, this King of Israel, come down now from the cross, that we may see and believe." Those crucified with him also heaped insults on him. At the sixth hour darkness came over the whole land until the ninth hour. And at the ninth hour Jesus cried out in a loud voice, "Eloi, Eloi, lama sabachthani?"—which means, "My God, my God, why have you forsaken me?" When some of those standing near heard this, they said, "Listen, he's calling Elijah." One man ran, filled a sponge with wine vinegar, put it on a stick, and offered it to Jesus to drink. "Now leave him alone. Let's see if Elijah comes to take him down," he said. With a loud cry, Jesus breathed his last. The curtain of the temple was torn in two from top to bottom. And when the centurion, who stood there in front of Jesus, heard his cry and saw how he died, he said, "Surely this man was the Son of God!" Some women were watching from a distance. Among them were

Mary Magdalene, Mary the mother of James the younger and of Joses, and Salome. In Galilee these women had followed him and cared for his needs. Many other women who had come up with him to Jerusalem were also there. It was Preparation Day (that is, the day before the Sabbath). So as evening approached, Joseph of Arimathea, a prominent member of the Council, who was himself waiting for the kingdom of God, went boldly to Pilate and asked for Jesus' body. Pilate was surprised to hear that he was already dead. Summoning the centurion, he asked him if Jesus had already died. When he learned from the centurion that it was so, he gave the body to Joseph. So Joseph bought some linen cloth, took down the body, wrapped it in the linen, and placed it in a tomb cut out of rock. Then he rolled a stone against the entrance of the tomb. Mary Magdalene and Mary the mother of Joses saw where he was laid. (Mark 15:21–47)

ONCE AGAIN WE SEE Mark simply giving a fast-paced glimpse of Jesus as he hung on the cross. His crucifixion account is simple and concise. We can find many more details by looking at the other Gospel writers.[1] But Mark gives us a different perspective from the others. Following his lead, I would like to change our perspective as we look at this passage. Normally, we look at this account and focus our attention on the cross of Christ. I would like for a moment to focus our view, not *at* the cross, but *from* the cross.

Mark gives us a glimpse of many people who are gathered around the cross and from these glimpses we can build several character sketches. Although the names, dates, and circumstances have changed, we can still identify these same characters in our world today.

Simon the Cyrene (Mark 15:21)

A man named Simon came to Jerusalem to celebrate the Passover. He originally hailed from a country in North Africa and if this were still his home,[2] he traveled a great distance to get to Jerusalem—for him, this may have been the pilgrimage of a lifetime. Whether he is a Gentile, a God-fearer, or a Jew who came to the feast is also uncertain. But this we know—his journey that day is interrupted by a strange processional

---

1. For example, Mark includes only one sentence spoken by Jesus from the cross. The other gospel writers record seven statements.

2. He was originally from Cyrene. It is unclear if he traveled from Cyrene or elsewhere. We will notice in a moment that he is later identified with Rome—which was also a great distance away.

that is winding through the streets of Jerusalem. Simon witnesses a man who is beaten, bleeding, and staggering. Suddenly, the man falls beneath the weight of a wooden cross. Before Simon knows what hit him, he is grabbed by Roman soldiers and forced into service. The Roman cross once belonging to another is now his to bear.

If we put ourselves in the sandals of Simon, it is not difficult to imagine a possible sentiment of resentment. To think that Simon may have resisted this task, complained verbally, or begrudgingly complied with the assignment is well within reason. But whatever his reaction, we know this one thing—Simon is forced to carry the cross of Christ.

At this point, we might be tempted to move on—Mark certainly does. But let me first ask a question: Why does Mark mention this account in the first place? Is it simply to provide an image of cross carrying by which we can insinuate that we, too, are to pick up our cross and follow Jesus? This thought certainly can inspire devotional applications. But notice Mark also mentions that Simon is the father of Alexander and Rufus (15:21). Why would Mark do this? It is uncharacteristic of Mark to give unneeded details. And yet, he mentions not only Simon, but his children, Alexander and Rufus, by name. Likely, Mark mentions them specifically because Mark's readers knew them intimately.

Many believe there is a hint in the Book of Acts that Simon of Cyrene remained in Jerusalem until Pentecost (Acts 2:10). The Book of Romans (a book also written to Rome) mentions that Rufus (could this be Simon's son?) is closely associated with the Apostle Paul and that Rufus' mother acted motherly to the Apostle (Romans 16:13).

If this is the same Rufus, and therefore Simon's son, (and many biblical scholars concur), far from being appalled for any length of time by carrying the cross of Christ, Simon is actually converted by it. Simon could have been angered, embittered, and missed out on a very important, critical moment. But it appears that he does not. It seems that Simon and his family are actually converted through watching Christ suffer. What was initially a burden to him became his salvation. Isn't it interesting how God can redeem our troubles if we will allow him to work in and through them? If our theorizing is correct, then Jesus' statement about "denying oneself and taking up his cross" (8:34) takes on new meaning for Simon.

Soldiers and Thieves (Mark 15:22-30)

Surrounding the cross, we also find the soldiers who crucified Jesus. They are the ones who nailed Jesus to the cross and lifted it into place. They are the ones we find throwing dice and gambling for Christ's garments (15:24). Their calloused indifference is demonstrated through the fact that they were more interested in the pleasures of a game and making money than they were in the death and blood of Jesus.

We also read of two robbers who were hung on either side of Jesus. John uses the same word "robber" (*lēstēs*) for Barabbas who was an insurrectionist. We can conclude that either they were thieves bent on killing and stealing, or they were angry men bent on overthrowing Roman rule in Palestine. In either case, they joined in with the crowds in hurling insults at Jesus (Luke 23:35).[3] "Those who passed by hurled insults at him, shaking their heads and saying, 'So! You who are going to destroy the temple and build it in three days, come down from the cross and save yourself'" (15:29-30).

Many people today operate by the soldiers' philosophy—they take what they want, are hardened to the concerns of others, and don't care who gets hurt in the process. Others are like the crowds who unknowingly shake their heads with derision at the very one who willingly dies for their sins.

Priests and Teachers (Mark 15:31-32)

The priests and the teachers of the law were the very men who plotted the death of Jesus. The priests had been frightened and jealous of Jesus as he taught throughout Israel. Now, they had accomplished their purpose—or so it seemed. This was their moment of triumph and they reveled in it. At the foot of the cross, they mock Jesus: "He saved others . . . but he can't save himself! Let this Christ, this King of Israel, come down now from the cross, that we may see and believe" (15:32).

There is an eerie symbolism in the teachers' taunts and a striking parallel to our modern world. They are calling for Jesus to separate himself from the cross and then they will believe. Their view of a Messiah cannot include this instrument of death. They will only believe in a Messiah who is free from the cross. Sound familiar? Many people want to associate with Jesus, but they cannot accept the cross. They accept the historical Jesus. They even accept many of his teachings. But they reject the cross. Theirs is a cross-less, and therefore a Christ-less, Christianity.

---

3. Luke also tells us that one of these robbers eventually repents of his wrongdoing.

The gospel is empty without the cross of Jesus Christ. The blood of Jesus is at the very core of the message of salvation. Paul says,

> "But we preach Christ crucified: a stumbling block to Jews and foolishness to Gentiles, but to those whom God has called, both Jews and Greeks, Christ the power of God and the wisdom of God. For the foolishness of God is wiser than man's wisdom, and the weakness of God is stronger than man's strength." (1 Corinthians 1:23–25)

The Centurion (Mark 15:39)

As Jesus calls out and breathes his last (15:37), we get one final reaction from the foot of the cross. We are introduced to the centurion. "When the centurion, who stood there in front of Jesus, heard his cry and saw how he died, he said, 'Surely this man was the Son of God!'" (15:39).

The Roman centurion was brought to a sobering realization at the foot of the cross. The men at his command had mocked, ridiculed, and crucified Jesus. To many, it had even been a joke. But to this centurion, the crucifixion was a ghastly mistake.

Much has been written about the statement we find here. Did the centurion acknowledge Jesus as the Son of God in a truly Christian sense, or was it simply this man's own expression that Jesus was a righteous man?[4] We can't know for sure. If the latter is true, the centurion expresses Christ's divinity. If only the former, he certainly acknowledges Jesus' innocence. In either case, there was something about the way Jesus died that the centurion had never seen before. Maybe he witnessed a dignity and composure in Christ that was unexpected—especially at a moment like this. Or maybe it was the fact that Jesus displayed a selfless compassion for others even at the moment of his death which tugged at the heart-strings of the centurion. Whatever the case, Jesus' conducted himself in a manner that transcended common explanation.

Yet, even with this profession, there is no glimpse of hope in the centurion's words. Surely this man "was" the Son of God. There is no expectation of resurrection. There is no glimmer of hopefulness. The centurion only knows that a horrible injustice has been committed that can never be undone. At this moment, the centurion does not comprehend what this Christ-event means for humanity. Unfortunately, this is the same scenario for many people today as they look at the cross. They might acknowledge

---

4. Luke 23:47.

either that Jesus was a remarkable man, or even confess that he was the Son of God, but they never personalize the fact that Jesus Christ died for their sins and never cling to the fact that he died for them. It is not enough to simply acknowledged that Jesus is the Son of God—we must go further. We must make the fact personal and not only accept Jesus as Savior, but we must trust him as Lord—and Lord means boss.

There are many who come close to the cross of Christ, but never fully submit. A Christian is a person who makes Jesus Christ Lord of his life and who faithfully seeks to follow all that Christ commands. Unfortunately, many make a right profession, but find themselves only in the proximity of Jesus.

Study Questions

1. What do we know about Simon the Cyrene and his sons Alexander and Rufus?
2. Summarize the scenes from each of the following characters' perspectives.
    a. Simon the Cyrene (15:21)
    b. The thieves (15:27)
    c. The priests, teachers, and passers-by (15:29–32)
    d. The centurion (15:39)
3. Which character from this passage do you relate to most?
4. What does Golgotha mean (15:22)?
5. Why do you think those who passed by Christ on the cross felt justified in saying what they did (15:29)?
6. How long was Jesus on the cross?
7. Did God really forsake Jesus (15:34)? Has God ever forsaken anyone else? Is there anyone else that God will forsake?
8. What is the significance of the temple curtain being torn in two from top to bottom (15:39)?
9. What do you think convinced the centurion that Jesus was the Son of God (15:39)?

For Further Study

10. See: Matthew 27:32–56; Luke 23:26–49; John 19:17–37.

39

See for Yourself

Mark 16:1–8

BLACK FRIDAY WAS THE darkest day in human history. Not only did a physical darkness come over the land from noon until three,[1] but there was spiritual darkness as the Son was separated from the Father. Also, an emotional darkness gripped the followers of Christ, whose hopes and dreams were shattered that Friday. The man whom they believed to be the coming Messiah had just suffered a cruel death on the cross. One can only imagine their broken hearts, their guilt, their shame, and their fear. What would they do now? Imagine the questions they must have wrestled with: "Why go on?" "Why bother?" Jesus was dead and the disciples had failed—how could they continue? Between the cross of Christ and the empty tomb, there was nothing but depression and hopelessness. As we come to our passage, we see three women, who in their sorrow, come to the tomb to show one last act of compassion for Jesus.

> When the Sabbath was over, Mary Magdalene, Mary the mother of James, and Salome bought spices so that they might go to anoint Jesus' body. Very early on the first day of the week, just after sunrise, they were on their way to the tomb and they asked each other, "Who will roll the stone away from the entrance of the tomb?" But when they looked up, they saw that the stone, which was very large, had been rolled away. As they entered the tomb, they saw a young man dressed in a white robe sitting on the right side, and they were alarmed. "Don't be alarmed," he said. "You are looking for Jesus the Nazarene, who was crucified. He has risen! He is not here. See the place where they laid him. But go, tell his

---

1. See Matthew 27:45.

disciples and Peter, 'He is going ahead of you into Galilee. There you will see him, just as he told you.'" Trembling and bewildered, the women went out and fled from the tomb. They said nothing to anyone, because they were afraid. (Mark 16:1–8)

As the women come to the tomb, they come expecting the expected.

Expecting the Expected (Mark 16:1–3)

With verse 1, we are again introduced to Mary Magdalene, Mary the mother of James, and Salome. They are an integral part of the connecting material between Jesus' ministry, his crucifixion, and the resurrection. They were part of the group that accompanied Jesus in Galilee. They followed him to Jerusalem. And as Jesus was crucified on the cross they watched from a distance (15:40–41). They also followed Joseph of Arimathea to the tomb where he wrapped Jesus' body in the linen shroud and laid his body to rest (15:46–47).

Now, these three ladies made plans to say their final goodbyes to Jesus, because they had been prevented from doing so on the Sabbath. So, sometime Saturday night after sunset, they bought supplies from one of the local shops that reopened briefly at the conclusion of the Sabbath. Since it was too late to go to the tomb that evening, they went "very early on the first day of the week, just after sunrise" (16:2).

The great devotion of the women is demonstrated first, by the fact that they purchased very expensive spices for the body of Jesus, and second, by their desire to anoint a body that had been dead for some period already. Interestingly, we know that Joseph of Arimathea and Nicodemus have already anointed the body with over seventy-five pounds of myrrh and aloes (John 19:39–40).[2] One might question why the women needed to bring spices and anoint the body a second time. Some suggest that the women might have been too far away to see that the men had actually anointed the body. Actually, being women, I think they probably wanted to anoint Jesus' body a second time precisely because Joseph and Nicodemus did it the first time—they wanted it done right!

Whatever the reason, the women left very early Sunday morning to head toward the tomb. "On their way to the tomb they asked each other, 'Who will roll the stone away from the entrance of the tomb?'" (16:3).

---

2. This was not, as some have imagined, a process of embalming the body. It was simply a reverent anointing. It also had aromatic purposes.

Burial in caves or chambers carved out of rock was much more common in Israel than burial in the ground. Matthew, Luke, and John all indicate for us that the tomb was new and had never been used. The reuse of tombs was quite common. John tells us that this particular tomb was in a garden. The tombs often had a disk-shaped rock similar to a millstone which rolled in a channel to seal the cave. The channel was sloped toward the opening so that it was easy to cover the hole, but very difficult to remove the stone and uncover it. This kept out both animals and grave robbers. Critics have questioned why the women did not think earlier about the problem of the stone. The simple answer is that love does not always foresee or deal with problems—it simply acts. The women were grieving and mourning, and the events were chaotic.

One thing is for sure, on their way to the tomb, they all expected to find the same thing. They expected to find a grave, and inside the tomb, they expected to find a lifeless body. There was no wishful thinking or devious scheming—they were expecting to find the expected. Instead, what the women found was altogether unexpected.

Experiencing the Unexpected (Mark 16:4-6)

As the women approached the tomb, they looked up and saw that the stone had been moved. Mark uses a trifecta of words which describe largeness. The very term that he uses for stone distinguishes it from being a small stone. Mark uses the common word for large stone (*lithos*). It is the Greek word from which we get our English words "lithograph" and "monolith." Mark, however, modifies this word by telling us that it is both *megas* (from which we get our word mega), meaning large relative to the norm; and, that it is *sphodra*—exceedingly much so. It is no wonder that the women were worried about how they might get the tomb open.

This question has often been asked: Why did the stone need to be rolled away? The answer is not so Jesus could get out, but so that the women (and later, Peter and John) could get in. "As they entered the tomb, they saw a young man dressed in a white robe sitting on the right side, and they were alarmed" (16:5). Mark identifies this person as a young man, but gives us a clue as to his true identity. The word translated "white" (*leukos*) means brilliant or shining. We learn from each of the other gospel accounts that this was indeed an angel, and that there are actually two present (John 20:12), but Mark is only interested in the one who speaks. When the angel greeted them they were alarmed (*ekthambeō*). This word is used only four times, and only in the Gospel of Mark. As we have seen previously, it can mean "to amaze, or marvel," but in this context—they are freaked out. This is not unexpected—how would you feel if you came to a tomb and an angel called out to you?

But while the fear of seeing the angel might not be unexpected, the angel's words certainly are. "Don't be alarmed . . . He has risen! He is not here. See the place where they laid him" (16:7). These words were unexpected. Understand, as the women approached the tomb, they were not expecting to find a resurrected Jesus. This is not a case of wishful thinking—in fact, the day's events came as quite a shock to their system. Mark even uses the word *phobeō* from which we get our word "phobia" (16:8) to describe their reaction.

Reacting to the Unexpected (Mark 16:7–8)

As the women encounter the angel, they are given specific instructions: "But go, tell his disciples and Peter, 'He is going ahead of you into Galilee. There you will see him, just as he told you'" (16:7). There are two questions that would be helpful for us to answer. The first is: Who are the women supposed to tell? Of course, it is clear that they are supposed to tell the disciples who had fled (14:50). But they are also to tell Peter. Peter is obviously singled out on purpose. The last time Peter was mentioned in the Gospel of Mark was at the courtyard of the high priest when Peter denied Jesus three times (14:72). What a sense of relief and encouragement these words would be to Peter—Jesus still wanted Peter, and Peter is included in the invitation to meet with Christ. The second question is simply: What are they to say? They are to include the message that Jesus Christ has risen and that he wants them to meet him in Galilee. This meeting spot takes them back home to familiar territory and is the fulfillment of a prearranged promise.

After Jesus predicted that all of the disciples would fall away and be scattered (14:27), he also promised that after he raised, he would go ahead of them into Galilee (14:28). This was actually Jesus' fourth prediction to them about his death, burial, and resurrection. He had previously said, "We are going up to Jerusalem . . . and the Son of Man will be betrayed to the chief priests and teachers of the law. They will condemn him to death and will hand him over to the Gentiles, who will mock him and spit on him, flog him and kill him. Three days later he will rise" (10:33; cf. 8:31; 9:31).

Although Jesus had predicted his resurrection and a future Galilean meeting, the angel's message still caught the women off guard. We read: "Trembling and bewildered, the women went out and fled from the tomb" (16:8). Here we find an interesting phrase. We first find the women "trembling" (*tromos*). The word literally means to shake or quiver in fearful response. As mentioned before, this reaction is understandable. The next word in the phrase, however, is curious. The NIV uses the word "bewildered." I am bewildered by this translation. The word is literally "amazed" (*ekstasis*). It is the very word from which we get our English word "ecstasy." While the women are trembling and afraid, the news of Jesus' resurrection creates a wonderful sense of astonishment. Both the NASB and the ESV translate it this way: "Astonishment had gripped (seized) them" (16:8).

The women are initially overwhelmed and confused and run from the garden. They are so befuddled that they do not speak to anyone—essentially ignoring the angel's command. After a brief delay, however, the women do indeed take the message of Christ's resurrection back to the disciples. Matthew records for us: "So the women hurried away from the tomb, afraid yet filled with joy, and ran to tell his disciples" (Matthew 28:8).

What began as the darkest day in human history, became the greatest story ever told—Jesus Christ risen from the dead. And yet, there are many who try, understandably, to dismiss this account. How can someone rise from the dead? Most who try to dismiss the account insist that Christians are blinded by their ignorance. I would assert, however, that Christians are not the ones with myopic vision. The evidence of the resurrection is strong and clear. The empty tomb baffles the unconvinced. The grave clothes wreak havoc on the skeptic. The evidence for the resurrection is substantia;l and we even find proof in the fact that Christianity grew so quickly in the very area that Christ was crucified, because it was also the very area in which Christ was raised from the dead.

Those who purport that the resurrection was the hallucination of a handful of hopeful women, miss the fact that these women were anything but hopeful—they were expecting the expected. Those who surmise that they went to the wrong tomb simply ignore the evidence to the contrary. The women had not only been to the tomb before, but the angel confirms the right location when he says, "You are looking for Jesus the Nazarene, who was crucified" (16:6). Besides, if the poor women were misguided, all the Roman authorities needed to do to squelch their unfounded belief in the resurrection was to point them in the proper direction and take them to the appropriate tomb. Some have suggested that the whole event was fabricated by the early church. But this ignores the fact that women were not considered as legal witnesses and would not have been woven so intricately into the narrative in a primary way if the story was merely a fabrication.

As you trace the arguments for and against the resurrection of Jesus, the evidence leads one toward rather than away from the Easter event. I am reminded of a story told by Lee Strobel, author of *The Case for Christ*. He tells of the surprise and animosity he expressed towards his wife when she came to know Christ as Savior. In his own words, he said, "I rolled my eyes and braced for the worst, feeling like the victim of a bait-and-switch scam."[3] But as an investigative reporter for the *Chicago Tribune*, he plunged into the evidence of history, science, philosophy, and religion for a period of over two years. He not only experienced the credible evidence of the resurrection, he became a Christian through his research. He began to see it for himself. Such is often the case for those who will see for themselves.

Throughout the Gospel of Mark, we have been listening as Mark has intricately presented to us the case for Christ. He has systematically answered two questions: Who is Jesus? And What did he come to do? He now has answered that question emphatically. Jesus is not just another teacher. He is not simply a good prophet or moral leader. He did not come to establish a political kingdom. Jesus is more than a man who was beaten, persecuted, and hung on the cross. Jesus is the Christ, the Son of God who was crucified but raised from the dead. This event is the crux of Christianity.

Mark has issued the challenge: "What will you do with Jesus?"

The angel has spoken: "Come and see!"

Now I am making the same invitation to you: "Come, see for yourself!" Come with an open mind. Sift through the evidence. Consider the testimony and credibility of the witnesses. Examine the facts. Then, after weighing the evidence, determine how you will respond. But please,

---

3. Lee Strobel, *The Case for Christ*, p. 16.

come and see how the darkest day in history became the greatest story every told.

Jeroslav Pelikan once said, "If Christ is raised, nothing else matters. If Christ is not raised, nothing matters." One of my professors, Bob Lowery, rephrased this to read: "Nothing matters but Christ's resurrection. And because nothing matters but Christ's resurrection, everyone and everything matter.[4]

Study Questions

1. What is the most incredible event you have ever seen?
2. What do you find sobering about visiting a cemetery or grave site of a loved one? Whose passing has been the most difficult for you? Why?
3. What day of the week is Mark referring to as "the first day of the week"? What importance, if any, does this play today?
4. What emotions were likely felt by the women as they discovered the empty tomb? Why were they so compelled to go and anoint Jesus' body?
5. Why was the stone rolled away? For Jesus? If not, for whom? What was the benefit of seeing the empty tomb (John 20:8)?
6. Mary Magdalene, Mary the mother of James, and Salome were never very far away during the crucifixion and burial of Jesus (see 15:40–41). What does this tell you about the faith of these women?
7. How did these women respond to the angel who said, "He has risen"? How would you have reacted? Would you have had trouble believing his words?
8. Why did the angel specifically tell the women to mention Peter (16:7)?
9. How does this account compare with Matthew 26?
10. Why do you think a woman, Mary Magdalene, was selected to first see Jesus?

---

4. This comes from a lecture by Bob Lowery at Lincoln Christian Seminary, 2009.

11. Who was Joseph of Arimathea and why did he take charge of Jesus' body?

12. How has the reality of the empty tomb changed your life?

13. How can you, in practical ways, show gratitude to God for sending his son Jesus to die on the cross for your sins?

For Further Study

14. See also: Matthew 28:1–7; Luke 24:1–12; John 20:1–9.

15. Compare Mark 16:7 with Mark 14:28.

40

A "Puzzling" Solution

An Introduction to Mark 16:9–20

[The earliest manuscripts and other ancient witnesses do not have Mark 16:9–20.] When Jesus rose early on the first day of the week, he appeared first to Mary Magdalene, out of whom he had driven seven demons. She went and told those who had been with him and who were mourning and weeping. When they heard that Jesus was alive and that she had seen him, they did not believe it. Afterward Jesus appeared in a different form to two of them while they were walking in the country. These returned and reported it to the rest; but they did not believe them either. Later Jesus appeared to the Eleven as they were eating; he rebuked them for their lack of faith and their stubborn refusal to believe those who had seen him after he had risen. He said to them, "Go into all the world and preach the good news to all creation. Whoever believes and is baptized will be saved, but whoever does not believe will be condemned. And these signs will accompany those who believe: In my name they will drive out demons; they will speak in new tongues; they will pick up snakes with their hands; and when they drink deadly poison, it will not hurt them at all; they will place their hands on sick people, and they will get well." After the Lord Jesus had spoken to them, he was taken up into heaven and he sat at the right hand of God. Then the disciples went out and preached everywhere, and the Lord worked with them and confirmed his word by the signs that accompanied it. (Mark 16:9–20)

As we begin, we find ourselves looking squarely at the largest disputed passage of Scripture in our Bibles—not only in terms of length, but also in terms of importance. This is the most significant textual variant in scripture.[1] If you are reading any of the modern translations of Scripture (i.e., NIV, NASB, ESB, NLT, etc), you will find a disclaimer to the effect that some manuscripts end with 16:8 while others add 16:9–20. You will find this reported either directly within the text itself (as is the case in the NIV), or located in a footnote or margin. The only exception of which I am aware is that of the King James Version of the Bible which includes 16:9–20 without comment.[2]

At this point, we are faced with several choices when considering how to proceed. First, we could simply end our discussion of the Gospel of Mark and not comment on either the passage itself or the editorial disclaimer. (This, by the way, is the approach of many preachers and commentaries.)

Second, we could play the ostrich, bury our heads in the ground and simply ignore the editorial comment by pressing on with the exposition of the text as if everyone was none-the-wiser about the deeper issue involved.

Or, third, we could deal with the issue head-on, grabbing it by the horns. It probably won't surprise anyone, that I prefer this final approach. I do realize that by doing so, I may place myself at odds with others who do not agree with my conclusions. How could I not? Competent scholars with fine pedigrees have come down on different sides of this very issue. (Still, I am a Crane and not an ostrich, and prefer not to bury my head in the sands of ignorance.)

We should begin by defining the issue itself.

The Argument Defined—"The earliest manuscripts and some other ancient witnesses do not have Mark 16:9–20" (NIV editorial comment).

Let me begin with the editorial comment itself inserted in the NIV.[3] It is true that two of the earliest complete manuscripts of the New Testament, ℵ and "B," (also known as the *Codex Sinaiticus* and the *Codex Vaticanus*),[4]

---

1. John 7:53—8:11 is the only other passage that could compare, but it does not raise the same number of issues as Mark 16:9–20.

2. The King James Version is based on the *Textus Receptus* (The Received Text), a late manuscript which includes this section of Scripture. The New King James Version does include a footnote about this section.

3. The editorial comments in each of the different translations vary slightly.

4. Some early Latin, Syriac, Armenian, and Georgian manuscripts also do not

do not contain Mark 16:9–20. It should, however, also be pointed out that the vast majority of ancient manuscripts do contain these verses—some very early (by the beginning or middle of the second century).[5] So the argument is not as cut and dried as it appears at first glance—there is a reason why this is the most significant textual variant in scripture.

Before moving on, I would like to reaffirm my confidence in the integrity of the Bible and state for the record that it is remarkably preserved and that over ninety-nine percent of it cannot be brought into question. Out of the literally thousands of manuscripts of the New Testament available, it is simply remarkable to discover how few textual variants there are in existence—especially when we consider that manuscripts were copied by hand.[6] Having affirmed my confidence in scripture, this passage remains the most significant textual variant in the New Testament. At its core, the issue deals with whether these verses originated with Mark or if they were added later. Asked succinctly: Did Mark end with verse 8 or with verse 20?[7]

As we begin, I would simply like to present the pros and cons of each view.

The Argument for Inclusion—That Mark 16:9–20 should be considered original material to the Gospel.

If the Gospel of Mark ends with 16:8, the story seems incomplete for at least three reasons. First, it seems unusual that Mark would not include some account of Jesus meeting his disciples in Galilee, especially in light of the promise given by the angel: "But go, tell his disciples and Peter, 'He is going ahead of you into Galilee. There you will see him, just as he told you'" (16:7). As readers, we expect Mark to narrate that event, especially for the sake of Peter, who has denied him. We would do well to remember, once again, that Mark wrote this book as Peter preached.

---

contain this section. Eusebius and Jerome note that this section was missing in most manuscripts of their time.

5. The manuscripts known as "A" (*Codex Alexandrinus*), "C" (*Codex Ephraimi*), and "D" (*Codex Bezae*), contain these verses and the early church father, Irenaeus, shows knowledge of it as well.

6. Even in the day of computers and spell check, I am confident that this manuscript still has a typo or two, even with several people proofing it.

7. A few manuscripts insert additional material after verse 14. One other manuscript adds a verse following verse 8 and then continues with 16:9–20. These, however, have very little textual support.

Additionally, Peter preached in Rome, the very audience to whom this book was written. This raises significant questions in my mind. Would Peter not preach about his restoration with Jesus at the conclusion of this story? Would Mark fail to record such a reunion of Peter with Jesus? Actually, this is exactly how the Gospel of John ends. John records for us a lakeside fish barbeque and Peter being commissioned into ministry by Jesus (John 21:1–19).

Second, it also seems unusual that Mark would end his story with the women paralyzed by fear and ignoring the words of Christ's messenger. The angel has just told the women not be alarmed (16:6), but to go tell the others what they have just experienced (16:7). If the story ends before verse 9, we simply read: "They said nothing to anyone, because they were afraid" (16:8). Period! That's it. Is there anyone else who is dissatisfied with that conclusion? How can a book which purports to be the good news about Jesus Christ, end with the women remaining silent and in fear?[8] Personally, I would be much happier if we found a verse like we find in a parallel section of the Gospel of Matthew: "So the women hurried away from the tomb, afraid, yet filled with joy, and ran to tell his disciples. Suddenly Jesus met them. 'Greetings,' he said. They came to him, clasped his feet and worshiped him" (Matthew 28:8–9).

Finally, the strongest argument is a grammatical one. It seems highly unusual, and even impossible for Mark to end a paragraph—let alone an entire book with a conjunction. And yet that is exactly what we find if we end the Gospel with verse 8.[9] How many of us got marked down in English class for ending a sentence with a preposition, let alone a conjunction? I can still remember Saturday morning cartoons with Schoolhouse Rock—"Conjunction Junction, what's your function? Hooking up cars and making 'em function." The same rules apply even more stringently in Greek than they do in English, and yet, if Mark ends this book with verse 8, we find him not only ending a sentence and paragraph with a conjunction, but this is how he ends the entire book.[10]

These arguments give sway to include 16:9–20 as part of Mark's original gospel. It just makes sense, doesn't it. There just has to be more!

---

8. Some do argue that Mark ends this way intentionally for dramatic effect.

9. Mark 16:8 reads, *ephobounto gar*.

10. It may be possible to find a rare instance in ancient Greek literature where a paragraph ends with a conjunction. There are, however, no cases where an entire book ends this way.

But, as persuasive as these arguments may be, there are equally compelling arguments against including the longer ending in the Gospel of Mark.

The Argument for Exclusion—That Mark 16:9–20 should not be considered original material to the Gospel (i.e., Mark's gospel ends with 16:8).

In this section, we find a number of interesting anomalies which would call for exclusion of this passage. The first is based on the vocabulary of Mark 16:9–20. In this section there are one hundred and one (101) different Greek words of the one hundred and sixty-seven (167) total words. By subtracting the unimportant words (words like the definite article, connectives, proper names, etc.) only seventy-five (75) words remain. Of these distinct words, fifteen (15) appear nowhere else in the Gospel of Mark, and eleven (11) are used in a different sense than the normal Markan usage. This means that slightly more than one-third (26) of the distinctive words of this section appear to be non-Markan. This is quite an anomaly. Some who attempt to reconcile this abnormality say that a different subject matter requires a different vocabulary. While there is some validity in this argument, few would agree there is enough to warrant the extreme divergence we find here.

Beyond the vocabulary argument, we also get a second anomaly, which is one of syntax. Simply put: the style is curious. For example: the transition between 16:8 and 16:9 is at best, awkward, and at worst unworkable. The NIV reads, "When [Jesus] rose early on the first day of the week" (16:9). In Greek, the word "rose" (*anistēmi*) demands an antecedent of "he," but it is strangely lacking. When we look back to verse 8 we find the story ending with the account of the women. The two verses do not fit grammatically together. To resolve the problem, the NIV literally inserts the proper name of "Jesus." It is necessary for them to do because verse 9 requires a masculine noun or pronoun. Verse 9 does not line up with what we expect to find, and need to find from verse 8 in Greek. The syntax simply does not work!

We also get a third interesting anomaly. Here we find Mary Magdalene, introduced to us as if it were our initial meeting. We read, "He appeared first to Mary Magdalene, out of whom he had driven seven demons" (16:9). But if this is part of the original text, Mary Magdalene has been part of the story line for some time. We find her mentioned twice specifically in chapter 15 (15:40, 47) and once more, just eight verses earlier in this very chapter (16:1). Why would Mark feel obligated to mention this fact about her now, rather than mentioning it when she first appears on the scene in his Gospel? We might categorize this as an anomaly of superfluous introduction. This comment is an unnecessary reiteration and is not typical of Mark's style of writing.

It is also interesting to remind ourselves of what we would expect to find following verse 8. We previously mentioned that we expect to find some Galilean appearance of Jesus to the disciples—especially Peter, as well as a note about how the women followed the instructions of the angel. These expectations were not met if we stopped the narrative in verse 8, but neither are they satisfied by the longer ending recorded for us in Mark 16:9–20.

The long and the short (sorry for the pun) is simply this: we need more information than we get from Mark 16:1–8, but we aren't satisfied with what we find in Mark 16:9–20, either. We need more, but not what we get! So, what are we supposed to conclude?

Answering the Argument

We have been asking the question: Did Mark end with verse 8 or with verse 20? Actually, I believe that this is a false dichotomy—a false choice. It is more likely that Mark wrote something (answering the first objection), but not what we find in the longer ending (answering the second objection). Mark wrote something, but we don't have it.

Then what happened to it? The best solution seems to be that Mark did write an ending to the Gospel (either in codex or scroll form), but that it was lost and what we have represents a very early attempt to provide what was once there. As the early church read through verse 8, they felt the same feeling of incompleteness that we get when we read only the first part of the chapter. Knowing "the rest of the story," they composed a longer ending based on what they knew happened.[11] But based on what? The answer is, they attached other scriptural material to it, primarily from Luke and John. I'll talk more about his in a moment.

---

11. The text itself supports this idea. Verse 20 is obviously written after the events of the Gospel of Mark.

What is truly remarkable is not that they wanted to complete the story (we would all feel that unresolved tension tugging at us), but the fact that we find this new conclusion to the Gospel of Mark as early the middle of the second century—that's very early. The longer ending (16:9–20) was likely penned sometime early in the second century, within just a few decades of the original autograph copy.

This leads me to ask an all-important question: If Mark 16:9–20 is not original (and I don't believe it is), is it therefore unscriptural? Actually, no! The early church abbreviated what they knew from scripture, primarily from the other Gospel endings and attached it to Mark to bring the story to its proper conclusion. What we find in Mark 16:9–20 is not new material, but material we find elsewhere in Scripture in passages that are not textual variants. Restated, we don't find any new doctrine or teaching in this section that we do not already have elsewhere in passages that are unchallenged. Let me demonstrate that for you.

In Mark 16:9–11 we find Jesus' appearance to Mary Magdalene. We find that same material recorded for us in John 20:11–18. In Mark 16:12–13 we read of Jesus' appearance to two men. A more detailed account can be found in Luke 24:13–35. The appearance to the Eleven and the Great Commission (16:14–18) is found in several parallel passages, including Matthew 28:16–20; Luke 24:36–43; John 20:19–25; 1 Corinthians 15:6; and Acts 1:6–8. Even the curious terminology of Mark 16:17–18 (of tongues, and snakes, and the laying on of hands) finds parallels in other places in scripture (Acts 2:4–11; 3:1–10; 5:12–16; 9:12–18; 10:46; 19:6; 28:3–6; Luke 10:19; and James 5:14–15). Finally, the ascension of Mark 16:19–20 is paralleled by both Luke 24:50–53 and Acts 1:9–12. While the ending of Mark's Gospel may not be the original ending, neither is it unscriptural, and it certainly is not in error. We find nothing new here that is not recorded for us elsewhere in our Bibles.[12]

This is true of every textual variant we find in Scripture. The critics of Scripture simply have no case. Actually, while many skeptics of the Bible try to use this passage to discredit its message, this section elevates my confidence. As I have stated several times—this is the greatest textual variant in Scripture! Yet we find nothing new, nothing unscriptural, nothing contradictory. Furthermore, although it is a textual variant, our Bibles identify the problem. They label it for us: "Here it is."

---

12. The reverse is also true—if we were to lose Mark 16:9–20, we would lose nothing!

When dealing with skeptics, this passage routinely comes up, and yet I can say that I know the issue, and I know what is at stake. And then I can boldly say to them, "Is this the best you've got?" Actually, it is!

If you find someone telling you that the Bible is unreliable, or suggesting to you that "many plain and precious truths have been removed," understand this one thing—they have failed to do their homework. Our problem is not whether or not the Bible is credible and reliable. Our problem is that often we don't act like it.

Study Questions

1. Are you the kind of person who reads the ending of a book first? Why or why not?
2. How did you react when you first saw the editorial comment on Mark 16:9–20?
3. Have you ever heard a sermon (or lesson) explain the editorial comment? In what context?
4. What does your Bible say (if anything) about this section of Scripture (16:9–20)?
5. Would you rather your Bible ignore or make you aware of textual variants like Mark 16:9–20?
6. How should the church respond to a section like Mark 16:9–20?
    a. Ignore the editorial comment and pretend it doesn't exist?
    b. Stop teaching the book at 16:8? or,
    c. Deal with the issue fairly and accurately?
7. How do you respond to Steve's handling of this section?
8. Explain the arguments, for and against, the longer ending of Mark (16:9–20).
9. In your opinion, what most likely happened to the ending of the Gospel of Mark?
10. What four post-resurrection events are described in this section?
11. Do verses 9–20 contain any information or doctrine not found elsewhere in the Bible?

12. How does the treatment of this section of scripture strengthen (or weaken) your view of the Bible?
13. Is it possible that God inspired both Mark's writing, and the addition of Mark 16:9–20? Why or why not?
14. Do you take the Bible for granted? Why or why not?
15. What aspect of the Gospel of Mark have you enjoyed or learned from the most? Explain.

For Further Study

16. The four sections of the longer ending each have parallels elsewhere. Take a moment and look up each.

    a. The appearance to Mary Magdalene: Mark 16:9–11 // John 20:11–18.

    b. The appearance to two Men: Mark 16:12–13 // Luke 24:13–35.

    c. The appearance to the Eleven and the Great Commission: Mark 16:14–18 // Matthew 28:16–20; Luke 24:36–43; John 20:19–25; 1 Corinthians 15:6; Acts 1:6–8.

        i. Tongues: Mark 16:17 // Acts 2:4–11; 10:46; 19:6.

        ii. Snakes: Mark 16:18a // Luke 10:19; Acts 28:3–6

        iii. Laying on of hands: Mark 16:18b // Acts 3:1–10; 5:12–16; 9:12, 17–18; James 5:14–15.

    d. The ascension: Mark 16:19–20 // Luke 24:50–53; Acts 1:9–12.

41

Missio Dei

THE MISSION OF GOD

Mark 16:9–20

> When Jesus rose early on the first day of the week, he appeared first to Mary Magdalene, out of whom he had driven seven demons. She went and told those who had been with him and who were mourning and weeping. When they heard that Jesus was alive and that she had seen him, they did not believe it. Afterward Jesus appeared in a different form to two of them while they were walking in the country. These returned and reported it to the rest; but they did not believe them either. Later Jesus appeared to the Eleven as they were eating; he rebuked them for their lack of faith and their stubborn refusal to believe those who had seen him after he had risen. He said to them, "Go into all the world and preach the good news to all creation. Whoever believes and is baptized will be saved, but whoever does not believe will be condemned. And these signs will accompany those who believe: In my name they will drive out demons; they will speak in new tongues; they will pick up snakes with their hands; and when they drink deadly poison, it will not hurt them at all; they will place their hands on sick people, and they will get well." After the Lord Jesus had spoken to them, he was taken up into heaven and he sat at the right hand of God. Then the disciples went out and preached everywhere, and the Lord worked with them and confirmed his word by the signs that accompanied it. (Mark 16:9–20)

WE'VE COME TO THE last words in the Book of Mark. As we reach this section, we find one further change in the writing style.[1] Up

---

1. If you come to this section wondering about the editorial comment, please see the discussion in the previous section. What we have here, regardless of whether or not they are Mark's words, are still scriptural. Everything we find in this section is found

to this point, Mark has written everything in narrative form. Now we get several overarching summations of events that occur over a period of 40 days. We find in this section four encounters with the risen Christ. We also see a wonderful transformation in the lives of the followers of Christ as they move from unbelief to belief, and then from belief into action. We see clearly the mobilization of God's people to accomplish the *Missio Dei*—the Mission of God.

Transformation: From Disbelief to Belief

One of the most powerful impressions left by this section, is the realization that the followers of Christ did not immediately believe in the resurrection of Jesus Christ—they needed to be convinced. Three times in the initial verses of this passage we read these words: "They did not believe it" (16:11); "They did not believe them either" (16:13); and we read of "Their lack of faith and their stubborn refusal to believe those who had seen" (16:14). Their disbelief is certainly a major theme of the opening verses of this section. But Jesus makes several post-resurrection appearances to transform them from disbelief to belief.

Jesus appears to Mary Magdalene
(Mark 16:9–11; cf. John 20:11–18)

We have already observed that Mary Magdalene, Mary the mother of James, and Salome did not expect to find a risen Savior. They were on their way to pay their last respects (16:1–2). When confronted with the message of the angel, they were at first, "trembling and bewildered" and "said nothing to anyone, because they were afraid" (16:8).

But shortly after this, Jesus personally appears to Mary Magdalene in the garden. Though her first response to the message of the angel was fear and bewilderment, her disbelief is turned to belief as she encounters the risen Christ. This section in Mark is an abbreviated account of what we find recorded for us in John 20:11–18. In John's gospel, Jesus approaches a distraught Mary and says to her, "Woman . . . why are you crying? Who is it you are looking for" (John 20:15). Mary, not expecting to see Jesus, initially mistakes him for the gardener. But as Mary turns toward him, and as Jesus speaks a second time, Mary realizes who it is, and cries out, "Teacher" (John 20:16). After this encounter, Mary runs

---

elsewhere in other New Testament passages.

back to the disciples, who are "mourning and weeping" (16:10) and informs them that Jesus is alive and that she has personally seen him, but they did not believe it (16:11).

Jesus appears to two disciples[2]
(Mark 16:12-13; cf. Luke 24:13-35)

Again, what we find in this section of Mark is an abbreviated rendition of what we find in another Gospel—this time from Luke 24:13-35. Two disciples (Luke mentions that one is named Cleopas) were leaving Jerusalem and heading to Emmaus, a town about seven miles to the northwest. They were talking about everything that had happened when Jesus appeared to them, but they were kept from recognizing him (Luke 24:16). The Gospel of Mark tells us that Jesus had taken a different form (16:12), which may indicate that Jesus' post-resurrection body, while similar to his incarnate body, was not exactly the same.

In any case, Jesus began to explain to them all the Old Testament prophecies about the Messiah, beginning with Moses and all the Prophets (Luke 24:27). Perhaps Jesus began with the promised offspring of Genesis (3:15), worked his way through the suffering servant of Isaiah 53, dialoged about the one who was pierced in Zechariah (12:10), and worked his way down to the messenger of the covenant in Malachi (3:1). His message could have included hundreds of other passages as well. But I know this—this is one sermon that I would love to have heard!

It was not until later that evening, as Jesus ate dinner with them that they recognized who he was. Maybe it was as Jesus broke bread with them (reminding them of the Last Supper) that their eyes were opened afresh to his true identity. Or maybe it was the moment they saw the nail-prints in his hands that everything became clear. Regardless, after he left them, they got up and traveled back to Jerusalem (Luke 24:33), but when they reported the resurrected Christ to the Eleven, "they did not believe them either" (16:13).

---

2. While the Twelve (i.e. Apostles) are often called disciples, the term disciples is often used of a much larger crowd of Christ-followers.

The appearance of Jesus to the Apostles
(Mark 16:14; cf. John 20:24–31)

When Jesus finally appeared to the Eleven, we read that Jesus "rebuked them for their lack of faith and their stubborn refusal to believe those who had seen him after he had risen" (16:14). Personally, I want to make a point of finding all the passages recorded for us in Scripture where Jesus rebukes[3] people and make a note not to do what they did! Notice the Apostles' stubborn refusal to believe the testimony of others. Jesus expected them to believe eyewitness accounts, even though they had not personally seen him. Evidently, Jesus felt that the Apostles had been given plenty of evidence to form an accurate conclusion.

Despite the fact that Mary Magdalene had told them she had seen the resurrected Christ, they did not believe. Despite the fact that two disciples had traveled from Emmaus to Jerusalem and told them they had spoken and eaten with Jesus, they did not believe. Despite the fact that Jesus had, on at least four occasions, predicted his impending death and resurrection, they did not believe. Despite the fact that they had seen miracle after miracle, including the raising of Jairus' daughter and Lazarus from the dead, they still did not believe.

Jesus rebuked them because he expected them to understand the words he had spoken. Jesus rebuked them because he expected them to believe in the miraculous power he had demonstrated. Jesus rebuked them because he expected them to believe the testimony of the reliable eyewitness he had sent. Why would they not believe the credible reports from the reliable witnesses of their friends and fellow Christ-followers? Jesus expected them to believe the evidence they had been given.

Often "doubting" Thomas gets a bad rap for not believing in the resurrected Christ. Thomas is known for his comment, "Unless I see the nail marks in his hands and put my finger where the nails were, and put my hand into his side, I will not believe it" (John 20:25). Of course, Thomas is also turned from disbelief to belief as sees Jesus. But Jesus told him, "Because you have seen me, you have believed; blessed are those who have not seen me and yet have believed" (John 20:29).

Mary Magdalene, the two disciples on the road to Emmaus, the ten Apostles, and Thomas, all were turned from disbelief to belief. But God's purposes were yet to be fulfilled. God desired that their faith be put into action.

---

3. This is among the most severe rebuke given in the Gospels. *Apistia* (without faith) and *sklērokardia* (refusal to believe) are nowhere else used of Jesus for the disciples.

Mobilization: From Belief to Action
(Mark 16:15–20)

Jesus not only expected the disciples to believe, but also expected their belief to impact their behavior. The gospel is not just something to be believed, it is something to be lived out. Actually, true faith is obedient response. This is clearly seen as Jesus gives the disciples their marching orders.

Jesus commissions the disciples
(Mark 16:15–16; cf. Matthew 28:19–20)

Notice the specific instructions Jesus gives: "Go into all the world and preach the good news to all creation. Whoever believes and is baptized will be saved, but whoever does not believe will be condemned" (16:15-16). In this passage, Jesus uses no uncertain language. What is required is clearly expressed—Jesus expects the disciples to go. The word translated "go" (*poreuomai*) is an aorist passive participle. Simply put, Jesus expects them to be going. One could even render it this way: As you are going. The word "go" here is actually not a command, but an expectation. The command in this phrase follows immediately after. Reading carefully, we come across what it is they are supposed to be doing as they go. They are to "preach" (*kēryssō*). This is in the imperative—this is the command. "As you are going—preach!"

The commissioning of the disciples found in Mark once again is a shortened version of an account in another gospel. Matthew records for us what is commonly called the Great Commission: "Therefore go and make disciples of all nations, baptizing them in the name of the Father and of the Son and of the Holy Spirit, and teaching them to obey everything I have commanded you. And surely I am with you always, to the very end of the age" (Matthew 28:19–20). Again, we find Jesus using an aorist passive participle (as you are going) and an aorist active imperative (make disciples). Jesus assumes that the disciples will go. His command is that as they go, they will make disciples. In Matthew's account we are also given two participles which describe what "disciple making" looks like. In order to make disciples they must baptize and teach. The true believer is one that puts faith into action.

In order to help mobilize the disciples, Jesus gives them supernatural gifts. In a highly misunderstood section of Scripture, Jesus promises to give the disciples supernatural spiritual help.

Jesus provides apostolic tools to help spread the gospel (Mark 16:17-18; cf. Acts 28:3-6; 2 Corinthians 12:12)

This section (about driving out demons, picking up snakes, and drinking poison) will raise more than just a few eyebrows unless it is taken in context. We must realize that these instructions were originally given to the Eleven as they were eating (16:14). Understand, these signs are not promised to all Christians who believe, but were designed for the Apostles, with the immediate confirmation and proclamation of the gospel in view. My own paraphrase might even include the phrase "among you" to clarify this point. "And these signs will accompany those [among you] who believe" (16:17).

Jesus has entrusted the gospel message to the disciples. If they die (i.e., are killed), the gospel will die with them. The disciples are promised divine protection. More than that, they are given tools that will not only confirm their message, but will enable them to spread that message rapidly. Four special signs are promised here. First, they will have the ability to drive out demons. We can clearly see in scripture that the Apostles were able to deliver people from demonic influence.

Second, they will be able to speak in new tongues, which was the ability to speak a language they have not learned (Acts 2:4-11; 10:46; 19:6). We all can see the benefit this would be for the immediate spread of the gospel. (I certainly wish that learning Greek or Hebrew had been imparted as a spiritual gift!)

Third, they will have the ability to survive personal attacks[4] in order that the gospel might go forward. Jesus is not suggesting that believers pick up snakes and drink deadly poison. Jesus' promise is that while taking the gospel forward, they will be protected. On this point, we have all heard tell of faith healers, rattlesnake handlers, and people who intentionally drink strychnine (although their numbers seem to be shrinking) to show the veracity of their faith. These signs were not intended to be public stunts or used at carnival sideshows. The gospel needed immediate protection and Christ promises supernatural protection.

---

4. Cf. Luke 10:19; Acts 28:3-6.

Finally, the disciples are able to place their hands on the sick to grant recovery.[5] In the first century, there was a one hundred percent recovery rate. It was a far cry from the hit and miss techniques of today's faith healers. Again, this was for the immediate confirmation and proclamation of the gospel message.

The fact that these signs were given to the disciples and that they are not given to all Christians can be demonstrated through three arguments. First, it was the Apostles who exhibited these signs. It can clearly be demonstrated that the Apostles could drive out demons, speak in new tongues and place hands on the sick for healing. Paul, especially, seems to have exhibited all of these signs. He cast out demons, he spoke in tongues, he was bitten by a snake which he harmlessly shook into the fire, and he placed hands on the sick who were healed.

Second, our passage supports this view. We have already pointed out that it was the disciples (in context) who were given these promises as they were eating a meal together. The last view of the Gospel of Mark reaffirms this when it says, "Then the disciples went out and preached everywhere, and the Lord worked with them and confirmed his word by the signs that accompanied it" (16:20).

Finally, the rest of Scripture supports it. There are many passages we could turn to, but allow me to give one in particular. Paul writes, "The things that mark an apostle—signs, wonders and miracles—were done among you with great perseverance" (2 Corinthians 12:12). These were Apostolic tools set in place for the immediate confirmation and proclamation of the gospel.

Far from needing to be embarrassed by these verses in Mark, we need to realize that the Apostles were given gifts which not only confirmed their message, but allowed the immediate spread of the Gospel and insured that it would move forward. Jesus provided Apostolic tools to ensure the spread of the gospel.

But Jesus gives one more convincing proof, through one more appearance to more than five hundred people at once, which serves to mobilize the disciples.

---

5. Cf. Acts 3:1–10; 5:12–16; 9:12, 17–18; James 5:14–15.

Jesus ascends (Mark 16:19-20; cf. Acts 1:9-12)

One last verification of Jesus' identity inspires the disciples on to action: "After the Lord Jesus had spoken to them, he was taken up into heaven and he sat at the right hand of God" (16:19). Once again, the Gospel of Mark gives us an abbreviated account of what we find elsewhere. Our passage is paralleled by Luke in both his gospel (24:50–53) and the book of Acts (1:9–12). In Acts, after Jesus was taken up to heaven before their eyes, two angels appeared and said, "Men of Galilee . . . why do you stand here looking into the sky? This same Jesus, who has been taken from you into heaven, will come back in the same way you have seen him go into heaven" (Acts 1:11). Notice that Christ's return will be both unexpected and dramatic, just as his departure was. But most of all, it was the culminating miracle that demonstrated who Jesus was. It was a vivid object lesson that Jesus was returning home.

This is what Mark has been showing us all along. Jesus is the Christ, the Son of God. This is a remarkable finish for the book of Mark. Jesus is the Son of God. He was not only crucified, buried, risen, but he ascended to his original and rightful place—next to his father in heaven. It is the culminating miracle that demonstrates once and for all who he is. Mark began his gospel by saying, "The beginning of the gospel about Jesus Christ, the Son of God" (1:1). Now the gospel is brought to its grand finale—Jesus Christ has ascended.

As I look at this passage, I am riveted with many applications, but let me simply close with two. After Jesus appeared to Mary Magdalene, and to the two disciples on the road to Emmaus, they went and reported to Jesus what they had seen and heard, but the disciples failed to believe them. Afterward, Jesus gave one of the harshest rebukes in scripture: "for their lack of faith and their stubborn refusal to believe those who had seen him after he had risen" (16:14). Jesus expected them to believe the credible testimony of others. Once again, I am reminded that we have been given far more evidence than they. We need to hold firmly to the reliable testimony of those who have gone before us concerning the message of Jesus Christ.

Second, we have seen demonstrated once again that true faith should mobilize us to action. Faith is obedient response. Faith makes demands of our lives as we live in faithful obedience to all God asks and commands. In fact, there are really only two things that God wants from us as we strive to fulfill *Missio Dei*—the Mission of God. God wants us first of all to become more and more like his son Jesus Christ. And second, he expects us to help others do the same. There can hardly be a more fitting end to the Gospel of Mark than to realize that we are responsible for taking forward the Gospel of Jesus Christ to others who have not yet heard.

Study Questions

1. What is the most unbelievable thing you have ever seen?
2. Why didn't the disciples believe the testimony of Mary Magdalene (16:11)?
3. Why didn't the disciples believe even after the testimony of the two disciples who encountered Christ on the road to Emmaus (16:13)?
4. If you place yourself in the shoes of Mary, or the disciples on the road to Emmaus, or the disciples, what would have been your initial response to the news of Christ's resurrection?
5. Read the account of Thomas in John 20:24–30. What does he demand before he will believe in the resurrection? Would you say you are very much like Thomas, or very different in this respect?
6. How did Jesus react to the Eleven's disbelief (16:14)? What ramifications might this have for us today?
7. How much evidence did you need in order to believe in Christ?
8. What keeps people from believing in Jesus today?
9. How have you applied verse 15 to your life?
10. What is the purpose of the signs listed in 16:17–18?
11. What four post-resurrection events are described in this section?
12. What seems to be the central theme of this passage? (Hint: it is synonymous with trust.)
13. What do you see as your role in spreading the gospel to all creation (16:15)?
14. What will you remember most from the Gospel of Mark? Explain.

For Further Study

15. Notice the other post-resurrection accounts recorded for us in scripture: the other women from Galilee (Matt 28:9–10);Peter (Luke 24:35); the Apostles minus Thomas (Luke 24:36–43; Jn 20:19–25); the Apostles with Thomas (Jn 20:26-31); seven of the Apostles by the Sea of Galilee (Jn 21:1–25); the Apostles on a mountain in Galilee (Matthew 28:16–20) and 500 disciples (1 Cor 1:6); Jesus' brother James (1 Cor 15:7); the Apostles at the ascension (Luke 24:44–53; Acts 1:9–11); and, Paul (Acts 9:4–6).

Bibliography

Beale, G. K., and D. A. Carson, editors. *Commentary on the New Testament Use of the Old Testament*. Grand Rapids: Baker, 2007.

Black, Allen. *Mark. The College Press NIV Commentary*. Joplin, MO: College Press, 1995.

Garland, David E. *Mark: The NIV Application Commentary*. Grand Rapids: Zondervan, 1996.

Hurtado, Larry. *Mark. New International Biblical Commentary*. Peabody, MA: Hendrickson Publishers, 1989.

Keener, Craig. *The IVP Bible Background Commentary, New Testament*. Downers Grove, IL: InterVarsity, 1993.

Kernaghan, Ronald J. *Mark. The IVP New Testament Commentary Series*. Downers Grove, IL: InterVarsity, 2007.

Kierkegaard, Søren. *The Soul of Kierkegaard: Selections from His Journals*. Edited by Alexander Dru. Mineola, NY: Dover, 2003.

Kittel, Gerhard. *Theological Dictionary of the New Testament*. 10 vols. Translated by Geoffrey W. Bromiley. Grand Rapids: Eerdmans, 1964.

Lane, William. *The Gospel According to Mark. The New International Commentary of the New Testament*. Grand Rapids: Eerdmans, 1974.

Lewis, C. S. *The Chronicles of Narnia: the Lion, the Witch and the Wardrobe*. Revised edition. New York: MacMillan, 1982.

Lewis, C. S. *The Screwtape Letters*. New York: MacMillan, 1961.

Schweitzer, Edward. *The Good News According to Mark*. Atlanta: John Knox, 1971.

Stedman, Ray, and James Denney, editors. *The Ruler Who Serves*. Grand Rapids: Discovery House, 2002.

———. *The Servant Who Rules*. Grand Rapids: Discovery House, 2002.

Strobel, Lee. *The Case for Christ*. Grand Rapids: Zondervan, 1998.

Wessell, Walter. *Mark. The Expositor's Bible Commentary*. Grand Rapids: Zondervan, 1984.

Wittherington, Ben, III. *The Gospel of Mark: A Socio-Rhetorical Commentary*. Grand Rapids: Eerdmans, 2001.